Working With School-Age Children

Marlene A. Bumgarner, Ed.D.

Gavilan College

Boston   Burr Ridge, IL   Dubuque, IA   Madison, WI   New York   San Francisco   St. Louis
Bangkok   Bogotá   Caracas   Kuala Lumpur   Lisbon   London   Madrid   Mexico City
Milan   Montreal   New Delhi   Santiago   Seoul   Singapore   Sydney   Taipei   Toronto

McGraw-Hill Higher Education

*A Division of The **McGraw-Hill** Companies*

WORKING WITH SCHOOL-AGE CHILDREN

Copyright © 1999 by The McGraw-Hill Companies, Inc., 1221 Avenue of the Americas, New York, NY, 10020. All rights reserved. No part of this publication may be reproduced or distributed in any form or by any means, or stored in a database or retrieval system, without the prior written consent of The McGraw-Hill Companies, Inc., including, but not limited to, in any network or other electronic storage or transmission, or broadcast for distance learning. Some ancillaries, including electronic and print components, may not be available to customers outside the United States.

This book is printed on acid-free paper.

3   4   5   6   7   8   9   0   BKM/BKM   9   8   7   6   5   4

ISBN 1-55934-948-4

Sponsoring editor, Franklin Graham; production editor, Melissa Kreischer; manuscript editor, Patterson Lamb; design manager, Jean Mailander; text and cover designer, Claire Seng-Niemoeller; art editor, Amy Folden; illustrator, Judith Ogus; cover photo, © Tom Rosenthal/Superstock; manufacturing manager, Randy Hurst. The text was set in 10/12 Plantin Regular by Thompson Type, and printed by Bookmart Press.

Text and photo credits appear on page 312, which constitutes an extension of the copyright page.

Library of Congress Cataloging-in-Publication Data

Bumgarner, Marlene A.
    Working with school-age children / Marlene A.
Bumgarner.
        p.   cm.
    Includes bibliographical references and index.
    ISBN 1-55934-948-4
    1. School-age child care—United States.   2. Child care services—United States   3. Child care workers—United States.   4. Child development—United States.   I. Title.
HQ778.6.B85   1999
362.7'0973—dc21   98-45605
                                                            CIP

www.mhhe.com

Contents

**PART ONE: SCHOOL-AGE CHILDREN AND THE
PEOPLE WHO WORK WITH THEM**   **1**

PART TWO: THE SETTING   87

5 The Adult's Role in Socialization and Development   87

6 Issues Facing Today's Children   109

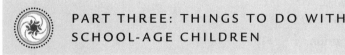

PART THREE: THINGS TO DO WITH SCHOOL-AGE CHILDREN   172

9   Cooperative Program Planning   172

11 Rainy Day and Snowy Day Projects: Especially Engaging Things to Do Inside   210

12 Working With Older School-Age Children and Teens   229

PART FOUR: ADMINISTERING A PROGRAM FOR SCHOOL-AGERS   246

Foreword

In the last few years, a sea change has been taking place in the way we think about children's out-of-school time. Now it isn't just a small band of advocates, parents, teachers, and researchers who are speaking out about the importance of children's "discretionary time"; policy makers, funders, government officials—even the President of the United States—want to see children safe, engaged in constructive activities, and making meaningful relationships with adults and other children. Finally, making the case for good programs and services during nonschool time has been heard. Could there be a better time for a new book about best practices? Timing is everything, as they say in the movies! Marlene Bumgarner has written such a book, and at the right moment. A major contribution is the expanded view of out-of-school time that is at the heart of the book; where are school-age children spending time? They are at home, in family child care (often marginalized by program advocates), in drop-in and library-based programs. In short, this book expands our picture of before- and after-school time to a more realistic one that is based on families' preferences and on children's ages and stages.

The blend of stories, anecdotes, research, and advice on practice comes from her experience in the field and in the classroom. Clearly Marlene also brings to this volume a caring, informed, and discerning eye. We know that what happens to children in good programs and other out-of-school time services makes a difference to children. And in this book the author presents us with the evidence, and more. It is a more than timely and very welcome addition to the literature of the field.

Michelle Seligson
Executive Director
National Institute on Out-of-School Time
Center for Research on Women
Wellesley College

Preface

This book has been written for people who work with school-age children when they are not in school. It is designed to be used in several ways—as an introduction to the increasing role communities play in providing out-of-school services to school-age children; as a text for college courses in child and youth work (including recreation, leisure studies, and school-age care); and as a reference for people who already work with school-age children as teachers, aides, camp counselors, coaches, service club leaders, recreational directors, or activity planners. It can also serve as a source of information for parents who are seeking high-quality out-of-school activities for their youngsters but are not sure what to look for.

The text begins by introducing several children, through their own words or those of parents and teachers. Most of these characters are composites of several children I have known, although some of them are actual individuals who have allowed me to use them by name. Moving into a different perspective, the book then describes some of the varieties of ways parents depend on other members of their community to assist them in the care and nurturing of their children while they work.

In these first chapters and throughout the text, I have drawn heavily from the experiences of real people, revealing a diversity of experience and needs, and defining the role of the professional child and youth worker in their lives. The text provides a thorough presentation of both theory and practice, for both of these aspects are necessary to create high-quality programming for children of any age. The necessary attributes and skills of the child and youth worker are described; also discussed are the issues faced by children in today's world and some strategies for helping children deal with the fear and anxiety that often result. The term *out-of-school* has been borrowed from my colleagues in the United Kingdom, where I first heard it during a sabbatical leave spent in Yorkshire. That term, also used in Canada and Australia, is now coming into use in the United States as child and youth professionals come to grips with the reality that all programs for school-age children are not "child care" programs, although caring for children is certainly one of the roles of people working with school-age children at any time. Out-of-school programs include before- and after-school programs designed primarily for the care and supervision of children whose parents cannot be with them for certain hours of the day. However, this new terminology also encompasses much more, such as recreational and competitive sports programs; art and music camps; homework clubs; youth centers; service organizations such as Scouting, 4-H, Junior Achievement, or Trailblazers; and a broad variety of other indoor and outdoor activities designed for school-age youth.

In response to the growing awareness of the need for out-of-school programs for older children, those 10 years old and above, a separate chapter addresses the ideal characteristics of those programs. Another chapter suggests ways in which staff in these programs can develop partnerships with parents and community agencies to develop cohesive and responsive programs that offer a wide range of activities and services to families. An additional chapter provides an overview of the administration function within programs for school-agers.

In Chapter 15, I present an overview of the new Standards for Quality School-Age Care developed by the National Institute for Out-of-School Time and the National School-Age Care Alliance. These standards, along with an improvement and accreditation process, form the core of a nationwide endeavor to raise the quality of out-of-school programs through self-assessment and peer-evaluation using criteria developed specifically for school-age programs. Both personally and professionally, I am committed to improving the quality of out-of-school time for the children in our world. I fervently believe that the development of these standards and the accreditation process is an important milestone on our journey to reaching that goal, and I am delighted to be able to include that information here. This text is a work in progress. If there is an area that needs to be expanded or added to future editions, please let me know.

Acknowledgments

In the preparation of this manuscript, I have had the help of many wonderful people. I am indebted to the professionals in the field who read part or all of the manuscript for this book and provided thoughtful and constructive comments and criticism. They include Ginger Barnhart, Bananas Resource and Referral Center; Meryl Glass, San Francisco City College; Janet Gonzalez-Mena, Napa Community College; and Liz Regan, Allan Hancock College. Thanks also to my production editor, Melissa Kreischer, who guided me through the production of this book with grace and patience.

A special thanks goes to the following Gavilan College students who read the text at various stages of completion and suggested additional topics or better ways to present the material: Venancia Chavez, Martha Hollis, Marlene Hughes, Dena Kehler, Kelly Thompson, and Jorge Zaiden. Other students allowed me to use curriculum planning ideas or material they had developed. Their names are cited at the appropriate places in the text.

Finally, I want to express my gratitude to the four young people who inspired me to write the book in the first place, who provided many of the stories and topics, and who lived through the years of writing and testing the material. They are experts indeed in the strengths and weaknesses of out-of-school care— my children, Doña, John, Jamie, and Deborah.

About the Author

The author, Dr. Marlene Bumgarner, taught elementary school when her oldest children were small. After completing her master's degree she began teaching child development at Gavilan College in Gilroy, California, where she was also the campus lab school director. For most of those years, one or more of her children (now aged 26, 22, 19 and 14) participated in licensed family child care, center-based before- and after-school care, and a variety of recreational and athletic programs. Their experiences provided the motivation and the means for writing this book. A single parent, Marlene was ideally situated to observe and listen to children and parents of children who were attending out-of-school programs. For many years she struggled along with other working parents who depended on community services and networks to keep their children safe and happy when they could not be with them. Her interest in developing high-quality out-of-school programs encouraged her to return to graduate school, completing a doctorate in early and middle childhood in 1993.

Marlene has developed and taught many courses and workshops for school-age staff and also created an associate degree in school-age programming at Gavilan College. A frequent conference speaker, she serves as a consultant to out-of-school programs in her community and on the governing board of the California School Age Consortium (CSAC). She is a member of the National Association for the Education of Young Children (NAEYC), the National School-Age Care Alliance (NSACA), and the World Organization for Early Childhood Education (OMEP).

To the four individuals who did most of the research—
Doña, John, Jamie, and Deborah.
Thank you for your memories, your insights, and your suggestions
for improving out-of-school environments for children.

Introduction

Anyone who reads a newspaper or watches the evening news should know that the child-care shortage has become an issue of crisis proportions. A network of high-quality child care that is both accessible and affordable is clearly needed before we can hope to achieve economic and social stability, and the development of that illusive dream has become the focus of child-care professionals and public policy advisers around the world.

What may not be apparent to people reading and hearing the reports of these efforts is that the child-care crisis affects families of children ages 6 to 18, not just families with the preschool-age children traditionally thought of as recipients of child-care services. Even if one discounts the fact that teenagers continue to need adult supervision and guidance, children between the ages of 5 and 12 account for two-thirds of the population needing care. Not only are there more children in that age group, but more of their mothers work than do mothers of younger children (Zigler & Lang, 1991).

Approximately 24 million school-age children in the United States need child care. The rising rates of divorce and single parenthood, as well as the growth of families where both parents work, has resulted in a tremendous growth in this figure. According to projections from the Bureau of the Census, in 1997 there were 38.8 million children between the ages of 5 and 14 living in the United States. Of these children, 23 million lived with a mother who was employed, unemployed currently seeking employment, or enrolled in school. In addition, an estimated 912,000 children in this age range live with a single employed father, 61,000 with an unemployed father, and 9,000 with a single father enrolled in school (SACC Project, 1996; Children's Defense Fund, 1998). According to research done at the National Institute on Out-of-School Time at Wellesley College, at least 5 million American children between 5 and 14 now spend too much time alone during a typical week (Seligson, 1997).

The good news is that a variety of solutions have been proposed and tried, and more are on the way. Before- and after-school programs on school sites, extension of services by child-care centers and family child-care homes, supervised recreation activities, drop-in tutoring centers, and other innovative programs are appearing, growing, and changing to meet new needs. What was once considered the private problem of divorced or poor families has finally been recognized as a broad social issue, one worthy of public consideration and perhaps even of public funds.

This book has been written for the career professionals and volunteers who will be working in the broad spectrum of programs serving school-age children. Because the field of school-age care and recreation is so new, many staff members come from a background of caring for younger children or have not received any training at all. A popular misconception that has existed in the child development professions for years is even more common in the emerging field of out-of-school care: "*Anyone* can take care of kids—it's easy!" The goal of this book is to extend the confidence held by those *outside* the profession to include people *inside* it—especially to those who work with and care for children between the ages of 5 and 12; not because it's "easy," but because they will know what it takes to be effective in the work they do.

Part One of the book, School-Age Children and the People Who Work With Them, introduces the various ways in which staff of programs for school-agers interact with children and their families. Perhaps you will see yourself in one of the scenarios described here.

Chapter 1 introduces some school-age children, their views on before- and after-school activities, and some of the problems and solutions surrounding their out-of-school time. The concept of school-age care is still quite new and, although children often protest that they "don't need a babysitter," our changing social environment makes it less and less safe for children to be unsupervised and unprotected. Chapter 2 acquaints the reader with his or her potential relationship to the children in out-of-school programs in order to answer the question, "Why do I need to read this book?" Other countries have found some solutions that we have not yet considered; individual communities have found some that are not well known. The many places in different communities where adults and school-age children spend time together are described in this chapter. In Chapter 3, anecdotal information and statistics combine to create a diverse view of the roles nonparental adults play with school-age children. Some of the roles described include classroom teachers and aides, bus drivers, yard duty supervisors and cafeteria staff, team coaches and managers, service club volunteers such as Scout leaders, 4-H club advisers, YMCA volunteers, and camp counselors. The new profession of before- and after-school caregiver is described as well as the characteristics of people who work successfully with children in each of these roles.

Chapter 4 provides a theoretical framework for understanding the school-age child. Many people enter the field of out-of-school care with little or no training in child development. This chapter describes the views of each major theorist on the development of children from early childhood through the school years for newcomers to the field. Chapter 4 may be skipped if the reader is already knowledgeable about these ideas, but newcomers to the field will find it a useful introduction to developmental theory and application.

Part Two, The Setting, presents several issues and influences on today's children which they bring to any out-of-school setting. Chapter 5 describes how adults can play meaningful roles in children's lives, and it also explains the influences adults have on the environment and experiences of school-age children. Topics include adults' roles in the development of the personality, social skills, problem solving, competence, moral reasoning, and values. Today's children worry about earthquakes and hurricanes, atomic wars and global warming, downsizing and homelessness, AIDS and substance abuse. They are heavily influenced by mass media presentations of changing ethics and values, and they live in a multicultural society their parents may not understand. Today's parents live with stresses their own parents never faced, and their children think about things children of previous generations could not even imagine. We can't change the world, but perhaps we can help our youngsters understand that it's not their job to fix it . . . at least not yet. Chapter 6 addresses this situation.

In addition to knowing what is on children's minds, fundamental to effective child care is an understanding of the environmental and emotional conditions that affect children's behavior. Chapter 7 describes a behavioral guidance system, setting and enforcing limits, and conflict resolution. An overview of learning styles guides readers as they plan activities and environments with school-age children.

Chapter 8 supplies the reader with a variety of ideas for creating environments for school-age children. School-age professionals use strategies that promote problem solving, competence, and responsibility in children as they work together to build settings for work and play. The way in which an environment is planned (i.e., autocratically or democratically) can determine its success as much as the final product. Not only is it important that the environment work; the children must feel comfortable in it. The environment should not only be nurturing and safe, it must also be attractive and interesting. Ideas for shared space, where nearly a third of all before- and after-school programs function, are also provided.

Part Three, Things to Do With School-Age Children, gives examples of developmentally appropriate activities for children during out-of-school time, beginning with an introduction to program planning in Chapter 9. It may seem strange at first to think in terms of "curriculum" for an environment most people think of as "child care," but that is exactly the point. For out-of-school activities to be successful, they must be intentional and well planned, and children must be an integral part of the planning process. Chapter 10 describes some indoor activities that children enjoy; Chapter 11 focuses on projects and activities that take place out of doors. Chapter 12 addresses the special challenge of designing programs for the older school-ager, youngsters from 10 to 18. Interesting and high-quality programs for this age group have been shown to have a strong impact on drug and alcohol usage, teen pregnancy, and crime.

Part Four covers the administration of school-age programs. Running a before- or after-school center or a baseball league requires a certain amount of administrative knowledge, yet state regulations do not always require program directors to take college courses in business administration. Chapter 13 addresses several critical areas: licensing, liability, funding, policies, procedures, and staff. Thoughtful policies and procedures are the core of an effective school-age program. Understanding the unique administrative requirements of a school-age center is an important element in successful programming.

Chapter 14 encourages a strong partnership between out-of-school programs and families as well as active participation in the local community. Children live and grow in the context of their families within communities, and one of the developmental tasks of the school-age years is to learn how to become an integral part of one's community. Well-articulated programs for school-age children develop ways in which family involvement can support their program goals as well as provide opportunities for the children in their programs to build relationships with members of the community in which they live.

Chapter 15 addresses program quality and accreditation. As communities struggle to address the acute need for programs for school-agers, they must be able to identify and monitor the components of out-of-school programs that result in desirable outcomes—for example, well-adjusted children who feel connected to their families and communities.

Appendixes contain useful resource material for program staff. We hope that the safety checklist and referral information will be helpful to staff for many years.

REFERENCES

Children's Defense Fund. (1998). *The State of America's Children, 1998.*

SACC Project. (1996). *Fact Sheet on School-Age Children.* Boston, MA: Center for Research on Women, Wellesley College.

Seligson, M. (October 23, 1997). *Panel Presentation.* Paper presented at the White House Child Care Conference, Washington, D.C.

Zigler, E. F., & Lang, M. E. (1991). *Child Care Choices: Balancing the Needs of Children, Families, and Society.* New York: The Free Press.

CHAPTER 1

PART ONE
....

SCHOOL-AGE
CHILDREN AND
THE PEOPLE
WHO WORK
WITH THEM

Who Are the Children in Out-of-School Programs?

Meet the Children

Twelve-year-old Jamal arrives home from junior high school each day at 3:00 p.m., stopping on the way from his bus stop to retrieve his 8-year-old brother Jesse from their neighborhood elementary school. Until their father arrives home about 6:30 p.m., Jamal is restricted from talking on the telephone, visiting friends, or having friends visit him. In the event of an emergency, Jamal has a list of numbers to call, including the local Red Cross and a neighbor who cares for younger children in her home. The afternoons are long, especially in the winters, when the darkness arrives long before their father. On Wednesdays, Jesse attends a Cub Scout meeting at the school, and Jamal goes to the library across the street until the meeting ends. The leader, Mrs. Espinosa, has seen Jesse's father only once, at the parent orientation meeting in the fall. However, Jamal sometimes stops to talk with her after a meeting, and he takes notes and permission slips home for their father.

Dianne and Kwame, both age 7, cross the street in front of their school and enter the public library. Selecting seats against the back wall, they take out paper and books and dutifully begin their homework. Their mothers, both teachers, will pick them up in an hour or so. Because there are so many unaccompanied children in the library each afternoon, the staff has been increased during these hours, and librarians alternate between helping children find books or magazines and running special programs to keep them from disturbing the other library patrons. Twice a week the librarians stage a puppet show for the younger children, and sometimes Dianne and Kwame help out.

Ten-year-old Stuart could go directly home after school if he wished. His parents have arranged for a neighbor to keep an eye on him until they come home from work, but Stuart feels that he is too old to be watched by a "baby-sitter." He prefers to play basketball at the YMCA for an hour, then stop at the video arcade around the corner from his house until dinnertime. On Tuesdays he has piano lessons, which take nearly an hour, including the walk to and from the teacher's house; and on Thursdays he plays in an after-school basketball league. By moving from one activity to another throughout the week, Stuart never has to do more than check in with the neighbor and rarely enters his own lonely house.

Eleven-year-old Gregorio has a 25-minute bus ride from his special day class to a developmental center on the other side of town. Gregorio has Down's syndrome. The extended day program teaches community living skills and offers recreation in community settings. Gregorio's mom is a bookkeeper at an auto parts store. She would rather have him in the after-school program at his own school, which is closer to her job, but the staff at the school was resistant to including a child with his particular special needs, which include a hearing deficit and a heart condition that requires him to wear a heart monitor. "I suppose I could fight it under the ADA," she says, referring to the Americans with Disabilities Act, "but I just don't have the energy. Besides, he can go to the developmental center until he turns 21."

Teresa and Espie are 9-year-old twins. Their 13-year-old brother is supposed to be watching them after school, but James is more interested in being with his friends and usually shoos the girls away. The row houses along their street are filled with unemployed and discouraged people, the alleys and culverts with homeless teenagers. Teresa and Espie are afraid to walk home alone and even more afraid to stay in their house when James brings his rough-talking friends over. But their mother works hard all day, and they don't want to make her life harder by tattling on James. A gang-prevention agency recently opened a drop-in recreation center for children in their neighborhood, and one afternoon the girls enter this safe haven. Soon they are dropping in after school, learning to make macrame hanging baskets and playing volleyball. There are even tutors there who know what homework assignments their teacher has given and who help them with their work, so they frequently stay at the center until long after dark. Eventually, their mother begins picking them up from there on her way home.

At the end of each school day, 8-year-old Deborah walks only a few yards to her after-school caregiver. An agency that operates care centers for school-age children throughout her state has placed a portable building in a corner of the school playground, and Deborah attends three afternoons a week while her mother, a hairdresser, completes her afternoon appointments. There she can do her homework at a table with her friends, play board games or use the computer, help make a snack or sew, or participate in construction or recreational activities outside as weather allows. An only child, Deborah enjoys this wind-down time until her mother comes to get her in the evening. She has been in group child care since infancy and seems to be content to continue doing so.

These scenarios illustrate some of the provisions made for the care of school-age children during the gaps between their school hours and the availability of their parents to care for them. Before- and after-school care of

Approximately 24 million school-age children in the United States need child care.

children is not new (Zigler & Lang, 1991), and there really never has been an "olden days" when all children had a parent at home to care for them. In earlier times, and even today in many communities, children have been cared for by grandparents, aunts or uncles, or siblings, as well as by governesses, tutors, and nursemaids, depending on the income and class of the family. Or they may have simply stayed home alone.

For a decade or so following World War II, the expanding U.S. economy allowed many middle-income mothers to remain at home until their children were grown, and the movement of families away from their birthplaces left many other families without nearby relatives to help with child care. Transplanted wives often had no choice but to stay in the suburbs with their children, and single mothers, unable to find child care, frequently requested governmental assistance to stay at home with their youngsters. A generation of these patterns left many people with the perception that it is—and always has been— the sole responsibility of women to care for the nation's children. This perception has resulted in a burden of guilt borne by the mothers who could not do so, and a persisting disinclination from other segments of society to share that responsibility with them.

However, at the same time many families were enjoying postwar prosperity, others were facing new challenges brought on by World War II and the Korean and Vietnam wars that followed it. Women joined the workforce in much larger numbers, new waves of immigration brought families from diverse cultures into communities and schools, and the mobility of families pursuing the American Dream resulted in unstable relationships, rising divorce rates, and single-parent households. An increase in female-headed households led to a drop in the standard of living for many families with children (Bailyn et al., 1992). Yet for many years we persisted in believing that mothers could, and should, raise their children without outside assistance.

Fortunately, attitudes are beginning to change, and this social issue, which has been regarded as a private family matter for so long, is now frequently the subject of public discussion, public policy, and community endeavor (Clinton, 1998; National Research Council, 1990; Petrie & Logan, 1986). Seeing a relationship between unsupervised children and growing juvenile crime rates, many communities are now addressing the need for out-of-school care and recreation programs, and some solutions are beginning to emerge.

Unfortunately, as the number of working mothers and single-parent families has grown (now including many male-headed households as well), so have the problems surrounding the supervision and care of their school-age children. Many after-school programs close during winter and spring breaks, and during summer vacation. Some do not provide services on teacher professional development days or school holidays, which may not be holidays for parents. Some schools close early one or two days a week for teachers to attend meetings or prepare lessons. Year-round schools offer a different kind of challenge, requiring full-day care for a segment of the community's children for several weeks at a time. Imagine the child-care nightmare of a family whose 8-year-old attends one school, grades K–4 from 8:00-2:00; whose 10-year-old attends a year-round mathematics magnet on the other end of town (3 months on-track, 6 weeks off), 8:30 to 3:15; and whose 12-year-old can walk to junior high but doesn't start until 9:00 a.m. or return home until nearly 4:00 p.m.

Parents of children with special needs face additional challenges. Like other parents, they want a safe, welcoming environment for their children while they work to support the family. Although the Americans with Disabilities Act prohibits child-care programs from discriminating against children based on disability, discrimination still exists. In addition, some children have extensive medical needs that make group care difficult or impossible. It is especially difficult to find programs for children over 12, with or without special needs. Even when programs for teens exist, they usually have few spaces and long waiting lists, and most youngsters over 10 or 11 resist attending any program labeled "child care."

Children who do not speak English or are learning it as a second language face many challenges in and out of school. Second-language learners frequently come from families whose culture is different from that of the majority of people in their community (although that is changing as we enter the 21st century). Cultural differences between parents and staff of after-school programs make for interesting encounters, both linguistic and social. Communication styles are likely to be different, as are some values and assumptions about roles and behaviors.

The problems have been identified, and many people are committed to help solve them. However, in order to develop and implement a system of care and recreation for children during their out-of-school time, it is important for

PERSPECTIVE

Working in La Fresa

José Luis Ríos

Nine-year-old José Luis Ríos lives with his large extended family in a small house in Las Lomas, California. All of his relatives work in the fields, including his brothers and sisters. José Luis is often taken out of school to work alongside his family. The owner of the land where the Ríos family works has been charged by the investigators of the Labor Department for violating some sixty provisions of the federal Migrant and Seasonal Agricultural Worker Protection Act.

My name is José Luis Ríos, and I am in third grade. I have nine brothers and sisters. We live with our parents and aunt and uncle and cousins in Las Lomas. My grandparents live in Michoacan, Mexico. If they were here right now, I'd ask them to come and visit because I don't know them. My parents told me they used to work in the fields picking strawberries, garbanzos, lentils, and corn. All my relatives that I can think of work in the fields.

My parents work in *la fresa* [the strawberries] and *la mora* [the raspberries], and my mom sometimes packs mushrooms. During the week, they leave in the morning around six o'clock. I go and help them, mostly on weekends. I help pick the strawberries and put them in boxes. Last year my father took me to the fields a lot during the week, too, instead of bringing me to school. I would find out I was going because he would say, "Let's go pick strawberries now." I like going to the fields with my family because it is pretty out there.

The longest day in the field was when we picked a lot of strawberries. I felt bad and it was getting dark. We were out there so long. I said to my parents, "Let's go home," and finally they said, "We're going." It was hard to work so long. My body gets tired, and when it is muddy, my feet get covered with mud and it is hard to walk. Also, when it is muddy, my uncle has to park the truck far away, and I get tired and cold when I have to walk back to the truck . . .

Sometimes when I'm there, my aunt and uncle that live with us are in the fields working. My cousins are there, too. I play with my cousin Andreas. He is seven. I like to play with him because he is a *buena gente* [good person]. We play tag in the fields. My brothers work in the fields but not usually my sisters. They go to school. Rogelio, my little brother who's two, comes to the fields, but he just plays. He doesn't make any trouble.

When I work in the fields, I don't get paid. I don't want them to pay me because it's not good. They pay my parents for what I pick. I like that my parents get paid because then they buy me toy cars and trucks or maybe a bicycle. My brothers get paid. Ignacio is eighteen, and he works during the week. He doesn't go to school now, but he used to go to high school. Manuel is the oldest, and he works in the fields in Salinas. I want to work in the fields like my brothers when I'm older, because I can eat a lot of strawberries and out there you can watch the birds.

But sometimes it is hard and I'm tired in school on Mondays because I worked on the weekend. I also get a lot of bad headaches, so sometimes I have to leave school early or go and rest in the nurse's office. When my father took me to the fields last year during the week, it was hard to study when I got home because I was tired. It is hard to work and go to school at the same time.

I like coming to school better than working in the fields. I go to school on the bus at seven-thirty. I like going to school to learn because then you know things. If you don't know anything and you go somewhere and somebody asks you to write something, you won't be able to. And when you're older you won't know anything. The people who haven't gone to school, they work in the fields.

I'm trying to learn English at school, but I like to speak Spanish because I'm understood better. I have more friends that speak Spanish than English. My parents tell me to study English, but I like studying the Native Americans best because they wrote, they did drawings, and they hunted buffalos. I like the Mayans. They made houses so the water couldn't get in when it rained. In school I like to write, too. I write about the birds because they are pretty and they fly. And I like to write about sheep and animals and also the Ninja Turtles.

When I get home from school, I have cookies. I eat most of my meals at school. My older brothers and sisters are there when I get home. They take care of me because my parents are working in the fields. My big sisters Carmela and Amelia help me with my homework and make cookies and coffee. Sometimes we take the strawberries from the fields home to eat. We make *fresa molida*—it's kind of a milkshake. Sometimes I take care of my little brothers and sister. I give them coffee and cookies. I have to watch out when I take care of them because cars come up our driveway and they could hit them. That's what happened to my little cousin. And sometimes we play right by the driveway. I play marbles with my brother Carlos and my cousin Jorge. I like to play hide-and-seek with my little sister Maria. My favorite place to hide is in the car.

us to understand all the factors that impact successful programs. First, we must meet the children and talk to them, get to know what matters to them, and what kinds of experiences they want to have when they aren't in school. Following are some examples.

The Children Speak

Billy, age 9: "My teacher has an iguana that she keeps in the classroom. Irma is really cool and likes to sit on our shoulders while we work. If we finish our assignments, sometimes we get to clean out her house or give her food or water. It's important to make sure that on cold days the light is close to the place she likes to sleep, and sometimes we put a blanket over the terrarium to keep in the heat. I really like taking care of animals. They're cool. We live in an apartment, and my mom works lots of hours, so we can't have a cat or a dog. Sometimes I get to visit my grandparents, who have horses. But I can see Irma every day, and I like that. If I were in an after-school center I'd like to have a pet that I could take care of every day, that knew me and loved me like I do Irma."

Moira, age 8: "Before Christmas, my dad got a job in another city, and now he only comes home on weekends. My mom cried a lot at first, and I was scared. Sometimes I'd go to bed and put my head under the covers because I felt safer there. I know it's silly, but since Dad's been gone, I feel littler. He used to take me places and stuff, and now when he comes home he just wants me to leave him alone. I hate it . . . maybe they'll get a divorce. I wish I could figure out what I did to make him want to leave. My mom has to work now, and I go over to Priya's house after school. That's OK, because I can do my homework with Priya, but we can't go out and play or anything because her mom is worried about us getting hurt or something. But sometimes when my mom comes home she's too tired to fix dinner and we get to have pizza. I wish I had someone I could talk to about this stuff, but I don't want to worry my mom."

Jorge, age 11: "When my little brother was born, I was really mad. I can remember it really well, even though I was only 3. I wanted my mom and dad to send him back where he came from. But now, Jimmy is on a little kids' soccer team. I can't play sports because I'm in this wheelchair, but he's really good, and I like to watch him. Jimmy makes it more fun to be outside. He's really funny, and sometimes he asks me to help him with his homework. Maybe I'll be a teacher when I grow up. I can teach kids stuff, then I could go watch them play their sports after school. Jimmy even suggested I could try out for the wheelchair basketball league. Maybe I will. My mom's a doctor, and she's gone a lot, but she's working on helping people not have to be in wheelchairs, so I like that. My dad sells insurance, and he works at home. It's nice to have him there when I come home from school. Lots of my friends' parents work and they go to day care after school, so I can't play with them. But Jimmy and I do our homework together and Dad takes us to the park so Jimmy can practice soccer. But when we don't have any school, he gets mad if we bother him while he's working, and sometimes he takes us to the park and leaves us there all morning. I like the park, but it's boring for such a long time. I wish we had other kids to play with when there's no school."

....

And what about the other children we met earlier? What would they like to have in an out-of-school setting? Jamal, for instance, has a science fair project to build this year. He has a computer at home, and his father has been helping him with ideas. But he has a friend, Aaron, who wanted to build something together with him—maybe a suspension bridge or an arch. Jamal can't have friends over after school, and Aaron's not allowed to go out after dinner or on Saturdays, so it's difficult for them to work together. Both Aaron and Jamal would like a place where they could work on their project together after school, with encyclopedias and other books about engineering as well as a workbench and tools.

Dianne and Kwame like going to the library, and they really enjoy working with the preschool children and the puppet shows; but they know the librarians don't like having children left there alone. They wish there was a special room at the library that was set up as a place where kids could study and talk, that was actually OK for them to be in, and where no one got upset because they were there without their parents.

Stuart has already found his way around the neighborhood, and most of the time he's pretty happy with his after-school arrangements. However, when pressed, he admits that he never starts his homework until after his parents come home, and then sometimes he gets involved in playing games with his dad or watching TV, and things don't get done that should. When the weather turns cold, he wishes there was a warm place where he could go right after school besides the neighbor's home or his empty house.

Gregorio likes his after-school center, and he likes the ride on the bus. He watches people, he'll tell you, and there are lots of trucks on the way. He likes trucks. But he misses being with Carlos, his best friend from school. Carlos can't go to the same after-school program where Gregorio goes, and Gregorio can't go to the after-school program at his regular school, where Carlos goes every day. He'd like it better if they could both be in the same program after school.

You can tell from the way Teresa and Espie regularly attend the drop-in center that they are happy it opened. But sit with them for a while and talk, and they will tell you that their favorite teacher, Ada, doesn't work there anymore. She left to work at a Head Start program where she can make more money. She explained it to the girls when she said good-bye; they understand, but they are sad she left. Last month Thea quit to work in a department store. She told the girls that it was because she had worked for the agency that ran the center for two years and never had a raise in pay. Their mother got a raise last December, and they remember how happy she was to be able to give them both new coats for Christmas. "It's not fair," Teresa wails. "Thea and Ada were really neat, and now they're both gone." These two children wish their teachers would keep coming to the center after school.

Most children prefer the company of their peers to going home alone.

Eight-year-old Deborah is content at her child-care center. However, one of her friends, Karolina, is not so happy. At 12 years old, Karolina is the only sixth grader in the after-school care program, and there are only four fifth graders. She complains that there's nothing to do there, and that all the toys are for "babies." She works on her homework most of the time, helping younger children like Deborah with their math or teaching them how to play card games. Karolina would like to go home alone after school, but her mother won't let her. She wishes there were more older kids, and something more interesting to do.

Because the concept of after-school child care is so new, probably very few staff members of child-care programs attended such programs when they were in elementary school. Think about how *you* spent your free time when you were 6, or 8, or 10, and consider the difference in the life of a child who has to spend 2 to 4 hours of "free" time every day in a group setting. Or ask children in group care how they would like to spend their time. School-age children have lots of ideas and often very strong opinions about what they want to do when they're not in school. One training manual (Newman, 1993) for school-age staff lists common answers to this question.

When I go to my center I want to . . .

- be left alone
- go home as soon as I can

- do whatever I want
- be with my friends
- call up my mom
- visit places
- play with my own toys
- have lots of junk food to eat
- watch TV
- be a Girl Scout
- read my book all afternoon
- play basketball all afternoon
- have lots of art projects
- have men teachers
- chew gum and eat candy
- have lots of time with the teacher
- go to the bathroom by myself
- learn how to play the drums
- work on my baseball card collection
- take my shoes off and get dirty
- have a break from homework and school
- get special attention
- play pool

Their Parents Speak

It's also helpful to hear from parents about their children, their likes and dis-likes, and how they view their children's out-of-school activities. After all, they know these children best, and they see them in a variety of environments. Parents also read books and talk to teachers and to one another, reassuring themselves that their children are developing and growing like other children do, or helping one another cope with behavioral changes or personality traits.

One father picking up his 7-year-old daughter from a Brownie meeting remarked to the leader, "I don't know how you can *stand* Melissa this week. She seems to be whining about something all the time. Everything is *boring,* or *dumb,* or *gross.*" Smiling knowingly, the young woman, the mother of Melissa's best friend agreed. "Yes, Melissa does like to dramatize events. But so does Lacey. I think it's just part of being a 7-year-old. However," she pointed out, "Melissa also gets just as intensely interested in something she wants to do as she gets intensely bored with something she doesn't like. For example, take those friendship bracelets we made last week. She didn't want to stop working on them even when you came to pick her up."

Parents need reassurance that their children are safe, and that they are developing and growing like other children.

Another parent, juggling a toddler and an infant as her 9-year-old opened the car door, praised her oldest child's cooperative spirit. "I don't know what I would do without Gurnoor. Since Jassim was born I never seem to have enough hands. But Gurnoor helps me get in and out of the house, and entertains his little sister while I feed and change Jassim. He's suddenly become so helpful!" School-age children are moving away from the dependence on adults that has characterized their early childhood. They are growing physically and like to show that they can be responsible and take on adult tasks.

A cluster of parents watching their 7- and 8-year-olds playing with super-hero characters at a park remarked on the complicated script the children had worked out. Each child had at least two different characters to move around, yet seemed to have no trouble remembering each of the other characters' names and extensive attributes, or the story line that had emerged during the last hour.

"You should hear all the rules they've made about this game," one of the fathers remarked. "If they jump from the picnic table it means they've transported to another galaxy, but if they're *under* the table they have their shields on. Only certain characters can be invisible, and if they get hit by a missile of some kind, they lose their powers. I'd need a rule book to keep it all straight."

"I know," agreed another. "But it gets even better as they get older. My 10-year-old daughter keeps reminding me of the moves whenever we play chess, and she's only been playing for a year. I have trouble remembering all the rules in *Jeopardy!*"

School-age children are also growing intellectually. They are developing logical thought and new social skills that allow them to think about people, places, and events that are far away from their daily lives, perhaps even imaginary, and they enjoy being involved in complex games, problem solving, and long-term projects.

Talking to parents can help us understand children's individual temperaments, developmental changes, and family dynamics. It helps us to to be aware of parents' need for reassurance—that their children are safe after school, and that they are developing and growing like other children. Talking to teachers can provide us with still other perspectives.

Their Teachers Speak

"I really enjoy teaching first grade," remarked a first-year teacher during a staff meeting at a small neighborhood school. "The children want so much to please you, and are loving and kind to one another. I did my student teaching in fourth grade, and found the kids really hard to handle."

"I would never want to teach 5- and 6-year-olds," disagreed the fourth-grade teacher. "They're still so needy; they follow you around all the time. By fourth grade the kids understand all the school rules and make sure their friends follow them. They can take care of their own emotional needs in the peer group, and don't need the teacher to be their nanny. But get much older than 9, and they are really a challenge. I definitely prefer teaching fourth and fifth graders."

"I really think the sixth graders are just as sweet as the first graders," interjected a third teacher. "But they don't think it's cool to let you know it. They're a lot more savvy about personal interactions and how friendships work, but they understand one another's strengths and weaknesses, and often allow for them. The only kind of thinking the little guys understand is "If you let me play with your toy, I'll be your friend." Watch the older children working in groups on a project and you'll see that they assign the slower kids things they can handle while the more capable children take on much more responsibility."

The Theorists Speak

Classroom teachers, more than any other group of people, see children in age-related ***cohorts,*** which allows them to see similarities among children of one age. Just as 2-year-olds have certain common traits, so do 6-year-olds, 9-year-olds, and 10-year-olds. There *are* some developmentally related behaviors and characteristics, and it is useful to know what they are, always keeping in mind that each child is unique and growing on his or her own timetable. Personalities and life circumstances also differ, influencing individual children's responses to similar situations, but some commonalities exist that are helpful to understand if you are going to spend much time with children.

For example, child psychologists and other researchers have observed that developmental changes in children are *orderly, directional,* and *stable* (Fischer & Lazerson, 1984). **Orderly** means that the changes occur in a sequence or series; they can usually be predicted because in many cases they are similar for all children. **Directional** means that these changes build on one another; they show some kind of progression or accumulation of the parts of development. **Stable** means that these changes stick around for a while once they appear (although with very young children the stages are often quite short). In general, once a child, for example, conquers his fear of the dark, he remains less frightened than before. Once a baby learns to walk, she continues to do so.

In addition, child development professionals tend to divide their analysis of development into separate areas. For example, *physical growth* and *motor development* are considered separately from *social* and *emotional development,* as are *cognitive* and *language development* and *ethics* or *moral development.* The study of normal children growing up in families around the world provides child and youth professionals with information that is helpful when they work with children of various cultures and abilities who are spending large portions of their growing-up time in child care and recreational environments away from home. Learning about development helps us apply the results of research to the development of programs for school-age children and the selection of guidance techniques to use in a variety of situations.

Researchers have developed theories to explain what they have observed about children at different stages of growth and development. Most theorists write about development in only one or two developmental areas, so it is important to consider the viewpoints of several different people in order to build a complete picture of the developing child. Chapter 4, Theories of Child Development, describes each of the major views on physical, social, cognitive, and moral development and summarizes the milestones identified by each theorist. Readers who have already completed a child growth and development course may be able to skip this chapter, but others will find it valuable as a reference point.

Chapter 2 describes the wide range of experiences known as "out-of-school care," and Chapter 3 introduces some of the people who work with school-age children.

SUMMARY
·············

Children whose parents cannot care for them after school face a wide variety of different circumstances. Some families allow their children to go home alone after school, others make informal supervision arrangements with neighbors, and still others pay for after-school child-care services.

People who work with school-age children can learn a great deal by talking with children, their parents, and their teachers. Child-care theorists study various aspects of child development, which is orderly, directional, and stable. A basic understanding of child development is necessary if you want to work in programs for school-age children.

REVIEW QUESTIONS

1. What do you think of the children described in this chapter? Do they sound like any children you know? Why or why not?

2. Make a list of the children described in this chapter. Which of them is under the care and supervision of an adult? Which are practicing self-care?

3. What is meant by the term *out-of-school care*? How does that differ from the earlier term *school-age child care*?

4. Describe the three characteristics of all developmental changes.

CHALLENGE EXERCISES

1. Interview members of a family in which both parents (or a single parent) work outside the home. Talk to the parent(s) separately from the children; ask what they think their children would like to do before and/or after school. Ask the child or children the same question. Compare the answers.

2. Create a composite child, age 5 to 12. Give the child a gender and a name. Describe him or her physically, behaviorally, and socially. What kind of scenario can you create for this child's before- and after-school situation? Is it realistic? Why or why not?

3. Who do you think should be responsible for the before- and after-school care of children? How about summer and holiday care? Who should pay for it? How should they raise the funds?

TERMS TO LEARN

cohort
orderly
directional
stable

REFERENCES

Bailyn, B., Dallek, R., Davis, D. B., Donald, D. H., Thomas, J. L., & Wood, G. S. (1992). *The great republic: A history of the American people* (4th ed.). Lexington, MA: D. C. Heath.

Clinton, W. (1998). State of the union address.

Fischer, K., & Lazerson, A. (1984). *Human development from conception through adolescence.* New York: W. H. Freeman.

National Research Council. (1990). *Who cares for America's children: Child care policy for the 1990s.* Washington, DC: National Academy Press.

Newman, R. L. (1993). *Trainer's guide, keys to quality in school-age child care.* Rockville, MD: Montgomery County (MD) Child Care Division.

Petrie, P., & Logan, P. (1986). *After school and in the holidays: The responsibility for looking after school children.* London: University of London Institute of Education.

Zigler, E. F., & Lang, M. E. (1991). *Child care choices: Balancing the needs of children, families, and society.* New York: Free Press.

CHAPTER TWO

Out-of-School Child and Youth Care

An Emerging Profession and a Challenge for Communities

Varieties of Care Options for School-Age Children

In Chapter 1 we met some children whose parents cannot always care for them before and after school. Seventeen million school-age children have both parents or their only parent in the workforce, according to Michelle Seligson, Executive Director of the National Institute of Out-of-School Time (NIOST), and experts estimate that between 5 and 7 million of these children go home alone each day after school (Seligson, 1997). Some of us who are adults today are lucky enough to remember childhoods spent climbing trees, combing the empty lots and parks of our communities for interesting things to do and friends to do them with, knowing that our mothers (or in some cases, fathers or aunts or uncles or grandparents) were home if we needed them. For most of human history, in nearly all cultures, extended families have helped to raise the society's children and keep them safe until they were old enough to do so themselves.

For a variety of reasons, in the United States and other industrialized nations, this is not happening as effectively as it once did. Families have changed; society has changed; children have changed; and somehow in that process, we have lost our ability to ensure that very important function of society and culture for our children. Families today tend to be nuclear (parents and children) more often than extended (several generations in one household), and they are more likely to live far away from other relatives than once was the norm. Family groupings may vary from father, mother, and child to single parents raising children alone, multigenerational households and variations on the "blended" or reconstituted family that include stepfamilies, unmarried couples, and gay and lesbian parents. However, they all have one thing in common: Most of the adults need to work outside the home to make ends meet.

Families also seem to be busier than they have ever been before, and so do their children, a trend that led David Elkind (1981) to coin the phrase "the hurried child." They also move more often. Neighborhoods, once the safe playgrounds of many children, have a different configuration when families move in and out of them in less than a generation (sometimes in less than a few years), and the alienation that comes from living among strangers seems to go hand in hand with statistics that tell us there is now much more violence committed by children and teens, more suicide, more depression, more eating disorders, and more drug and alcohol abuse than in previous years (Ollhoff, 1996).

What this means in many communities is that children are no longer safe wandering about unsupervised for long periods of time. Rising involvement of young people with alcohol, drugs, and crime tells us that our youth need the guidance of caring adults, support of their communities, and interesting things to do in their out-of-school hours. The good news is that, in many places, those things are available to them. Some can be found by looking in the telephone yellow pages, or the newspaper child-care directory. However, many out-of-school recreational and care settings exist outside the community child-care system and look a little different from what we might expect. To understand the framework within which programs for school-age children function, we need to be aware of the whole picture of child rearing and supervision during out-of-school hours.

The following descriptions outline several kinds of solutions developed by parents and communities to address some of the child-care and safety challenges facing them. Some child-care professionals might find certain of these alternatives outside their scope or not even desirable, but it is important that we examine the present situation before attempting to work within it.

IN-HOME CARE

Dad's Home: Have Some Milk and Cookies   Even on the brink of the year 2000, some children do have one or more parent at home to welcome them after school and to supervise their activities. Although in more families than ever it is now necessary for both parents to work, many parents have jobs that permit flexible hours, shift work, or work at home; these parents manage to combine earning a living with supervising their own school-age children. Increasingly, both fathers and mothers seize the opportunities to run small businesses from their homes or take work home so they can be with their children after school. Other parents receive child support or government assistance that allows them to care for their children.

While visiting families with school-age children, I met a Midwestern doctor who has for several years made hospital rounds in the early morning while her husband Dane stays at home to prepare breakfast for the children. Phuong sees patients in her office until noon, when she returns home to care for their 5-year-old after he returns from kindergarten. In the late afternoon when the older children come home, she eats a snack with them and listens to the events of the day. Then they go out to play or begin their homework and Phuong reviews patient files and prepares the evening meal. After Dane arrives home, about seven, Phuong returns to the hospital for evening rounds, sometimes returning in time to help with baths and bedtime stories. Prior to this arrangement, Dane, an insurance salesman, made evening sales appointments; now he uses the evenings at home to make telephone calls and do paperwork while the children study or watch TV.

Joan Harper and her husband separated 2 years ago. Since leaving her job as a supermarket checker 10 years earlier for the birth of their first child, Joan has not worked outside the home. The terms of her divorce allowed her 3 years to attend college and develop job skills, and she receives additional assistance from a state agency because one of her three children is under 5 years of age. While her youngest child is in a preschool program paid for by the agency, Joan attends computer and English classes at a community college. Two nights a week her former husband cares for the children while she participates in a special job readiness program at the local high school. For the moment, Joan is home in the afternoons when her two oldest children arrive from school, but soon she will be required to seek employment and will need to make other arrangements for child care.

Another couple I observed had four children, 7 to 14 years old, attending three different schools. This particular family lives in a city in the north of England, but they could have been living in any urban setting. Peter, an independent educational consultant, plans meetings away from his home office around the week's teaching and meeting schedule of his partner Susan, a lecturer at a local college. As most of his commuting is done on the train, he uses the time spent riding the train to complete reports and other paperwork. In the afternoons, while Peter or Susan work at the kitchen table or read in a nearby chair, their children, frequently accompanied by friends, wander in and out, sharing experiences or preparing snacks; they also move freely about the neighborhood, checking in from time to time for more food or permission to ramble further afield.

Another family was made up of two women and their two daughters. Stephanie, mother of 10-year-old Danielle, is a technical writer at a small computer company. Her partner, Dianne, works at a 24-hour resource and referral agency. Both women drive nearly an hour to work but have chosen to live in a community that has excellent schools and where they feel supported in their lesbian lifestyle. Together the couple adopted 5-year-old Tasha after her parents were killed in an airplane accident. To be sure that one of the women is with their daughters, Dianne works nights. She arrives home in the morning just as Stephanie and the girls are getting up and usually eats breakfast with them. She sleeps after they leave, rising about 2:30 p.m. to meet Danielle at school and pick up Tasha from the activity program she attends after kindergarten. Sometimes she has a chance for a nap in the evening after Stephanie arrives home from work, but much of the time Dianne catches up on missed sleep during her days off.

Watching these parents juggling work-related responsibilities and commuting with car pools, Scout meetings, doctors' appointments, trips to the swimming pool or football field, and meals, we see their need for organization, good communication, and commitment to a family-centered life. However, we also see some of the advantages of a regular parent presence; communication was enhanced by day-by-day interaction, regular supervision of homework, and awareness of social ups and downs that are sometimes missed when parents are away from their children until the dinner hour or later. This is a gap that staff must try to close when working in out-of-school care.

Even with their willingness to "flex" working hours and work together to provide care, Peter and Susan depend on the help of other people to be sure that someone is always available; a complicated schedule involving neighborhood parents (who receive child-care assistance in return), childminders, or holiday play schemes is worked out each week to be sure all the gaps are covered. A child-development college student is Dane and Phuong's backup assistant; he is called in when the children are mildly ill and cannot attend school, or when one of the parents has a work-related responsibility during the hours he or she is supposed to be "in charge." Occasionally, when Dianne must work a daytime shift and Stephanie can't stay home, they depend on a network of other parents to retrieve the girls from school and care for them until one or another parent gets home.

Clearly, all at-home care is not the same. Zigler found a tremendous variety of ways in which parents interact with their children while they are caring for them after school (Zigler & Lang, 1991). In homes with one or more parents present in the daytime, the general pattern is for children in the early primary years to spend most of their time engaged in activities with or close by the parent, gradually becoming less reliant on direct adult interaction and engaging in more independent play. Eventually, children age 9 and older begin to use the parent as a base, checking in as needed or as instructed, but roaming the neighborhood in search of social activities. Eleven- and twelve-year-olds in parental care are often requested to run errands or do short stints of babysitting; gradually they gain more freedom to organize their own time and activities. The most effective school-age child-care models seem to allow this same kind of developing autonomy to take place.

Some parents may be at home, but they are too involved in their own worries, responsibilities, or interests to be emotionally available to their children; these parents offer little in the way of social interaction, guidance, or companionship, and expect even their very young children to amuse themselves. At the other end of the continuum, some parents structure every waking moment of their children's lives, scheduling dancing lessons, piano lessons, soccer and swim practice, and closely supervising homework and the children's social activities (Elkind, 1981). In the same way, school-age care arrangements vary in their structure and direction.

Neighbor Care   In close-knit neighborhoods, parents who are available to their children for some or all of the afternoon hours may share the responsibility with other parents nearby, facilitating the increased freedom of movement desired by older school-age children. This arrangement, used by Susan and Peter

School-age programs in cities may share playground space with schools and public parks. Here, children return from the public park where they have been playing.

as described above, replicates the pattern of rural and suburban child rearing of earlier decades, when groups of children would flow from one backyard, tree house, or empty lot to another, passing by one another's kitchens for snacks on the way. Some at-home parents, voluntarily or not, absorb the occasional care of several children in the neighborhood as the balance changes from one or two children whose parents cannot be home in the afternoon to one or two children whose parents *can.*

Benny and Bill, both soccer coaches, work from home and have become focal points of many children's afternoon activities in their neighborhoods. Benny runs a janitorial service but schedules his work around school hours. His blue van is a regular sight in the school parking lot, as he ferries several families' children to music lessons, the library, or home for a snack before soccer practice. Once home, Benny helps neighborhood children with homework, or fixes a flat bicycle tire, or just offers a listening ear. On the other side of town, Bill runs a graphic arts business in his garage; from 2:30 until dinnertime children flow in and out of his kitchen and backyard (temptingly equipped with a tennis court, basketball hoop, and soccer net). During this period of his day, Bill alternates between sitting at his computer and handing out food.

Just a few houses away from Bill, Miss Joan, who teaches piano in her home, remembers when parents brought their children to lessons and picked them up promptly afterward. Now, because their parents are not home, many children come directly after school, even if their appointment is not until much later. Responding to the ever-present groups of children sitting on her front lawn, Joan has begun setting out bowls of nuts and raisins on her dining room table and allowing children to come in (quietly) and study or read together while they wait for their turn at the piano, sometimes returning to the table after their lesson until parents come from work to pick them up. Miss Joan has become, in effect, a part of the child-care solution for many parents who would, she realizes, be forced to stop their children's lessons altogether if she were not responsive to their needs. She works closely with both parents and caregivers to schedule appointments at convenient times, and she follows up on children who do not arrive for appointments to be sure they are not stranded between school and home. One might argue that child care is not her job, but Miss Joan believes her help is a boon to the community, and the parents of her students would agree with her.

Relative Care   One single father in a rural Minnesota community does not have the luxury of being able to work from home. However, as an electrician he can flex his days as long as he achieves the total hours needed to earn an acceptable income and satisfy his supervising contractor. For 5 years Nels has arisen at 4:00 a.m. each day and carried his two sleeping children to his mother's nearby home so that he can be home with them after school and allow them to participate in athletic activities and music lessons. He has never missed a first day of school or a parents' night, and the only outside care his children have received has been in summer recreation programs to relieve the burden on his mother of 3 uninterrupted months of her high-spirited grandchildren. The regular family presence is an important component of his relationship with his children, who are very close to him and appreciative of the interesting life and varied activities he and his mother afford them.

Traditionally, grandparents and adult siblings have helped young parents care for their children; increasingly, grandparents are managing offices and even younger aunts and uncles are working as many hours as the mothers and fathers. However, when working patterns allow families to help, and when families live close enough to one another, they often do. Grandparents take children to the dentist after school, drive them to baseball practice, help them with their homework. Often this care takes place in the child's own home; at other times, children walk or take public transportation to the relative's home after school. In either case, relative care provides an important support system for working parents and can help to keep families functioning during the years when children need more supervision than their parents can provide.

The Mary Poppins Alternative   The nanny, once the private domain of British upper-class children, has entered American prime-time television as a regular character. Increasing in popularity, nanny training programs in private institutions and public colleges prepare child and youth workers to interact with parents and children of a variety of ages within a home setting. One researcher reports that over 100,000 trained nannies are employed in the United Kingdom alone, and 6% of American children younger than 5 were being cared for by

PERSPECTIVE

White House Child Care Conference Panel Presentation

OCTOBER 23, 1997

Michelle Seligson, Executive Director of the National Institute on Out-of-School Time

President and Mrs. Clinton, I want to thank you both for the honor of asking me to participate in this conference. It is tremendously exciting to know that you are interested in this vital issue, and that you want to help.

I first got involved in school-age child care more than 25 years ago when I needed after-school care for my own children, Sally and Jon. I was lucky to connect with other parents and we started a parent co-op center with a small after-school program. My experience starting a program, going on to help others in my town begin school-based programs, and hearing from schools and families around the country about their concerns, led me to establish the School-Age Child Care Project at the Center for Research on Women at Wellesley College. Foundations and other funders and colleagues have helped us over nearly 20 years conduct our research and apply it. We are now calling ourselves the National Institute on Out-of-School Time because we want to expand definitions of care to include older children—no self-respecting middle school kid wants to be thought of as being in child care!

Where do children go after school? Is this a problem? What do they do? Many adults over the age of 30 remember out-of-school time as time to play with friends, explore the neighborhood, play records, ride bikes, and above all, eat! Someone's mother or relative was home but mostly kids entertained themselves. People remember feeling safe. Things are different now. Kids don't speak about feeling safe in their neighborhoods, or even at home. Twenty-five million children in America have working parents, many of whom work full-time once their kids reach school. Children spend less than 20% of their waking hours in school. Risks to health and even life are now common

among young children. According to the National Center on Juvenile Justice, newly reported data from eight states on peak hours for violent juvenile crime show nearly half of crimes taking place between 2 p.m. and 11 p.m. A 1990 University of California study and other studies found unsupervised children are at significantly higher risk of truancy, stress, receiving poor grades, risk-taking behavior, and substance abuse.

Children spend more of their out-of-school time watching television than any other single activity, and we know the impact of that on kids—kids read less, play less, and are more aggressive. On average, American children spend 40 hours a week watching television and playing video games, more hours than they spend in school, and children in low-income households are estimated to spend 50% more time watching television than their privileged peers. Our best estimates tell us at least 5 million children between 5 and 14 spend too much time on their own during a typical week.

What does research have to say about what makes for healthy kids who feel good about themselves and others, and who are competent in school? The key studies point to two factors: caring relationships and constructive activities.

An evaluation of after-school programs conducted by Deborah Vandell at the University of Wisconsin finds that the single most important factor is *the quality of children's interactions with the program staff*. Kids do better in school, are more self-assured—if they attend carefully planned but flexible programs where the primary work of the adults is caring about and for the kids. Jerome Bruner has written compellingly that what helps kids learn is the nature of their relationships, our capacity to listen and to hear their stories. We develop a sense of self not in a vacuum but in relation to others. Other studies have found how well a child gets along with other children to be a better predictor of adult adjustment than academic performance or classroom behavior (Hartup, Early Childhood Research Quarterly, 1990).

Informal learning environments offer an opportunity to build good social relationships with other children, and the chance to try to learn something you don't know how to do—physical or artistic or intellectual—in a safe place where you don't pass or fail. Good after-school programs make that possible, as do appropriate ratios of adult staff, who understand the age group, who are comfortable in a relaxed setting that is different from the regular school day, who use their unique talents and personalities and their capacity to engage the children. Good after-school programs respect the power of play as children's work, and the unique characteristics of an individual child. These are the fundamentals of quality.

How are communities dealing with this issue? Schools, churches, parks and recreation centers, youth-serving agencies, child-care centers and family day care homes—every community institution including libraries and public housing and corporate headquarters are potential sites and potential partners in this enterprise.

- Some states have enacted enabling legislation so schools can partner with community agencies; others have financed training and new programs

- There has been generous funding from the American Business Collaboration that has helped to develop more programs and improve quality.

- A privately funded initiative of the Dewitt Wallace Readers Digest Fund, called MOST (Making the Most of Out-of-School Time) focuses on three cities as a logical locus for building and improving the supply of school-age care. In Chicago, a new partnership with the city's Park District is creating new school-age child-care spaces for several thousand children; in Boston, Parents United for Child Care has leveraged hundreds of thousands of dollars from the private and public sector to support low-income families' school-age child care; in Seattle, anyone can go to a public library or 88 other community access points to log on free to the data base and get information about 300 out-of-schooltime programs like art centers, sports and recreation, tutorial services.

But there are some big problems.

- This is not just about some working families needing after-school child care. This is an issue that cuts across all income groups, including families preparing to enter the out-of-home workforce. Every family that on this very day is managing the work and family and school and child-care whirlwind knows what I mean. Yet some Americans are more in need of help with school-age child care than others. Some don't have the resources to pay for lessons, after-school sports, academic programs, summer camps. Some kids don't get the same exposure to ideas, skills, positive relationships with adults and their peers.

  The National Before and After School Program Study clearly shows this discrepancy—83% of approximately 50,000 school-age child-care programs depend on parent fees for their survival. Many families simply can't pay. We know very little about how immigrant and refugee families manage their children's out-of-school time.

- While there is widespread agreement on standards of quality and a new national accreditation system, quality is uneven at best.

- It is more and more difficult to recruit qualified school-age child-care staff. Salaries are low and turnover is high, and people move on quickly to better paying work.

- Programs often pass along to parents the cost of having to lease school facilities and pay for custodial services. There is a huge transportation problem—who should pay to bus children from school to after-school programs? Parents? The school district?

- Some school boards have welcomed partnerships with community-based organizations, or are running their own programs; others resist them.

- Many families have even more trouble than others finding good care: families whose children have special needs, rural families, parents with middle school children—an underserved group that has some of the most pressing needs.

Conclusion

We know what to do to solve some of these problems. There are three ways national leadership could help:

1. First, following up on this conference, keep the spotlight on this issue both inside and outside government.

2. Finance more school-age care for low- and moderate-income parents, regardless of their relationship to welfare. Good school-age care benefits society—the investment will pay off in terms of producing long-term benefits in children and especially as a prevention strategy.

3. Fund community-level strategies to enable groups to work across institutions to collaborate on discovering and meeting local needs and expanding services to meet those needs. An official incentive encourages people to cross institutional lines, and funding is an additional incentive.

Thank you.

nannies in 1985 (Leach, 1994). Some nannies have the luxury of a private room and a bath; others prefer the freedom of living elsewhere, arriving each morning before breakfast to help ready children for the day and leaving in the evenings when parents return.

Hired most often by parents of very young children, well-chosen nannies can become devoted companions to older children and provide the peace of mind necessary for parents to meet their professional responsibilities away from home. When trained in child development and health and safety, the nanny can become a respected member of a parenting team and assist in family decisions surrounding homework, chores, bedtimes, and allowances.

Christopher Robin Milne, of *Winnie the Pooh* fame, had this to say about the importance of his nanny:

> She had me when I was very young. I was all hers and remained all hers until the age of nine. Other people hovered around the edges, but they meant little. My total loyalty was to her. To the extent that I was a "good little boy," to the extent that my prayers had real meaning for me at a very early age and continued to have meaning for many years afterwards, and to the extent that all this was something acquired rather than inherited, this was Nanny's doing. Was she a brilliant teacher? Not specially. She was just a very good and very loving person; and when that has been said, no more need be added.
>
> —Milne, 1974, p. 2

Nanny placement agencies, however, report that there is a great variation in training of nannies. Some have had professional training and experience; many have not. Although many young people enter the profession with high ideals, a nanny or *au pair* position is also sometimes seen merely as a route out of a small town, or into the United States from Europe (Hofferth & Phillips, 1987; Hostetler, 1984). The demand for in-home caregivers is so great that regulation is difficult, and nanny care is generally ignored by child-care information services. This is an area in which **resource and referral agencies**— which help parents find appropriate care for their children, provide support and education to providers, and report data regarding child-care need and supply to local agencies—can provide a helpful service.

All the variations of care discussed so far offer children a regular adult presence and more or less healthy opportunities for normal social development within a home environment. However, an in-home caregiver is a very expensive child-care option, out of reach of most families, and some families are without friends or family who can help them care for their children. What about these families? What is their solution to the before- and after-school dilemma?

Home Alone: It Really Isn't Funny   In Chapter 1 we met 12-year-old Jamal who takes care of brother Jesse each day after school. According to researchers, over a third of all school-age children go home to empty houses each night (Seligson,

1997). In contrast to the experiences described so far is the loneliness encountered by many of these youngsters, often labeled **latchkey children** because of the key they carry to open their home's door latch. The popular film *Home Alone* romanticized the notion of self-care, but in reality many children find it a rather unpleasant experience. Interviews with children who enter empty houses, heat snacks in the microwave, and spend their afternoons in solitary confinement do not often result in praise for this option (Alexander, 1986; Bumgarner, 1995). To be fair, most parents do not usually *choose* self-care, but rather *settle* for it when their working arrangements preclude their presence before or after school and no economic alternative is available. And, to make matters worse, as children enter the 9- to 12-year-old period they may resist being enrolled in supervised care, believing that they can take care of themselves and urging their parents to allow them to do so.

Whatever the reason, according to a variety of reports, as many as 7 million American children appear to be in self-care arrangements, with more to come (Coleman, Rowland, & Robinson, 1989; Seligson, 1997; Thiel, McCroskey, & Marquart, 1988; Todd, Albrecht, & Coleman, 1990; Zigler & Lang, 1991). In the United Kingdom, the Kids Club Network estimates that 1 out of 5 children between the ages of 5 and 10 is left alone at home during school holidays, and 1 in 6 goes home at the end of each school day to an empty house (Leach, 1994).

There are conflicting opinions on the effects of latchkey arrangements (Lamb, 1982; Long & Long, 1981; Robinson, Rowland, & Coleman, 1986), but four types of adjustment risks have been identified as associated with extended hours of self-care. Children who are home alone may *feel badly, act badly, develop badly,* or *be treated badly*. In other words, children who spend long periods of time alone may begin to feel rejected and alienated from peers and family or possibly experience high levels of fear. Left to their own devices, and frequently bored, such children may begin to engage in antisocial or delinquent behavior. Additionally, children with no feedback or regular interaction with peers or adults may develop emotional or health problems or begin to fall behind in their schoolwork. Finally, children without supervision may become victims of crime or abuse; they are at a higher risk for accidents than are children in care (Coolsen, Seligson, & Garbarino, 1985; Galambos & Garbarino, 1983; Todd, Albrecht, & Coleman, 1990).

Todd (Todd et al., 1990) developed a conceptual framework for organizing the variety of experiences school-age children may have while their parents work. Table 2-1 presents that framework. Using Todd's analysis, children in solitary self-care fall at the lowest end of the supervision continuum and probably suffer the greatest vulnerability to the risks described above. Some communities, having discovered the large numbers of children in such jeopardy, have initiated telephone help-lines, family education programs, or "check-in" programs, in which qualified staff run drop-in or call-in centers to assist children in self-care to deal with loneliness, fear, or specific problems such as homework, preparing meals, or first aid for simple injuries. These children would be considered to have "distal supervision," or supervision from a distance.

TABLE 2–1   A Continuum of School-Age Child-Care Options

HIGH ──────────────── Degree of Adult Supervision ──────────────── LOW			
Adult supervision with full accountability	Adult supervision with *some* accountability	Distal supervision	No supervision
Relative care	Short-term recreation programs	Self-care with parental monitoring	Self-care with no parental monitoring
Family child care	Enrichment activities (e.g., music/art lessons)	Sibling care	Telephone help-lines
Formal before- and after-school care programs	Youth groups (4-H, Scouts, sports)	Check-in programs (neighbors or community-based)	

Source: Adapted from Todd et al., 1990.

This is an area of need that deserves to be explored in communities where it is not yet an option.

Another way some communities have approached the large number of self-care arrangements appearing in their midst is with education programs designed to make parents aware of the risks and help children become more able to care for themselves. Often these programs utilize one of the self-help books that have been designed to help children in self-care handle routine events or emergencies that might occur while they are alone. A sampling of these books is listed at the end of this chapter. Support systems for latchkey children such as check-in programs, educational workshops, and books can help to increase children's safety and welfare; however, children, parents, and the entire community need to understand that the best place for children before and after school is not alone but in the care of a responsible adult.

OUT-OF-HOME CARE

Licensed Family Child-Care Homes   Licensed family child care accounts for nearly a quarter of American school-age children in out-of-home care (Bureau of the Census, 1987). In the United Kingdom and Australia, childminders (who care for children under 5) and playworkers (who work with children 5 to 15) are trained and registered separately, and the latter are in short supply in most communities (Brady & Graham, 1993; Leach, 1994; Petrie & Logan, 1986). If they adapt their environment and activities to the needs of school-age children, licensed family homes and playschemes can be excellent arrangements. Ideally, the caregiver would live in the same neighborhood as the children being cared for, so that the children can participate in school-sponsored activities and play with children who live nearby.

Unfortunately, some regional licensing requirements make it difficult for providers to profit as much from school-age care as from the care of younger children; these restrictions also limit the circumstances under which the providers care for school-agers. The number of child-care slots allowed per provider is often the same for 2-year-olds as for 10-year-olds even though school-age children need less intense care than infants and young children. Licensing capacities also usually include providers' own school-age children, and may disallow "drop-in" children who need care only one or two afternoons a week.

One commonly heard complaint about family child care of school-agers is that many caregivers, accustomed to the needs of small children, do not plan activities or design environments suitable for older children (National Research Council, 1990; Zigler & Lang, 1991). Too many school-age children, they say, are forced to compete for attention and space with younger children, or spend large portions of their day watching television and eating. Actually, there are some excellent arguments for mixed-age grouping of children, and knowledgeable family child-care providers will address the needs of *all* the children in their care.

For example, sensitive caregivers listen to older children's requests for private spaces away from toddlers, respond to their need to talk about the events of the day, and provide them challenging games and a chance to socialize as well as study and work on homework. Younger children may require closer supervision and more one-on-one attention from the caregiver, but when those children are asleep or quietly occupied, caregivers can turn their attention to the older children, using that time to help them plan future activities, assist with problem solving, or simply listen. When developmental issues are taken into consideration, most school-age children thrive in the multiple-age groupings and familylike settings that emerge in family child-care homes.

Some school districts prohibit transportation of children to sites other than their own homes (Zigler & Lang, 1991), and licensing regulations frequently stipulate "line of sight" supervision, restricting school-age children from going home first, then checking in with a caregiver, and perhaps returning home or to a friend's house later. Active efforts from day care associations and parents have successfully changed some of these restrictions, and innovative planning can result in programs that meet children's needs and also satisfy lawmakers' concerns. (See the description of the Family Satellite Program for an example.)

School-Administered Before- and After-School Group Care   For over a decade, government reports (Robinson, 1982; U.S. Congress, 1989) and educators (Petrie & Logan, 1986; U.S. Department of Education, 1997; Zigler, 1987; Zigler & Ennis, 1988) have repeatedly identified publicly funded school systems as the agencies best equipped to provide communities with before- and after-school child-care services. The number of such programs presently operated by individual schools or school districts is difficult to determine because they are usually administered locally and the data are not reported to a single agency. However, surveys indicate that these numbers are growing as pressure from parents needing help with child care produce task forces and needs assessments that support their demands (Marx & Seligson, 1988; National Research Council, 1990; Seligson & Allenson, 1993). Marx and Seligson (1988) reported that

**CONSIDERING SCHOOL-AGERS' DEVELOPMENTAL NEEDS:
THE FAMILY SATELLITE PROGRAM**

The Family Satellite Program in Reston, Virginia, is an innovative approach to family day care after-school programs. There the Reston Children's Center (RCC) operates a network of family day care homes in conjunction with its center-based preschool and school-age services. The family care-givers become employees of RCC and receive benefits including paid holidays and sick time. They are also given program support in the form of field trip planning, materials and supplies, and activity plans. This assures that children will have something interesting to do after school and will be active rather than sitting for hours in front of the television. After the age of 9 or 10, children and their parents may opt instead for a check-in program. In the RCC Check-In model, which was designed with the help of a federal grant, a written contract lists specific places the child has permission to go, including his or her own home. This model provides an appropriate transition for the child too old for many of the activities offered in the day care home and too young for self-care.

Source: From Zigler & Lang, 1991, p. 138.

in 1986, twelve states provided some form of funding for school-age care. For the most part, families cannot pay anywhere near what agencies need to provide high-quality, well-staffed, developmentally appropriate care. It seems likely that part of this cost will have to be provided by state or federal government in the form of tax credits, reimbursements, or outright grants to serve most of the children who need care.

One example of how government support for child care can work is found in California. Since 1985 the state of California has funded school-age child care under the auspices of the School Age Community Child Care Act. Designed to begin to address the need for extended day care for the children of working parents, the California State Department of Education distributed $15 million in grant funds to 190 programs in its first year of operation. State-funded school-age programs are administered by school districts, county offices of education, cities, colleges and universities, and private nonprofit agencies. Not all facilities are located on school sites, but the majority are (Thiel et al., 1988).

One major advantage of school-site care for school-age children is transportation. In ideal situations, before- and after-school centers are located at each school in a district. However, even if only certain schools are designated as care sites, shuttle service between schools can usually be arranged by the district transportation office. A second advantage is utilization and safety of publicly owned facilities. Many school districts have been challenged for their **underutilization** of school buildings, which are at risk for **vandalization** during the hours when they are unused. One of Zigler's strongest arguments for school-site care is that the community-education model of facility usage creates a natural buy-in or "protection" role for community members who use the facility outside school hours (Zigler & Ennis, 1988). Because 75% of vandals are between the ages of 7 and 18 (National Crime Prevention Council, 1996; Winnipeg Police Service, 1996), it also makes sense that providing programs for children in that age range will help to reduce the total amount of vandalism in the community.

In 1997, $1 million was allocated to a Department of Education after-school initiative called 21st Century Community Learning Centers. This number was increased substantially, to $40 million in 1998, and the Clinton administration proposed an additional increase, to $200 million, in fiscal year 1999. This initiative gives grants to local middle and elementary schools in rural and urban areas to provide after-school opportunities, including education and recreation (Children's Defense Fund, 1998). There is appropriate concern among child and youth professionals that this money will be used simply to provide more hours of the educational experiences children now receive during the school day, but the potential exists for creativity and innovation. It will be interesting to see how President Clinton's support of the 21st Century Learning Centers proposal will influence states to implement this means of providing out-of-school care in their own communities. However, much more than $200 million will be needed to provide before- and after-school and summer programs for the millions of children who are not now being served by such programs.

Agency-Administered Child-Care Centers   As federal block grant money and state-initiated funding become available for the creation and implementation of school-age child-care programs, a common approach to the disbursement of funds has been the competitive bid process. Agencies that have entered the field of ***publicly funded*** care for school-agers include community park and recreation centers, nonprofit child-care centers, and established youth organizations such as the YMCA/YWCA, Campfire, and Boys' and Girls' Clubs. Private corporations previously offering care for younger children also compete for these funds.

Federal provision for school-age child-care services primarily takes the form of funding for planning, development, establishment, expansion, and improvement of programs. A total of $3 million was distributed to states and territories between 1986 and 1989 under the Human Services Reauthorization Act, with the stipulation that the funds be used for school-age child-care services (National Research Council, 1990).

In 1990, the Omnibus Budget Reconciliation Act created the Child Care and Development Block Grant, which provides child-care services to low-income family members who work or attend school, or who are receiving or need to receive protective services. However, as changes in the welfare system push more and more mothers into the labor force, the already unfilled need for before-school or after-school care and full-day care during holidays and school vacations will dramatically increase. For welfare-to-work to succeed, federal dollars will have to be made available to meet this need.

Many established agencies have recently entered the field of out-of-school care.

Programs for school-agers may also use U.S. Department of Agriculture funds to reimburse the cost of children's meals. However, there are two shortcomings in federal nutrition programs that need attention. The mechanics of reimbursement systems tend to discourage many schools from using this money for after-school programs, and it is available only for children under 12. The Children's Defense Fund recommends federal action to make meal reimbursement readily available for after-school programs, and to extend reimbursement to programs serving at-risk adolescents in low-income areas (Children's Defense Fund, 1998).

In addition to programs operated or augmented with tax money, large corporations have opened for-profit school-age centers, or added school-age care to their existing offerings. Care may be offered before and after school for children age 6 and older, half-days for 5-year-olds, and all day on holidays, release days, and school vacations (Coleman, Robinson, & Rowland, 1991). Care provided by contractors may not be located on the school sites and more often is housed in large buildings built specially for the purpose; these providers may offer a greater variety of activities, materials, and equipment than is found in public school–sponsored care.

On the down side, contractor-provided child care is profit driven. Training of staff is frequently done on the job or at corporate-sponsored in-service training, and cost considerations sometimes keep salaries so low that highly educated child-care professionals are not willing to apply for positions. Although some for-profit programs for school-agers are excellent, many others are simply warehouses for bored children. These agencies need enthusiastic, dedicated program managers to create developmentally appropriate programs that will nurture rather than merely warehouse children while their parents work, and a clearly delineated career ladder must be developed to attract and keep professional staff.

Grassroots Solutions   Sometimes pressure from parents demanding care for their school-age children can result in dramatic successes. The American Home Economics Association (AHEA) solved a problem for working parents by organizing an after-school program in rural Arkansas after they were approached for help. One parent, after requesting information from the county department of human services regarding after-school care for her child, was dismayed to discover that not only were there no centers offering care for school-age children in the rural town of 671 people, there was no resource and referral system to locate family day care providers or even baby-sitters.

Following discussions with other parents, the AHEA was contacted. Under the umbrella of Project Home Safe—sponsored by the Whirlpool Foundation and designed to provide training, technical assistance, materials, and other resources to promote solutions to the school-age child-care problem—the AHEA conducted a three-day workshop and followed up with guidance to launch an after-school child-care program. The formulation of a community coalition, fund-raising plan, facilities location committee, and publicity package was the responsibility of the interested parents, each of whom gave far more than the required 40 hours of community service necessary to qualify for Project Home Safe assistance. The result was the opening of a summer program for 42 children, followed by an after-school program the following fall (Warnock, 1992).

Parents in Native American communities have also worked with funding agencies to integrate solutions to child-care challenges and other needs. In Leelanaou County, Michigan, the Benodjehn Child Care Center provides Head Start (preschool) and school-age care for approximately 100 Ottawa and Chippewa families. The Grand Traverse Band established the combination facility and keeps it open 21 hours a day so that parents can work at the community's major revenue source, the casino/hotel. The Benodjehn Center also offers education, medical and dental services for the whole family, meals and nutritional information, and transportation. Beginning at 7:00 a.m., children are provided breakfast as they arrive on the center's bus:

> By 9:00 all children have eaten a healthy breakfast, and are either in the Head Start/preschool program or have been picked up at the Center by the local public school bus and taken to school. Many of these children then attend the on-site, afternoon latch key program from 1:00 p.m. to 7:00 p.m. Again, the school bus transports the children from the public school back to the program. From Wednesday to Saturday, child care services are available from

7:00 p.m. to 2:30 a.m., which is essential for those parents working in the gaming facility.

—Krohn, Charter, Beniak, Anderson, & Sordelet, 1993, p. 36

Grassroots development of school-age care provision takes place in urban areas, too. In 1986, a citywide pressure group began to raise the profile of the need for before- and after-school and holiday care in the city of Bradford, an industrial city in the north of England.

In 1989, residents and professionals voiced concern about drug and alcohol abuse by the youngsters on the Holmewood Housing Estate, a 30-year-old development housing nearly 8,000 people (Brady & Graham, 1993). Application to the City of Bradford Metropolitan Council Urban Programme Unit resulted in funds for a research project, which was carried out by a student at a local college of education. The result was an impressive report, which formed the basis for a grant application in the following year. Before- and after-school and holiday care is now provided in two locations and serves nearly 100 children from several different schools (Austin, 1996).

Many such stories exist. The National Institute for Out-of-School Care at Wellesley College is a good source of models and expertise for parents who wish to develop their own community-based programs (Seligson & Allenson, 1993).

Nontraditional Hours, Nontraditional Services   As demonstrated by the tribal child-care center described earlier, parents don't always work during the "traditional" daytime hours. The Labor Department reports that about 1 in 5 U.S. workers, 14.3 million people, do not follow a 9:00–5:00 work schedule whereas most child-care centers continue to operate during traditional work hours. In a report issued in 1995, the Labor Department stated that this problem affects about 7.2 million working mothers with 11.7 million children under the age of 15 (Lewis, 1995).

Providing evening or nighttime care of school-age children presents significant challenges, but some programs are now beginning to address them. In Florida, for example, there is a heavy service industry, and parents are often employed in hotels, hospitals, and restaurants that are open 24 hours. Many family child-care homes offer evening care in the Tampa Bay area, and at least one after-school center does also. *Kid's Time,* owned by Greg and Nanette Brosius, has been operating late-night hours for years. According to a parent whose children attend the facility, they are also open on Saturdays, including late at night, and have been quite successful in their venture (Angelone, personal communication, 1998). In response to welfare-to-work legislation, the Hispanic American Organization of Allentown, Pennsylvania, opened a program for school-age children that runs until 11:30 p.m. (Genco, personal communication, 1998). This program serves a population of people new to the workforce, primarily working in fast-food jobs and entry-level factory positions that require them to work the latest shifts. In Minnesota, Diane Bales, now with the Cooperative Extension Service at the University of Georgia, once

Child-care needs exist outside the 9-to-5 workday.

worked for a small program that provided evening care for children through early school age. Bales reports that Minnesota has developed a full set of licensing guidelines for overnight care centers, sorely needed for parents who work all night (Bales, personal communication, 1998).

When working parents must attend out-of-town meetings or conferences, 24-hour child-care challenges emerge. *Kids Along,* the brainchild of Shelley Matheny of San Rafael, California, helps parents by allowing them to take their children on business trips. The number of parents using the service is large; for instance, in 1995, Kids Along entertained 1,600 children at a New York Life conference in Manhattan. While their parents were talking about insurance and investments, their children attended a carnival, played virtual reality games, and did arts and crafts. A four-day session costs $350 to $400 per child. Sometimes the employer pays, reports Matheny; sometimes the employee does (Kahn, 1996).

Just down the highway, *KidsPark* provides drop-in child care in locations near shopping malls. Originally conceived as a service to baby-sit while parents shopped, *KidsPark,* which now has seven locations in the San Francisco Bay Area, serves children age 2 to 12 while parents work, run errands, or go out to dinner and a movie. "The family-support structure that we used to have is no longer there," explains Debra Gorenberg, founder of *KidsPark.* "We have replaced grandparents in the family infrastructure." Open days, evenings, and weekends, *KidsPark* provides meals, a play structure, toys, crafts, videos, and computers. It offers an adult-child ratio of 1 to 8 and equips parents with pagers so they can be reached in an emergency (Kahn, 1996). Another late-hours program, "Take a Break," in the Boulder/Lafayette area of Colorado, provides care until midnight and offers children (once they finish their homework) activities such as rollerblading, basketball, computers, Nintendo®, and air hockey.

If parents can't get away from work to pick up their children from *KidsPark* and get them to soccer practice or the orthodontist, *Kids on the Move* will pick them up. *Kids on the Move* is a children's shuttle service, charging $7 for a prearranged one-way trip of up to 4 miles. The owner, Kim Burt, says she is meeting the needs of many area families, most of whom have two parents working (Kahn, 1996). A similar shuttle service called *Kids Around Town* operates in St. Paul, Minnesota. Barb Ruprecht used a severance package from 3M to help finance her business, which she opened in September 1992. She started with two vans and two part-time employees when school opened that year, and by the following year she had six vehicles and nine employees. Her clients include children who must be taken to and from school, those who stay late for activities, and those with doctor appointments. *Kids Around Town*'s vans feature car phones and seat belts, and uniform-clad drivers are instructed to make sure they are delivering the children to another adult. A one-time, one-way trip within a 20-mile radius costs $8, but Ruprecht charges only $8 for a round trip to and from school, which is reduced for those under contract (Merrill, 1993).

The emergence of these niche companies reflects a real need among families to get help with caring for their children around the clock and under some rather challenging circumstances. It also raises some important questions. As the service sector becomes the core of U.S. industry, and parents are increasingly away from home at times that are difficult for their families, who will take care of their children? At the present time, most licensing agencies do not regulate short-term care and transportation services as closely as they do other child-care settings. It would be wise for school-age advocacy organizations to take the lead in developing needs assessments, guidelines for programming, and training of staff for these extremely extended day settings. Subsidized programs must also be developed for families that cannot afford the high cost of this scarce new kind of child care.

Drop-in Programs   Although they have now entered the field of school-age care as formal on- and off-site providers, the YMCA/YWCA and Girls' and Boys' Clubs continue to offer the valuable drop-in programs for the youth of urban areas that they have provided for generations, and they have added many programs in suburban areas as well. In addition, community-based antidrug and gang-prevention programs are beginning to fund recreational and social activities based on the successful drop-in model. One such program is *Friday Night Jams* in Morgan Hill, California. It began simply—by opening a middle school gymnasium for basketball on Friday nights. Soon the program grew to include activities for younger children. A similar program was developed in the neighboring community of Gilroy that offers a video room, a game room with a pool table, tutors and counselors, and an open kitchen with sodas and snacks available at modest prices. Starting out with 20 participants, *Friday Night Jams* quickly grew to almost 200 boys and girls arriving each week to play pick-up basketball, participate in arts and crafts, or simply hang out with their friends in a safe place (Gruner, 1994). A homework club started by a single mother living in subsidized housing in Charleston, South Carolina, is now recognized and receiving external funding. The program is supported by the Save the Children Out-of-School Time Rural Initiative and the Trident Literacy Association, a nonprofit organization serving disadvantaged children and families in public housing (Chung, 1997). Programs like these offer youngsters an alternative to gangs, violence, and other negative behaviors that too often result from endless weeks and months of loneliness and boredom.

Athletic and Recreation Programs   Activities that offer adult supervision but are not commonly thought of as "care" programs include community-sponsored or after-school athletics teams, such as swimming, gymnastics, basketball, baseball, soccer or football, or recreation programs that meet once or twice a week to play games or make arts and crafts. Additionally, in some communities, open gyms offer the use of a trampoline, basketball courts, or swimming pool on a drop-in basis. The most formal of these arrangements is the competition team, as coaches are likely to require two or more practices a week and usually let parents know if their children do not show up regularly, or if a child seems troubled or behaves in an unusual way. The less-structured programs do not usually involve regular communication with parents, who may not know if their child fails to arrive or leaves early. However, the activities in and of themselves are beneficial to school-age children, and the interaction with adult staff is a valuable part of the community care network.

Enrichment Programs and Youth Groups   Art or music lessons, choir practice, Trailblazers, Scouts/Guides, Campfire, 4-H, and Junior Achievement are examples of the enrichment programs and youth groups available in some communities. In earlier times, Girl and Boy Scout meetings and choir practices were generally held at night after dinner, and parents typically drove their children to them. Increasing pressures on families in which both parents work have made the little time they have to spend with their children too precious to share with others. As a result, more and more of these kinds of activities are taking place immediately after school and in this way have become part of the community network of care.

One example of an excellent community-sponsored school-age program is Girl Scout Troop 1900 of the Los Angeles Girl Scout Council. It charges no dues and meets daily from 2:00 to 6:00 p.m. in a back room of the Gramercy Place homeless shelter. Boys and girls age 5 to 11 are led by volunteers, generally college students or recruits from other community agencies, in a variety of activities, sports, songs, and creative endeavors. Members of this troop do not wear uniforms, rarely complete badge work, and do not sell cookies door-to-door. The goal? To be allowed to act like children, and to experience some continuity and security in their lives. The leaders of Troop 1900 are, in a sense, emissaries from a society that has let these children down, trying to give them a "slice of normalcy" more than a traditional Scouting experience (Hall, 1995).

In many communities, organized sports programs provide children with challenging activities during out-of-school time.

Some school-age care programs contact sponsoring organizations to initiate a group to meet at their site; others make transportation arrangements so that their children can participate. Many children can walk to meetings, especially if the groups meet in a room at their school or at an easily accessible location such as the public library. As demonstrated by the Los Angeles example, Scouting, YMCA, Campfire, and other such groups can be chartered to meet in homeless shelters, youth centers, and group-care facilities; they can also include both boys and girls.

In most cases, the leaders of community service enrichment programs are volunteers, often with little or no training, although sometimes they are retired teachers or social workers. This can be a fulfilling kind of work, one whose reward is an unending stream of children who feel connected to their communities and the adults who live in them. It also can provide valuable experience for students preparing to work in the field of out-of-school care.

After-School Programs at Libraries   Some communities have begun to respond to the large number of students congregating after school in public libraries. In many of these, special programs, often run by volunteers, address the interests and needs of these children. For example, historical associations, Explorer Scouts, and business leaders may develop programs on local history, fingerprinting, or getting a summer job. Increasingly, children's librarians are becoming involved.

In her report of a national study conducted in 1990, author Frances Dowd revealed that most of the 110 large public libraries surveyed were regularly visited by unattended children whose families used the library for child-care purposes after school. Surprisingly, only a minority of libraries reported "significant" problems or concerns regarding medical emergencies or accidents, the need for increased security measures, re-allocation of staff to cover after-school hours, or legal liability. Many of the libraries polled by the study have increased their drop-in activity programs, story hours, and clubs; some also offer information and referrals to licensed child care and other out-of-school activities (Dowd, 1991).

The public library association in New London, Connecticut, is one of many that have developed programs for children after school. Once filled with often-unruly, unsupervised children each afternoon, the library now offers an organized after-school program, staffed by the YWCA; the children's librarian supplements the program with films and reading materials (Zigler & Lang, 1991). Dowd described a program at the Fort Erie Public Library in Ontario, Canada, which is funded by the Ministry of Community and Social Services and coordinated by the Boys' and Girls' Clubs of Ontario. This program features before- and after-school programs at two of the library sites, transportation of children from schools to the libraries, snacks, field trips, and coordinated activities such as swimming and basketball at the YMCA. In Georgia, the DeKalb County Public librarians wrote letters to parents when children were left unattended in their libraries. Out of the exchange that followed came designated Homework Libraries, which provided typewriters, computers, read-along books, and learning games (DeKalb Public Library, 1990).

A particularly notable program for otherwise unsupervised children is Seattle's After School Happenings (SPLASH), which is conducted at several branches of the Seattle Public Library. The activities, which include making dollhouse furniture, gardening, hearing stories, participating in sing-alongs, and getting help with homework, are tailored to the needs of the particular community served. Three of the 10 goals of SPLASH are to (1) promote reading as a lifelong pursuit, (2) establish services for new immigrants, and (3) provide activities that help develop self-esteem, self-worth, and creativity (Hogan, 1998; Seattle Public Library, 1998).

CHILD CARE IN OTHER COUNTRIES

Many Western industrialized nations are still developing clear public child-care policies, although most countries permit working parents to remain at home for a time following the birth of each child to recover physically and psychologically and take care of their infants. Most European countries, as well as the United States, Australia, Canada, and Israel, have publicly acknowledged the importance of early childhood education and care for all children under 5, although cost has been a limiting factor in the development of wides-cale arrangements for these children (Zigler & Lang, 1991).

School-Age Care in Europe, Canada, and Australia   Over the last several decades, with the involvement of municipal and state governments, Denmark and Sweden have developed comprehensive systems of after-school care serving children and youths from age 7, when they enter school, to age 21. These programs are staffed by educators who are trained in special colleges. In Sweden, parents are entitled to 18-month parental leaves and 6-hour workdays from the birth of their first child until their youngest child is 8 years old. This parental leave policy, combined with school schedules that closely match the working hours of parents, reduces the need for formal child-care programs for most school-age children.

Different nations, however, because of differing ideas about work and school, have varying responses to the child-care challenge. Many European schools, for example, have traditionally scheduled long lunch breaks, when children would return home for the main meal of the day. French schools meet from 8:30 a.m. to 4:00 p.m., with a 2-hour break; Spanish schools run from 9:00 a.m. to 5:00 p.m. with a 3-hour break. In the Netherlands and Portugal, it is common for schools to run from 9:00 to 4:00 with a 2-hour lunch. In Germany, Italy, and Luxembourg, many schools have 4-hour days, either all week, or for certain days of the week. In France there is no school on Wednesdays. Nearly all countries with an agricultural history have a break of 3 months in the summer; in France and Greece the break is 4 months. None of these schedules were designed with two working parents in mind (Jensen, 1991; Meijvogel, 1991; Moss, 1991).

A group of parents in the Netherlands, faced with school hours and time-tables that differed for each level of schooling, petitioned to have the same hours for children at all ages, the same holidays for all schools, and no unsched-uled school closures (previously a common event). Assisted by a Dutch femi-nist campaign entitled "Time for Mothers," then tactfully renamed "Time for School," the attempt to free mothers from the tyranny of the school timetable was diverted to the socially safer subject of appropriate school hours for chil-dren. The result was more consistent scheduling within age ranges and permis-sion for the parents to organize child care on the school sites during the lunch hour and over holidays (Meijvogel, 1991).

Denmark has seen a phenomenal increase in child care provision—from 300 children recorded in care in 1972 to 41,500 in 1986. Supervision is pro-vided for children from a few months of age to 14 years, primarily in mixed-age groupings, often using primary school facilities. School-based care is funded by the education sector whereas center-based care is funded by the social wel-fare department. A small number of children are cared for by salaried childmin-ders who are paid for through the welfare system by local authorities (Moss,

1991). Twenty percent of the children age 7 to 10 attend youth centers known as *fritidshjem*—"leisure homes," or literally, "free-time homes" (M. Seligson, personal communication, March 24, 1998). These child-care services are reportedly professionalized and aim at the highest quality (Jensen, 1991).

Some large French schools employ graduate students from related university courses to lead play sessions after school (Leach, 1994). This is not such a new idea; in the 1920s and 1930s after-school recreation programs were common in industrial cities in Europe, and they were often staffed by teachers and college students (Skirrow, personal communication, 1996; Trevelyan, 1919). What is new, however, is that all professional child-care workers in France are integrated into the total economy and enjoy the same benefits as other French workers, such as social security, illness and vacation pay, and retirement benefits (Zigler & Lang, 1991).

The United Kingdom, Canada, and Australia have extensive networks of programs for school-age children, supervised by government agencies and child-care advocacy groups. Efforts are being made to expand the availability of out-of-school care into all communities and to develop a comprehensive method of program assessment and improvement.

School-Age Solutions in Africa, Asia, and Latin America   In countries where children become part of the family labor pool as soon as they are able, compulsory education laws are difficult to enforce. Such is the case in parts of Kenya and Liberia, where social agency personnel struggle to provide child-care centers for very young children of low-income families (Hildebrand, 1997). School-age programs are nearly nonexistent there.

Japanese and Chinese schools are open from 8:00 a.m. until 5:00 p.m. in many areas, and youngsters are encouraged to play actively after the noon meal, then sleep for 1 to 2 hours. When school hours stretch to fill the adult workday, separate programs for before- and after-school care are not necessary. In rural areas of these countries, children return to their homes after school and participate in doing the tasks necessary to running the household.

In Vietnam there is a big difference between the city and the rural areas. Very few rural children stay in school past fifth or sixth grade—especially girls, who are encouraged to work around the house and/or on the farm. All children return home immediately after school, whether someone is there or not. In Ho Chi Minh City, a few programs exist for older children, but almost without exception relatives take care of school-age children (Play, personal communication, 1996). In Sri Lanka, the situation is reported to be similar (Sivakumaran, personal communication, 1997).

The Family and Child Welfare branch of the Ministry of Community Development in Singapore provides a guide to setting up before- and after-school centers as well as financial support for those programs. Assistance is available to nonprofit organizations for conversion or renovation of premises, purchase of furnishings and equipment, fee subsidy for eligible parents, and start-up funds during the initial low enrollment period. The Ministry of Community Development reports that its recent promotion of before- and after-school centers is directly related to the results of research on dysfunctional families, juvenile delinquency, and drug abuse in Singapore. One typical program, housed at the Bukit Ho Swee Community Center, offers the following services:

- Daily review of schoolwork under supervision
- Indoor and outdoor games
- Enrichment programs such as storytelling and educational TV/Video shows
- Regular meals including breakfast, lunch, and tea
- Instruction and encouragement in developing good habits and self-discipline
- Supervised learning and playing with other children
- Enrollment for School Holiday Program

—Bukit Ho Swee Community Center, 1997

In India and Latin America, thousands of children live on the streets, eating from garbage cans and sleeping in railway stations (Aptekar, 1988; Kumar, 1995). Trying to address this problem, the YMCA opened a night shelter in Visakapatnam, India, which offers informal education and training in carpentry, car and cycle repairs, bookbinding, welding, tailoring, and office work. Because street children have in a sense lost their childhood, the YMCA program also encourages children to play volleyball, kabaddi, and chess, and to go on trips to the beach, zoo, and park (Kumar, 1995).

Louis Apteker, who lived and worked among the street children in Colombia in order to study them, described the need for both macroprograms—which are on a larger scale and are concerned with changing people's attitudes about childhood and street children in particular—and microprograms, which serve the needs of the children themselves. Yet even as he proposed solutions for the community, the anthropologist expressed a respect for the culture of the children called **gamines,** who functioned independently of family and society yet exhibited many healthy characteristics of a working social group. These children, he reported, had taken on many of the rights of adults and would not easily or happily respond to efforts to return them to childhood (Aptekar, 1988). Clearly, there is a great deal of variation in the lives of the world's children. And there is much work to be done developing appropriate out-of-school programs to serve them.

In modern India, the number of working women in all the major cities is increasing tremendously. Many of these mothers face the "insecurity of leaving the child behind at home in the care of unwilling relatives or untrained, unreliable domestic help who have little idea of cleanliness, hygiene or the knowledge of how to deal with an emergency" (Dolna Day School Trust, 1996, p. 2). **Crèches,** or child-care centers for very young children, have been present in India for many years. In recognition of the many problems faced by this new generation of working parents, some crèches in Calcutta, which had previously cared for children from 3 months to 5 years of age, have been extended to include children up to 16 years old. In addition to keeping the school-age children safe, these crèches, run by Dolna Day School Trust, offer painting, drawing, singing, instrumental music, dancing, and even computer studies.

Other centers, operated by a voluntary organization known as "Mobile Crèches," operate in Delhi, Bombay, and Pune to care for the children of migrant construction workers. Older children on the sites lack access to school or health centers and prefer to stay with their younger siblings, so the mobile crèches now include children up to age 12 and employ nonformal education methods to introduce these children gradually to the skills they will need should they ever be able to enter the formal education system (Anandalaskshmy, 1995).

Elements of an Effective Before- and After-School Program

We still have much to learn about the best ways to provide supervision and guidance for children during the out-of-school hours, but some common threads can be found from the examples presented. The most effective arrangements accommodate the often inflexible working schedules of parents and school calendars of children. For children who attend structured school settings, effective programs allow them to feel that "school is out" and that this is their "free" time rather than simply more of what they have been doing all day. For other children, this "out-of-school" time is the closest they will get to a formal education. Most important is that all programs allow children to grow in responsibility and freedom as they develop in reliability and trustworthiness.

When parents are asked what they want in an after-school program, they are likely to emphasize the need for a safe and pleasant environment, for adequate care, and for the opportunity for their children to do their homework. Children tend to vote for recreational games, plenty of time to talk to their friends, free choice of a variety of activities, and usually no homework. Knowledgeable caregivers also plan for a private space and time for each child who needs it and for an opportunity to exchange confidences with and receive reassurances from other children and nurturing adults.

The Wellesley School-Age Child Care Project (now known as the National Institute of Out-of-School Care) has since 1979 sought to "improve the quality of life of school age children, their parents, and their caregivers" (Edelman, 1993, Foreword). Michelle Seligson, the founder of the project, has identified several characteristics that should be present in programs for them to meet the needs of children and keep them interested. She describes the optimum environment as an atmosphere of informal learning that allows children to (1) make choices, (2) expand their cultural horizons, (3) achieve a gradual sense of independence as they grow, and (4) participate in peer culture (Seligson & Allenson, 1993; Zigler & Lang, 1991).

In the United Kingdom, the National Out-of-School Alliance stipulates that after-school clubs "should be warm and welcoming places where all children and staff are valued and respected equally. Club rules and staff should promote safety, enjoyment, comfort, and positive behavior . . . [the club] recognises and values children as individuals, builds good relationships with them and includes them in the running of the club to ensure it meets their needs" (National Out-of-School Alliance, 1995, p. 146).

A task force in Toronto, Ontario, Canada, envisions a system of care for school-age children within the metropolitan area in which "children are cared for in ways that assure their safety, security and health and respect their individual differences, backgrounds, and needs . . . parental choice is respected . . . , service to families is affordable, flexible and responsive to changing needs . . . and fees are geared to income, level and type of service required" (Metro Task Force on Services to Young Children and Families, 1996, p. 1).

In a description of the Dolna Crèche program in India, the author writes:

All over the world today, life has become a whirlwind of activities and in the general hustle and bustle no one has any time to "stand and stare." Parents are losing the enjoyment of watching their children grow-up and children are losing out on the comfort, solace, understanding and guidance that they need, from their grandparents and parents, especially in their formative years. A direct result is the increase in the number of children straying from acceptable norms in society and adopting wayward habits and culture.

It is because of these reasons that value-oriented education is assuming a special place in modern-day society. Institutions like Dolna have come forward to give the children those inputs that will instill a clear sense of values in them, teach them that they have positive responsibilities towards their families, their culture and their heritage. The children must appreciate Indian culture and the values that are its heritage, especially since its very existence is endangered by strong influence from the West. At the same time they should also learn to glean the best of what the modern western world has to offer.
—Dolna Day School Trust, 1996.

These are very diverse cultures, yet the goals for our children are not so different.

To attain these important goals, a continuum of care arrangements needs to exist within each community, and private and public agencies must work together with parents and youngsters to assure that these arrangements suit them. Judith Erickson of the Center for Youth Development and Research at the University of Minnesota, St. Paul, disparages American society for turning children into "symbols of inevitable loss for adults who fear their own aging processes" (Erickson, 1988, p. 87). She calls for developers of after-school programs to "find ways to bring youth of all ages together in creative activities that will allow them access to caring, supporting people, to interesting and challenging activities, and to productive and meaningful roles in their communities in the here and now" (p. 100). Erickson maintains that if programs for school-age youth are to work, they must connect families with the community; they must connect individual children with their own dreams, thoughts, and capabilities; and they must connect actions with consequences.

The field of school-age child and youth work offers a broad range of employment and volunteer options. It is extremely important for the future of children in our society that the adults doing this work perform it with a clear understanding of their roles, their significance, and their responsibility to the society as a whole. If so-called child-care programs can become integrated into the life of the community, if youngsters and their lives can be connected with those of policy makers, businesspeople, and other people of their own age, they will be better able to develop a sense of the continuity of life and of the manner in which they fit into it. Only then, concludes Erickson, "will supervised after-school programs constitute a viable alternative to the television set, the refrigerator, and the street" (Erickson, 1988, p. 101); in other words, to essentially no care at all. Far too many of the world's children face that situation every day. We must work together to change things.

SUMMARY

Communities in all industrialized nations are facing the need to provide care and supervision of school-age children before and after school and during holidays. The varieties of ways in which these needs are being met in the home include flexible working hours for parents; assistance from relatives, neighbors, and community volunteers; and the employment of nannies or *au pairs*. Many children are left to fend for themselves, sometimes with telephone numbers they can call in case of loneliness or emergencies. Some communities offer telephone help-lines or drop-in activity programs for these children. Out-of-home care can include licensed family child-care homes; center-based programs on and off school sites; and a variety of activity, sports, and enrichment programs. Professional child-care organizations for school-age children have developed guidelines for supervision and care programs that can guide community agencies, program planners, and parents in the development of new programs and the evaluation of existing ones.

REVIEW QUESTIONS

1. Referring to the scenarios given, identify some of the times during a typical school day and a school year when children are most likely to benefit from having care and activity programs.

2. How can communities meet the needs of families who need care for their children only part of the time?

3. Describe the various kinds of in-home care described in the chapter.

4. What are the advantages and disadvantages of family child care for school-agers?

5. Why is public funding necessary if communities are to have adequate school-age care programs?

CHALLENGE EXERCISES

1. Interview a parent, a school-age child, and a community member about the out-of-school programs in your community. Ask them what they think *should* be available, and compare it to what *is* available.

2. Visit a school-age child-care or activity program while it is in progress. If possible, interview the leader and identify the goals of the program. List all the different ways children are occupying their time. Note where the adults are and what they are doing. Describe what you observed. Does this program appear to meet the guidelines given by the two professional school-age care organizations?

3. How do you feel about coaches, music teachers, and librarians being referred to as "caregivers"? Ask one of these people what he or she thinks about being thought of in this fashion.

4. What do you think are the responsibilities of facilities that offer out-of-school programs? List four things you think they should provide.

TERMS TO LEARN
....

crèche

gamine

latchkey children

publicly funded program

resource and referral agency

underutilization

vandalization

SELF-CARE BOOKS FOR CHILDREN AND THEIR PARENTS
....

Coolsen, Peter. (1989). *I can take care of myself: The family handbook on self-care.* Work/Family Directions.

Kyte, Kathy. (1984). *In charge: A complete handbook for kids with working parents.* Knopf.

Long, Lynette, & Long, Thomas. (1983). *A handbook for latchkey children and their parents.* Arbor House Publishing Company.

Long, Lynette. (1984). *On my own: The kids' self-care book.* Acropolis Books.

Swan, Helen, and Houston, Victoria. (1985). *Alone after school: A self-care guide for latchkey children and their parents.* Prentice-Hall.

REFERENCES
....

Alexander, N. P. (1986). School-age child care: Concerns and challenges. *Young Children, 42*(1), 3–10.

Anandalaskshmy, S., & Balagopol, I. (1995). *Mobile crèches at Delhi, Bombay and Pune, India: ECCD at the construction sites.* Delhi, India: The Consultative Group on Early Childhood Care and Development.

Aptekar, L. (1988). *Street children of Cali.* Durham, NC: Duke University Press.

Austin, H. (1996). Child care services manager: Child care challenge.

Brady, S., & Graham, K. (1993). *Out of school—out of care.* Bradford, West Yorkshire, England: Holmewood Out of School Project.

Bukit Ho Swee Community Center. (1997). Before and after school care for primary students (Brochure). Bukit Ho Swee, Singapore: Author.

Bumgarner, M. (1995). Interviews of parents and children in a variety of after-school arrangements; conducted by students as a class assignment, Gavilan College.

Bureau of the Census. (1987). *Who's minding the kids?* (Series P-70, no. 9). Washington, DC: U.S. Department of Commerce.

Children's Defense Fund. (1998). *The state of America's children yearbook 1998.* Washington, DC: Author.

Coleman, M., Rowland, B., & Robinson, B. (1989). Latchkey children and school-age child care: A review of programming needs. *Child & Youth Care Quarterly, 18*(1), 39–48.

Coleman, M., Robinson, B. E., & Rowland, B. H. (1991, Summer). School-age child care: A review of five common arguments. *Day Care & Early Education,* 13–17.

Coolsen, P., Seligson, M., & Garbarino, J. (1985). *When school's out and nobody's home.* Chicago: National Committee for Prevention of Child Abuse.

DeKalb Public Library. (1990). Dear Parent form letter and brochures. Decatur, GA: Author.

Dolna Day School Trust. (1996). *Dolna's services today.* Calcutta, India.

Dowd, F. S. (1991). *Latchkey children in the library and community: Issues, strategies, and programs.* Phoenix, AZ: Oryx Press.

Edelman, M. W. (1993). Foreword. In M. M. A. Seligson (Ed.), *School-age child care: An action manual for the 90s and beyond.* Westport, CT: Auburn House.

Elkind, D. (1981). *The hurried child: Growing up too fast too soon.* Reading, MA: Addison-Wesley.

Erickson, J. (1988). Real American children: The challenge for after-school programs. *Child and Youth Care Quarterly, 17*(2).

Galambos, N., & Garbarino, J. (1983). Adjustment of unsupervised children in a rural ecology. *Children Today, 12,* 2–4.

Gruner, A. (1994, August 12). Kids find themselves in a jam. *The Dispatch,* pp. 1, 8.

Hall, C. (1995, July 10). At home in Troop 1900. *Los Angeles Times,* pp. B1–B3.

Hildebrand, V. (1997). *Introduction to early childhood education* (6th ed.). Columbus, OH: Merrill.

Hofferth, S., & Phillips, D. (1987). Child care in the United States, 1970–1995. *Journal of Marriage and the Family, 49,* 559–571.

Hogan, J. (1998). Director of SPLASH program.

Hostetler, L. (1984, January). The nanny trap: Child care work today. *Young Children,* 76–79.

Jensen, J. J. (1991). School-age child care in the Danish social context today. *Women's Studies International Forum, 14*(6), 607–612.

Kahn, H. (1996, April 5). Two-career couples pay to shuttle the children. *New York Times,* Business News section.

Krohn, S., Charter, M., Beniak, T., Anderson, J., & Sordelet, G. (1993). Tribal child care innovations. *Children Today, 22,* 35(3).

Kumar, M. (1995). *Street life.* Visakapatnam, India: YCARE International.

Lamb, M. E. (1982). Maternal employment and child development: A review. In M. E. Lamb (Ed.), *Non-traditional families: Parenting and child development.* Hillsdale, NJ: Erlbaum.

Leach, P. (1994). *Children first.* New York: Alfred A. Knopf.

Lewis, D. (1995, May 11). Child care scarce for parents who work odd hours. *Boston Globe.*

Long, T. T., & Long, L. L. (1981). *Latchkey children: The child's view of self-care* (ED 211–229). Urbana, IL: ERIC Clearinghouse on Elementary and Early Childhood Education.

Marx, F., & Seligson, M. (1988). *The public school early childhood study: The state survey.* New York: Bank Street College of Education.

Meijvogel, R. (1991). School-age child care in the Netherlands: The shift from equality aims to the interest of the child. *Women's Studies International Forum, 14*(6), 557–560.

Merrill, A. (1993, September 21). Shuttle service helps kids get to and from after-school activities. *Knight-Ridder/TribuneNews Service.*

Metro Task Force on Services to Young Children and Families. (1996). *Pilot projects for restructuring school-age child care in metro Toronto.* Toronto, Ontario, Canada: Council of the Municipality of Metro Toronto.

Milne, C. (1974). *Enchanted places.* London: Methuen.

Moss, P. (1991). School-age child care in the European community. *Women's Studies International Forum, 14*(6), 539–549.

National Crime Prevention Council. (1996). *Vandalism/graffiti prevention: Don't close your eyes to vandalism.* McGruff Web Site.

National Research Council. (1990). *Who cares for America's children: Child care policy for the 1990s.* Washington, DC: National Academy Press.

Ollhoff, J. A. L. (1996). *School-age care providers: Extended day or extended family.* St. Paul: Minnesota Department of Children, Families, and Learning.

Petrie, P., & Logan, P. (1986). *After school and in the holidays: The responsibility for looking after school children.* London: University of London Institute of Education.

Robinson, A. (1982). *Latchkey schemes* (Briefing Paper 2). London: National Children's Bureau.

Robinson, B. E., Rowland, B. H., & Coleman, M. (1986). *Latchkey kids: Unlocking doors for children and their families.* Lexington, MA: Lexington Books.

Seattle Public Library. (1998). *S.P.L.A.S.H. flyer.* Seattle, WA: Author.

Seligson, M. (1997, January–February). School-age care comes of age. *Child Care ActioNews, 14.*

Seligson, M., & Allenson, M. (1993). *School-age child care: An action manual for the 90s and beyond.* Westport, CT: Auburn House.

Thiel, K., McCroskey, J., & Marquart, D. (1988). Program and policy considerations for school-age child care: The California experience. *Child & Youth Care Quarterly, 17*(1), 24–35.

Todd, C., Albrecht, K., & Coleman, M. (1990, Spring). School-age child care: A continuum of options. *Journal of Home Economics,* 46–52.

Trevelyan, J. P. (1919). *Evening play centres for children.* London: Methuen.

U.S. Congress. (1989). *The act for better child care services of 1989 (S.5).* Washington, DC: 101st Congress.

U.S. Department of Education. (1998, December 6). 21st Century Learning Centers Application Package. Washington, DC: U.S. Department of Education, Office of Educational Research and Improvement.

Warnock, M. (1992). After-school child care: Dilemma in a rural community. *Children Today, 21*(1), 16.

Winnipeg Police Service. (1996). *Online crime prevention handbook.* Winnipeg, Ontario, Canada: Author.

Zigler, E. F. (1987, March). Formal schooling for four-year-olds? No. *American Psychologist, 42,* 254–260.

Zigler, E. F., & Ennis, P. (1988). Child care: A new role for tomorrow's schools. *Principal, 68*(1), 10–13.

Zigler, E. F., & Lang, M. E. (1991). *Child care choices: Balancing the needs of children, families, and society.* New York: Free Press.

CHAPTER THREE

Who Are the People Who Work With School-Age Children?

Meet the Adults

In the course of a single day, most school-age children come in contact with many different adults. After leaving home in the morning, they may pass neighbors and businesspeople on their way to the school bus or public transit; they may be driven to school in a neighborhood car pool or slip into a friend's house for a snack or a greeting before walking to school with the friend.

Once at school, in addition to teachers, children encounter custodians, librarians, attendance clerks, the school secretary, the nurse, perhaps the principal, yard duty supervisors, cafeteria staff, building and ground maintenance staff, and parent volunteers. In the afternoon, children may stop for a snack at the convenience market, buy a magazine at a bookstore, or play video games before heading home, exchanging conversation with each of the adults they see.

When I was a child, I spent many after-school hours talking to the ice cream man or to Mrs. Mayer, who ran a 1950s version of a neighborhood convenience store. Some of my friends took piano lessons after school and told their piano teachers about the events of the day; one of my own daughters shared confidences with a friendly coach who transported her from school to soccer practice twice a week.

Each of the people with whom these children interact has a role in the raising of a child. Some of them do it better than others, and some have greater influence than others, but everyone has a part. Some of them are aware of their influence; some are even paid to spend time with the children they help to shape; but many more are unaware of the impact they have on the young people whose lives they touch. Most children benefit from interaction with a variety of adults in different settings. They grow and learn as they see different ways of

Adults need to remember that children's relationships with adults shape their values, morals, and self-perceptions.

doing things, hear different ways of explaining things, watch people of different cultures and nationalities work and play together. Before- and after-school programs of all kinds complement the structured school day that most children experience. Often, due to their varied roles, adults outside of school can permit themselves to be somewhat warmer and more personally responsive in style than can regular classroom teachers and staff (National Research Council, 1990).

Although many people who work with school-age children do so intentionally, following a well-planned career path, others find themselves supervising children almost by accident, perhaps because they agreed to help a friend run a Brownie troop or coach a Little League team, or because they answered a newspaper advertisement promising "challenging work with youthful clients."

Occasionally, parents whose own youngsters are school-agers decide to take extra children into their home as a way to earn an income without being away from their family; or family child-care providers who have previously accepted only babies may find themselves continuing to care for children when they reach kindergarten age and beyond.

Ironically, some people wind up caring for school-age children because they had been trained to work with much younger children, and answered a position announcement that called for ***early childhood education units*** (postsecondary coursework in child growth and development that is required in some states for employment in both preschool and school-age care programs). In some large child-care centers, caregivers rotate between the different age groups and may find themselves with 10-year-olds when they're used to working with 4-year-olds. When that happens, it's not uncommon for them to feel unprepared for the activity level and behaviors common to school-age children. Here are some examples.

CLASSROOM AIDE

When her daughter Karen entered kindergarten, Penny Neilson volunteered to work in her classroom on Fun Fridays. Karen's kindergarten teacher planned arts and crafts activities and a cooking project each week, and she depended on parent volunteers to help carry them out. After a year of working in Karen's classroom, Penny answered an ad for a teacher's aide in a second-grade class, where she helped children with their reading and math projects while the teacher took small groups of children for oral reading.

Penny has now worked as a paid aide at the elementary school for 4 years. She enjoys her work, but sometimes she worries that she is not saying the right things to children and doesn't always feel she is successful when she encourages them to do their best. Many children come to school without the skills she thinks they need to succeed, and she could help them better if she knew more about children and how they learn. Penny reads everything she can find about children, and now she is even thinking about taking a night class at the local community college to see if that would help her know what to do and say.

NANNY

Rose began working for a dual-career family as a live-in nanny when their first child was an infant. Now that infant is in second grade and the new baby just entered kindergarten. Although Rose considers that the bulk of her child-care work is over, these children's parents so value her that they continue to pay her the same salary she received for full-day care to awaken the children each morning, take them to school, and be there for them in the afternoons. Rose is flattered and is enjoying working in the youngest child's kindergarten once a week, or driving for second-grade field trips, but these children are presenting new challenges that she doesn't quite know how to handle.

"What do I tell Marjory when she tearfully describes how the kids called her 'fat girl'? Or explain to Sally that it's OK for her to know how to read better than the other children? That they'll catch up, just like she will soon learn how to catch a ball better? How do I explain to the other parents who I am and why I'm at school with these children instead of their mother? Will they think she doesn't love them? *Does* she love them?" Rose is afraid that the children will be disappointed with her lack of ready answers. *She* certainly is.

SCHOOL-BUS DRIVER AND YARD DUTY SUPERVISOR

Sondra began driving a school-bus after being laid off from a computer assembly job several years ago. She is a good driver, and she loves her work. She transports high school students starting at 6:20 a.m., followed by grades K–6 and finally the junior high group. When she returns her bus to the yard at 9:30 a.m. and completes the checkout procedures, she drives to a nearby elementary school, where she supervises recess and the cafeteria during first lunch. Then it's back to the bus to pick up the afternoon kindergartners and take the early group home before returning for the senior high, elementary school, and junior high youngsters.

Sondra studied the statutes provided by the Department of Motor Vehicles and passed both a written and a road test before obtaining her license. She is certified in cardiopulmonary resuscitation and first aid. She considers herself a good bus driver. "But," she confides, "I had no idea that the kids were going to be so rude, or so loud, or so mean to each other." She finds herself breaking up fights in the bus and on the playgrounds, and soothing hurt feelings at the lunch tables. Occasionally, she overhears things about the children's lives or neighborhood turf battles that make her worry. Sometimes she wishes she had taken a ***child guidance*** class before accepting this job.

COMMUNITY VOLUNTEER

Luke volunteers at a homeless shelter several evenings a week; Chibi helps out at the Friday night basketball games held for any youths who wish to attend. Both young adults grew up in communities where gangs claimed many of their schoolmates, and they are trying to keep that from happening in the town where they hope to raise their own children. But the youngsters who spend time in these places "aren't much used to trusting adults," explains Luke. "They figure we think there's something in it for us, even though they don't know what it is. It really gets to me, you know? I give up my nights to go to that place, and most of the time it's like they don't really care if I'm there or not."

Chibi disagrees. "No," he says, "these kids appreciate having us there. You just have to understand that they'll never really show it, because that's not cool."

SECURITY GUARD

Norma has been standing in the junior high parking lot every school day for five years. As a security guard, she has the job of patrolling the faculty and visitor parking areas to prevent vandalism and theft during class hours. She finds herself witnessing students cutting classes, pursuing romances, and experiencing emotional ups and downs that often send them to the parking lots for refuge. "It's not in my job description to send a student back to class," she explains, "but I know these kids, and I hate to see them mess up. I try to talk with them, see what's eating them, and get them back on track. Sometimes I feel like their mother."

ATHLETIC COACH

Benny and Bill coach a girls' soccer team. Maria and Carlos, a husband/wife team who are friends of the two, coach a boys' team. Over pizza one night, the conversation centered around children asking to play specific positions, and how to balance the needs of the team with the individual needs of the children. Maria commented that she had been a Cub Scout leader, and the training program she had attended had been very helpful. Carlos remarked that he wished there was a youth coach's training program available in their community. "It's not so much that I feel unprepared to teach these kids how to play *soccer*," he explained; "it's more that I don't understand the personal interactions that take place on and off the field that get in the way of team cooperation. There's something about these girls that I just don't get."

SERVICE CLUB YOUTH LEADER

Scouting is not unique in offering training for its leaders. Kyle, who has accompanied both his children to YMCA-sponsored activity programs for several years, has attended many workshops for group leaders. However, he is quick to add, those programs usually emphasize technical details like collecting dues, leading crafts activities, and planning field trips. They give some basic information about children's skill levels and safety precautions with children of different ages, but they leave the leaders to deal with the varieties of interpersonal relationships between parents and their children.

Eric, Kyle's 16-year-old son, agrees. "I've been working with the Trailblazers now for 2 years and sometimes I just want to quit. I think I'm pretty patient, but they argue with one another, or they're rude to their parents or the other adults in the program, and sometimes they don't come when they say they will or remember to bring snacks or craft materials. It's very frustrating."

FAMILY CHILD-CARE PROVIDER

Gloria has cared for other people's children in her home since she was a new bride 14 years ago. At first she took only babies and toddlers, and asked parents to find a new place for them when they entered preschool. But then her own two children were born, and when they entered preschool and kindergarten she encouraged parents to leave their older children in her care so her own children would have friends to play with after school.

Now her licensed family child-care home has 12 children age 2 to 11 years. "I took some child development classes when I first started doing day care, but they only talked about children under 5. This older kid thing about 'I won't be your friend if you don't let me play with your ball or your truck' really gets me. The kids always seem to be fighting!"

Training programs for coaches of community sports leagues are helpful because many first-time coaches have no experience with the personal interaction dynamic involved.

SCHOOL-AGE CHILD-CARE CENTER DIRECTOR

When Scott's wife died 5 years ago, their three children were 5, 7, and 12. They attended two different schools, and there were no family child-care providers near their home who could arrange to pick them up from school and care for them. "I wished desperately then that there had been someplace near the elementary school where the two youngest children could go," he remembers. "Instead, they walked home together and their sister took care of them when she got home from junior high. I hated it, and lived in fear that something bad would happen before I got there."

Today, Scott directs a before- and after-school child-care program on the grounds of the elementary school where his youngest child is now in sixth grade. "Our program received funds from the school district to lease a portable classroom, and a local resource and referral agency wrote a proposal to fund the day-to-day operation of the center. Some parents pay full cost and others pay a sliding fee. It's hard to believe that we didn't think of this earlier, but finally children in our neighborhood have a safe place to go to after school. The only problem is that they're bored much of the time, and some actually say they would rather walk home to an empty house just like my children did. I wish I knew how to keep them interested, but all my training has been for work with younger children."

The Common Need: Knowledge of Child Development

Whatever the reason they came into their situation, these adults and young people recognize the need for information on child development and the need to understand the developmental characteristics of school-age children. Within that framework, they could put their charges' often confusing behavior into context and develop activities and experiences for them that will be ***developmentally appropriate,*** meaningful, and fun.

A common belief is that all you need to work with children is to "like kids." Nothing could be farther from the truth. In fact, it is the people who are most sensitive to the needs of children and who enjoy spending time with them who voice the loudest frustration when they act up. The 2-year-old child throwing a temper tantrum has the charming quality of being cute, at least at nap time or when he snuggles in your lap for a story. A 9-year-old may not be quite so charming, especially when she is challenging the authority of the adult in charge or calling a 6-year-old disgusting names.

Adults who work with school-age children and youths actually get paid to play.

Characteristics of People Who Work Successfully With Children

Some common characteristics occur in people who work successfully with children. Reviewing them can guide you in your personal development and reassure you that your goal of working with school-age children is achievable. For example, a Canadian guide for parents selecting care for their children advises them to seek adults who

- Listen to children when they speak and respond with interest and respect
- Accept and value children's ideas and suggestions
- Display a sense of humor
- Respond with care and understanding to a child who may be fearful, shy, upset, hurt, or angry
- Encourage children to be cooperative with each other
- Promote the development of problem-solving skills and a sense of independence
- Set reasonable limits for behavior and respond to inappropriate behavior in a fair, consistent, and nonpunitive manner
- Initiate conversations with the children other than giving instructions, announcements, and commands
- Take time to be alone with individual children
- Encourage children to make choices
- Make the children feel good about themselves and other people
  —*Parents' Guide to Selecting Day Care,* 1997, Province of British Columbia

All these characteristics can be learned. Understanding *why* children act as they do can reduce the tension; understanding what is reasonable to expect of children at different ages can prevent us from putting them in situations where they fear failure, or where they are bored for lack of challenge—both of which are circumstances that lead to difficult behavior. If you value children for their individual differences; respect their language, culture, and personality; and nurture their friendship, they will learn to behave similarly to other people. Learning how to plan activities that are appropriate for children's ages and abilities as well as their interests will ensure that children enjoy spending time with you, and you with them. Perhaps most important, respecting children and their thoughts and ideas means that you will put their feelings and needs before your own, something that sometimes becomes more difficult as a tiring day wears on.

Another aspect of child development is understanding that children's relationships with community members, especially their families, shape their values, morals, and motivations. Understanding the way in which family and culture influence children's beliefs about the world helps us to be more accepting of individual differences and more respectful of diverse opinions.

PERSPECTIVE

The Ecology of a Chicano Student at Risk

Milagros Seda and Dennis J. Bixler-Marquez

While the nation contemplates what to do about our "failing" education system, researchers and educators continue to examine the most important component of the education system, the students.

José's Family and Background

José resides with his mother, older brother, and younger half-sister. The father of José and José's older brother left home when they were infants.

José has a 15-year-old uncle who communicates with him about twice a month. The mother claims that both of her sons look up to their uncle, who gives them a lot of positive support. The uncle shares with José an interest in wrestling and often instructs José and his brother on various wrestling holds. José also is in contact with the maternal extended family; at Christmas, José normally visits his grandparents, from whom he receives some of the presents on his Christmas wish list. Sometimes his mother cares for some of her relatives' children in her home, which allows José to socialize and establish rapport with his extended family.

José loves and respects his mother. She in turn demonstrates great concern over his well-being but is at times unable to obtain for him necessary school services or community services, such as taking him to the public library, swimming pool, or recreation center because of the burden of using public transportation in a suburban area; she does not own a vehicle. The mother does attempt to provide a home environment where the family can function with limited excursions into the new neighborhood. Most of José's outings are limited to the homes of family members.

The mother related that she uses a system of charts to monitor and control her children's behavior; her children collect points for showing good behavior and performing household chores, while points are taken away for misbehavior. José does well at home under this management system.

José's Academic History

The relationship between school and José's mother was filled with conflict from the onset, yielding negative academic results for José. José attended preschool for only a few months, since his mother had trouble picking him up on time due to employment and transportation constraints. When the assistant principal threatened to not allow José to return, she withdrew him from school. This meant he did not attend preschool or kindergarten. His formal schooling began in the first grade, indicating that he may have started out in school with academic and socialization deficits.

There was no information in José's cumulative folder regarding first-grade academic performance. In the second grade José had a B average in math, social studies, science, art, music, and PE, but was below grade level in reading. He transferred 16 days before the end of the school year to his current school, where he completed the remainder of the term.

The home language survey completed on José in second grade indicated that English is the language spoken most often in his home. We corroborated this finding via direct observation and an interview with the mother at home; she used fluent English with us and with her children. José and his siblings also have a good command of English, which they use almost exclusively among themselves at home and with peers in school during noninstructional periods. In addition, present and former teachers never indicated language among the at-risk factors associated with José's academic standing.

In the area of sports his mother reports that José is the "outdoors type," who would rather go out to the park than watch TV. She said that, although he would like to participate in organized sports, she cannot afford to have him join due to the cost involved. Before moving to this school, José had participated in sports activities that did not require fees or uniforms. The school José now attends has a very good physical education program but no organized sports activities at his grade level. The physical education teacher identified José as a natural athlete who behaves like most of the other fourth-grade males. He reports that in his class José follows the rules, obeys the teacher, and does not pick fights.

Follow-Up Findings

During the follow-up research conducted in 1990, we interviewed the fifth-grade teacher and suggested that one way to continue helping José might be if he were part of a sport team in the school or neighborhood; football is José's favorite sport. At first she thought it might be a good idea, but after giving it further thought, she stated that he might have trouble being a team member and probably would not last long. This opinion of José's potential for participation in group sports may have been shaped by his continued horseplay in class, which she found annoying.

We believe it is essential for José and his family to receive counseling and empowering social skills. The school should also consider the intervention of social agencies to ameliorate situations out of the realm of school responsibility. In addition, he should be provided with a part-time tutor to help him continue to improve his reading ability. The stable presence of supervisory and counseling personnel is essential for José and students like him. We feel José has an excellent chance of succeeding in school if his progress continues to be monitored during the critical transitions to middle school and high school and active steps are taken to meet his academic and emotional needs.

This study suggests at least two fundamental changes that schools could make to improve the education received by students like José. First, schools need to become more like communities where students gain a sense of belonging, and parents and teachers have a strong sense of joint ownership, responsibility, and accountability. Second, once students have been identified as being at risk of educational failure, mentors should be assigned to these students to lead them through the path of academic success.

Note: This information was originally published and provided by the Bilingual Education Teacher Preparation Program at Boise State University, Boise, Idaho. Every attempt has been made to maintain the integrity of the printed text.

Pacific Oaks College formed a School-Age Child Care Task Force to identify needs and barriers unique to school-age program staff. Their 1994 report listed 12 competencies recommended for leaders of programs for school-age children. In addition to knowing basic child development, health, safety and emergency procedures, licensing regulations, and curriculum preparation, the task force recommended that leaders show

- Ability to interact, coordinate, and work effectively with school personnel
- Ability to communicate and develop liaison skills with parents
- Sensitivity to a broad variety of cultural and family life styles
- Ability to model and teach positive discipline and conflict resolution skills
- Ability to relate culturally and linguistically to children, staff, and parents
- Child observation skills
- Knowledge of specifics of creating and managing appropriate indoor and outdoor environments

—Cohen, Sharpe, & Sprague, 1994

Many of the competencies listed above are similar to those in the Canadian list, and they can be *learned*. Research has shown that postsecondary education in child development and early education makes an important difference in the quality of adult behaviors directed toward children, as well as in the likelihood that people working with children will remain happily employed in their chosen profession (Berk, 1985).

But how about personality and aptitude for child and youth work? A publication of the California School Age Consortium identifies the ideal candidates for working with school-age youngsters as

people who truly enjoy interacting with this age group, and who can serve as
positive role models for children. They should have a basic understanding
of the developmental needs of school-agers and of how to meet them. They
should bring energy, flexibility and a sense of humor to the job. They should
have an effective and positive style of guidance and discipline with children,
and an ability to work well with other adults—both co-teachers and parents.

—Bellum, 1990

Let's try to understand what this means. The following sections address each
of these valuable characteristics.

ENJOY INTERACTING WITH SCHOOL-AGERS

School-age children require a high level of interaction with their adult companions if they are to build relationships that work well when difficulties arise.
Younger youth workers may find that interaction easier because the age difference between them and their charges is relatively smaller, although many wonderful friendships have been forged between 9-year-olds and their adult Scout
leaders, coaches, choir directors, or bus drivers. The trick seems to be the
adult's self-confidence and ability to be himself or herself with young people.

If you have ever ridden with a busload of children traveling to summer
camp or on a ski trip, sat in the same booth with them in a fast-food restaurant,
or sung silly songs all the way home from the beach and actually enjoyed yourself, then you are probably on the right career path. Ask yourself if you would
ever spend time with 6-year-old children for *fun;* if not, how can you be sure
you will enjoy doing it just because someone offers to pay you?

Watch a group of children visiting the local zoo, museum, or other educational or recreational spot in your community. Now, watch the adults accompanying the children. Some of them probably look harried, tired, or out of
sorts. Others are animated, engaging in conversations with the children about
what they are seeing. For you to be successful working with school-age children, you must be like the second group of leaders more often than the first
group. Adults who lose patience with children's normal behavior or whose
energy level flags after a few hours have more difficulty managing groups of
children. Just like adults, children who sense that you don't enjoy being around
them will often not enjoy being around you, either. Adults may have learned to
mask their emotions or to simply avoid people who don't like them, but
children—especially children who are required to remain in the same place
with you for long periods of time—tend to be less tactful and may even go out
of their way to irk you if they think it might make things more interesting.

A few things can help the inexperienced child and youth worker to enjoy
working with school-age children. One is to try remembering your own childhood and replay feelings you had about experiences and people. Journal writing, group discussion, or role-playing are often helpful. Another important tool
for enjoying children at any age is understanding what is normal for their developmental stage and what you can do to encourage movement to the next.

SERVE AS POSITIVE ROLE MODELS

What often comes to mind when the term "role model" is mentioned are impeccable morals and examples of good citizenship, such as not smoking, drinking, or swearing around the children. However, some of the most important examples youth workers can provide for youngsters are dispositions for cooperation and models of problem solving. By *dispositions,* I mean personality traits such as integrity, persistence, creativity, enthusiasm. Children who see adults working out their differences of opinion learn useful techniques for personal interaction. When they watch you repair a broken game box, they learn economy and patience; as you share with them your plans for the future, they may begin to develop their own dreams.

Working with children is a way to build foundations for the future. Very young children need caregivers who provide consistent nurturing so the children can develop trust; toddlers need adults who allow them to develop independence and autonomy. School-age children are trying out different personalities and demeanors as they search to find the ones that fit them best. The adults around them, at home, at school, on television and in movies, provide the *models* for this experimentation. As children develop their ethnic identity, they benefit from having role models within their own culture. The more effective the models, the more likely children are to emulate them long enough for the values they represent to become habits. Role modeling is a very big responsibility, but it's well worthwhile.

UNDERSTAND THE DEVELOPMENTAL NEEDS OF SCHOOL-AGERS AND HOW TO MEET THEM

A few years ago, I visited Disney World with my two youngest daughters. While waiting for them to return from a ride, I watched a group of school-age children interacting with their adult chaperones. They were apparently on a class trip, about 25 fifth graders who obviously knew one another quite well and were in high spirits on arriving near the long-awaited scary ride. Their teacher was cheerful and enthusiastic, but when she accompanied a group of girls to the restroom, she left the rest of her class with one of the parents traveling with them. Immediately the tone of the group changed. "Everyone get in line," the woman said loudly, her large straw hat flapping as she waved her arms. "I want you to be ready to move as soon as your teacher gets back." The response was underwhelming; a few children came toward the mother, but most continued their talking, joking, and people-watching. One child quipped, "The lady in the big yellow hat lost her Curious George."

"Hurry up, or I'll leave you here while we go on the ride!" was the reply. Now the youngsters began to pay attention, and to grumble. "Who died and made her God?" was heard from within the ranks. "Who said that?" she demanded. "We're not moving until I hear an apology." No one answered. It was during this stalemate, which lasted another 5 minutes, that the teacher returned. "Who's ready to go on the ride?" she asked, on approaching the group.

An important role of staff is to help school-age children learn how to resolve conflicts.

Waving hands signified that most of the children were interested and ready, but once again a few did not respond.

The teacher walked closer to two of the youngsters without hands up. "What would *you* like to do?" she asked. There were several ideas—buy a drink, go to the gift shop, wait somewhere in the shade; these were clearly children who did not want to go on the ride with the others. In short order, the teacher divided them into small clusters with an adult for each and left for the ride with the rest. "Last one in line has to load the suitcases," the teacher called as she broke into a trot. In contrast, the woman in the yellow hat could be heard calling "Don't run . . . wait for me . . . you won't be able to go in the gift shop if you don't mind what I am saying!"

What was happening here? Clearly, the parent barking out commands was *not* comfortable working with 10-year-old children. She appeared to feel out of control and tried to impose order with commands and threats. The teacher, on the other hand, felt comfortable enough with the children to suspend her authority over them and give them reasonable choices—even to play with them. That kind of confidence and enjoyment takes a while to develop, but understanding children's normal developmental traits is a big part of it.

When a 10-year-old child wisecracks, he is performing for his peers, not necessarily challenging authority. And even when mid-age children *do* challenge authority, they do it to build themselves up, not to tear down the one they are challenging. The confident adult understands this and provides opportunities for children to grow into leadership rather than trying to squelch their budding confidence. School-age children, especially from age 7 to 11, are trying to learn how to act like older people in authentic roles while struggling with the fear that they don't know what to do (psychologist Erik Erikson called this period a conflict between ***industry and inferiority***). This is as true of children with disabilities as with all other children.

Erikson and the adult who understands children's need to master the world around them would encourage us to offer children lots of chances to make choices and decisions. The opportunity to do that, especially in situations in which a wrong decision may be inconvenient or uncomfortable but not disastrous, provides valuable information for the growing child and enhances his or her confidence in facing future dilemmas (Erikson, 1985). Additionally, confident children are usually much easier to get along with than children who feel they must always be challenging authority in order to stretch their wings.

HAVE ENERGY, FLEXIBILITY, AND A SENSE OF HUMOR

Even adults who enjoy spending time with children may be short on energy if they are overworked, short on sleep, or in less than optimum health. Energy is one of the most important ingredients in a working relationship with active children, so child-care professionals should revitalize themselves often. A well-balanced diet, regular exercise, and sufficient sleep go a long way toward creating energy; each individual will need to develop a suitable schedule of work, study, and play that allows for sufficient vigor to make it through several intense hours of interaction with children each day. If all else fails, take vitamins!

Flexibility, however, does not come in a vitamin bottle. Flexibility means the ability to see more than one way to accomplish a task and the willingness to change the order of events or even throw out your plans if they don't seem to be working. The children in one after-school program decided to stencil and paint murals on classroom windows during one holiday season. The adult in charge helped a planning group come to agreement about the choices of designs and colors of paints, who would draw the stencils, and who would paint the windows. Three creative fifth and sixth graders were assigned by their peers to sketch the large stencils on butcher paper; third and fourth graders were given the task of mixing paints and taking orders from the teachers; first and second graders would sponge-paint the lower portions of the windows, and third, fourth, fifth, and sixth graders would paint with brushes around the edges of the stencils and stand on step stools to sponge-paint the upper portions of the pictures.

Once the painting began, several children decided they were really not interested in doing this after all. One second grader became quite upset that she was not allowed to use a brush; she didn't want to use only a sponge. In the interest of fairness, the youth leader at first insisted that everyone should participate in the project, and that the second grader should use the sponge like everyone else her age. The children balked, the teacher insisted, and they eventually complied. However, after thinking it over later that evening, he decided to try presenting the problem to the children who had set up the division of labor in the first place.

The next day the adult leader presented the problem to the group as one both of fairness and of matching skills to tasks. The second-grade girl was thought of by her classmates as an artist, and they believed she deserved this exception. When they learned this, the older children didn't mind at all letting her use a brush. In fact, one of them suggested that she also be given a chance to draw a stencil. An unexpected outcome of the group meeting was that the children who were no longer interested in the project were freed from participating. There were plenty of hands still left to do the work, and the whole process went much more smoothly now that willing painters were painting.

Two important things happened here. In the first place, more children ended up satisfied with the results. A less flexible adult might have insisted on equality/fairness at the expense of *everyone*. Additionally, by modeling flexibility (but not insisting on it, which is a kind of inflexibility in itself), the adult leader taught the children a valuable skill. Some rules, even when arrived at thoughtfully, are arbitrary and can be changed. This young leader also showed an ability to put his own ego aside and accept the children's decision with a good sense of humor, even poking a little fun at himself for his initial desire to "play fair and hang tough."

USE AN EFFECTIVE, POSITIVE STYLE OF GUIDANCE AND DISCIPLINE

No school-age gathering will be entirely without problems. It would be naive to assume that if all the adults working with children are energetic, cheerful, and flexible, and enjoy being with children, everyone will get along with everyone else all the time. Another important tool in the skills kit of a child and youth worker is knowing how to develop a reasonable set of behavioral guidelines and implement them. Once again, understanding the developmental characteristics of school-age children is imperative, because what works for a 6-year-old won't work for a 10-year-old, and the reverse is also true. However, it is also important to understand the conditions that affect children's behavior and how to regulate these conditions to optimize the classroom climate. (This is discussed at length in Chapter 8.)

BE ABLE TO WORK WELL WITH OTHER ADULTS

Don't overlook the reality that working with children does not preclude the necessity of also working with adults. Parents, classroom teachers, and other adults in the school-age program itself will each play a part in your daily work. If you are to be successful working with school-age children, you will need to communicate often and clearly with their families about all their individual needs and contributions. Classroom teachers can hold the secrets to children's moods, the key to the copy machine, and the availability (or not) of the very space used for your program. Parents know what is happening in a child's personal life. And day after day you will be working with others just like you who are trying to understand the behavior of growing children, trying to develop an effective program, and trying to develop their own abilities to work with both children and adults. Each of these groups and others with whom you will come in contact have good and bad days; all will need from you the very best you have to offer.

The goal of this text is to help the reader understand how adults influence children's lives, what makes school-age children unique in the human development continuum, and why it is important to develop the competencies you need to succeed in work with school-age children.

As you move through the challenge exercises at the end of each chapter, you will have many opportunities to interact with children and adults in different circumstances and different ways. Gradually, you will learn which strategies work best for you, and you will develop a style of interaction that will facilitate your work with children in any role. In the next chapter, we discuss some basic principles of child growth and development.

SUMMARY
. . . .

The lives of school-age children are affected by many adults, some of whom work with them for several hours a day in a variety of roles. School-age children interact with adults on the school playground, in organized athletic or recreational programs, and drop-in youth centers. Others attend before- and after-school programs in family child-care homes or child-care centers. It is important for child and youth workers, if they are to be successful, to understand the basics of child growth and development and the unique characteristics of school-age children. It is also important that students considering a career working with school-age children evaluate their aptitude for this work and develop a set of competencies that will allow them to succeed.

REVIEW QUESTIONS
. . . .

1. Referring to the scenarios presented in this chapter, describe some similarities and differences in the responsibilities of school-age staff in each of the following settings:
    a. A classroom aide working inside a regular classroom or on a field trip.
    b. A child-care worker in a before- or after-school child-care center.
    c. A recreational leader in a drop-in youth center.
    d. A school-bus driver.

2. In what ways do you think early childhood development courses prepare someone to work with school-age children? In what ways might that training be limited or inadequate?

3. What kinds of problems and challenges might an athletic coach face with members of team that are similar to those encountered by Scout leaders or summer camp counselors? What *different* kinds of problems might they face?

4. List four characteristics of child and youth workers that appear in at least two of the three lists in this chapter.

CHALLENGE EXERCISES

1. Seek out three people in your community who work at least occasionally with school-age children. Prepare a set of questions to ask them how they came to be doing this work, what kind of training or education they have had, and what they like best or least about their work. Interview all three people, and summarize your findings.

2. If you kept a journal or diary as a child, dig it out and review some of the passages. Note feelings, attitudes, and emotions. Summarize an event, identifying those characteristics. If you do not have a written source to draw on, try to recall a major event from your childhood—for instance, getting a new puppy, being bilingual, the birth of a sibling, or moving to a new home. Summarize the event as described above.

3. Research the educational requirements for school-age child-care professionals in your state. Do those requirements apply only to child-care centers, or do they also include family child-care homes, before- and after-school "drop-in" programs, or recreational activities?

4. Find out what the after-school options are for school-age children in your community. How many different places can they go after school where they will be safe and supervised by adults? Visit one of them and report back to the class.

TERMS TO LEARN

child guidance
developmentally appropriate activities
dispositions
early childhood education units
industry and inferiority
models

REFERENCES

Bellum, D. (1990). *Staff issues: Training, retention and recruiting.* San Francisco: California School Age Consortium.

Berk, L. (1985). Relationship of caregiver education to child-oriented attitudes, job satisfaction, and behaviors toward children. *Child Care Quarterly, 14*(2), 103–129.

Cohen, R., Sharpe, C., & Sprague, M. (1994). *Advancing careers in child development: California's plan—School age child care task force draft recommendations.* Pasadena, CA: Pacific Oaks.

Erikson, E. H. (1985). *Childhood and society* (3rd ed.). New York: Norton.

National Research Council. (1990). *Who cares for America's children: Child care policy for the 1990s.* Washington, DC: National Academy Press.

Provincial Child Care Facilities Licensing Board. (1988). *Parent's guide to selecting day care.* Vancouver, B.C.: Province of British Columbia, Ministry of Health.

CHAPTER FOUR

Theories of Child Development

The study of child development can help out-of-school-care professionals design more effective and interesting programs and curricula for children who spend large portions of their growing-up time in environments away from home. It's helpful, for example, to know that 10-year-olds are more likely to be skillful enough to enjoy the competitive aspect of a roller blading derby than are 6-year-olds; or that certain craft activities enjoyed by most kindergartners may be too simple for many third graders. Studying physical development will help us to understand this better.

In the area of social development, knowing that children experience friendship in different ways at different ages can help us communicate more effectively with groups of children who seem to be excluding others from their activities. With the media bringing detailed descriptions of every world event into family homes, knowing what fears and concerns are likely to impact children at different ages can guide us in helping children handle them. In all these cases, studying children's development has provided the clues.

Child development researchers tend to divide their analysis of development into separate areas—usually divided into physical growth and motor development, social and emotional development, intellectual or cognitive development (memory, language, thinking, and problem solving), and moral development. Although we know that children's development does not occur separately in these different domains, sometimes studying children is a little easier if we look at these areas one at a time. That is the order followed in this chapter.

Physical Growth and Development

ARNOLD GESELL (1880–1961)

Best known for books about children's ages and stages bearing his name, Arnold Gesell held doctorates in both psychology and medicine. Combining these two areas of expertise, he directed the Clinic of Child Development at Yale University from 1911 to 1948 while simultaneously holding a teaching position in the School of Education.

Gesell was very interested in the characteristics of children at different age levels; by encouraging parents to bring their children to his clinic for well-child visits, he was able to collect data over three decades (Gesell, 1955). Gesell and his staff created tests, measuring procedures, and observation techniques that allowed them to describe children's status in a wide range of growth areas. The research team gathered information about children in the clinic up to the age of 10. They also interviewed parents to learn about the children's behavior at home. Colleagues and students continued Gesell's work at the privately funded Gesell Institute of Child Development established after his retirement from Yale, where they concentrated on the childhood ages from 10 to 16.

Gesell's Growth Gradients   Gesell proposed a development theory with three parts:

1. Development is primarily a result of genetic factors.
2. Each age produces certain predictable characteristics and behaviors (stages).
3. Alternating periods of equilibrium and disequilibrium result in "better" and "worse" years in a child's life with his family.

Heavily influenced by the thinking of his day, Gesell all but ignored environmental factors, instead interpreting the collected data in terms of the unfolding genetic calendar. His presentation of the material is known as ***maturational theory;*** although it is considered overly simplistic by many child development professionals today, generations of parents and child-care workers have found Gesell's time lines helpful, even comforting. Parenting books published by the Gesell Institute remain popular after four decades. Table 4-1 outlines some of the age-graded characteristics of school-age children observed by Gesell's research staff. These characteristics represent experiences common to children of Gesell's day and may seem somewhat gender-biased to us. However, they are remarkably accurate even today. Remember that each child develops on a unique schedule, and some developmental milestones may appear earlier or later in different ethnic groups as well.

Psychosocial Development

SIGMUND FREUD (1856–1939)

Freud was a physician and neurologist who became interested in the role of early experiences in the development of personality. He experimented with the newly developed technique of hypnosis and gradually adopted the use of the

TABLE 4-1   Gesell's Growth Gradients

5 years	6 years	7 years	8 years	9 years
Control over large muscles is more advanced than control over fine ones. Like to climb fences and go from one thing to another. Can skip. Attempt to roller skate, jump rope, and walk on stilts. Like to march to music. Want to hold adult's hands when unsure of themselves as when descending stairs.	Very active; in almost constant motion. Activity is sometimes clumsy as children overreach and fall in a tumble. Bodies are in active balance as children swing, play active games with singing, or skip to music. Balls are bounced and tossed and sometimes even caught. Enjoy walking and balancing on fences. Have trouble choosing between two alternatives.	Show more caution in many gross motor activities. Repeat activity persistently. Have great desire for a bicycle, though only ready to handle it within limits. Beginning to be interested in group sports. Girls may have a desire for dancing lessons. Fears stimulated by TV and reading.	Bodily movement is more rhythmical and graceful. Now aware of posture in self and others. Like to play follow the leader. Learning to play soccer and baseball with a soft ball and enjoy the shifts of activity within the game. Ready to go out to meet the world but often overestimate own ability in meeting new challenges.	Work and play hard. Apt to do one thing until exhausted, such as riding bicycle, running, hiking, skating, or playing ball. Interest in own strength and in lifting things. Boys like to wrestle and may be interested in boxing lessons. Great interest in team games and in learning to perform skillfully. More self-sufficient than 8-year-olds.

10 years	11 years	12 years	13 years	14 years
Prefer to be active, and love the outdoors. Poised and congenial. Girls show signs of approaching adolescence during this year or the next. Even poor eaters are eating more than they used to. Both girls and boys seem positively to dislike washing, especially their faces. Love old clothes. Some fears from past may reappear. Great interest in "smutty" jokes.	Egocentric and energetic. Always on the go—eating, talking, moving about. Slow to respond and quick to criticize. Have trouble sitting still for long periods. Fiddle with things in hands; when standing, shift from one leg to other. Need lots of physical activity, yet also fatigue easily. Increased need for sleep. Most girls are growing quickly. Do not like to be alone.	Energy levels beginning to calm down. More capable of organizing their energy. Enthusiastic about things they like, especially sports. Occasional periods of extreme fatigue and bad temper. Rapid growth in height for girls. Appetites vary, but most children are hungry by midmorning and again after school even with adequate meals. Beginning to be conscious of clothes.	Withdrawn, physically as well as emotionally. May actually seem unfriendly. Need privacy to brood and think about all the changes taking place. Appetite calming down. Like to be involved in lots of things. Responsibility for chores increasing, as skills develop. Unexplainable tears occasionally happen, usually behind a closed door. Rapid growth in height for boys.	Boundless energy, optimistic enthusiasm and goodwill. Enjoy their friends and extracurricular activities, usually far more than school. Intellectual confidence in most cases. Generally criticize parents and family freely and often. More outgoing, more straightforward, less on the defensive than earlier. Trying to find their own way, decide what paths are best.

Source: Selected and adapted from Gesell, Ilg, & Ames, 1977; and Ames, Ilg, & Baker, 1988.

"talking cure," what we now know as *psychoanalysis,* in which the patient talks about his experiences from early life.

The Id and the Ego   Freud's analysis of his patients' childhood memories and also of their dreams provided the basis for his theory of psychosexual development. Freud believed the human personality consisted of three parts: the id, the ego, and the superego. The *id,* according to Freud, is the source of all desires and produces the energy to obtain the desired objects (food, love, sex, etc.). The id wants immediate satisfaction but cannot create the thought processes necessary to figure out how to get it. The *ego,* which has been called the "mind's avenue to the real world" (Miller, 1993), produces the more organized and logical thought necessary to evaluate, recall, consider, and predict all necessary actions for reaching a goal.

Defense Mechanisms   However, all things that we desire cannot be attained, and Freud included in his theory an explanation for how the personality addresses that situation. When the id cannot be instantly gratified, Freud explained, the ego provides a *defense mechanism.* By distorting reality to the id, defense mechanisms such as repression, reaction formation, projection, regression, and fixation reduce anxiety. These terms have become part of the common language of Western society, and understanding them can be helpful. Sometimes we see behaviors in schoolchildren that may be explained by others as defense mechanisms at work.

Repression, preventing a frightening or threatening thought from emerging into awareness, is a common aftereffect of a traumatic or unpleasant experience. *Reaction formation,* behaving in a way that is opposite to the emotions actually felt, may cause a child to obey slavishly the commands of a feared bully, acting devoted instead of fearful and angry. Reaction formation also may cause siblings to demonstrate intense love toward a younger child for whom they feel acute jealousy.

Projection turns things around. "He hates me" is easier to say than "I hate him." More to the point, "I hit him because he was mean to me" is more acceptable than "I hit him because I hate him." In *regression,* children revert to an earlier stage of development. It is quite common for a first grader, for example, to begin sucking her thumb or for a second grader to begin wetting his bed when life presents challenges too great to bear, such as the departure of a parent or the arrival of a younger sibling.

In *fixation,* one area of personality development stops moving forward. Freud explained excessive drinking and smoking, for example, by relating it to sucking on a breast or a bottle of milk, a need that for some reason did not get completely satisfied in the adult's infancy. A child's version of that particular fixation could be thumb or finger sucking, constant gum chewing, or excessive attachment to a blanket or other love object.

The Superego   The final component of personality to appear, according to Freud, is the *superego.* He considered this part of the personality necessary for socialization to take place. The superego contains two parts: the **conscience** and the **ego ideal.** Conscience is developed when a child is taught about good and evil by adults in society, whether the teaching is intentional or unintentional. The ego ideal refers to the standards of behavior for which the child strives. The superego is the member opposite to both the ego and the id. It rewards, punishes, and makes demands (Miller, 1993).

Freudian Stages of Development   Freud's theory of child development included another important component—that this development takes place in discrete stages. Most students will have at least heard the names of Freud's psychosexual stages of development: oral, anal, phallic, latency, and genital. His theory was originally shocking to the public and continues to attract controversy. However, knowing it is useful if only because other theorists have built on it, and so a brief discussion follows.

ORAL STAGE (BIRTH TO 1 YEAR)   Babies love to suck, and Freud believed that the mouth was the center of all sensation. Sucking, he said, is soon joined by biting, chewing, and eventually eating—all pleasurable activities. Freud believed that babies experienced sexual pleasure through these oral activities as well as sexual tension and frustration when the desire for oral experiences was not satisfied.

ANAL STAGE (1 YEAR TO 3 YEARS)   The anal stage is the much discussed toilet training period. Predictably, Freud described the act of defecation as satisfaction (pleasure), and the need to delay that gratification until it is convenient, frustration (anxiety). Following this stage comes the *phallic stage* (3 to 5 years), during which children work out their gender roles; a period of *latency,* or waiting; and then the *genital stage,* whose goal is mature, adult sexuality.

Freud expanded his stage theory of development by explaining that the way children developed during each stage—how they responded to the various levels of satisfaction with which they were presented—determined their later personality. Each stage arrived as the child reached the appropriate age, but each aspect of personality development built on whatever happened during the previous stage.

ERIK H. ERIKSON (1902–1994)

Entering clinical practice at the end of Freud's life, Erik Erikson accepted most of Freud's work as valid. However, three major differences set his theory apart from Freud's:

1. The use of healthy personalities in his research
2. A stage theory of development that allows for revisiting earlier stages
3. A series of identity crises he believed each person must face

Erikson built on Freud's psychosocial theory, showing how life events influence children's personalities. Here an Indian boy stacks newly-baked bricks.

Erikson's Life Crises   Critics of Freud, both during his lifetime and later, pointed to his work with neurotic personalities as inadequate foundation for a theory of *normal* personalities. Erikson studied healthy people instead. Like Gesell and Freud, Erikson originally believed that children and adults develop in predetermined ways, determined primarily by genetic code (**epigenesis**). However, his description of the eight stages of development, and the emotional conflict associated with each, clearly shows that he came to believe that environment was crucial. One way of viewing this theory is that whereas individuals work through each "crisis" on a fairly predictable timetable, the circumstances of their lives determine how they will interpret the event.

STAGE ONE: BASIC TRUST VERSUS BASIC MISTRUST   During the first year of life, children develop their attitude toward the people and circumstances of their world. Erikson described the eight stages as if each involved two emotions on opposite ends of a seesaw. In the case of *trust verseus mistrust,* for example, a child who experiences inconsistent caregiving or outright neglect is likely to decide that life is not too dependable. As a result, the child either ceases to interact much with adults (assuming, probably correctly, that they won't meet his or her needs) or learns that acting out is the only way to get any attention. On the other hand, if most of the basic needs of this first year are met, and especially if they are met in a caring and loving manner, the child might well decide the world is a nice place to live. Thus, children develop either a trusting

TABLE 4–2 Comparison of Stages of Development According to Freud and Erikson

							Years of life								
	0	1	2	3	4	5	6	7	8	9	10	11	12	13	14
Freud	Oral		Anal		Phallic			Latency					Genital		
Erikson	Trust vs. mistrust		Autonomy vs. shame or doubt		Initiative vs. guilt			Industry vs. inferiority					Intimacy vs. isolation		

or a mistrustful outlook on life based on their experiences with it, and they develop adaptive behaviors to match their conclusions.

Is the result permanent? A common question. Each crisis carries with it the likelihood of a permanent influence. However, there seems to be evidence— for example, with children removed from abusive homes into caring adoptive families—that a great deal can be done to temper these initially formed attitudes. Children who develop one way of behaving as a result of neglectful or inconsistent surroundings may change their behaviors gradually when they discover that the environment of their after-school program is predictable, caring, and fair.

STAGE TWO: AUTONOMY VERSUS SHAME AND DOUBT **Autonomous** is a good adjective to describe most healthy American 2-year-olds; the stereotypical toddler generally has two favorite expressions: "No!" and "*I* do it!" According to Erikson, this healthy try at autonomy can be threatened by overly harsh caregiving, especially surrounding the issues of self-care, which typically begins during the second year of life in European-influenced American homes. This stage is chronologically similar to Freud's anal period (see Table 4-2).

The way Erikson explained the crisis faced by the 2-year-old child is that he is caught in a double bind. He can't yet dress and undress himself or control his bowel functions; yet when he tries and fails, he often feels ashamed. If he refuses to try, he feels powerful or autonomous, but at the cost of his self-image when he ends up soiled and scolded. Gentle teaching, Erikson cautioned, produces the best results: a confident child, able to control his bodily functions and begin to take care of himself with pride. Cultures that do not value early autonomy present a more mellow environment for their children, and this may be a less stressful period for such children.

STAGE THREE: INITIATIVE VERSUS GUILT Caregivers responsible for kindergartners may experience a crisis of initiative versus guilt with some of their charges; the 4- and 5-year-old child has learned to build, to climb, to talk, to reason, to imagine. All these new skills bring creativity, and it is great fun to explore them. **Initiative** is Erikson's term for the process; the other side of the seesaw is **guilt,** invoked when a creation gets out of hand somehow, perhaps gets broken, or spilt, or too loud. The role of the adult with stage three children is to guide them safely through the exciting stuff without letting it get out of control. The conscience develops during this period, which is important, but a heavy dose of guilt can be produced by overly harsh responses to childish initiative.

STAGE FOUR: INDUSTRY VERSUS INFERIORITY   Freud called this period *latency,* a time when not much was thought to be happening except that time was passing before the child entered puberty. Erikson noticed that children between 6 and 12 years of age are not just marking time; they are actually tiring with the business of play and want to learn how to do useful things. Children in this stage form attachments to teachers and to parents of their friends, and they playact at doing grown-up work like those people do. Successful development during this period enhances self-esteem and gives children an accurate sense of their ability to work at useful tasks. If things do not work out so well, children's sense of inferiority can cloud their school years and stay with them for a very long while afterward.

It is important, believed Erikson, that school-age children have many opportunities to complete tasks they consider interesting and that the "real world" of adults considers worthy. It is especially helpful if children see adults working on the same or similar tasks and if they receive (gentle) guidance when they hit rough spots. Projects that involve cooking or making things with tools, for example, are very attractive to children 7 to 9 years of age. If a way can be found to make money off the creations, you'll also have the interest of the 10- to 12-year-olds!

Feelings of inferiority develop in children who rarely succeed at the tasks they set themselves or those that are set by others. These negative perceptions of self may also occur if most of the things the child has learned to do well are considered insignificant by important adults and classmates (Thomas, 1992). You may have children in your program with a very negative view of their own abilities and worth; a challenge for you is to involve children in activities at which they can succeed, at least occasionally, even with all their self-doubts.

STAGE FIVE: IDENTITY VERSUS ROLE DIFFUSION   People who work with children in sixth grade or above know that adolescence brings with it a whole range of new and confusing changes to many children, in both their bodies and their personalities. Erikson coined the term **identity crisis** to explain what is happening during this period.

This is the period when a child's **persona** seems to change weekly; hairstyles, favorite type of music, and clothing take on entirely new and very significant meanings for the young adolescent. Sometimes we say that a youngster *identifies* with a particular character in a movie or book, or with a group of people who characterize themselves by dressing or acting in a particular way. This is a reference to Erikson's term and often signals a youth's desire/need to try out several different roles before deciding on the one he or she will wear for the rest of his or her life.

Anthropologist Margaret Mead and social learning theorist Albert Bandura have expressed skepticism that adolescence is a distinct stage of development. There is some evidence to indicate that this period of life is much less stressful in some cultures than in others (Bandura, 1964; Mead, 1928/1973), and so it wouldn't be surprising if it is also less difficult for certain *individuals* than others. (The personality formation theories of Mead, Elkin, and Piaget, which are described in Chapter 5, are also helpful in explaining what is going on during this time.)

How we dress, speak, and act has a direct influence on the people around us. How they respond to us tells us important things about ourselves. One of the crucial tasks of this period is for a young person to succeed in finding a role to play that results in feedback from the society that matches his or her own perception of self—in other words, a role that *fits*.

At this point, what has gone before has a powerful influence on what happens next. Erikson said it this way: "The sense of ego identity, then, is the accrued confidence that one's ability to maintain inner sameness and continuity is matched by the sameness and continuity of one's meaning for others" (1959, p. 89).

In Erikson's view, children who consider themselves to be competent, connected with society, and attractive to others will feel most comfortable in roles that reflect those characteristics. If, on the other hand, children have learned to believe that they are "troublemakers," "lazy," and "no good," they will be more likely to take on demeanors and costumes that consistently bring those messages from people around them and, sadly, reinforce the negative self-perception developed during an earlier stage. Understanding this process can help a child or youth worker to interrupt the cycle, avoiding overreacting to this week or this month's hairstyle or fashion statement, and, when possible, even providing some gentle feedback to youngsters that will help them behave or dress so as to elicit desirable responses from the world around them. But be aware that older school-agers may consider this to be "selling out." A lively discussion can continue for months on this topic.

ROBERT HAVIGHURST (1900–1991)

Coined by the Progressive Education Association in the 1930s, the term *developmental task* is usually attributed to Robert J. Havighurst, who popularized it in the 1940s and 1950s. Developmental tasks are

> those things a person must learn if he is to be judged and to judge himself to be a reasonably happy and successful person. A developmental task is a task which arises at or about a certain period in the life of the individual, successful achievement of which leads to his happiness and to success with later tasks, while failure leads to unhappiness in the individual, disapproval by society, and difficulty with later tasks.
>
> —Havighurst, 1953, p. 2

Havighurst identified five stages of development in 10 categories of behavior, but in its simplest form the developmental task theory integrates well with Erikson's life-crisis approach. The attainment of certain tasks (such as

The Middle Years: Piddling, Plundering and Posturing

Herb Kohl

Everyone interested in starting after-school programs needs to understand who the middle years' child is. This is the perspective of Herb Kohl, author of 36 Children, Growing with Your Children, *and* Growing Minds. *Kohl is a strong advocate of progressive and alternative education and is a keen observer of human nature. He speaks from his experience as a classroom teacher.*

Different children reach maturity in different ways and in different orders of growth. Some speak much more precociously than they walk, while others walk much more confidently than they speak.

In terms of who these kids are, the age spread is so enormous and the needs so diverse until it's best to look at the 5–8 year olds separately from the 9–12 year olds. The 5–8 year olds have their internal needs related to growing, strength, independence and exploration of the world. They're discovering the mastery of the world that surrounds them and the mastery of their local world causes tremendous anxiety for adults. They no longer have to look around for approval. This is a period when fundamental detachments occur and they deal with a real sense of individuation, much of which is culturally determined.

In certain class and cultural settings, kids are given a great deal more freedom. The more freedom that abounds, the earlier the individuation sets in. In many ways, the safety valves of middle class communities often stifle that kind of individuation. In working class communities, necessity often facilitates the independence much earlier.

Another developmental characteristic is the desire for them to have the same power as the adults by whom they are surrounded. You often see it in 5 year olds when they pretend to read. That is a power that most adults have over children. Playing house, making a store, driving a car are also ways of modeling the adult world. A real instinctive use of the body occurs as well and it is during this phase a fairly sophisticated coordination takes place, i.e. running, chasing, throwing or catching a ball.

With the 9–12 year olds, especially the 11 and 12 year olds, sensitivity to and towards peer affection becomes important. Friendship and sexuality become an obsession. The onset of a very self-conscious and acute, almost microscopic, awareness of the body and sexuality emerge. The casual and easy play that exists amongst the younger group becomes complicated by the peer and sexual dynamics. . . .

I'm not so certain that we really understand how far kids' minds can really grow. That's why the fullest humanistic education possible between the ages of 5–8 is essential. Exposing them to numbers learned through manipulation and to the real world will encourage their minds to flow freely from one subject to another: music to math and poetry to physics. They really don't deserve to be drilled or turned into people who hate the development of the mind.

Nine–twelve year olds are fully capable of sophisticated production of work and experimentation within literature and science. They also have the ability to articulate what they are doing. The age of in-depth inquiry is most apparent in the 10, 11 and 12 year olds. That kind of creative inquiry certainly needs to be encouraged. But I feel we're doing the opposite and that is closing down minds instead of opening them up. . . .

Compassion as well as budding political and moral consciousness also begin to play a significant role during the middle years. Unfortunately, institutions are driving people towards the discouragement of their compassions. Schools often destroy its development through teachers humiliating some and overpraising other students. Television and sports function in a similar manner . . .

This is also a time in which kids have to learn to sort out relationships. For one of the more sensitive issues at this point is the relationship between affection and sexuality. Two girls who love the same boy find it hard to like one another. Or two boys become enemies because they have a crush on the same girl. . . .

The fact that they are older means they're often left out of experiences and situations that do continue to nurture them and help them grow. The after-school environment is an important part of those experiences. That environment can often be an oasis in the midst of the desert that school sometimes becomes. Some of the more sensible ways of providing that care would be through activities like music, reading, theater; noncompetitive or judgmental group events should be encouraged as well. The fact must be stressed that we want them to have education as opposed to schooling and nurturing as opposed to care.

Maybe if we put ourselves on notice to the fact that our children are in the process of becoming the people they will ultimately be, we might move differently in terms of fulfilling the needs they really have and not the ones we imagine they have. There is no time when it is more important to demonstrate compassion and hope.

establishing oneself as a very dependent being or beginning to adjust to expectations of others) can serve as signals that the goal of that first life crisis (basic trust versus basic mistrust) is being achieved. Havighurst was, in fact, influenced heavily by Erikson as he developed his matrix of tasks (Thomas, 1992).

Examples of developmental tasks of 5- to 7-year-old children (initiative versus guilt; industry versus inferiority) include "freeing oneself from primary identification with adults," "establishing peer grouping and learning to belong," "improving skill in use of small muscles," and "learning more realistic ways of studying and controlling [the] physical world." Table 4-3 shows some of the developmental tasks Havighurst felt were important in the school-age years.

Although the exact nature and timing of these developmental tasks are influenced by culture and life circumstances (and Havighurst limited his study to the developmental tasks of mid-20th century, middle-class American children), an awareness of the tasks themselves can be very helpful to people working with children of different ages. The developmental task model can be used to help us recognize the *nature* of children's tasks at each age level, provide opportunities for them to practice the tasks, be patient with their attempts, and furnish information and training necessary to promote their success (Thomas, 1992).

Intellectual Development

JEAN PIAGET (1896–1980)

Piaget's work has heavily influenced the fields of psychology and education, and with good reason. His interpretation of children's intellectual growth stages provided a vocabulary and a framework for understanding much that goes on inside children's heads. For professionals in school-age child care, Piaget's most important contribution may be the observation that many children do not begin to overcome perceptions with logic until after the age of 7, and that most children are unable to work effectively with hypothetical situations until after the age of 11. Knowing this, it becomes easier for us to help children communicate with others by avoiding confrontations that result when we assume that these cognitive processes are in place.

Piaget identified four periods of cognitive development: sensorimotor, preoperational, concrete operational, and formal operational. Each period is characterized by a different way of thinking and knowing, and every child passes through each stage in the same order (although not necessarily at the same ages—or at the ages Piaget first theorized).

Sensorimotor Period   In the beginning of postnatal life, the **sensorimotor** period, we are dependent on our senses to provide all our knowledge. Babies seem to lose interest in objects and people when the object or person moves away from them. They experience things by sight, sound, or touch, so when a

TABLE 4–3   Some Developmental Tasks of Childhood

	Early childhood (2–3 to 5–6–7	Late childhood (5–6–7 to pubescence)	Early adolescence (Pubescence to puberty)
I. Achieving appropriate dependence-independence pattern	Adjusting to less attention; becoming independent physically.	Freeing oneself from primary identification with adults.	Beginning to establish independence from adults in all behavior areas.
II. Achieving appropriate giving-receiving pattern of affection	Developing ability to give affection; learning to share affection.	Learning to give as much love as one receives; forming friendships with peers.	Accepting oneself as worthwhile person; worthy of love.
III. Relating to changing social groups	Beginning to develop ability to interact with age-mates; adjusting to family expectations for child as member of the social unit.	Clarifying adult world versus child's world; establishing peer grouping and learning to belong.	Behaving according to shifting peer code.
IV. Developing a conscience	Developing ability to take directions, to be obedient in presence of authority; developing ability to be obedient in absence of authority.	Learning more rules; developing true morality.	
V. Learning one's psycho-socio-biological sex role	Learning to identify with adult male and female roles.	Beginning to identify with same-sex social contemporaries.	
VI. Accepting and adjusting to a changing body	Adjusting to expectations based on improving muscular abilities; developing sex modesty.		Reorganizing self-concept in the face of significant bodily changes; accepting one's appearance.
VII. Managing a changing body and learning new motor patterns	Developing large muscle control; learning to coordinate large and small muscles.	Improving skill in use of small muscles.	Controlling and using "new" body.
VIII. Learning to understand and control the physical world	Meeting adult restrictions on exploration and manipulation of expanding environment.	Learning more realistic ways of studying and controlling physical world.	
IX. Developing an appropriate symbol system and conceptual abilities	Improving one's use of the symbol system; great elaboration of concept pattern.	Learning to use language to exchange ideas or to influence; beginning to understand casual relationships; making finer conceptual distinctions; thinking reflectively.	Using language to express and clarify more complex concepts; moving from the concrete to the abstract; applying general principles to the particular.
X. Relating oneself to the cosmos	Developing a rudimentary notion of one's place in the cosmos.	Developing a scientific approach.	

Source: Adapted from Havighurst, 1953.

4-month-old accidentally pushes a rolling toy under the couch and can no longer mouth it or see it, it appears no longer to exist for her.

Somewhere around the end of the second year, children begin to learn how to think symbolically; we know this because they search for objects that have disappeared, or imitate actions that they saw on the previous day, and they "pretend." These actions signal the beginning of preoperational thought.

Preoperational Thinking **Preoperational** children do not think logically, and they are **egocentric,** which means not only that they believe the world turns around them, the literal meaning of the term, but also that they are not able to consider another person's perspective, either physically (determining which is the right hand of a person facing them, for example) or emotionally. An egocentric child will frequently select a birthday present for a friend (or a parent) using the criterion that "I'd like one." It is nearly pointless to ask a preoperational child "How do you think Billy feels when you hit him?" because the child cannot yet put himself in another person's place and imagine how that person might feel. He can only tell you how *he himself* feels, and this explains why a common response to this question is "angry" or sometimes "sorry."

Because young children are trying very hard to understand their world, these limitations on their thinking processes can cause them to oversimplify categories, making them appear quite stereotypical. For example, Jill might not understand why her brother Brian is disappointed when he fails to get into nursing school. She may not yet be able to understand either (a) why a boy would want to be a nurse or (b) what "failing" really means. As children move from simple sorting of people and things into social categories (clothing styles, gender roles, race, age) and into more complex understandings of social roles and behaviors, these stereotypes are gradually modified. That is one of the positive results for children of experiencing the world outside the constraints of family and neighborhood, as they do in school-age programs; it also suggests that child and youth workers should offer challenges to oversimplified categories of ideas whenever they occur.

Concrete Operations By the time children are 6 or 7, most are using **concrete operational** thought at least part of the time. The significance of this step is that the child can now think logically, at least about concrete and familiar things. In earlier stages of cognitive development, a child would **centrate** on one attribute of an object (such as its color, its shape, its purpose) and be unable to consider other attributes at the same time; now the child can think about more than one characteristic at the time.

The most commonly published example of centration is the **conservation of liquid** task, in which a child is asked to decide whether a container of water that is tall and thin holds the same amount as one that is short and wide. Even after being shown that they hold the same amount, by pouring water from one to the other, preoperational children will insist that the tall one holds more because it is tall (or sometimes, the short one holds more because it is fat). A child who is a concrete operational thinker will think, "If the water can be poured from one to the other with no spilling and no space left over, they must hold the same amount." The same kind of thinking appears in dividing up cookies of different sizes, cutting sandwiches into several pieces, making change for coins, and deciding who gets to use the swing next and for how long. Understanding the limitations of preoperational thought can help caregivers mediate disagreements between two children at different levels of thought— for example, between a kindergartner and a second grader.

Formal Operations   Children who exhibit *formal operational thinking* (roughly age 11 to age 15) are no longer constrained to thinking about what they have experienced directly. They can deal with physical impossibilities ("imagine that this car ran on milk . . .") in order to consider plausible possibilities. This ability allows the study of higher mathematics, physics, the solution of social and political problems, and the enjoyment of arguing for the sake of experiencing the logical argument process. It can make working with older children a real treat if you understand what is going on. However, for adults who have poor ego concepts or who do not understand the developmental tasks the children are working through (using language to express and clarify more complex concepts, moving from the concrete to the abstract, applying general principles to the particular), this period can be quite challenging.

Developmental psychologists of today question some of the specific details of Piaget's theory, but there is no doubt that he has caused people to think about childhood in a different way. He gave us a new vocabulary and a new respect for children's thought. His description of how children acquire knowledge is an example of this. To explain the process, he coined two terms, *assimilation* and *accommodation*. When faced with new information, children either ignore it or *assimilate* it into their existing view of the world. I think of assimilation much like picking up a pinecone or other object and placing it on a shelf or in a drawer of the mind. If, however, the information is at odds with the existing understanding (or doesn't fit on the shelf or in the drawer), children either reject it or *accommodate* to it; in other words, they change existing perception to adapt to the information (build a new shelf or choose a large drawer).

For example, if a child is learning to spell a list of words, each new word is assimilated or added to each of the words that came before it. Imagine, however, that the child comes to a word she thinks she already knows how to spell, and discovers that she doesn't. A good example, one which always troubled me when I was a child, is *accept* and *except*. If the child has been using these two words interchangeably, understanding the two different meanings but believing them to be spelled the same, she is liable to stop for a moment to ponder this new information. Assuming she trusts the word list from which she is working, she will change her *schema* (another Piagetian word), or mental model, of the word that is pronounced *ek-sept* (or perhaps she will learn to pronounce one of them *ak-sept*). This is accommodation. We don't always accommodate new information quickly. Sometimes the process is painful. Remember algebra?

LEV SEMENOVICH VYGOTSKY (1896–1934)

Lev Vygotsky was a young literature teacher who began studying developmental psychology following the Russian revolution near the close of World War I. The Marxist-Leninist political philosophy of the time emphasized the equality of people. Some of Vygotsky's early research findings, contrary to the Freudian-influenced psychological thought of the time, seemed to parallel this belief and secured him high regard in the Soviet Union. Vygotsky taught that the social and cultural context in which the child grew up and learned was the critical factor in intellectual development. Vygotsky's theory is known as *contextualism.*

Although his work was not widely accepted in the United States until recent years, Vygotsky has had a strong following in Europe since 1962, when his text *Thought and Language* was translated into English. Many of his ideas are helpful in explaining development, but two concepts are especially useful for people working with school-age children—the zone of proximal development and scaffolding (Vygotsky, 1962, 1963).

The **zone of proximal development** describes the range of difficulty within which a child can learn a new task or concept. Within this zone, Vygotsky explained, the task or concept is difficult, but not too difficult. Often, the child needs a little help to understand the concept or master the task; this assistance, which usually comes from a helping adult, Vygotsky called **scaffolding.** Parents and teachers use scaffolding all the time by asking questions ("How do you think you could turn that puzzle piece so it will fit?"), sounding out the beginning of a word but not the end, suggesting two words that a third word might be between on a dictionary page. The important message that Vygotsky and the Russian contextualists gave to those of us who work with children is that there is a strong relationship between social experience and intellectual development. In other words, by encouraging growth toward problem solving and thinking in these ways, we are making a positive contribution to children's competence.

HOWARD GARDNER (1943–)

Gardner reframed the concept of intelligence itself. In 1983, the Harvard professor published *Frames of Mind,* a book outlining the notion that there are at least seven separate human capacities (Gardner has recently added an eighth intelligence: naturalistic). These range from musical intelligence to interpersonal intelligence and spatial intelligence to logical intelligence. A compelling idea to educators, Gardner's theory presents a strong case for multisensory education at all ages and brings into question the single-strand assessment that has been in place since intelligence tests were first introduced to the public schools in the early 1950s. Gardner's view of intelligence explains not only how children learn best but also why different cultures might value forms of intelligence differently.

Some children prefer to do their homework with their friends; others prefer to study alone.

Most of us agree that 21st-century pilots should have strong *logical/ mathematical* intelligence. However, Gardner explains that if he were in a boat in the middle of the ocean without navigational instruments, he would rather have a navigator with well-developed *spatial* intelligence. That way he could find their way home by using the stars (Gardner, 1983). Gardner's theory of multiple intelligences is represented in Table 4-4, along with related activities that can easily be incorporated into programs for school-age children.

Moral Development

LAWRENCE KOHLBERG (1927–1987)

A Harvard University professor of psychology and education, Kohlberg was particularly interested in moral development that has to do with the establishment of a conscience and understanding right from wrong. His doctoral work focused on the moral reasoning skills of North American boys age 10 to 16, but he later studied girls in North America and children of both genders from Mexico, Thailand, kibbutz communities in Israel, Malaysia, Turkey, Taiwan, and other areas. Following his lengthy research, Kohlberg concluded that the stages of moral development he identified are present in all cultures, but youths move through the stages at different ages in different societies.

TABLE 4–4 Gardner's Theory of Multiple Intelligences in Activity Planning for School-Age Children

Intelligence	Description	Appropriate activities, materials to offer
Verbal/Linguistic	Likes to talk, listen Enjoys writing Likes rhymes, jokes	Keep a journal; write a newspaper; play word games Read books, magazines; write poetry, stories Debate hot topics; work crossword puzzles
Logical/Mathematical	Recognizes patterns Works with abstract symbols Solves problems	Keep stats for after-school games Play checkers, chess, backgammon Measure things; do science experiments Run a math lab for younger children
Visual/Spatial	Likes color and design Describes scenes Likes to build things	Match nail polish color with fabric swatches Build castles/forts with cardboard cartons Make a wheat-paste topographic map; create 3-D art
Bodily/Kinesthetic	Likes physical games Takes things apart and fixes them Is good at sports Might play instrument	Play relay races; sprints; hide & seek; sports Make sandpaper numbers/letters for new readers Work with play dough, clay; jewelry-making, weaving Study dance/gymnastics Rearrange the furniture
Musical/Rhythmic	Enjoys listening to music Plays instruments Possibly also dances	Play Name that Tune; Freeze Dance Play Simon (musical version of *Concentration*) Listen to music while doing homework Play piano, rhythm instruments
Interpersonal	Works well with others Notices others' feelings Is high communicator	Be group leader for planning session Be Jeopardy host; Bingo caller; Conflict Manager Make phone calls to price food for party
Intrapersonal	Likes quiet corner Tends to play/work alone Is thoughtful	Keep journal; have access to earphones; lots of books Do Jigsaw puzzles; start Pen Pal project; Have quiet spot for homework

Source: Adapted from Bumgarner, 1993.

A self-identified Piagetian with roots in George Herbert Mead's sociology of thinking (see Chapter 5), Kohlberg identified a direct relationship between the child's passage through cognitive stages of thought and the potential for achieving certain moral reasoning stages (Kohlberg, 1984, 1987). However, after recognizing that relationship, he acknowledged that intellectual development alone is not enough to determine moral judgment. A major portion of his theory is devoted to describing and explaining three additional factors (desire, social role-taking, and justice structure) that interact with mental maturity to determine the way a child is likely to behave in any given situation.

Kohlberg arrived at his conclusions by presenting children with moral dilemmas. Probably the most famous dilemma is whether or not it would be acceptable to steal medicine for a loved one if it was impossible to purchase it and the loved one would die without the medicine (Kohlberg, 1969). By presenting children with these quandaries, many of which had no real solution, he was able to identify the components of decision making and to observe how those components changed with experience and maturity.

Following his observations of 75 young American males over a 10-year period, Kohlberg developed a hierarchy of three moral levels—***preconventional, conventional,*** and ***postconventional***—each consisting of two stages. Kohlberg's hierarchy is presented in Table 4-5. The contrived nature of the questions and the limitations on gender and culture have been raised by other researchers; however, an understanding of Kohlberg's hierarchy can help us realize that children's moral decisions are indicators of a developmental stage process and of local influences and do not necessarily reflect the inherent "moral fiber" of the child. Exactly what the children decided—whether or not the husband should steal the drug—is not important; what is of interest is the way they came to their decision.

After completing his original set of interviews, Kohlberg concluded that the levels and stages occurred in a regular sequence and were age related. He determined that most children under age 9 thought about moral dilemmas in a preconventional way, placing a heavy emphasis on rewards and punishments; but by the time they became young adolescents, they began to reason in more conventional ways, more actively supporting the moral order. By early adulthood, a small number of people were using postconventional or universal reasoning to sort out moral problems. Most people, predicted Kohlberg, would never use postconventional reasoning. Many cross-cultural studies have been undertaken to test Kohlberg's ideas, and most have found them to be useful in understanding the development of moral behavior (Snarey, 1985).

CAROL GILLIGAN (1936–)

Harvard psychologist Carol Gilligan has suggested that Kohlberg's work is male-value-laden. Girls and boys are socialized differently, she pointed out, and consequently develop different codes of morality. A woman's view of ethics "centers around the understanding of responsibility and relationships, just as the [male's] conception of morality as fairness ties moral development to the understanding of rights and rules" (Gilligan, 1982, p. 19). She believes that differences in moral reasoning between males and females are based primarily on the fact that girls are generally raised by same-gender caregivers (mothers, grandmothers, and nannies, for example) whereas boys are generally raised by opposite-gender people. This leads to differences in personality structure, resulting in different kinds of decision making in moral/ethical matters. Thus the male view of morality is based on ***objectivity*** (justice) and the female view on ***connectivity*** (caring). Gilligan suggested that women's responses on Kohlberg's scale were lower than men's because their moral thinking was more oriented toward interpersonal relationships. Kohlberg did not seem to find Gilligan's ideas inconsistent with his. Instead, he challenged her research team to "determine whether there is a stage-type development in dilemmas of care, and whether stage development in such dilemmas is synchronous with stage

TABLE 4–5   Kohlberg's Stages of Moral Judgment

I. Preconventional Level. The subject follows society's rules of right and wrong but in terms of the rewards and punishments, and only when someone is watching.

> **Stage 1. Punishment and obedience orientation.** Whether an action is good or bad depends on whether it is punished or rewarded. If the person is going to be punished, it's *bad,* so he shouldn't do it. If no punishment will result, then it's all right.

> **Stage 2. Naive instrumental orientation.** There is some aspect of fairness or reciprocity at work here, although it is quite concrete, not motivated by loyalty, gratitude, or justice. For example, "I'll trust you with the contents of my locker if you let me share your gym clothes."

II. Conventional Level. People at this level conform to the expectations of their family, group, or nation. They actively support and justify the existing social order.

> **Stage 2. Good-boy, nice-girl orientation.** People act in ways that please or help others and are approved by them. Now the *intention* of the judged person becomes important, not just the results of the action.

> **Stage 3. Law-and-order orientation.** People are doing the right thing when they act according to the rules set up by the existing social order (e.g., show respect for authority, do their "duty," etc.).

III. Postconventional Level. In this level, there is a clear attempt to identify universal values of morality. By identifying commonalities between different groups and authorities, people narrow their moral code to include the values that "everyone" seems to agree on.

> **Stage 5. Social-contract orientation.** One of the tests of this level is how a person acts when there is a conflict between the society's standards and individual rights. Generally, there is a recognition that sometimes individual rights need to be put aside "for the good of the order." However, people functioning at this level are frequently challengers of laws that violate human rights, believing that just government does contain the means to adapt and adjust when necessary.

> **Stage 6. Universal ethical principle orientation.** Moral judgments of the person in Stage 6 are framed by universal principles of justice, based on the reciprocity and equality of human rights and on respect for the dignity of humans as individual persons. *Right* and *wrong* are internally arrived-at convictions, defined by general principles of ethics and morality.

Source: Adapted from Thomas, 1992.

development in justice reasoning or whether they are radically asynchronous" (1987, p. 305).

Gilligan's questions encouraged research by others. Stanford researcher Nel Noddings, in her book, *Caring: A Feminine Approach to Ethics & Moral Education* (1984), carried the morality concept a step further with her work on the **cared-for** and the **one-caring,** as she described a morality based on natural caring, a classical feminine view rooted in **receptivity, relatedness,** and **responsiveness.** Noddings encouraged schools to realign educational goals so that they would more openly encourage and reward sensitivity in moral matters.

Another study found that men are also capable of displaying an orientation toward care and relationships; when they do, those men have scores similar to

Children develop their moral reasoning by engaging in a reciprocal exchange of ideas with others.

the scores of women (Cole, 1996). Additional research revealed that there are more differences in approaches to solving ethical dilemmas between people of diverse cultures than between genders.

WILLIAM DAMON (1944–)

Damon also questioned the appropriateness of Kohlberg's hypothetical dilemma methodology for studying young children—mostly because he thought the questions were irrelevant to most children's experience. He developed a different set of questions, using children's own games (such as marbles), and questioned children's reasons for certain actions that were related to their interests (Damon, 1977). Later, Damon and Killen (1982) studied the process of change in children's moral reasoning when they had opportunities to discuss ethical dilemmas with an adult or groups of other children. Various scenarios were presented to the children and coding schemes were devised to assess the way in which children presented their arguments and how they responded to others' statements. Peer discussions were videotaped for later analysis, much of which is contained in Damon's book, *The Moral Child* (1990).

Damon's most useful discovery may have been that children grow and develop in their moral reasoning in a much more complex fashion than was earlier believed. Simple exposure to other people's opinions, even those of respected adults, is not, *in and of itself,* sufficient to determine the kind of ethical decision making children will use. This is great news, especially in light of the declining availability of high moral standards in the public media, a major contender for children's free time. Damon concluded that one of the more effective change-agents in children's thinking is ***reciprocal interaction***—the exchange of ideas with adults and one another in a two-way fashion, "extending, clarifying, or compromising with the other's statements" (1982, p. 365).

Talking with children about real quandaries in their lives and the options available to them appears potentially to be a very valuable exercise—both to increase your understanding of children's moral thinking and to help the children progress in it. Gilligan's, Noddings's and Damon's views, although they have not yet been widely accepted, have important implications for adults working with school-age children. They provide explanations for differing styles of communication, thinking, and decision making and remind us to be wary of any psychological model that is based on a single worldview. Having an understanding of Kohlberg's hierarchy of moral judgment is a useful tool, but it should be used carefully. There is still no consensus on its general applicability to a dual-gendered and multicultural society.

Table 4-6 summarizes some of the major milestones in school-age child development. Periodically referring to this chart and the text that explains it will help you keep your expectations of children reasonable.

Learning Theory

B. F. SKINNER (1904–1990)

Harvard research psychologist B. F. Skinner was for 40 years the best-known person in learning theory. His behaviorist approach to the solution of educational, personal adjustment, and social problems resulted in four decades of controversy and notoriety. Teachers and parents, behavioral psychologists and prison wardens have applied his principles of ***operant conditioning*** to increase desirable behaviors and decrease less desirable ones, sometimes with excellent results but often with disastrous ones.

At the base of his theory is the principle that a behavior will increase if it is followed by a ***reinforcer*** and decrease if followed by a ***punishment.*** Reinforcers can be a pleasurable event (an ice cream cone) or the removal of an unpleasant event (a ban on watching television); punishment is always something the child perceives as an unpleasant occurrence. The difficulty comes in identifying what is pleasant and what is unpleasant. The most common misconception among adults trying to use these principles is that children do not like to be scolded or singled out in a group. In actual practice, any attention is sometimes better than none, and so the child who is berated for his misbehavior in a particular setting may feel that he has been rewarded (simply by being noticed) and repeat the same behavior in order to receive the "reward" again.

TABLE 4–6   Milestones in Development of School-Age Children 6 Years Old and Older

Age	Physical	Cognitive	Language	Social-Emotional
6 yrs.	Has 90% of adult-size brain Reaches about two-thirds of adult height Begins to lose baby teeth Moves a writing or drawing tool with the fingers while the side of the hand rests on the table top Can skip Can tie a bow	Begins to demonstrate concrete operational thinking Demonstrates conservation of number on Piaget's conservation tasks Can create series operationally rather than by trial and error	Might use a letter-name spelling strategy, thus creating many invented spellings Appreciates jokes and riddles based on phonological ambiguity	Feels one way only about a situation Has some difficulty detecting intentions accurately in situations where damage occurs Demonstrates Kohlberg's preconventional moral thinking
7 yrs.	Is able to make small, controlled marks with pencils or pens due to more refined finger dexterity Has longer face Continues to lose baby teeth	Begins to use some rehearsal strategies as an aid to memory Becomes much better able to play strategy games May demonstrate conservation of mass and length	Appreciates jokes and riddles based on lexical ambiguity Begins to read using a print-governed approach, but cueing systems are still imbalanced	May express two emotions about one situation, but these will be same valence Demonstrates Kohlberg's conventional thinking Understands gender constancy
8 yrs.	Plays jacks and other games requiring considerable fine motor skill and good reaction time Jumps rope skillfully Throws and bats a ball more skillfully	Still has great difficulty judging whether a passage is relevant to a specific theme May demonstrate conservation of area	Sorts out some of the more difficult syntactic difficulties, such as "ask" and "tell" Integrates all cueing systems More conventional speller	Expresses two same-valence emotions about different targets Understands that people may interpret situations differently but thinks it's due to different information
9 yrs.	Enjoys hobbies requiring high levels of fine motor skill (sewing, weaving, model building)	May demonstrate conservation of weight	Interprets "ask" and "tell" correctly	Can think about own thinking or another person's thinking but not both at the same time.
10 yrs.	May begin to menstruate if female	Begins to make better judgments about relevance of a text Begins to delete unimportant information when summarizing	Becomes good conventional speller	Can take own view and view of another as if a disinterested third party
11 yrs.	May begin preadolescent growth spurt if female	May demonstrate conservation of volume	Begins to appreciate jokes and riddles based on syntactic ambiguity	Still has trouble detecting deception Spends more time with friends
12 yrs.	Has reached about 80 percent of adult height if male, 90 percent if female Has all permanent teeth except for two sets of molars Plays ball more skillfully due to improved reaction time Begins to menstruate if female	Shows much greater skill in summarizing and outlining May begin to demonstrate formal operational thinking		May begin to demonstrate Kohlberg's post-conventional moral thinking.

Source: J. Schickedanz et al. (1998). *Understanding Children.* Needham Heights, MA: Allyn & Bacon.

One advantage of after-school programs is that, unlike regular classrooms, children at different stages of physical, social, and cognitive development play and work together.

Skinner provided a technique for undoing this problem once it is recognized. When the reinforcer is eliminated, basically, by ignoring the behavior, the likelihood that the behavior will occur again decreases (after a short period of increase as the child tries repeatedly for the expected reward). Once that decrease begins, the continued refusal on the part of the adult to reinforce it will eventually result in the ***extinction,*** or disappearance, of the undesirable behavior.

Opponents of those who would use learning theory to modify children's behavior claim that the techniques are manipulative and violate human rights. Supporters point out that parents and teachers have always used these techniques; Skinner and others merely observed the process and gave it a vocabulary.

ALBERT BANDURA (1925–)

Bandura and his colleagues expanded Skinner's approach to explain how children learn social behaviors. Social learning theorists, as they are called, propose that most of a child's learning comes from actively copying, or *modeling,* the behavior of others. Reinforcement of behavior still occurs, but sometimes it can be vicarious reinforcement. In other words, if Zeke hears Kyle being rewarded for trying out a new play during basketball practice, he learns to do the same when he has the opportunity. Skinner felt that the process of learning from modeling occurred *only* in cases where the child was reinforced directly for the new behavior. However one approaches the argument, understanding learning theory can be helpful in understanding children's (and adults') behavior.

SUMMARY

Children grow and develop in a variety of areas—physical, socioemotional, cognitive, and moral. Psychologists and educators have observed children and formulated theories about the way development progresses and some of the contributing factors. Arnold Gesell collected data from children for 30 years and developed guides for parents containing growth gradients and behaviors likely to occur at each age and stage. Psychoanalyst Freud studied his patients, developing a complex theory of personality development. One of his students, Erik Erikson, proposed a revisionist view based on a series of life crises influenced by environmental factors at work during each stage. Havighurst identified developmental tasks mastered at various stages of growth and development. Jean Piaget classified stages of logical thought, which provided a scaffold for Kohlberg's view of moral development. Lev Vygotsky and Howard Gardner have expanded our understanding of children's thinking. Carol Gilligan proposed a feminist alternative to Kohlberg's theory, and Noddings and Damon identified factors that contribute to optimal growth in moral reasoning. Skinner offered a behaviorist approach to the solution of educational, personal adjustment, and social problems. Albert Bandura expanded on that approach to explain how children learn social behaviors.

REVIEW QUESTIONS

1. What are the four domains of development studied by most theorists?

2. Match each of the following development areas with a theorist:

Growth (maturational theory)	Gilligan
Psychosocial development	Erikson
Cognitive development	Gesell
Moral development	Piaget

3. Match the theorist below with the correct phrase:

Erikson	developmental task
Havighurst	life crises
Vygotsky	growth gradients
Kohlberg	stages of moral judgment
Gesell	zone of proximal development

4. Explain how the moral development theory of Gilligan differs from that of Kohlberg. How might it affect children's decisions surrounding right and wrong?

5. Describe how one theorist's ideas influence another. Trace, for example, the roots of Kohlberg's ideas about moral development and Erikson's ideas about personality development.

6. How might physical development of children influence social development? How might social development influence children's ability to make friends?

CHALLENGE EXERCISES

1. Interview three parents of school-age children. Ask them questions about their children's behavior, their thinking, their ethical decision making. How closely do these children match the developmental stages presented by the theorists?

2. Interview three children about school, favorite activities, and friendships. What can you say about their moral development from their answers?

3. Design a project to build with a group of school-age children. Work with them to plan the project, obtain the necessary materials, and construct it. Describe what you observe about their developmental differences as you work together.

TERMS TO LEARN
········

autonomous

cared-for

centrate

concrete operational thinking

connectivity

conscience

conservation of liquid

conventional

defense mechanism

developmental task

ego

ego ideal

egocentric

epigenesis

extinction

fixation

formal operational thinking

guilt

id

identity crisis

initiative

maturational theory

objectivity

one-caring

operant conditioning

persona

postconventional

preconventional

preoperational thinking

projection

psychoanalysis

punishment

reaction formation

receptivity

reciprocal interaction

regresssion

reinforcer

relatedness

repression

responsiveness

scaffolding

sensorimotor

superego

zone of proximal development

REFERENCES
········

Ames, L. B., Ilg, F. L., & Baker, S. M. (1988). *Your ten- to fourteen-year-old.* New York: Dell.

Bandura, A. (1964). The stormy decade: Fact or fiction. *Psychology in the School, 1,* 587–595.

Bumgarner, M. (1993). *Improving the understanding of learning styles in prospective early childhood education teachers through self-study and observation.* Ft. Lauderdale, FL: Nova Southeastern University.

Cole, M. C. S. (1996). *The development of children.* New York: Freeman.

Damon, W. (1977). *The social world of the child.* San Francisco: Jossey-Bass.

Damon, W. (1990). *The moral child.* New York: Free Press.

Damon, W., & Killen, M. (1982). Peer interaction and the process of change in children's moral reasoning. *Merrill-Palmer Quarterly, 28*(3), 347–56.

Erikson, E. H. (1959). *Identity and the life cycle in psychological issues.* New York: International Universities Press.

Gardner, H. (1983). *Frames of mind: The theory of multiple intelligences.* New York: Basic Books.

Gesell, A., Ilg, F. L., & Ames, L. B. (1977). *The child from five to ten* (rev. ed.). New York: Harper & Row.

Gesell, A. (1955). Foreword. In F. L. Ilg & L. B. Ames. *The Gesell Institute's Child Behavior from Birth to Ten.* New York: Harper & Row.

Gilligan, C. (1982). *In a different voice: Psychological theory and women's development.* Cambridge, MA: Harvard University Press.

Gordon, A., & Browne, K. W. (1996). *Guiding young children in a diverse society.* Boston: Allyn & Bacon.

Gould, K. H. (1988, September–October). Old wine in new bottles: A feminist perspective on Gilligan's theory. *Social Work,* 411–415.

Havighurst, R. J. (1953). *Human development and education.* New York: Longmans, Green.

Kohlberg, L. (1969). Stage and sequence: The cognitive-developmental approach to socialization. In D. A. Coslin (Ed.), *Handbook of socialization theory and research.* Chicago: Rand McNally.

Kohlberg, L. (1984). *The psychology of moral development.* San Francisco: Harper & Row.

Kohlberg, L. (1987). *Child psychology and childhood education: A cognitive-developmental view.* New York: Longman.

Mead, M. (1973). *Coming of age in Samoa: A psychological study of primitive youth.* New York: American Museum of Natural History. (Original work published 1928)

Miller, P. H. (1993). *Theories of developmental psychology.* (3rd ed.). New York: W. H. Freeman.

Noddings, N. (1984). *Caring, a feminine approach to ethics and moral education.* Berkeley: University of California Press.

Schickedanz, J. S., Schickedanz, D. J., Forsyth, P. D., & Forsyth, G. A. (1998). *Understanding children.* Boston: Allyn & Bacon.

Snarey, J. R. (1985). Cross-cultural universality of social-moral development: A critical review of Kohlbergian research. *Psychological Bulletin, 97,* 202–232.

Thomas, R. M. (1992). *Comparing theories of child development* (3rd ed.). Belmont, CA: Wadsworth.

Vygotsky, L. S. (1962). *Thought and language.* Cambridge, MA: MIT Press.

Vygotsky, L. S. (1963). Learning and mental development at school age. In *Educational psychology in the USSR* (pp. 21–34). London: Routledge & Kegan Paul.

CHAPTER FIVE

The Adult's Role in Socialization and Development

Chapter 3 described some of the varieties of people who work each day with children. Many of these people are conscious of the important part they play in children's lives; others, however, are not. Yet the adults with whom children come in contact each day can have a tremendous influence on their lives. People who work in out-of-school programs need to understand the interaction that takes place between children and adults and the role they play helping children to grow and develop. Jim and Laurie Ollhoff, professors of school-age child care at Concordia University, see adults in out-of-school programs as professionals

> with the knowledge to know why a child is misbehaving, to know why children have a hard time with this activity, to know why children will enjoy this activity. When confronted with a new situation, [professionals] can go into their base of knowledge and figure out what *should* work, and then try it. If it does not go as expected, the professional should be able to evaluate the situation and figure out why it didn't work, and what should work next time.
>
> —Ollhoff, 1994, p. 8

In other words, adults behave as professionals in out-of-school settings by studying the theories that seek to explain human behavior and by using that theoretical framework to guide their own behavior as they design environments, plan activities, and relate to adults and children in their programs.

Marian Marion, a specialist on children's behavior, believes that the way children function in group settings is determined by the interaction between the three components of what she calls the *guidance system*. Those components are the *adults,* the *children* themselves, and the *environment* (Marion, 1987). Marion believes that when adults understand this relationship, they can more easily become effective leaders and mentors and create the kind of environment in which positive interaction with and between children takes place. Anyone who works with children should understand some of the ways these components influence behavior. This chapter explores the role of adults in out-of-school settings. Chapter 4 discussed the development of children, and Chapter 8 describes the influence of the environment.

Adults as Agents of Socialization

The earliest lessons on how to live in the world are given to children by parents, grandparents, siblings, other family members, and caregivers. In a loving environment, children are taught that the world is a predictable and safe place, and they soon learn how to ask to have their needs met in ways that adults find acceptable (Erikson, 1985). They eventually also learn how to take turns and wait for things (lunch, a toy, going to the bathroom), how to do some things for themselves (eat, get dressed, go to the bathroom), and how to share. Each of these social skills is learned through interaction with members of the household or caregiving team. Sociologists call this process *socialization.* After a while, other people enter the picture.

Socialization is formally defined as "the process by which we learn the ways of a given society or social group so that we can function within it" (Elkin,

Children learn how to live in their world by watching members of their family.

1989, p. 2), and it is accomplished both *intentionally* and *unintentionally* by the agents of socialization. ***Intentional socialization*** might include "Don't put your feet on the furniture," or "Say please," or "Before you can play a new game, you need to put the parts to the game you were playing back into the box." ***Unintentional socialization*** takes place when children observe other people (often when these people are unaware of being watched) and absorb lessons from what they see and hear. An example of unintentional socialization would be observing the inclusion (or exclusion) of a child with leg braces in a game of tag, or eavesdropping on a phone conversation in which someone comforts a discouraged friend or calls to report that he will not be at work because he is ill.

Sociologist Frederick Elkin describes the role of others in the process of socialization:

> In the course of growing up, a child must acquire varied knowledge and skills, such as what utensils to use when eating specific foods; how to greet strangers; how to show or conceal emotion in different settings; when to speak and when to be silent. As children grow they move into a widening world of persons, activities, and feelings—all shaped by encounters with others who help define a socially organized world. These *others* will establish standards of right and wrong, and as a result children will come to have certain feelings if they are inadvertently rude, fail an examination, upset a friend, or in some other way do not measure up to their own expectations or the expectations of others.
> —Elkin, 1989, p. 1

As children enter school, the ***others,*** or ***agents of socialization,*** become the peer group, the media, and adults such as teachers, bus drivers, after-school caregivers, and recreation workers. As socialization agents, they help children learn to get along with one another, to cross streets and behave in elevators, to carry on a conversation, and to play "fair." They do this both by what they *do,* and by what they *say.* Children learn more than just ***behaviors*** through socialization; they also learn ***attitudes,*** related ***emotions,*** and ***motivations,*** and after a while they begin to *internalize* what they have learned, creating a kind of rule book for life. During this process, some lifelong assumptions about the world are formed. Culture plays an extremely important role in this process. Each culture socializes its children to function within that culture. In a multicultural society, the socialization process may lead to confusion for children as they receive one set of messages from family members, different ones from school, and still others from the media.

By being aware of these overlaps, adults who work in out-of-school settings can provide opportunities for children to discuss conflicts between the various parts of their lives and help them discern what makes sense for them. It's also very important for children to see examples of fashion, clothing, and role models from their own culture. Make a point of subscribing to several ethnically focused magazines such as *Essence, Hispanic, Face, Tribal Arts, Heart & Soul,* and *Orient* and develop a culturally rich selection of music, books, and posters.

Attitudes, or the feelings one has about facts or conditions, can reveal a great deal about a child. "Nah, I can't do that. It's *stupid,*" reflects an attitude. So does the omnipresent "Yeah, right. . . ." Be watchful for comments like "He talks funny," or "Lisa is a pretty good runner, for a girl." Developers of the antibias curriculum at Pacific Oaks College tell us that ignoring such slanderous words effectively validates them (Derman-Sparks, 1989). To teach antibias attitudes, we need to notice biased statements and challenge them. For example, Marika, a worker in an after-school tutoring program, heard one of the fifth graders say, "But of course Tina scored higher than I did. Asians are better in math!" Marika immediately took the child aside and explained to her that Tina was good in math because she studied very hard. Tina's achievement did not come because of her Chinese ancestry.

Adults who work with children also occasionally hear statements of a political or economic nature. We need to be wary of assuming, as may once have been likely, that children's words reflect attitudes they hear at home. Given the strong influence of media in today's society, these attitudes are learned in many different places (Barbour, 1997). In fact, unless children initiate conversations with their parents about specific issues, they may not have any idea where their parents stand. Honesty, dishonesty, and respect (or lack of it) for other people can also be learned in a wide variety of places—including programs for school-agers.

Emotions of shyness, sadness, anger, embarrassment, and pride are feelings, often experienced so intensely they seem physical. Most children experience a full range of emotions whatever their age, language, or condition. Where the socialization process comes into play, however, is in determining which emotion is triggered by which situation. One child may feel grief at the death of a living creature; another may feel pride as he pulls off its wings. As with so many other things, these emotions are learned by observing other people as they respond to various events in their lives. Adults play a very big role in helping children to develop appropriate emotions for the society in which they live, by giving words to their feelings, accepting the feelings of others, and helping children explore their feelings when they are confused.

Motivations are also learned. One child may study hard in school to please his parents; his best friend may do so to feel superiority over a sibling. A child may play with a blind classmate because she feels sorry for him; another may do so because she enjoys his company. Some children tell the truth because they fear punishment; others may be truthful because they believe it is a moral thing to do. Motivations for social behavior are based on stages of development and on beliefs that children learn through interactions with the socializing influences in their environment (Dreikurs, 1990). We can help teach the "usefulness" or appropriateness of certain attention-getting aggressive behaviors, for example, by ignoring them and giving positive attention to children when they exhibit prosocial and cooperative behaviors. Keep in mind as you do this, however, that different behaviors (such as giggling, avoiding eye contact, or staring directly at you) may have different meanings in different cultures. An excellent resource for this kind of information is *Developing Cross-Cultural Com-*

petence: A Guide for Working With Young Children and Their Families (Lynch & Hanson, 1992).

Adults and the Development of the Personality

Related to socialization, or learning how to be a member of society, is the development of personality, or learning how to be an individual. Social behaviorist George Herbert Mead was one of the first to offer an explanation for how children internalize society's rules and values. For Mead, the outcome of the socialization process that makes *self-regulation* possible at all is the development of the *self*. He described the self as having two parts: the *I* and the *me*.

Only humans, Mead asserted, can purposefully decide what they wish to represent of themselves to others (Mead, 1934). As "me," we accept the images of others into our personality ("You are a pretty girl"; "You are so clumsy"), but as "I," we regulate our own behavior and present to others the view we wish them to see ("I am an intelligent young woman"; "I can do this"). Mead believed a cognitive process takes place, consciously or unconsciously, of modeling ourselves after what we think *others* wish us to be as well as after what *we* wish to be. He called this thought *internalized conversation.* (You may know it as "self-talk.")

Children accomplish this cognitive process, wrote Mead, through two stages—*play* and *games.* In play, children mimic what they understand adult roles to be (such as Mom going to the office and Dad teaching school, or the postal worker delivering letters). Games are more complex, requiring a set of rules and other people to play opposite parts. ("Pretend you're the spaceship captain and I'm the engineer and I have this cool navigating tool that lets us change solar systems but you get hit by an enemy virus and I have to figure out how to pilot the ship.")

The role played by adults in the development of a child's personality (the self) is explained slightly differently by different theorists. Freud, for example, believed that normal personality development depended on a son's identification with his father, a daughter's with her mother. In other words, by imitating behaviors, expressions, even mannerisms of the same-gender parent, a child would gradually learn the appropriate way to "be" a man or a woman in the society, and he or she would incorporate many of those adopted personality characteristics into the self. Freud's explanation of personality development also included various parts of the self (the id, the ego, and the superego), and viewed the child as a passive recipient of the identification process (Freud, 1960, 1963).

Like Freud, Erik Erikson also used the term *identification* in his interpretation of personality development. However, Erikson believed, as did Frederick Elkin, that children draw their models from many different people during childhood and adolescence, not just their parents, and incorporate bits and pieces of each of them into their developing personalities. As children's cognitive and physical capabilities grow, they try new ways of interacting with other

Talking About Racism

Leonard Pitts, Jr.
PARENTING Magazine

An African American father struggles with how to explain racism to his children.

My youngest daughter, Onjel, already knows that she is black. It was well over a year ago that I first heard her referring to "that white girl" or "that black girl." So I know that she has a sense of herself as someone different, someone apart. That bothers me. I wish she could have had a few more years just to be who she is. A few more years of freedom. Is that so much to ask? After all, she's only four years old.

I already know what will happen next, how she'll discover what black means. One day, too soon, she'll have a falling out with one of her playmates. And in the heat of the argument, the other child will brand my daughter with an ancient epithet that will make my pretty baby feel low and unclean and despicable. The other child will call my daughter a nigger.

And I know what will happen after that, too—I know it by heart. I'll take my anger to the child's parents. They'll profess astonishment, apologize, and tell me they haven't a clue where their little cherub picked up such foul language. Maybe I'll believe them. Probably I won't.

Then I'll lead my daughter back home. We'll find a quiet place to talk. She'll look up at me, waiting for Daddy to make sense of her pain. And my brain will become as empty as a politician's promise.

What do I say to my children about racism? I ought to have it down by now. Certainly I've had enough practice. Markise, who is now 20, was in grade school when he had his first brush with racism: A bully called him a nigger when my son refused to give up his place in line.

Monique, 17, was in second grade when another girl got angry because Monique wouldn't lend her a crayon. The other child said her father had always told her niggers were stingy.

Marlon, 12, doesn't even remember his first experience with prejudice because, he says, "it's happened so many times."

Bryan, who is 9, had his first encounter last year: A playmate's father said that because Bryan is black, the two children can't play together anymore.

At some point, it comes to every black child: Not just the knowledge that he or she is black, but the terrible understanding of what being black in America means. And then the child goes to the parent, who tries to explain it all but ends up relying on clichés.

What do I tell my children about racism? I tell them that they are good people. I tell them that anyone who seeks to judge them without knowing them is a fool. I tell them that there are many such fools in the world, but that they must dare and dream and aspire anyway. I tell them that the ignorance of others is always an obstacle but never an excuse.

As I said, clichés. Your child is hurting and looking to you to make it stop. But you can't. All you can give her is homilies. Few situations in the world have such an ability to make you feel so utterly useless, so completely impotent.

In a way, I'm almost thankful to have been raised in the racial isolation of inner-city Los Angeles. Yes, I grew up without the advantages my children enjoy, but I also never experienced the pain they have. Where I came from, everybody was black. I thought white people lived only on television, where they wore suits and dresses all day long and smiled in perpetual contentment because they had tigers in their tanks, Dodges in their garages, and Ty-D-Bol men in their toilets.

If my parents ever talked to me about racism, I don't remember it. More likely, it went unremarked, like air. You don't talk about air. Air just is. As racism just is. That is what makes it so hard for me to explain it to my own kids. Racism just is.

Racism is stupid, atavistic, a sure sign of an underdeveloped mind and a malnourished spirit. But for all that, it is. And likely always will be. The challenge is in teaching a child not to let it consume her. Because if you dwell on it, if you look for logic along its twisting, dimly lit passageways, you'll just make yourself crazy.

And if you let it define you, you let it defeat you. So I tell my children that they must learn to distinguish between what other people think of them and what they know of themselves—and to always put their faith in the latter. I tell them to never play out a role scripted for them by somebody else.

Sometimes I think I harp too much on that point. Markise, a quiet, thoughtful young man, used to get so angry at his black friends when they were loud and rowdy. "They act just like white people expect them to!" he would seethe. Which is true enough. But, then, teenagers are supposed to be loud and rowdy. And white kids can act this way without fear that someone is going to project that behavior onto their entire race.

Is that fair? Of course not. But fair has got nothing to do with it. Never has.

There is something stubborn within all of us that refuses to yield to logic on this subject: Even though we should and do know better, we go right on hating and fearing that which is different from us simply because it is different.

"Can we all get along?" asked a shaky-voiced Rodney King at the height of the 1992 riots in Los Angeles. The question was too profound in its very simplicity for us to take seriously. It was too stark, too innocent, struck too close to the bone. It embarrassed us the way a child does when she asks the boss about his toupee at the dinner table. We resented King for not knowing better than to ask. So we made fun of his innocence and made a mockery of his question; better to hold it at a distance and avoid its ominous implications.

But was there anyone who, hearing King's question, didn't tremble a little in his own soul and fear that the truthful answer is no?

Sometimes I feel so bad for Markise. It seems like there's something more I could have told him that would make it easier for him when security guards follow him around department stores. Or when police officers handcuff him at the curb, claiming, as they always do, that he looks "just like" the suspect in a recent robbery. Instead, I gave my son clichés, and now he gives me back potent frustration and a stunned bewilderment that things have to be this way, that people can hate and distrust him on sight without the minor inconvenience of getting to know him.

I know just how he feels. One day, on the way to taking my family to dinner, I stopped at an automatic teller machine. I was driving a minivan full of kids—including Onjel in her car seat. In the parking lot, the guy in the car next to mine looked at me and didn't see a family man. He saw a nigger and a thief.

So he called out to his female friend, who was at the machine. As I got in line behind her, she abruptly aborted the transaction and fled to the car.

I felt shamed. I felt furious. I felt tired. My frustration was older than I am. But I told myself the same thing I always do: Live with it. Racism just is. So how am I supposed to know what to say to Markise? How am I supposed to make it easier for him to accept moments like that when I don't even know what to say to myself?

From time to time, I read articles in which whites attempt to justify their fear of black people by claiming they are just being prudent—statistics, after all, suggest that blacks are criminally inclined out of proportion to their numbers. I always wonder why these people who have such faith in the statistics don't cite the rest of the equation, the part that shows that the primary victims of black criminals are, overwhelmingly, themselves black. Similarly, whites are most likely to be victimized by other whites.

Why doesn't it play that way on the evening news and in the arena of public perception? The answer is obvious, of course. Racism just is.

What do I tell my children about racism? I try to give them the tools that will make it possible for them to deal with it. Such as laughter: I laugh when I can't

do anything else. Such as self-knowledge: When television hauls out the archival footage of the civil rights movement, I call the kids into the living room and make them watch. Afterwards, we talk. I take them to see *Glory* and Spike Lee's film *Malcolm X*. And we talk some more. When a local museum displays artifacts of black suffering in America, my family visits the exhibit. I explain to them the sacrifices their grandparents made for the freedoms we take for granted.

I try to give them some sense of perspective, too. Bigotry, I want them to understand, is a universal disease. I want my children to see it in context, to know that they are not hatred's only victims. I want them to remember the terrible feelings that racism engenders, to use that knowledge to understand why they must never make someone else a victim of that pain.

That's why I told them about Anne Frank, to broaden their perspective. And that's why, on a trip to Los Angeles, I took my two youngest sons to the Simon Wiesenthal Center Museum of Tolerance. My boys walked through the displays on hatred and civil rights, sat through the horrific films on genocide in the 20th century, toured the Holocaust exhibit. When we were finished, I asked them what they thought. They replied with some variant of "cool."

Sigh. That, of course, is the eternal conundrum with kids. You never know how much they're taking in and how much is just sliding between their ears without making an impact. You don't know if you've made a difference with your kids until they're not kids anymore. And then it's too late.

Still, I have reason to be hopeful. Markise is frustrated by the unfairness of life, but he's moving forward in the face of it. He's a college man studying for a career in law. I have high hopes for all of my kids.

I've spoken harshly of clichés, but that's frustration talking. It's just that I want to give my kids more than words—I want to make my children's pain go away. But I can't. All I can do is teach them how to use it.

"Let the pain motivate you to be better," I told Marlon just the other day. "You will need to be better than the best, my son." Why? Because growing up black is like growing up in a minefield: It takes courage, resolve, and no small amount of luck to make it safely to the other side. It calls on a person to be bigger, nobler, and grander of spirit than any of the low, mean forces that would bring him down.

But a parent can only tell children so much. Then they must go out there alone, away from your shelter, to live among those who would harm them, to make their own way. That's the hard part. That's when the frustration becomes acute. And you want to sweep your kids back in and tell them just one more thing—something that will keep them safe and well.

Instead, you let them go and you curse the impotence of homilies.

What do I tell my children about racism? Same as you. Not nearly enough.

Children need to see authentic images of themselves portrayed in classrooms and out-of-school environments in order to develop a healthy self-image.

people. They watch how respected adults play certain roles, such as aggressor, peacekeeper, or comic, and they imitate those people's actions. This is also how they learn their ethnic identity.

In his classic work *Childhood and Society,* Erikson presented the following scenario:

> I know a colored boy who, like our boys, listens every night to Red Rider. Then he sits up in bed, imagining that he is Red Rider. But the moment comes when he sees himself galloping after some masked offenders and suddently notices that in his fancy Red Rider is a colored man. He stops his fantasy. While a small child, this boy was extremely expressive, both in his pleasures and in his sorrows. Today he is calm and always smiles; his language is soft and blurred; nobody can hurry him or worry him—or please him. White people like him.
>
> —Erikson, 1985, p. 241

Erikson's point here, of course, is that seeing a conflict between the adventurer Red Rider and his own Black flesh, the child halted his fantasy—eventually permanently. At that time, and in that place, it was not realistic—or even safe—for a Black child to aspire to such expressivity. Today we know it is imperative that African American children see African American adults in positive and exciting roles if they are to believe they can have high aspirations as well.

Erikson also spent a significant amount of time with Sioux people and integrated what he learned into his psychoanalytic construct. He describes a rich tapestry of traditions, beliefs, and principles of child rearing, which one by one were ridiculed, overruled, and defeated by the White men and women who imprisoned the Sioux on reservations, ran their schools, and demanded that their children be raised like White children. "Thus, step for step, the Sioux has been denied the bases for a collective identity formation and with it that reservoir of collective integrity from which the individual must derive his stature as a social being" (Erikson, 1985, p. 154).

Social learning theorists such as Albert Bandura believe that young children learn attitudes and behaviors by observing models who are powerful and nurturant and who reward and punish the child. Children actively imitate or *model* what they see or hear other people do (Bandura, 1969). According to the identification concept, as explained by Erikson and Bandura, the child is not a passive observer but is actually trying to be like his or her parents and other adults who have authority and whom the child respects. While this may be true, it would be hard to deny that imitation can also be unintentional and unnoticed by the imitator.

Your role as an agent of socialization or as a model for a developing personality is clearly significant, whether the children with whom you work are mimicking behaviors on purpose or accidentally. In addition, Native American children and Chinese children, African American children and Hispanic children—in other words, all children—need to see authentic images of their own people to develop a feeling of pride in their heritage and have a healthy self-image and racial identity (Native Child, 1997). As adults working with children, we can all use theoretical frameworks to guide our practices and help us remember the value of modeling culturally relevant and morally sound behavior.

Adults as Teachers in Out-of-School Settings

Traditionally in most cultures, teaching children to become productive, independent adults has been the primary task of families and schools. However, recent observers of modern youth have challenged those institutions, declaring that many young people are not learning the basic skills they need to live and work productively (Blair, 1995; Glenn & Nelsen, 1989; Wallace, 1991). One explanation for this situation may be that in most families, especially those in which both parents work outside the home or only one parent is present, time is at a premium and family members spend less time together than they did in earlier generations. Whether family time is being stolen by long commutes to and from work, by the emotionally exhausting search for employment, by children's social and athletic activities, or by working a second job, most parents agree that they have less time available to spend teaching their children the skills of adulthood.

Schools also face a time problem. As our society has changed from a manufacturing-based economy to an information-based one, teachers have been asked to add more and more material to their curriculum. Often this is done at the expense of traditional, practical pursuits, such as woodworking, cooking, sewing, or money management.

Another reality of today's society is the poverty of many children, often because of divorce and the resulting single-parent, female-headed households (Bureau of the Census, 1986). Poverty may impede the development of children in many ways, related to the stresses that it generates within families. As a result of this stress, poor children have a higher incidence of disability and illness, diagnosed or undiagnosed, which may interfere with normal development (Kasheff, 1997). Unassisted poor children also tend to do badly in school and often drop out before high school graduation (Erickson, 1988). Children from low-income families may be unable to participate in costly enrichment activities such as scouting, sports, or music lessons, and they cannot always get to community-based programs intended to help them. Poverty means that high-quality, for-profit, school-age child-care programs may not be readily accessible to this group of children; it also means that the impact of such programs could be tremendous if sliding-scale fees were made available. Child and youth workers in publicly funded drop-in recreational or tutoring programs may want to consider this as they design their programs: If the programs are accessible, interesting, enjoyable, and affordable they will be more effective at attracting the children who need them most.

LIFE SKILLS AND JOB SKILLS

In this modern family, in which both parents probably work or in which only one parent is trying to meet all the financial, emotional, and physical needs of the household, opportunities to teach domestic skills are often scarce. These are the skills everyone needs in day-to-day life, such as balancing checkbooks, buying groceries, cooking, cleaning, doing laundry, and mending clothes. Nor are there long stretches of family time available in these busy homes to spend building go-carts or boats in the garage, hanging curtains, repairing bicycles or broken lamps, or even planting a garden.

Some skill training has been transferred to schools, where vocational courses teach résumé writing and how to find housing, but because of budgetary problems or the crowding of the curriculum by "high-tech" subjects, offerings of life skills classes may be limited. Also gone are lessons in manners and etiquette—the social graces. Some people may argue that these things have gone out of fashion, but the business pages of any major newspaper report the value of appropriate dress, polished manners, and grammatical speech in employment interviews.

"Someone has to teach the skills now needed by both men and women, future fathers and mothers, to keep family households running smoothly," warns Doris Wallace, a senior research psychologist at Bank Street College (1991, p. 160). For adequate socialization to take place, Wallace believes, someone must model the skills and attitudes desired and the children need to spend a certain amount of time with those models if they are to absorb the messages. Thus adults working with children in any capacity become the agents of socialization for the time spent with these children.

Katharine, a counselor in a summer camp, teaches bed making and other self-care skills to the children in her cabin. "I remember my mother teaching me how to make hospital corners," she explains, "but even if that skill hadn't been made unnecessary by fitted sheets, most of these children's parents are up at dawn and out the door before 7:00 a.m. I suspect they don't have time to make their own beds, let alone teach their children how." So Katharine does it instead. The issue here is not for a child to learn how to make a bed so that a quarter bounces on it, as a Marine sergeant may require, but to learn the value of orderliness and how to bring it into his or her life. Katharine also stages formal luncheons where she teaches children how to select a meal from a menu of different types of food as well as how to use cloth napkins, numerous forks, or chopsticks. There are other ways to teach such things, and some people might even argue that there is no longer a need for them, but Katharine reports that the children beam with pride when they demonstrate their knowledge of "fancy food stuff" to their families at the end of camp.

Diego Esparza grew up in a home with child-parents. His mother was only 14 when he was born; his father was barely 15. After struggling to keep their household together for several years, Diego's father abandoned his wife and three children when Diego was 7. Diego's mother began working long hours, leaving the two younger children with her mother for several days at a time. In the after-school homework center where Diego went each afternoon, the tutor had a point system for special projects that children could complete when their homework was finished. Diego liked baseball cards and he found he could earn them by sorting school papers, shelving books, and labeling file folders. By the time he left elementary school, Diego could type and file and knew how to use the lab computer. He returned to the homework center as a tutor while he was in middle school and when he went to high school, he worked in the school library. Diego's teachers see a college education in his future. Thanks to an adult who knew the importance of teaching life skills, Diego got a lot more than just baseball cards from attending that after-school program.

SOCIAL SKILLS AND STRATEGIES

Social skills include getting along with others—on the school bus, in the super-market, at a baseball game. Learning how to enter a group, how to make someone else feel comfortable when he or she is the "new"or "different" one, working out disagreements, solving problems, and cooperating on a task—all these are social skills that must be learned and are heavily influenced by the actions and attitudes of the models of socialization children have around them.

It is important that adult caregivers get along with the other adults in the program in ways that teach positive lessons. They don't have to agree all the time, but they need to work out their disagreements in friendly ways. You are "on" all the time when you are working with children. Negative attitudes among staff in a child and youth setting can be tremendously harmful and should be handled as soon as possible. Adults encourage growth and independence in children when they teach the skills necessary for working with others.

Opportunities for children to learn the things they need to live effectively in society do not happen naturally in the course of a normal child-care day, so caregivers need to use imagination to create situations in which their charges can practice these skills. I saw one excellent example of this at an after-school center. A parent was working as a substitute caregiver during the summer, and she had noticed that the children were getting bored. It was hot, and the weeks stretched in front of them. Searching for something interesting to do, Julie brought in a book that her own children had enjoyed, *From the Mixed-Up Files of Mrs. Basil E. Frankweiler* (Konigsburg, 1967), and began reading it to a small group of youngsters in the shade of a tree. The main characters in the story secretly leave home, travel by bus to the Metropolitan Museum of Art, take up temporary residence in the museum, then become involved in solving a mystery.

As Julie talked to the children about the story, she realized that most of them had never ridden on a bus, nor did they know how to read a transit schedule or a map. The next day she brought in a map of their local community and they pored over it together, searching for familiar landmarks. Julie helped each child to find his or her home on a map, which they put on the wall with colorful pins marking all their locations. A few days later, continuing with her daily reading of the book (to an increasing number of children), she brought in a map of the nearest medium-size city and helped the children plot a route from each of their homes to places they liked to visit, such as the hockey stadium, the mall, and the park. Finally, she obtained a bus schedule for each child, and together they planned routes to the city art museum, using the map and the schedules. As a culmination of the summer project, they traveled together to the museum and ate lunch together in a nearby park.

As Julie talked with me about her experience, she explained that she had been at the same time appalled at the children's lack of knowledge about how to get around and behave in public and amazed at how much they had learned in one trip. As a young mother, she had stayed at home until her youngest child entered elementary school and had traveled widely with her brood. At first she expected that all children would know, as hers did, that you do not run up and down the street while you are waiting for the light to change, or trade seats constantly on public transportation. However, she discovered that for many of these children, this was their first outing other than family vacations. She had then accepted more willingly the role she played as a "parent," taught them what they needed to know, and rejoiced as they modified their behavior accordingly. In this circumstance, the caregiver learned as much from the interaction as did the children.

Many out-of-school settings offer opportunities for socialization. Coaches of athletic teams often travel to other cities for games; they can help children learn reasonable ways of behaving in motels, restaurants, rest stops, buses, airports, and airplanes. Scout leaders and youth-group leaders take their charges to ski slopes, camps, fairgrounds, or other public places; in each case, they become agents of socialization. Sometimes child and youth workers find themselves feeling frustrated and even angry, believing that parents have been remiss by failing to teach their children to behave "properly." It is more useful, however, to consider the role of socializing agent as simply being shared by the parents with others, and one of those "others" is you. Consider yourself part of the socializing team and take your role seriously.

PROBLEM SOLVING AND COMPETENCE

Closely related to a knowledge of social skills is knowing how to solve problems. Knowing what to do in a social situation and what to do to solve a problem both contribute to a child's feeling of *competence,* which in turn builds *self-esteem* (Coopersmith, 1967). Adults in the child's life have many opportunities to model problem solving; they can also create situations in which children have opportunities to practice solving problems on their own.

Preschool teachers frequently ask children to set the table for a snack; through repetitive trips for cups, crackers, napkins, and juice, the youngsters learn about one-to-one correspondence and other elements of mathematics. Similarly, school-age children can be asked to develop a list of materials they need for a construction project or be given the task of scheduling the computer so that everyone has an equal opportunity to use it. Many children do not have the confidence in their own capabilities that comes from succeeding at these kinds of day-to-day tasks:

> Because children are motivated to learn and perform from birth, they can come to view themselves as capable at a very young age. Scott, for example, at eighteen months would constantly pester his mother to let him help. "Me do it," he would declare enthusiastically as he followed her around the house. He wanted to push the vacuum, dust the furniture, crack the eggs, and help with all the cooking.
>
> "No, honey," his mother would answer. "You are too little to help me. Go play with your toys or watch TV now."
>
> In this way, Mom had started undermining Scott's sense of capability very early, and Scott learned his lessons well. When he was ten years old, Mom would say, "Come into the kitchen and set the table." Scott would either ignore her or reply, "I'm busy playing with my games, Mom." Mom didn't realize he was only doing what he had been trained to do.
>
> —Glenn & Nelsen, 1989, p. 72

Simply being asked to *do* a task is not enough. Children may need help to solve these problems, and it helps to see adults solving their own problems, too. Chances are that lots of learning—on both sides—will occur in your time together.

"No one brought the soccer net? Perhaps we could set up the traffic cones to designate the goal area." "Whoops, we're out of wheat paste for the papier-mâché? Let's see if we have some flour. I remember my teacher making paste from flour and water. Perhaps we can figure out how to do that, too." "The printer isn't working? Well, what are some of the things that can go wrong? Let's check the cables." "Annie can't reach the easel from her wheelchair. How can we set it up so she can paint, too?"

How many times in a day do you go through the problem-solving process? Do it out loud, let the children know what you are doing, and accept their suggestions as you brainstorm possible solutions. This is how they learn to do the same thing, and in the long run, whether your activity is playing soccer, making a Kwanzaa craft, adapting a project for a child with special needs, or producing a newsletter, it will run more smoothly as the children begin to feel more capable, more in charge of their own actions, more connected. The less children depend on adults to solve problems or give direction to their activities, the more independence and motivation they will begin to exhibit.

LITERACY AND A LOVE OF LEARNING

From age 5 to 8, children learn to study, to reason, to use the information coming in on all sides to develop concepts and ideas about the world. In spite of research that supports a different approach, most North American, European, and Asian schools are still curriculum-centered rather than student-centered. Such schools may leave children with a sense of failure at a very early age, to the point that they may become discouraged easily (Erickson, 1988). Discouraged or not, most children will put in their time until they finish their state-mandated education and then they are turned loose on the society, unprepared to work and uninterested in learning (McGrath & Spear, 1991). The attitudes and motivations learned in schools that place an emphasis on achievement over development do not prepare children for lifelong learning, an absolute necessity in this technologically based society (Secretary's Commission on Achieving Necessary Skills, 1991). Even schools that have kept children's developmental needs at the center of their planning are often unable, due to class size or pressure for high test scores, to devote much time to nurturing a love of learning.

Recreational and care programs for school-age children, however, can offer opportunities for them to try new things, to stretch their wings and choose their own activities. Although attitudes toward literacy and learning begin early in life, the process is ongoing and can be sparked by interesting experiences and enthusiastic adults. Learning to read and write, for example, is a developmental activity, and a child can progress from where he or she is to the next stage at any age, even if the school curriculum has passed beyond the skills the child needs to learn.

Child and youth workers who read interesting books, to themselves or to collected groups of children, and who share their own love of learning by seeking answers in libraries or on-line databases, provide models and motivations for children. These examples can have a tremendously positive influence on the children's future lives. Informal educational programs such as merit badge programs in scouting, project work in 4-H club, or mock business management

Children with a wide range of physical skills can play together in out-of-school settings. Their growing bodies need frequent workouts.

in Junior Achievement or Future Farmers of America offer excellent models; later chapters suggest specific ways school-age children can be helped to overcome their fears and discouragement and to experience the enjoyment of learning. School-age programs are also ideal environments in which young people can learn about individual and cultural differences, as they develop solutions to problems within their microsociety. Their experiences working and playing together can serve as rehearsals for the very real problems our multicultural world faces in the next few decades.

LIFELONG HEALTH AND FITNESS HABITS

The topic of health-related fitness in children has received great attention in recent years. Western society has put enormous emphasis on physical appearance; this focus, combined with many youngsters' belief that they must follow in the footsteps of talk-show guests and fashion models and hurry into adulthood, seems to have made eating disorders such as *anorexia* and *bulimia* permanent fixtures of the middle years (Elkind, 1981, 1984).

Additionally, researchers studying elementary school children have discovered that many children have low aerobic endurance and high levels of body fat. Researchers at the National Center for Health Statistics studied data on children age 6 to 17 collected by the National Health and Nutrition Examination Survey between 1988 and 1994; they compared the information with earlier surveys and concluded that approximately 1 in 5 children in the United States in that age range is overweight. In the years since the first of these surveys was conducted, the number of overweight children in this country has more than doubled (Mayo Foundation for Medical Education and Research, 1997). Unfit and overweight children are more liable to show early signs of coronary heart disease, high cholesterol levels, and high blood pressure (Rosenbaum & Leibel, 1989) as well as the social and psychological stresses that come from appearing "different" from their peers. The greatest risk, however, according to the Mayo Foundation, is that many obese children become obese adults; then they are at a greater risk, at a younger age, for developing heart disease, diabetes, high blood pressure, high cholesterol, gallbladder disease, arthritis, and certain cancers.

Two causes are usually suggested for this trend toward childhood obesity: Many children watch too much television, and they do too little of anything else. A third explanation, that eating disorders are related to low self-esteem, is also significant.

According to recent figures, most children between the ages of 2 and 12 watch approximately 28 hours of television per week, and that's not including time spent playing video and computer games (American Medical Association, 1996). Additionally, they spend a very small portion of each day participating in high-intensity physical activity. The American College of Sports Medicine reports that, due to financial constraints, only about one-third of all elementary schools now offer a physical education program. Even when these programs exist, many students participate in as little as one hour of planned physical activity a week (Endres & Rockwell, 1994). In addition, sports played during physical education periods are typically those that promote agility and specialized skills, such as baseball, basketball, or volleyball. More useful to children's overall fitness would be activities that include proper warm-up and cool-down exercises and develop *cardiovascular fitness.* Such activities are cycling, swimming, running, or playing tennis. The U.S. Surgeon General's Report on Physical Activity and Health recommends 30 minutes of moderate to vigorous physical activity per day for normal healthy children (U.S. Surgeon General, 1996).

So how do adults fit into this picture? Once again, the adults in a child's life model behaviors, attitudes, and values that are internalized and eventually become part of the child's own personality. Parents who commute long hours and work all day may have difficulty modeling physical fitness to their children. Even if physical activity is a regular part of their lives, it may take place away from home, out of the child's view (an aerobics class on the way home from work, for example, or a racquetball game at noon).

Additionally, parents who work some distance from home may be less in control of what their children eat than those who have the time to cook nourishing breakfasts and be waiting with healthy snacks after school. Their children's eating habits, not to mention television and movie-viewing patterns, are usually influenced by their friends, teachers, coaches, and after-school program staff.

The adults with whom children spend their daytime hours, therefore, need to model good eating patterns and healthy levels of physical activity. It is also helpful if they regularly participate directly with youngsters in physically challenging games and activities.

Rich Scofield points out that children "play" in response to their natural developmental needs. For example, children 7 years old and older want to do "real work with the real tools" of the adult world, such as woodworking tools, the stove and vacuum cleaner, and paintbrushes. They also "strive to become competent at a particular skill." This could include throwing a football, playing hopscotch, jumping rope, in-line skating, and learning tricks with a yo-yo as well as bending wire, cutting cloth, hanging a picture. These activities become "not only skills to learn but also social statements as they strive for peer acceptance" (Scofield, 1987, p. 2). Adults working with school-age children can—and should—capitalize on children's natural physical development. It is very important to provide materials, equipment, and opportunities for different kinds of physical activities—not just outdoor sports, but also dancing, dramatic performances, building projects, and furniture arrangement. It is also important to provide activities in which children with a wide range of physical capabilities can be successful. Simple cooking projects and nutrition education can also be a part of the school-age program. Later chapters discuss how to plan and schedule some of these activities.

SELF-ESTEEM

The importance of positive self-esteem has received more than its share of attention. Depending upon what you read, having it can lead to happiness, success, and possibly a lucrative contract with your favorite football team. Lack of self-esteem, we are warned, is likely to result in alcoholism or drug abuse, school failure, teenage pregnancy, and unemployment. Nothing is quite that simple, and neither is the human quest for significance, purpose, or value (Curry, 1990). However, knowing oneself is an essential first step in being a valuable and competent member of society.

Contrary to the popular view that self-esteem can be "fed" to a child with regular doses of praise and compliments, a child's feeling of self-worth actually develops from repeated self-evaluation. A well-accepted definition of self-esteem is "a personal judgment of worthiness that is expressed in the attitudes the individual holds toward himself" (Coopersmith, 1967, p. 1). Researchers have come to believe that self-respect is based on two main convictions: "I am lovable," and "I am worthwhile" (Briggs, 1970, p. 3). Different cultures view this concept in different ways, and the European/North American version has a tendency to slip into self-preoccupation and narcissism, especially when it is perceived as resulting from an unending flow of happy-grams, smiley-face stickers, "participant" ribbons, and other similarly superficial rewards (Curry, 1990; Katz, 1993).

In measuring one's self-worth, a child looks at several different parts of himself, commonly referred to as the *dimensions* of self-esteem. Dr. Stanley Coopersmith, one of the earliest students of the conditions that enhance self-esteem emphasizes these elements:

- *Virtue*—adherence to moral and ethical standards
- *Significance*—a feeling of connection to other people whom the child considers significant
- *Purpose*—a feeling of power—the capability to control one's life and influence others
- *Competence*—a feeling of success, particularly in things the child regards as important or valuable

—Coopersmith, 1967, p. 38

I find it interesting to compare these four dimensions of self-esteem with the description by a teacher in New Delhi, India, of traditional rituals for welcoming children into the society. At the first, fourth, and sixth months, she describes, children were prayed over, bathed, dressed in beautiful clothes, and celebrated. God's blessings were invoked for the child's health, well-being, and longevity, and the child was gradually made aware of his relationship to his environment, including his family, members of the community, and the sun and the moon. Poetry relating to the 10 stages of childhood include descriptions of the child being gently encouraged to creep and crawl, clap to songs, kiss his parents, and walk. In the seventh month, the mother asked the moon to be a playmate to the child. *Pillai Tamizh,* this poetic tradition, is described by the teacher as "domestic and intimate and [focusing] on close relationships, rather than on individual development." Yet the resulting effect is "an appreciation for how integrated each of us is within ourselves" (Anandalakshmy, 1997, p. 10). Self-esteem here is not a result of the idolization of the "I" but rather the integration of the "we."

Similarly, traditional beliefs of Native Americans that influence the education of children emphasize the unity of the universe; giving value to plants, animals, and people; holding the land in sacred trust; waiting for a speaker to finish and thinking deeply about what was said before formulating a response—these traditions help develop young people who hold a solid sense of significance, purpose, and value through their bond with their culture and the entire world.

Dr. Michelle Borba, a psychologist specializing in esteem issues, considers the role of adults in the development of a child's self-esteem to be the sources of "building blocks," or life experiences that allow a child gradually to acquire the dimensional feelings listed above (Borba, 1988, 1989). It might seem that the goal would be to have a high level of each dimension, but researcher Coopersmith discovered that many individuals with high self-esteem arrived at that feeling through notable success in only one or two areas. However, if the areas in which success is achieved are not perceived by the child to be *important*—for example, being the lead in the school play, or knowing how to play marbles better than anyone else in the neighborhood—the success will go unrecognized by the child.

The most important contributors to the development of competence seem to be opportunities to *do* things, and opportunities to *evaluate* the results of those doings. We do no good to offer empty praise to children; they are smart enough to know it is valueless. In fact, self-esteem-building exercises can backfire, resulting in a kind of narcissism, if they do not teach children to acknowledge and deal with their shortcomings as well as their strengths (Damon, 1991; Katz, 1993).

Borba identified 10 ways child and youth workers can provide experiential building blocks for children whose self-esteem is under construction:

1. *Help children form a clear picture of themselves.* This can be done by giving honest feedback and encouraging children to voice their own strengths and weaknesses.

2. *Help children see success.* Plan activities that can be accomplished by children with differing skills.

3. *Be a model of positive self-esteem.* Let children see your confidence in your ability to find solutions to problems.

4. *Instill a positive attitude and atmosphere.* Be a change agent for optimism.

5. *Teach children to evaluate themselves.* After an activity or interaction is over, ask questions such as Would you do that the same way next time? Are you happy with the results? What do you think you need to learn to succeed the next time you try it?

6. *Teach children to praise others.* An easy way to do this is to do it yourself.

7. *Teach children to praise themselves.* Encourage them to enjoy their successes.

8. *Build up children's positive attributes in the eyes of others.* But never compare one child to another.

9. *Help children develop awareness of their capabilities and strengths.* A variety of opportunities for doing real-world activities is helpful here.

10. *Be specific in your feedback to children.* "I really appreciated the fact that you wrapped up the soggy bedding from the hamster cage before putting it in the trash."

—Adapted from Borba, 1988

Also, pay attention to the wisdom of other cultures and study the way they have traditionally integrated each generation of children into their society. While you're at it, watch for inappropriate images of ethnic and cultural groups (as well as of people with differing mental and physical abilities) within your program. Children who frequently see and hear stereotyped images of someone they relate closely with may be discouraged from developing pride in their heritage and racial or social identity. Obviously this would discourage the development of a positive self-esteem. Engage in dialogue with groups of children whenever you encounter negative images; rewrite them together, and construct your own version of Borba's building blocks to self-esteem.

MORAL REASONING AND VALUES CLARIFICATION

"SHAME" cried out the cover of *Newsweek* magazine in two-inch-high letters on February 6, 1995. Subtitled *"How do we bring back a sense of right and wrong?"* the collection of articles inside described a society in which convicted murderers show no remorse, unmarried welfare recipients continue to bear children at public expense, and fathers openly avoid paying support for their families. Newspaper and magazine articles frequently report on the decline of decency in daytime television, prime-time sitcoms, popular music, and videos. Most editions of the evening news provide plenty of material for those reports.

The burden of teaching right and wrong is appropriately placed with the family, but once again we need to acknowledge that adults who work with school-age children become an extension of those families, partners with the parents in the socialization process. Positive role models can have a strong influence on children's ethical decision making, and an environment in which children can talk about the confusing sets of values they see around them can add greatly to their moral development. It is also important to understand the way children of different ages perceive ethical dilemmas and how they arrive at their decisions.

Lawrence Kohlberg has proposed a widely accepted theory of children's moral development. He outlined three levels of moral thinking, which are related to children's understanding of rules, justice, and social order. Other theorists who have developed explanations for the way children develop their moral codes include Piaget (1932/1965), Gilligan (1982), and Damon (1990). Their theories are discussed in detail in Chapter 4. Chapter 7 suggests ways you can provide school-age children with opportunities to develop moral values and self-control.

SUMMARY
. . . .

Socialization, which can be intentional or unintentional, is the process by which children learn the ways of their society so they can function in it. Agents of socialization include parents, caregivers, teachers, peers, and the media. Outcomes of socialization include behaviors, attitudes, emotions, and motivations as well as language, culture, ethnicity, and gender. When both parents work, the workers in the school-age program become especially influential in the socialization process. Child-care professionals need to understand the socialization process and provide models, activities, and opportunities for reflective communication to the children with whom they work.

REVIEW QUESTIONS
. . . .

1. How do "others" function in the socialization process?

2. Give one example of intentional socialization and one of unintentional socialization.

3. List three agents of socialization.

4. Name four influences on children's eating and physical activity patterns.

CHALLENGE EXERCISES

1. Define socialization and share examples from your life.

2. Select a person you know to be a model for socialization. Describe the person, then try to imagine how a child might behave if he or she identified with that person.

3. Observe a group of strangers riding together in an elevator. Describe how they act. Do they talk with one another? Which way do they face? How do you suppose they all learned how to behave in this situation?

4. Imagine that you are about to embark on a road trip with 20 children, age 7 to 10. What preparation would you give the children for the trip? What kind of ground rules would you set?

TERMS TO LEARN

agents of socialization
anorexia
attitudes
behaviors
bulimia
cardiovascular fitness
competence
emotions
games
intentional socialization
internalize
internalized conversation
model
motivations
others
play
self
self-esteem
self-regulation
socialization
unintentional socialization

REFERENCES

American Medical Association. (1996). *Physician guide to media violence.* Chicago.

Anandalakshmy, S. (1997, March 1). *Thinking with the heart and feeling with the brain.* Paper presented at the Fifth National Lecture on Child Development, Lady Irwin College, New Delhi.

Bandura, A. (1969). *Principles of behavior modification.* New York: Holt, Rinehart & Winston.

Barbour, C. B. N. (1997). *Families, schools, and communities.* Columbus, OH: Merrill.

Blair, M. (1995, August 11). Class on manners alerts kids to changing times. *The Dispatch,* p. D4.

Borba, M. (1988). *Building blocks for self-esteem.* Unpublished lecture handout.

Borba, M. (1989). *Esteem Builders.* Torrance, CA: Jolmar Press.

Briggs, D. C. (1970). *Your child's self-esteem.* Garden City, NY: Doubleday.

Bureau of the Census. (1986). *Poverty in the United States, 1986* (Series P-70, No. 9). Washington, DC: U.S. Department of Commerce.

Coopersmith, S. (1967). *The antecedents of self-esteem.* San Francisco: W. H. Freeman.

Curry, N. J. C. (1990). *Beyond self-esteem: Developing a genuine sense of human value.* Washington, DC: National Association for the Education of Young Children.

Damon, W. (1990). *The moral child.* New York: Free Press.

Damon, W. (1991, Fall). Putting substance into self-esteem: A focus on academic and moral values. *Educational Horizons.*

Derman-Sparks, L. (1989). *Anti-bias curriculum: Tools for empowering young children.* Washington, DC: National Association for the Education of Young Children.

Dreikurs, R. S. V. (1990). *Children: The challenge.* New York: Plume Books.

Elkin, F. (1989). *The child & society: The process of socialization* (5th ed.). New York: Random House.

Elkind, D. (1981). *The hurried child: Growing up too fast too soon.* Reading, MA: Addison-Wesley.

Endres, J. B., & Rockwell, R. E. (1994). *Exercise and physical fitness: Food, nutrition, and the young child* (4th ed.). New York: Merrill.

Erickson, J. D. (1988). Real American children: The challenge for after-school programs. *Child & Youth Care Quarterly, 17*(2), 86–101.

Erikson, E. H. (1985). *Childhood and society* (3rd ed.). New York: Norton.

Freud, S. (1960). *The ego and the id* (J. Riviere, Trans.). New York: Norton. (Original work published 1923)

Freud, S. (1963). *General psychological theory.* New York: Collier.

Gilligan, C. (1982). *In a different voice: Psychological theory and women's development.* Cambridge, MA: Harvard University Press.

Glenn, H. S., & Nelsen, J. E. D. (1989). *Raising self-reliant children in a self-indulgent world.* Rocklin, CA: Prima Publishing & Communications.

Kasheff, Z. (1997). What's ailing our kids: Five health issues. *Essence, 28*(1), 184.

Katz, L. (1993, Summer). All about me. *American Educator,* 18–22.

Konigsburg, E. L. (1967). *From the mixed-up files of Mrs. Basil E. Frankweiler.* New York: Dell.

Lynch, E. W., & Hanson, M. J. (1992). *Developing cross-cultural competence: A guide for working with young children and their families.* Baltimore: Paul H. Brookes.

Marion, M. (1987). Guidance of young children (2nd ed.). Columbus, OH: Merrill.

Mayo Foundation for Medical Education and Research. (1997, May 5). *Childhood obesity: Healthier lifestyles needed to treat this growing problem. Health Oasis* (Online newsletter). Available http://208.240.'53.40/mayo/9705/htm/overweightm

McGrath, D., & Spear, B. (1991). *The academic crisis of the community college.* New York: SUNY Press.

Mead, G. H. (1934). *Mind, self and society.* Chicago: University of Chicago Press.

Native Child. (1997). *Stereotypes.* Available www.nativechild.com/stereotype.html

Ollhoff, L. J. (1994). *Giving children their childhood back— Discussion guide.* Rosemount: Minnesota Department of Education.

Piaget, J. (1965). The moral judgment of the child (M. Gabain, Trans.). New York: Free Press. (Original work published 1932)

Rosenbaum, M., & Leibel, R. L. (1989). Obesity in childhood. *Pediatrics in Review, 11*(2), 43–57.

Scofield, R. (1987). Why school-agers act as they do. *School-Age Notes* (Newsletter). Nashville, TN.

Secretary's Commission on Achieving Necessary Skills. (1991). *What work requires of schools; A SCANS report for America 2000.* Washington, DC: U.S. Department of Labor.

U.S. Surgeon General. (1996, July). *Report on physical activity & health.* Atlanta, GA: Centers for Disease Control and Prevention.

Wallace, D. S. (1991, September). Are we preparing our kids for the real world? *Good Housekeeping, 157,* 160.

CHAPTER SIX

Issues Facing Today's Children

One does not need to be a parent or caregiver to know that the nature of childhood has become an issue of major proportions all over the world. The *social revolution* that has changed gender roles and confused individual and family responsibilities in many nations has also resulted in the questioning of traditional child-rearing patterns, leaving many parents and their children feeling confused and unsupported in their respective roles. One of those roles, of course, relates to the care and nurturing of the children themselves, especially when both parents work and have responsibilities away from home, or when one parent alone cares for the children of the family.

Entrepreneurs, in both the private and the public sector, have responded fairly well to the challenge of providing increasing numbers of out-of-school programs that serve the needs of working parents. However, it's still a common misconception in many quarters that school-age child care is simply a custodial service that allows mothers to take tennis lessons or have a part-time job outside the home.[1] More accurately, before- and after-school programs have become environments in which much of the nurturing, socialization, and education of children is now taking place, and out-of-school program staff serve an important role as partners with parents in the rearing of their children.

Developmental Issues and Generational Issues

As the demand for child-care services shifts from the care of very young children to that of school-age youngsters, understanding some of the specialized needs of the children in that age range becomes important (Zigler & Lang,

[1]Even as I was writing this chapter, I received a call for help from a small southwestern community where, upon applying to the school board for the use of a classroom, a group of after-school program organizers (nonprofit) were told that the mothers of these kids should be home at 3 p.m. to watch their own kids, that it is not the role of the school to provide care, and so on.

1991). These "specialized" needs include ***developmental needs*** such as the ones discussed in Chapter 5, which require child-care professionals to understand different ways children interact, how they use their bodies and minds, and how they view logical or moral dilemmas at different ages. In addition, each decade brings different ***generational needs,*** needs that change according to the changing social circumstances, budgetary priorities, and media coverage in the nation as well as the cultural and ethnic demographics at any given time and place.

For example, public school teachers reported the following kinds of activities as top disciplinary problems in the schools of the 1940s: talking out of turn, running in the halls, chewing gum, making noise, not putting paper in the wastebasket. Today, the schools are faced with such offenses as assault, robbery, rape, drug abuse, alcohol abuse, teenage pregnancy, vandalism, and even murder (Teen Help, 1996). Many school-age children must learn strategies to deal with difficult decisions and frightening situations in their daily lives.

CONCERNS OF PARENTS

A 1991 survey of Armenian American teenagers reported that parents and teachers considered the most serious problems facing their youths to be "excessive concern with material possessions (specifically name-brand clothing, cars, stereos, CD players, etc.); susceptibility to media influence; susceptibility to peer pressure; fear of responsibility; and unwillingness to assume responsibility for their own actions."(Yeghiayan, 1991, p. 155)

Not only newly assimilated families worry about these things. In 1988, *Better Homes and Gardens* magazine asked their readers: "Do you think the American family is in trouble?" Of more than 100,000 people who responded, 77% said "Yes." Issues worrying those readers included drug and alcohol abuse, the absence of a religious/spiritual foundation, inattentive parents, divorce, moral decay, materialism, and both parents working (Greer, 1988).

In an article in *Essence* magazine, Ziba Kashef (1997) listed health as one of the most critical issues for African American children; she links the most common health problems (obesity, high asthma rates, accidents, and substance abuse) to behaviors that can be changed through modeling and education. But some realities cannot be changed simply by educating the children. *Jet* magazine reported in 1996 that extreme poverty continues to be an urgent problem for Black children. The article, citing a report from the Columbia University Center for Children in Poverty, stated that 30% of young Black children live in families that have incomes below 50% of the federal poverty threshold (National Center for Children in Poverty, 1996). Additionally, far too many children of all races live with the fear of violence in their homes, their communities, and their schools. Children who grow up in neighborhoods where violence is common find it difficult to concentrate and to learn; they may also show signs of depression and learned helplessness because they see no way of escaping their personal nightmares (Womble, 1993). Personal safety rates high on almost any survey of family concerns.

A 1995 application for federal funding written by a consortium of parents, teachers, school administrators, and community agency staff in an apparently affluent California community reported that the parents' major concerns for their children, evidenced from interviews and questionnaires, were the availability of affordable "decent" housing, personal safety in their neighborhoods, help with the rising cost of health care, children's school failure, affordable out-of-school care and recreation, and the negative effects of parent stress (Yinger & Ceely, 1995). Parents, it seems, could see past the city planners' vision of the community to the reality faced each day by their families.

CONCERNS OF CHILDREN

In contrast, children's statements about what concerns and frightens them are not necessarily related to the realities their parents recognize—and they are not very different today from what they have been in the past. In Laura Ingalls Wilder's fictionalized biography *On the Banks of Plum Creek*, Laura faces roaming long-horned cattle who were eating the family's stored hay; she nearly drowns in a creek that overflows its banks; and she nearly freezes carrying food to the barn full of animals during a snowstorm. Yet it is the invasion of grasshoppers that frightens her most because they had the power to cause her family to lose their home (Wilder, 1937/1965). Wilder was living on the prairie in the mid-1800s. In 1942, Anne Frank, in the famous journal written while she was being hidden from Nazi soldiers, was more troubled about families being torn apart than about the possibility of death, and she wrote with true pathos about the difficulty of getting along with her relatives, forced to live in close quarters day in and day out, even when they had become her most valuable possessions (Frank, 1939/1993).

My mother, growing up in the north of England in the 1920s, was afraid of "dark places, especially down cellar, where the rats were." There was no electricity in her childhood home, so there were lots of "dark places." Her other fears were related: a "bad man who would take us away if we were naughty," and "running out of coal." In her memory book about that time, she recalls also being frightened of losing her school exercise books, being late for church, and getting her one good pair of shoes wet.

In 1968, a group of researchers asked school-age children to rank their fears, using a list of 80 items. Three of the top 10 were getting poor grades, being sent to the principal, and having their parents argue. In 1985 the same list was presented to children over 7. Only two new fears had joined the top 10: a burglar breaking into the house, and falling from a high place. In both lists, however, Schachter and McCauley, 1988, point out that more than a third of the children were afraid of "bombing attacks—being invaded." Eighty percent of the children in a 1983 study listed being killed or a family member dying, and 70% worried about the house burning down, being followed by strange people, and being kidnaped (Ollendick, 1985). In 1993, 50,000 children in grades 3 to 12 took part in the Scholastic Magazine Poll of American Youth. Sixty-one percent of the respondents rated crime and violence as the national issue that most concerned them. Other top concerns were the environment (52%) and education (45%) ("Scholastic Magazine Poll," 1996).

Maslow's Hierarchy of Needs

Children's fears don't always reflect issues facing their parents or the wider society. Some predictable things are feared by all children at certain ages; these include losing their security, whether it is home, family, or a pet. One theory of human motivation proposes that each of us has a *hierarchy of needs,* the foundation of which consists of basic survival needs (food, clothing, shelter, air) (Maslow, 1970). Resting on those needs are the basic safety needs, which would include a feeling of security about home and family. This hierarchy, developed by Abraham Maslow in 1948, is depicted in Figure 6-1.

Until the first set of needs is satisfied (food, clothing, shelter, etc.), the second set has little meaning. If you're hungry, for example, it's difficult to think about much else. Once the survival needs are met, the need to secure that survival—hold on to your food—becomes the most important consideration in the life of the child until that need is satisfied, also. Only when children are warm, fed, and housed, with some security of maintaining that condition, can they begin to move up the pyramid and start to think about social needs (having friends, being loved and appreciated) and esteem needs (trying to earn respect,

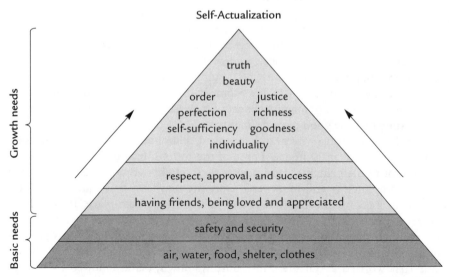

FIGURE 6-1   Maslow's Hierarchy of Needs (*Source:* Adapted from Maslow, 1970, p. 74)

approval, and success). For children to be able to form friendships and develop a culturally sensitive morality—two of the developmental tasks of this period (Havighurst, 1953)—they need to be relatively free from worrying about their physical safety and comfort. That, of course, is one of the roles played by out-of-school care.

Common Fears of Childhood

As part of a school assignment, several child-development college students asked youngsters in child-care centers what they worried about at night. Answers ranged from "I'm scared I won't pass my spelling test on Friday" and "Who will take care of Fluffy (a rabbit in the third-grade classroom) during summer vacation?" to "My daddy might lose his job and we might have to move to Arizona" or "What happens if our house catches on fire during the night?"

Common childhood fears do not seem to differ much from generation to generation or culture to culture, but they may differ considerably by age and by gender (Dong, Yang, & Ollendick, 1994; Ollendick, Yule, & Ollier, 1991). In other words, as children develop and grow, they experience changes in what frightens them and how they react. Very young infants do not usually express fear when their parents or caregivers leave the room; 8- or 9-month-old children, on the other hand, develop quite normal *separation anxiety* as they develop an understanding of their own separateness and vulnerability to abandonment. Before learning how to crawl, children do not seem to show a fear of heights, but after they are about 6 or 7 months old, they refuse to crawl across a "visual cliff," an illusion made by suspending a sturdy piece of plastic across a floor with checkerboard coverings (Gibson & Walk, 1960). (When half the plastic is covered with the same checkerboard fabric, the floor appears to drop off halfway across.) Both these examples remind us that children become frightened of things only after they begin to understand the possibilities for hurt or sadness, and that their understanding changes as they develop cognitively.

Two-year-olds may be frightened of being flushed down the toilet or sucked down the drain of a tub or being eaten by monsters living in their closets or under their beds. By the age of 5 or 6, children begin to understand and fear real-life dangers, such as fire, burglaries, or national disasters. Twelve-year-olds worry about their hair, their clothes, their skin, but they also fear economic problems such as layoffs for their parents, homelessness, and hunger, and by this time they are very much more aware of the potential for chaos and inequity in the world.

Some fears occur as part of a child's normal development. Children will outgrow most common childhood fears of animals, loud noises, doctors, or the dark. Fears they develop from watching television can be explained and the children reassured. Other fears reflect reality in an uncertain world: What if Daddy or Mommy doesn't come home? However, certain unreasonable fears, such as the fear of getting dirty or being left forever at the child-care center, may, if they persist, be the result of anxiety disorders or other emotional problems. Children troubled by these worries should be referred to a family therapist. It is important to recognize that sometimes even normal fears or concerns may grow beyond your ability to help and that encouraging families to speak to professionals can be the first step toward resolving these problems.

Events and fears that concern children may not be the same as those that keep adults awake at night, but they are often quite intense, troublesome, and definitely *real;* they should never be ignored. As children mature, fears about thunder, dogs, doctors, or the dark begin to give way around age 8 or 9 to *social anxiety* or worries about measuring up to their peers (Feiner, 1988). Is my hair OK? How about my skin? I can't remember my spelling words! What if I forget my lines (or the music, or miss the ball . . .)?

It's also about this time that *societal concerns* enter children's consciousness. Now worries about homeless people, people with AIDS, leukemic children in Chernobyl, and personal fears of family bankruptcy, divorce, or burglary appear. The natural process of developing a conscience carries with it a gradually dawning awareness of unfairness, the unevenness of wealth and opportunity, and eventually a more global view of people's inhumanity to humankind. The first symptom many children have of this new feeling is fear or anxiety.

GENERATIONAL FEARS

Like children of every generation, today's children reflect the traumatic events and conditions they encounter in the anxieties they develop. Television coverage of the 1991 Gulf War focused for several days on a missile strike that landed directly on target; children who were preschoolers during that event can still describe it and often relive that scene in their dreams. More recently, the 1995 bombing that killed preschoolers in Oklahoma and the 1996 gunfire attack on a class of young children in Dunblane, Scotland, caused many school-age children to worry about the safety of their younger siblings as well as themselves. Following the 1989 earthquake in California, hundreds of children refused to sleep in second-story bedrooms; parents reported sleep disorders for as long as a year following the quake. The riots in Los Angeles following the 1992 Rodney King trial also had far-reaching impact on children who watched them on television.

Even parents can be a source of concern for children. Parents of children who regularly attend a school-age child-care center probably work outside their home. The parents of many children in after-school recreational programs are divorced. At some times during their lives, almost all parents are less attentive than they should be. Statistics on the use of drugs and alcohol lead us to believe that a substantial number of children face unpleasant situations with these elements in their homes (Bissell, 1994). There are about 300,000 homeless children under 10 in the United States (Leach, 1994); in California alone, over 1 million children are either hungry or on the brink of hunger (Standish, 1994).

Consequently, in today's world, as in eras past, children are frequently—and justifiably—frightened.

THE ROLE OF THE ADULT IN THE FEAR CYCLE

So, whose job is it to fix all this? How do you, as a professional youth worker, respond to parents' worries and children's fears? Knowing what frightens children is a big help. So is understanding the changes that are taking place in society and how some people are learning to handle children's worries and fears. It is also helpful to know what you *cannot* do.

A school-age play group or after-school program can be a good environment in which to help children handle some of their fears. Caregivers should never denigrate children's concerns. Belittling the anxieties will likely lead the frightened child to keep his or her feelings locked up inside, not only afraid of what was originally frightening, but now also afraid of sharing the fear with others. And as the adults model respect for children's fears, the other children in the program will learn sensitive ways to respond to their friends' private monsters.

SOME STRATEGIES THAT CAN HELP

Sometimes play activities, such as "let's pretend," can help children master specific fears—fear of animals or of the dark. Very young children love playing "We're Going on a Bear Hunt" (Rosen and Oxenburg, 1989); older children can pretend to be marooned on a desert island or at summer camp and play out their individual fear scenarios with their friends. In this way, children can work on the fear while maintaining a boundary between fantasy and reality (Berger, 1971); these activities can also allow them to release, in an appropriate way, angers and hostilities that may have been generated by the fear (Moracco & Camilleri, 1983). Other methods for working through fears in a group include painting the frightening situation, then talking about it, and performing puppet shows with one character acting out the frightened child and another a helpful friend.

A valuable resource for parents and adults who work with children with troublesome fears is *Taming Monsters, Slaying Dragons* (Feiner, 1988). This book describes a broad selection of children's normal developmental fears along with several strategies for helping frightened children overcome or manage their fears. A discussion of family systems and support networks contained in the book is also helpful for child-care professionals working with children whose fears may be realistic (such as fearing loss of a home when a parent is out of work or fearing a bully who lives in the child's neighborhood). Sometimes it is not possible to remove the situation causing the fear; but life does need to go on, and fear can be crippling and paralyzing. Schachter and McCauley's book *When Your Child Is Afraid* (1988) contains useful suggestions for helping children develop strategies for coping with the frightening

PERSPECTIVE

Proof That After-School Programs Work

Marian Wright Edelman, Children's Defense Fund President

Jennifer Lowery sings in her church choir, acts in school plays, coaches swimming, volunteers at the Baltimore Aquarium and the National Zoo, and dreams of becoming a marine biologist. Diego Ivan Duran works part-time, mentors a small group of eighth graders, runs an advocacy group for Latino students at his school, and is aiming for college and then graduate school.

As remarkable as these Maryland students are, what's even more amazing are the obstacles they have overcome to accomplish so much. That's why CDF recently honored them for *beating the odds.* Jennifer and Diego have reminded me once again that avoiding school failure, alienation, too-early pregnancy, and resisting violence are possible when young people possess reserves of inner strength, have positive adult role models, and are engaged in productive activities when they're not in school. It is these extracurricular activities that have boosted their self-esteem and given Jennifer and Diego a feeling of connectedness to the community, despite the daunting circumstances in their personal lives.

Jennifer, 17, grew up in a home where her father battered her mother and regularly hurled verbal insults at his two children. When Jennifer was a sophomore, her father announced that he had put the house into foreclosure and allowed the car to be repossessed. Then he abandoned the family.

A shelter was home for the family until Mrs. Lowery—who had never worked outside the home—got a job managing a retail store. Making ends meet is still hard. Yet Jennifer, thanks to her mother, guidance counselor, and math teacher, has maintained her focus. "Involvement really keeps people out of trouble," notes Jennifer, after reciting her range of positive after-school activities that mean so much to her.

Diego struggled to learn English after he emigrated to the United States from Venezuela to join his mother when he was 9. At age 13, he received a partial scholarship at a private boarding school. Then his mother suffered a spinal injury, and Diego had to leave boarding school and go to work to support the family. His shaky English skills mistakenly landed him in a school for emotionally disturbed children.

Determined to get into the educational mainstream, Diego taught himself how to read and write English, and within a year he was attending his local public high school. Now 18 and a senior, Diego has devoted himself to helping others by forming a school-based tutoring and community service project.

"There are things you can learn from after-school activities that you can't learn from a book, like how to deal with people," says Diego, who credits his adviser Daniel Garcia and his mother for keeping him on the right track. "It prepares you for life."

These two are living proof that after-school programs are one of the essential keys to a bright future. They not only offer emotional support and positive friendships for young people but also provide a sense of community that is so often lacking today.

circumstances of their lives. For example, if a child has experienced real violence in his or her neighborhood, Schachter and McCauley advise the following:

1. Seek professional help for effects of stressful trauma that do not abate within a reasonable time after the incident.

2. Demonstrate the security measures of the child's house or apartment building to prevent unlawful entry.

3. Use the anxiety to help the child remember to use locks and keys, not to divulge information or display money to strangers, and so forth.

Some of these options might not be available to children in certain situations, but concerned adults may be able to help reduce children's vulnerability in several ways by working in the community. They might develop neighborhood watch groups and other support services for parents and youths to help them cope with situations that threaten their safety. An example is a walk-to-school program that helps children get to and from school safely.

Six-, seven-, and eight-year-old children are testing reality, and their fears frequently reflect ***magical thinking,*** or believing that their thoughts can influence circumstances around them. Schachter observes that older children respond well to appeals to their growing logical notions of cause and effect; historic and present time; and ability to discriminate size, weight, and volume of objects, including fearsome ones. It is harder to fear something, he notes, if you are busy analyzing how it works. A third book that is helpful both to parents and to child-care workers is *How to Talk to Your Kids About Really Important Things: Specific Questions and Answers and Useful Things to Say* (1994), by Charles E. Schaefer and Theresa Foy DiGeronimo. Topics covered include adoption, alcoholic parent, death of a loved one or pet, hospital stay, repeating a grade, sleep-away camp, HIV/AIDS, homosexuality, Santa Claus, war, and many others.

Violence in the Home and Community

Some children in school-age programs may truly be at risk from violence, not only in their neighborhoods but also in their own homes. These children may develop behaviors such as biting, hitting, or destroying other children's property, or they may turn within themselves, cry easily, lose their appetites, or cling to a toy or a trusted person. The more violence they experience, the more serious these behavioral clues may become (Paul, 1995).

Child-care and recreation professionals should be trained to recognize signs of abuse and neglect and work with families at risk to seek help whenever possible. Invite a social worker or counselor from the child protective services in your community to present an in-service workshop to staff and interested parents. Beyond practicing reasonable awareness, we do not have the power to prevent or to cure the hurts inflicted in the hearts of children by family violence. However, helping children to develop relationships with children and adults in their after-school program is a valuable role and one that can work to offset the negative effects of violence in their lives (Wallach, 1993). Organized schedules, within a clear structure of boundaries and expectations, can provide a sense of security for children in chaotic environments. Other helpful strategies focus on supporting the families themselves (Sonquist, 1994):

Know the parents, know the community. Child and youth workers who know the families they serve, and drive through the communities in which they live, are more in tune with the lives of the children they serve. When

Violence is a harsh reality that many children live with every day.

violence occurs, it is more likely they will sense whether it is coming from the community, the home, the media, or a combination.

Offer parenting advice. Model good practice with children and share with parents what you know about the ways children of different ages respond to scary things. Encourage parents to restrict children's viewing of violent videos and television shows and discuss alternatives to violence-oriented action figures. Parenting workshops combined with potluck dinners can be good settings for presenting some of these ideas and also for initiating friendly relationships with parents.

Improve referral networks. Child and youth workers can serve as bridges to community support services. You might provide a telephone number; offer to make an appointment for a parent; or arrange for the social worker, psychologist, or other professional to meet the parent after work at your site. When children are frightened, their parents are often frightened, also. You can help the child by helping the parent.

Media-Induced Fear

Periodically, several children in a program will experience anxiety or fear sufficiently for it to become a concern of the program staff. This is common after a major cataclysmic event, such as a hurricane, earthquake, economic setback, or major news story. Dinner-table conversation and the evening news may have

Television news coverage of frightening events may be a source of stress to some youngsters.

a strong influence on school-age children's concerns, especially when these relate to fears already present in their minds. Some programs have had good success with a structured, group approach to calming children's fears at these times. Following the Oklahoma City bombing in 1995, many child and youth workers struggled with the impact on the children in their programs. Psychologists associated with Scholastic Inc. and the National Association for the Education of Young Children (NAEYC) felt the emotional impact was serious enough that they sent guidelines to parents and teachers to help them talk to children. Rich Scofield framed the NAEYC suggestions for older children and printed them in the bimonthly newsletter he publishes for school-age care professionals (Scofield, 1995). Many programs found the suggestions helpful, so they are included here with some additional comments.

If you can help it, do not expose young children to TV or radio broadcasts about the disaster. But don't make a big deal about it, either. Just don't turn on the TV. Find alternative activities. If the children do happen to see broadcasts, reassure them that the event happened far away (if it did) or is over (if it is).

Convey stability and calm. Children respond well to calm adults; conversely, they pick up the uncertainty, anxiety, and fear of distressed adults. We can't very well deny our own emotions, so the best approach is honesty and doing our best to remain calm in the presence of children. The Scholastic message (Brodkin, 1995) suggested bringing in psychologists to help with children who show "sudden changes in behavior or a generalized increase in fearfulness."

With respect to what particular children need in a particular situation, take your cues from the children themselves. Don't initiate discussions with children about events they might not even know about or might be upset by. If children have heard about the event and their behavior or words convey their difficulty dealing with it, talk with them in a low-key way. Ask a few questions to see what they have heard and find reassuring ways to deal with the information. Explain that "people are helping her to get out" (such as when 18-month-old Jessica McClure spent 56 hours trapped in an abandoned Texas well in 1988), or "We'll collect some blankets to send to the flood victims."

Focus on positive steps for prevention. When a car smashed into an urban child-care setting near our home, the children in my daughter's after-school center set about redesigning the fencing and the traffic pattern of the center as it had been depicted in the newspaper. Unknowingly, they were helping themselves work through their own fear and anger at the unnecessary event. Wherever possible, help children brainstorm ways of doing things so the disaster does not happen again ("The baby-sitter should cover the well"; "They should move the road further away from the building so a bomb can't be hidden in the car"; "The fence should be replaced with a concrete wall, and the playground should be moved away from the street side of the building").

Family Issues—Divorce, Loss, Relocation

When fears or concerns arise out of personally experienced circumstances, individual children may not find a large group brainstorming session to be helpful or even desirable. Sometimes small groups of children experiencing similar problems can support one another as they deal with frightening changes in their lives or possibilities that have not yet materialized.

One such approach, *Rainbows for All Children,* is a peer support program originally developed for use with children grieving over the loss of a parent through death, divorce, separation, or abandonment. The aim of the program is to help troubled children believe in their own goodness and the value of their own family, whatever its form. Child-care professionals and teachers attend training sessions where they learn to provide emotional support for the children by listening with empathy and compassion, sharing feelings, involving them in planning and decision making, and helping them to reach forgiveness and acceptance. *Rainbows* is also effective in helping children deal with the sale of the family home, parental unemployment, siblings who go away to college, or pets that die. Operating much like a weekly club for anyone who wishes to participate, programs such as *Rainbows for All Children* can provide a helpful tool for adults working with normal children living through troubled times (Charlet, personal communication, 1995; Yehl, 1987).

Divorce is an issue that troubles many children, even long after the grieving and anger have begun to fade. The day-to-day mechanical issues of living in two homes (or traveling long distances to visit a relocated parent) can test a child's patience. Sometimes, parents' failure to figure out how to do this in an organized way can lead to lost homework assignments, missed appointments,

Divorce, single parenthood, and remarriage all bring with them stresses on children.

late arrival at school, and other events that signal a downward spiral of discouragement and often failure.

School-age program staff can help children adjusting to divorce by being patient listeners and by understanding the complications of life that lead to late pickups, lost possessions and homework, short tempers, and unexpected tears (not just of the child but sometimes also of the parents). Divorce usually is accompanied by a change of residence, parents changing their usual patterns of work and play, a loss of old and trusted friends, and an expectation that children will make new friends as the parents' new social connections bring new people into their lives. Assurances that things will be better in 6 months or a year can sometimes help; these are realistic time frames that children can look forward to. Things probably *won't* be much better in a week or a month. Such adjustments take a long time.

A strategy for use with children who are worried or frightened about events in their lives was developed by an Australian psychologist whose own daughter sometimes couldn't sleep at night. Dr. Doris Brett developed a series of stories that mirror many of the real-life situations that make children anxious: nightmares, the birth of siblings, starting school for the first time, coping with divorce or the death of someone close (Brett, 1988). Designed to calm the fears and build the confidence of her daughter, Brett fashioned "Annie" stories to allow children to explore the situations with an adult storyteller through the experiences of an imaginary boy or girl much like the child listener. Storytelling is an art that takes some practice, but the stories in Brett's collection make it easy for the caregiver to get started if he or she is willing to give the technique a try.

In addition to telling stories, reading books to children about potentially frightening events or creatures can help youngsters develop a stronger sense of control over their own safety. For instance, reading about natural disasters such as earthquakes, tornadoes, and hurricanes can show how rarely these events actually occur. One writer suggests reading books that praise the effectiveness of seatbelts to help a child overcome his fear of auto accidents (Murray, 1994); equally effective are geographical atlases (to show how far away any military action is) and books about reptiles, spiders, or dogs.

Societal Issues

Sometimes the issues that trouble children are outside their own personal spheres. One 9-year-old became distressed about a homeless man she and her mother passed each day on their way to school. Watching him each morning, sitting on the side of the road near the edge of town, blowing on his chapped and cold hands, she worried that he would become ill or be hungry all day. The youngster shared her concern with a staff member at her after-school center and after some discussion they decided to learn more about the man. Eventually, they discovered that this particular person had turned down an offer of shelter in town and preferred to stay where he was. In fact, he had been sleeping in a grove of trees nearby for several weeks. He did accept the offer of a warm jacket and some bread and cheese that the children at the center provided, and the worried child felt comforted that they had done something to help him.

As a result of this incident, however, the anxious young girl learned what provisions were being made in her community for homeless people and troubled adults like the person she had helped and how she and her classmates could assist in fund-raising or other activities. Finding an avenue of service gave her a way to channel the concern she felt for the homeless man and other needy people. As discussed in a later chapter, this is a role that can and probably should be taken by school-age child-care programs: to be a resource to children who have questions about their communities and to help connect them with other people in their community who are interested in or concerned about the same things as they are. Parents may be at work during the hours when community agency telephones are answered, and this kind of research often needs to take place during that time. Helping children to feel that they are useful members of their communities is part of the broad role we can play in the socialization process. It can have very far-reaching and long-term positive outcomes.

Tobacco, Alcohol, and Drugs

So far we have discussed fears and concerns of children about things that are happening around them or to them. We should also consider some of the issues of school-age children that result from things they do themselves. Drinking, smoking, using drugs—any one of these behaviors can signal problems in children's lives, and the behaviors themselves can lead children into fear-producing circumstances. The Gesell Institute of Human Development polled children from 10 to 14 about how much "their friends" used tobacco, alcohol, and drugs. Table 6-1 below shows the results of those interviews.

Children were asked whether they or any of their friends smoked, drank, or used drugs. Ten- and eleven-year-old children reported only on usage by "their friends"; 12- and 13-year-olds answered the question by saying that *either* they or their friends used these substances. The percentages shown reflect the numbers of children who said that either they or their friends used the substance (Ames, Ilg, & Baker, 1988). Self-reporting does not produce reliable statistics, but it does reflect perceptions. In this case, the perception, supported by other studies, is that these troublesome habits are commonly found among school-age children.

Drug and alcohol prevention programs are beginning to appear in the public school systems, fueled by the rising cost of health and rehabilitation care. More recently, tobacco education programs have been introduced in the early elementary grades with the hope of reducing the number of new smokers in coming years. One program, developed specifically for after-school recreation and care programs, addressed the self-esteem component that is believed to contribute to drug, alcohol, and tobacco usage in children. The *Nancy Reagan Afterschool Program* consisted of a series of videos portraying school-age children in a variety of situations from encountering peer pressure to breaking laws. A valuable leader's guide included suggestions for follow-up activities for each scenario and many other group or individual activities (art, getting along with others, imagining, journaling, music, movement, skits, storytelling) designed to give young people tangible alternatives to drug use (BEST Foundation for a Drug-Free Tomorrow, 1994). Even if you decide not to implement a formal curriculum designed to help children resist pressures to use tobacco,

TABLE 6-1   "Some of My Friends Use This Substance"

	10 years		11 years		12 years		13 years	
	Girls	Boys	Girls	Boys	Girls	Boys	Girls	Boys
Tobacco	51%	34%	75%	46%	80%	68%	84%	68%
Alcohol	30%	30%	<30%	<30%	52%	52%	66%	64%
Drugs	12%	12%	21%	31%	32%	39%	46%	48%

alcohol, or drugs, the resource material that accompanies this kind of curriculum often contains valuable statistics and information that you can use in informal conversations with children and parents. Develop relationships with children and their families; be aware of community programs; and be accessible to children when they need help in decision making or problem solving. Your availability and assurance may be the deciding factor.

SUMMARY

School-age youngsters face many different and frightening situations as they grow and develop. Although childhood has always brought some fears, today's children live with media scenes of war and violence, which make their fears more graphic. Frequently they also live with violence in their own neighborhoods and even their homes. Child and youth workers can help by listening to children, setting up activities and environments that are conducive to reflection and reassurance, and allowing children to voice their worries and act out their fears or anger in appropriate ways. Consistent boundaries within the school-age program and a regular routine can also help children who may have chaotic home lives. Many resources are available to families and professionals who want to help children deal with their fears. Tobacco, alcohol, and drug abuse are also factors that intrude into children's lives. Their families may struggle with addiction; the children themselves may be pressured to try these substances. Once again, caregivers can model ways of making decisions and resisting pressure. Drug-abuse prevention programs that teach strategies and build children's self-assurance can help staff develop their own awareness of these societal issues and ways to help today's children cope with them.

REVIEW QUESTIONS

1. How have changed gender roles resulted in parents feeling unsupported in their roles?
2. Distinguish between developmental needs and generational needs. Give some examples.
3. What issues troubled parents in 1988?
4. List two needs from each level of Maslow's hierarchy of needs.

5. List three local events reported in the media that may have elicited fear in school-age children in your community.
6. Distinguish between social anxiety and societal concerns.
7. List five normal fears of childhood.

CHALLENGE EXERCISES

1. Interview three parents of school-age children. Ask them what has frightened or worried their children in the last year. How did the parents handle the situation? What did they say? Did it help?

2. Try to remember something frightening from your childhood. How did you handle it? Did you talk about your fear or keep it to yourself. What frightens you now? How do you deal with your fears?

3. Do you believe school-age program staff should take a stand against smoking, drinking, and/or drug use when they serve children who may be using these substances? What approach should they take?

4. Interview someone who works in a program for school-age children. How does this person feel about helping children to deal with family violence? With drug abuse issues?

TERMS TO LEARN

developmental needs
entrepreneurs
generational needs
hierarchy of needs
magical thinking

social anxiety

social revolution

societal concerns

REFERENCES
·················

Ames, L. B., Ilg, F. L., & Baker, S. M. (1988). *Your ten- to fourteen-year-old.* New York: Dell.

Berger, A. S. (1971). Anxiety in young children. *Young Children, 27,* 5–11.

BEST Foundation for a Drug-Free Tomorrow. (1994). *For ME guidebook: Video guides and creative activities for ages 7–9.* 725 South Figueroa Street, Suite 1615, Los Angeles, CA 90017.

Bissell, J. (1994). Children exposed to alcohol and drugs. *CSAC Review, 8*(1), 1–2.

Bredekamp, S. E. (1987). *Developmentally appropriate practice in early childhood programs serving children from birth through age 8.* (Expanded ed.). Washington, DC: National Association for the Education of Young Children.

Brett, D. (1988). *Annie stories.* New York: Workman Publishing.

Brodkin, A. (1995, April). The Oklahoma tragedy: Helping children cope. New York: *Scholastic, Inc.*

Dong, Q., Yang, B., & Ollendick, T. (1994). Fears in Chinese children and adolescents and their relations to anxiety and depression. *Journal of Child Psychology and Psychiatry, 35*(2), 351–363.

Feiner, J. (1988). *Taming monsters, slaying dragons: The revolutionary family approach to overcoming childhood fears and anxieties.* New York: Arbor House.

Frank, A. (1993). *Anne Frank: The diary of a young girl.* New York: Bantam. (Original work published 1947)

Gibson, E. J. & Walk, R. (1960). The "visual cliff." *Scientific American, 202,* 64–72.

Greer, K. (1988). Are American families finding new strength in spirituality? *Better Homes & Gardens, 66*(1), 16–22.

Havighurst, R. J. (1953). *Human development and education.* New York: Longmans, Green.

Kashef, Z. (1997, May). What's ailing our kids: Five health issues. *Essence, 28*(1), 184.

Leach, P. (1994). *Children first.* New York: Knopf.

Maslow, A. (1970). *Motivation and personality* (2nd ed.). New York: Harper & Row.

Moracco, J. C., & Camilleri, J. (1983). A study of fears in elementary school children. *Elementary School Guidance & Counseling, 18*(2), 82–87.

Murray, M. (1994, January). What your child fears most. *Reader's Digest,* 109–112.

National Center for Children in Poverty. (1996). About one-third of black children live in poverty. *Jet, 91* (7), 33.

Ollendick, T. H. (1985). Fears in children and adolescents: Normative data. *Behavioral Research Therapy, 23*(4), 464–467.

Ollendick, T. H., Yule, W., & Ollier, K. (1991). Fears in British children and their relationship to manifest anxiety and depression. *Journal of Child Psychology & Psychiatry & Allied Disciplines, 32*(2), 321–331.

Paul, J. (1995, January-February). Violence and young children. *Children's Advocate,* 2–3.

Rosen, M. & Oxenbury, N. (Illustrator) (1989). We're going on a bear hunt. New York: Margaret McElderry.

Schachter, R., & McCauley, C. S. (1988). *When your child is afraid: Understanding the normal fears of childhood from birth through adolescence and helping overcome them.* New York: Simon & Schuster.

Schaefer, C. E., & DiGeronimo, T. F. (1994). *How to talk to your kids about really important things.* San Francisco: Jossey-Bass.

Scholastic Magazine Poll of American Youth. (1996, October). *Instructor.*

Scofield, R. (1995). Helping children cope with tragedy. *School-Age Notes, 15*(9), 2–6.

Sonquist, H. (1994). *Helping families cope with violence.* Paper presented at Successful Strategies: Addressing Violence and Young Children, conference sponsored by Action Alliance for Children, Oakland, CA.

Standish, M. (1994, May-June). Children hungry when breakfast is available. *Children's Advocate,* 3.

Teen Help. (1996). *How times have changed* (Pamphlet). St. George, UT.

Wallach, L. B. (1993). 4 ways to help children cope with violence. *Young Children, 48,* 4–11.

Wilder, L. I. (1965). *On the banks of Plum Creek.* New York: Scholastic. (Original work published 1937)

Womble, M. (1993, March). Our children's safety is everyone's business. *Midwest Forum, 3,* 1–3.

Yeghiayan, G. D. (1991). *Pathfinders for posterity: Armenian-American youth in transition.* Los Angeles: American Armenian International College.

Yehl, S. (1987). *Rainbows for all children.* 913 Margret Street, Des Plaines, IL 60016.

Yinger, J., & Ceely, S. (1995). *Healthy start funding proposal.* Morgan Hill Unified School District, Morgan Hill, CA 95037.

Zigler, E. F., & Lang, M. E. (1991). *Child care choices: Balancing the needs of children, families, and society.* New York: Free Press.

CHAPTER SEVEN

Conditions Affecting Children's Behavior

Understanding the Behavior of School-Age Children

One of the most common challenges faced by child and youth workers is understanding and moderating the behavior of the children in their care. Several factors contribute to the way children behave in small and large groups. Children in out-of-school programs may come from widely differing family settings, reflecting a variety of cultures, values, and communication styles. The social development of some of the younger children may limit their ability to understand what is expected of them or how to practice the give-and-take necessary to get along with other children. Youngsters of the same age vary individually, also. Some seem to have grasped the concept of shared space and time better than others. They differ in conflict-resolution skills. They also come with varying self-concepts, which in turn influence their motivation to work things out and their ability to do so.

Most school-agers are feeling increasingly able to take care of themselves, and they are eager for opportunities to try out their new independence and physical skills. They are also widening their social horizons, making new friends and trying on new roles within their school and neighborhood. They need the guidance of adults as they take emotional risks and especially as they face rejection or, worse, hostility from others. Insecurities lie just under the surface in most school-age youngsters, even when they appear to be confident or even rude to adults.

To work effectively with school-age children, adults must understand and consider these factors. Within a framework of mutual understanding, children and adults can work together to create an environment, a set of expectations, and a system of strategies that will allow them to coexist (most of the time) in harmony.

The physical environment can influence children's ability to behave in acceptable ways.

The Guidance System

The process of influencing children's behavior has been called many things. Parents usually call it **discipline.** Some educators and psychologists refer to **behavior management** or **behavior modification.** More frequently in recent years this process has been called **guidance.** This last term is helpful because it reminds us that the process of helping children learn to behave in socially (and situationally) appropriate ways is ongoing. The goal of guidance is not to control children's behavior but to help children learn how to control their *own* behavior.

Marian Marion, a frequent conference speaker and writer on the subject of children's behavior, has described a **guidance system** that consists of *children, adults,* and *the environment* (Marion, 1987). She believes that effective interaction with and between children develops when adults understand the workings of this system, accept the responsibility for behaving as leaders and mentors rather than as dictators, and create a self-help environment. Marion's ideas are highly adaptable to before- or after-school settings as well as recreation programs and drop-in centers. Some of her suggested strategies are described later in the chapter.

DEVELOPMENTAL CHARACTERISTICS OF SCHOOL-AGE CHILDREN

Chapter 4 described the physical, intellectual, social, and moral development of children. When you are developing a guidance plan for school-agers, it is important to consider these developmental characteristics as they occur at different ages and stages:

Five- to Seven-Year-Olds   Unlike younger children, many 5-, 6- and 7-year-old children can begin to think about problems in a logical fashion, but they may still have difficulty controlling their behavior in groups. There is a shift during this period from the kindergartner's dependence on adults to the second or third grader's tight-knit friendships (sometimes territorial and controversial) with one another (see Table 7-1). Most of the younger children in school-age programs will be in Kohlberg's Level 1 of moral reasoning, which means they follow the rules mostly because they want to avoid punishment, or because they think there might be a reward (extrinsic or intrinsic) for good behavior. This is seen in the intense but often short-lived friendships, which usually have a per-

TABLE 7–1   Developmental Stages of Friendship

Approximate age	State	Characteristics
Under 4	Momentary playmateship	Can't yet consider the viewpoint of another person; can only think about what they want from the friendship. Define friends by how close they live or by their material possessions ("He's my friend; he lives next door" or She's my friend; she has a doll house and a swing set").
4–9	One-way assistance	Can now tell the difference between their own perspective and that of another. Friendship is based on whether someone does what the child wants ("He's not my friend anymore; he doesn't want to play cars").
6–12	Two-way, fair weather cooperation	Understand that friendship involves give and take, but mostly as it serves each one's individual interest rather than both working cooperatively toward a common interest. They emphasize similarities between friends ("We both collect rocks"). Children also understand that friendship involves getting along with one another.
9–15	Intimate, mutually shared relationships	Friendship is now viewed as an entity in itself; an ongoing, committed relationship that is treasured for its own sake and may involve possessiveness and jealousy ("How can she go to the movies with Jenna—she's my best friend"). Older children in this stage may defend one another against others.
Above 12	Autonomous interdependent friendships	Youngsters can now respect their friends' needs for both dependency and autonomy.

Source: Selman, R. L., & Selman, A. P. (1979). Children's ideas about friendship: A new theory. *Psychology Today, 12*(4), 71–80; also Youniss, J., & Volpe, J. (1978). A relational analysis of children's friendship. In W. Damon (Ed.), *Social cognition.* San Francisco: Jossey-Bass.

sonal gain involved for one or the other child ("I'll be your friend if you let me play with your video game").

Eight- to Ten-Year-Olds   By the time children are 8, 9, or 10 years old, they are growing stronger, have greater endurance, and are often ready for more physical challenges. Moving into Level 2 of moral reasoning, they develop their own games with complicated sets of rules and hold one another to compliance, although competition is often complicated by close friendships. Children who are 9 or older are beginning to be able to see another's point of view fairly well and can empathize with children whose feelings have been hurt or who are different in some way. Ten-year-olds need things to be "fair," and arbitrary rules or enforcement of them will often set off tears of frustration and anger.

Between 8 and 10, children are still frequently troubled by fears of snakes, spiders, heights, and large bodies of water and may stubbornly refuse to hold the visiting boa constrictor or dive into the pool. Child and youth workers who understand the resulting conflicts (being good and following the rules juxtaposed to the gripping sense of fear) can better help children work through their difficulties. If adults scoff at their inability to "get with the program," troubled youngsters, already feeling helpless and frozen in place, may now feel worthless as well.

Most children in the 8- to 10-year-old range are now able to work without much adult supervision or direction and are learning to accept responsibility for their own actions.

Eleven- and Twelve-Year-Olds   Children over 10 can seriously challenge inexperienced youth workers. Secure in their self-perceptions, children in these older ranges may test program rules and the authority of anyone around. Twelve-year-olds often think it's "cool" to swear or use rude words and frequently talk back to teachers, coaches, parents, and program staff just to see how it feels. At the same time, older school-agers have learned the two-way street of friendship and are more willing to adjust to one another's individual likes and dislikes.

Piaget and Kohlberg both found that around 12 years of age children's reasoning changes and they begin to take intentions into account when determining how badly someone has behaved. They find it possible, and even attractive, to consider the reasons behind an action and decide that sometimes "ends justify the means." Although they can now think realistically about the consequences of their actions, they sometimes find their judgment being tested by peers and may need the uncritical ear of a caring adult to help them sort it all out.

Thirteen- to Sixteen-Year-Olds   Young teens are often happier in school than in previous years, although not necessarily because they've suddenly begun to love learning. Social interactions have become the most important part of their life, and school is where most of these encounters take place. If their moral development is continuing on track, they may be in Stage 4 or even 5 of Level 3 reasoning. Characteristics of these stages are a willingness, even a desire, to meet one's agreed-on obligations, to keep the social order going, and to uphold the "social contract"[1] of the institutions in which they exist. (Unfortunately, those "institutions" can include cliques and gangs as well as classrooms, schools, athletic teams, or other community groups.)

Younger teens become extremely busy with friends, outside activities, and school sports or clubs; if college is a goal, older teens begin to settle into heavy study patterns. The use of a telephone seems to be almost a necessity to this age group, both for homework discussions and for keeping in touch with social doings; in more affluent areas, or areas of heavy drug traffic, pagers and cellular telephones are carried in backpacks along with textbooks and gym shoes. Fourteen-year-old girls are more interested in boys than boys are in them, but by age 16 their interest is being reciprocated. Peer pressure and group pranks are not uncommon. Teens have lots of complaints about the way the school (or the government, or their house, or their soccer team) is being run. Youths in this age group definitely do not believe they need before- or after-school supervision. Many people, unfortunately, agree with them.

TECHNIQUES USED BY ADULTS TO INFLUENCE CHILDREN'S BEHAVIOR

The goal of guiding children's behavior is to encourage ***prosocial behavior*** and discourage ***antisocial behavior.*** Prosocial behavior can be defined as any behavior that makes others feel good or benefits others (such as sharing, cooperating, or exhibiting ***altruism,*** or selflessness). Antisocial behavior is the opposite—behavior that makes people feel bad or harms them in some way (such as aggression, violence, or criminal activity).

Psychologists have proposed various theories to explain aggressive behavior in children. We can see this behavior in infant/toddler centers, in preschools, and certainly in school-age settings. Two children want a toy and one of them takes it by force, sometimes hurting the other child. Or one child destroys another's block tower, or painting, or math homework. Aggression among older children sometimes takes the form of putdowns, hostile postures, or the "cold shoulder." When it is allowed to build up, aggression can lead to far worse consequences.

Freud (1930/1957) believed that children are born with an aggressive drive, but the way they express it is learned in childhood—for example, by watching their parents argue with a neighbor. Konrad Lorenz was responsible for publicizing the ***aggressive instinct*** idea; he believed it was necessary for evolution and the "survival of the fittest." Although he thought aggressive behavior patterns were instinctual, he maintained that they were no longer necessary for survival and could be altered to become socially useful behavior

---

[1]The social-contract theory concerns the origin of organized society, holding that the state originally was created through a voluntary agreement entered into among individuals living in an anarchical state of nature. This contract defines and regulates the relationships among the members of society and between the individual and the governing authority. Our understanding of this concept was primarily crafted by Thomas Hobbes, John Locke, and Jean Jacques Rousseau in the 17th and 18th centuries.

Effect of Discipline May Differ for African American and European American Children, Says New Research

Ethnic background seems to play a role in how children react to physical discipline from their parents. According to a new study in the November issue of the American Psychological Association's *Journal of Developmental Psychology,* European American children who are physically punished become more aggressive in school. In contrast, African American children do not become more aggressive when they are punished physically by their parents.

"The meaning attached to the physical discipline could be the reason for this ethnic group difference," said psychologist Kirby Deater-Deckard, Ph.D., of the Institute of Psychiatry in London, England, and lead author of the study. "We have speculated that a child from an European American family may interpret harsh physical discipline—not physical abuse—as parental hostility and lack of warmth. But a child from an African American family may not view the same punishment as hostile or showing a lack of warmth or caring."

Dr. Deater-Deckard and psychologists Kenneth A. Dodge, Ph.D., John E. Bates, Ph.D., and Gregory S. Pettit, Ph.D., found this out by first asking single and married mothers of 466 European American and 100 African American kindergartners from various socioeconomic levels if they used physical punishment as a way to discipline their children. The mothers along with the children's teachers and peers were then asked how often and to what extent these children acted in an aggressive way and whether they had conflicts with their teachers. The children were monitored through the third grade.

"Single mothers, mothers with fewer socioeconomic resources and African American mothers reported using more physical punishment," said Dr. Deater-Deckard. "But even though the African American children were more likely to be living in single-mother and lower income households, these children did not behave more aggressively in school even though it appeared they would be at risk for it."

It seems likely that there are ethnic and cultural variations in the ways children view the meaning of parents' behavior, explained the authors. For example, "among European American families, the presence of harsh discipline may imply an out-of-control, parent-centered household for some, whereas a lack of discipline among African American parents may indicate an abdication of the parenting role to others."

"We are currently exploring African American and European American children's view of physical discipline," said Dr. Deater-Deckard. "Future studies should tell us whether these ethnic group variations are due to cultural differences in the meaning of physical discipline."

Article: "Physical Discipline Among African American and European American Mothers: Links to Children's Externalizing Behaviors" by Kirby Deater-Deckard, Ph.D., Institute of Psychiatry; Kenneth A. Dodge, Ph.D., Vanderbilt University; John E. Bates, Ph.D., Indiana University; and Gregory S. Pettit, Ph.D., Auburn University, in *Developmental Psychology* (1996, November), *32*(6), 1–8.

(Lorenz, 1966). Bandura conducted research to support the idea that children learn from their early environment *when* it is appropriate to act aggressively, *what forms* of aggression are acceptable, and *toward whom* they can act aggressively and get away with it (Bandura, 1969, 1973). He believed that aggression is a behavior learned through reinforcement and imitation, and therefore, it can also be unlearned. Dreikurs and Solz (1990) attributed hostile or aggressive behavior to mistaken goals pursued by many children. No matter whether aggression is learned or instinctual, part of the process of socialization is learning to keep it under control.

Eva Essa, child psychologist, (1990) presents nine techniques to deal with misbehavior, including aggression: reinforcement, ignoring, time-out, self-selected time-out, prevention, redirection, discussion, special time, and star chart. Levin (1994) encourages adults to share power with the children so they can "learn from daily experience how to take responsibility for themselves and their classroom community" (p. 29). Marion (1987) describes the use of modeling, direct instruction, rewards and punishments, stating expectations of desired behaviors, and cognitive modification strategies. These three behavior specialists are all saying essentially the same thing, which is also the title of an excellent book about discipline: *Control the Climate, Not the Children* (Fink, 1995). All four views are incorporated into the strategies described below.

Modeling and Instructing   All psychological theories dealing with aggression emphasize the role of adult models and teachers in shaping children's behavior. It is important that adults in school-age programs *model,* or demonstrate, positive behaviors such as respect, generosity, cooperation, thoughtfulness, and helpfulness in their dealings with all the children and other adults in the program. It is especially important to model acceptance of individual differences such as cultural practices, conflicting values, and unusual appearance or style of dress, and to avoid retaliatory or aggressive statements such as "I'll get him for that!"

Child and youth workers can also **instruct,** or teach, the use of problem-solving and conflict-resolution techniques, how to control aggressive feelings, how to confront other people appropriately, how to make friends by being a friend, and other social skills. It often seems quicker and easier to intervene in children's difficulties, telling them to "take turns," or "use your words," but those short-term solutions do not help children learn to solve problems or resolve future conflicts. It is also helpful to comment positively when children *do* choose appropriate behaviors.

Several problem-solving strategies have been developed that can be taught to school-age children. A fairly simple one, developed by Thomas Gordon, can be outlined on poster board and referred to whenever there is a conflict. The first step is to determine "Who owns the problem?" For example, if Jorge is trying to finish his book report and Susan wants to play on the electronic keyboard, it could be Jorge's problem if he is working on his homework during free activity time, or Susan's if she wants to play during the study hour. If it is Jorge's problem, he needs to be encouraged to follow these steps:

1. Define the problem ("I can't concentrate when Susan plays the keyboard").

2. Generate possible solutions ("Susan uses the earphones; I find another place to work; I wear earplugs").

3. Evaluate and test the various solutions.

4. Decide on a mutually acceptable solution (this depends both on Susan's willingness to compromise and Jorge's persuasive skills).

5. Implement the solution.

6. Evaluate the solution.

If it is Susan's problem, it becomes *her* responsibility to work through the process. Guiding children through problem-solving strategies takes longer than imposing your own solution, but it has longer-lasting results (Gordon, 1974).

Conflict-Resolution Strategies　Problem solving works for solving problems. However, if the problem appears to have led to a serious emotional conflict, a more appropriate technique to use is ***conflict resolution.*** This is a process that helps people see a situation more objectively, consider the other person's viewpoint, and resolve conflicts without violence (Fink, 1995). A familiar way of solving conflict between two or more children is for the nearest adult to intervene, ask what happened, and try to make a fair judgment. This approach teaches children that "teachers solve conflicts" and often leaves them feeling frustrated; it also teaches them that we think they are unable to resolve conflicts on their own. This approach may keep the school-age environment superficially harmonious; however, several small differences that are resolved unsatisfactorily probably go to a scoreboard in children's heads, waiting to fuel future conflicts, which may escalate as a result. Also, the teacher-intervention model does not prepare youngsters for resolving conflicts *outside* the after-school program when there is no adult to help. Conflicts on the playground, on the school bus, in the neighborhoods, and elsewhere are usually resolved using the "might makes right" rule; here, those with more power simply impose their will on those with less. The whole world would be better off if children everywhere were taught the skills necessary to negotiate and resolve differences peacefully.

To teach conflict-resolution skills, adult leaders need to learn them. There are many institutes, workshops, classes, and books available, fueled by the reasonable belief that children who possess these skills are less likely to succumb to gang-related and other types of violence. Many elementary schools hire trainers to come on-site to train teachers and student leaders, who in turn train others. The basic structure of conflict resolution is similar to the problem-solving technique presented above. However, because serious conflicts usually cause heightened emotions, effective programs include training student facilitators to guide the process and keep the children with the conflict on track. Another model, used at the Friends School of Minnesota, encourages all students to become proficient in conflict resolution through private conferences and group gatherings. "Conflict resolution is part of the school's culture. When children experience a conflict, they ask for a conference. When group problems arise, a group gathering is called and students discuss the issue and possible solutions" (Friends School of Minnesota, 1997, Introduction).

In this context, a conference consists of the children experiencing a conflict as well as an additional person they mutually accept who has agreed to help them resolve their dispute. The Friends School training material suggests that they choose a comfortable place to sit and arrange themselves so everyone can see

Whenever possible, children should be allowed to work out their differences without interference from others.

everyone else. The children then follow a set of steps that include agreeing on the rules, laying out the rules for talking (listen, take turns speaking, speak respectfully, etc.), clarifying the issue (behaviors, conflict, feelings), and making a plan. The process is complete when the parties agree on how they will proceed.

Violence-prevention programs such as Peacebuilders® and Adventures in Peacemaking include conflict-resolution strategies in their curriculum. These programs are often brought to school districts by antigang task groups, who believe "that by changing the social climate in the schools and community, it can make a positive difference and can have a long term effect on behavior and can become a positive way of life" (Beall, 1996, p. 1). Programs for school-agers provide an ideal environment in which to practice peace-building and conflict-resolution skills; they may even be models for local schools that experience problems with conflicts.

Reinforcing, Rewarding, and Punishing   Adults **reinforce** children's behavior both knowingly and unknowingly. (B. F. Skinner defined a *reinforcer* as anything that causes a behavior to be repeated.) Realize that what we may think of as punishment (such as placing a child in a time-out chair or delivering a stern lecture on the importance of taking care of the furniture) may actually feel like a

reward to a child who is seeking attention; consequently, it may encourage the behavior. However, when one child helps another find a game piece, and the adult says quietly, "Brian, I really appreciated the way you helped Gillian," this can be a very effective reinforcer. *Ignoring* a child's inappropriate behavior, which can be done if the actions do not threaten to injure anyone or anything, is essentially the withholding of a reinforcer; this strategy will weaken the undesirable behavior or decrease the likelihood of its repetition.

Dreikurs and Solz (1990) identified four **mistaken goals** that children sometimes pursue in their quest for a feeling of belonging. They described these goals as **undue attention, struggle for power, retaliation and revenge,** and **complete inadequacy.** As adults struggle with children's behavior, they may inadvertently reward and punish behaviors without really understanding what they are reinforcing. Dreikurs and Solz's classic text, *Children: The Challenge* (1990), is a useful handbook of guidance techniques for parents, child and youth workers, and teachers; in it, Dreikurs and Solz suggest ways children can be encouraged to pursue more appropriate goals in their social interactions. Through observation, study, and practice, we can learn to identify the reasons behind many confrontations or situations that confuse us. By reinforcing and rewarding behavior that contributes to the harmony of the environment, we can begin to help children reduce their instances of inappropriate behavior. Even when we do not truly understand *why* unsuitable behaviors occur, we can still use guidance techniques to decrease their frequency and increase the occurrence of desirable ones.

Stating Expectations of Desired Behaviors   Thoughtful classroom teachers do not surprise their students. Instead, they prepare them for what is to come that day, the next day, and during the following weeks. In the same way, adults who work with school-age children in less formal surroundings show respect for them by involving them in planning activities and posting these activities ahead of time. It is also important to develop and clearly state behavioral guidelines. Whenever possible, present expectations as *positive*, rather than *negative* ones. For example, say "In this program, we are considerate of one another" rather than "Don't hit." Or "While we are inside, let's keep our voices quieter" rather than "Stop yelling." If there are designated times for certain activities, make sure they are clearly posted; if materials or equipment need adult supervision, keep them in locked cabinets, clearly labeled. If some children seem regularly to stretch or ignore the program guidelines, speak to them privately to be sure they understand the expectations and consequences of repeated infractions.

Dale Fink, in his book *Discipline in School-Age Care: Control the Climate, Not the Children* (1995), suggests this approach to communicating expectations about appropriate behavior:

> *Be concise and be positive.* Rules stated simply are easier to learn and remember, rules stated positively set a better climate. Which sounds better to you: "Respect other people's private space and property" or "Keep your hands on your own body, and stay out of other people's cubbies"?

Put rules in writing and post them prominently. Important rules which need to be frequently invoked should be neatly printed and posted in a place that allows staff and children to easily refer to them. Of course, children who do not read will need to have them explained orally. This is a good demonstration to young children of the power and importance of written communication.

Ask parents to assist in clarifying important rules. Some SAC [school-age care] programs send home a copy of the rules, others go a step further and turn a list of important rules into a written contract between the child and the program. They send two copies of the contract home with the child and ask the parents to read it over and discuss it with the children. The children then sign one copy and return it to the program, keeping the other copy for themselves and their families. [Author's note: if the child goes home to more than one house, it might be a good idea to send a copy for each parent or guardian.]

Make only rules the staff plans to respect! How many times does it happen? The rule says, "We sit on chairs, we use tables for games and activities." But the staff member sits on the table! The message to children is that "might makes right," rules have no intrinsic value and it's fine to break rules if you can get away with it.

Be sure discussion of rules in a large group is only the beginning. Do you rely exclusively on *large group* discussions of important rules and behavioral issues? Some children "tune out" during large group discussions and will miss everything you say. You may take the attitude, "well, if they can't listen, that's their problem," or you might recognize that we all have different learning styles. If you take the latter approach, you will find opportunities to explain the rules in *small groups* or even *individually* for those children who don't concentrate well in a group.

Do you rely on discussions held at the beginning of the year and after that it's "Hey, you know the rules! We went over this in September!" Many children have a lot on their minds in September—new school classrooms, new friends, new after-school arrangements. They need many more opportunities to become familiar with your expectations.

Clarify expectations immediately prior to specific activities. It would be unrealistic to explain the rules of the gym while you are in the cafeteria and expect all the children, once they actually get into the gym, to remember all the rules and comply with them. Instead, sit down inside the gym and discuss behavioral expectations prior to beginning the play or activity period. Do this, not just once, but the first several times you bring your group into the gym—or into any other space that is new to them.

When you are introducing unfamiliar craft materials, a new game or any other new activity, follow a similar pattern. Make sure children have a chance to understand your expectations before they "get themselves in trouble" by using the material or playing the game in a way that you regard as inappropriate.

Provide individual guidance for individual children. You will become familiar over time with the behavior of individual children. Since you are more interested in "prevention" than "treatment," you will want to devise your own strategies for helping individual children avoid misbehaving. There is nothing wrong with calling Terry aside at the start of the outdoor play period (out of earshot of the other children) and saying "Terry, remember what happened yesterday in the sandbox? I want you to have a good time today and not have problems out here, so why don't you repeat to me the rules for the sandbox area?" To follow up, you may want to seek out Terry a few minutes later, ask how things are going, put your hand on his shoulder, let him know he is doing fine. You will always find prevention less costly than treatment—in your time, energy and morale!

—Fink, 1995, 20–22

Using Cognitive Modification Strategies   Marion (1987) encourages adults seeking to change children's behavior to (1) arouse their empathy, (2) help them alter their self-perceptions, and (3) focus on their own values and actions. These are examples of **cognitive modification strategies,** which involve teaching youngsters how to think about a situation, consider several related factors, and change their behavior based on that thinking process.

One example of this technique was successfully used by a basketball coach whose 12-year-old players began to arrive late for practices or miss them altogether. Taking the players aside one by one, the coach pointed out how important it was to the others that each player show commitment to the team (arouse *empathy*). As he discussed the problem with each child, various reasons were given for the lateness or absence. Conflicts with music lessons or schoolwork, problems with rides, illness, or fatigue were among the various reasons stated.

Modeling problem-solving strategies, the coach encouraged each player to think of ways to get to practice more regularly. Ideas such as using better planning, rescheduling music lessons, car pooling, and getting to bed earlier were discussed (altering *self-perception*). Finally, he pointed out that the players wore their team shirts to school, invited friends to their games, and wanted very much to win games—all circumstances that seemed to conflict with the lack of interest they had been showing at practice. Working with players privately was important because that allowed them to save face and change their behavior seemingly of their own accord. Helping them to see the discrepancy between their behavior, their personal values, and the team goals was all that was necessary to change most of the players' behavior.

There is a delicate balance between urging compliance with program expectations and encouraging healthy autonomy. Remember, however, that the grown-ups are responsible for protecting children's health, safety, and feelings; sometimes they must use stronger measures such as suspension or expulsion to deal with out-of-bounds or unsafe behavior.

THE ENVIRONMENT

The world has always been a dangerous and, in spots, a violent place. One difference today, however, is that in addition to whatever real circumstances exist in the community, danger and violence are also broadcast into our homes by television, radio, and newspapers:

> Two generations ago only a few unfortunate children ever *saw* anyone hit over the head with a brick, shot, knifed, rammed by a car, blown up, immolated, raped or tortured. Now all children, along with their elders, see such images every day of their lives and are expected to enjoy them.
>
> —Leach, 1994, p. 152

The effects of violent news reporting and entertainment on children's behavior are still unclear, but undoubtedly they are significant. Children who frequently watch videos or television shows in which people kill or hurt one another, who regularly view national news programs, and who often play video games with a violent content inevitably learn a different set of ideas about conflict resolution than do children whose television and video viewing is restricted and guided. In addition, if children spend their time in passive pursuits such as watching televison or videos rather than participating in sports, music lessons, or academic enrichment programs, they lose valuable learning time. To become a responsible member of a group setting in which people act in caring, respectful, and helpful ways to one another and everyone is treated with respect, children need many opportunities to learn how to behave in prosocial ways (Levin, 1994, p. 17).

We cannot control the home environment, but we *can* control the setting in out-of-school programs. When children are offered the opportunity to play strategic games, such as *Othello, Connect Four,* or *Stratego* (especially if program staff play along with them), they are encouraged to develop thinking skills necessary for working through interpersonal problems. Teaching children to knit, sew, weave, make paper, construct projects out of wood or plastic, or cook also strengthens their cognitive skills and helps them develop patience. Encouraging children to participate in cooperative activities, such as soccer, basketball, cat's cradle, construction, or mural making, builds friendships and teaches youngsters to work together. So does group brainstorming about the furniture arrangement, the daily schedule, or how the computer equipment will be shared.

None of these activities alone will solve children's interpersonal problems or teach conflict-resolution and problem-solving strategies. However, if you encourage these kinds of pursuits while you minimize the availability of action figures, violent arcade or video games, and television and video presentations as well as practice the other guidance techniques in this chapter, you will help children behave in less aggressive, more cooperative ways. Other considerations, covered in greater detail in Chapter 8, include arranging the environment to accommodate changing needs and interests. This should be done so that it encourages flexibility, allows children to participate in a variety of different activities without getting in one another's way, and encourages the development of self-help skills. Over time, a well-thought-out environment will influence children's behavior positively.

Setting and Enforcing Limits

Even though programs for school-age children should encourage participation in decision making by the children in the program as much as possible, the final responsibility for setting and enforcing limits on children's behavior falls on the adults in charge. Keep rules to a minimum and consider the following guidelines as you develop the limits for your program:

A good limit will do the following:

* Help children achieve self-control
* Help children develop positive interactional skills
* Protect a child's health and safety
* Never degrade a child
* Have real meaning
* Be developmentally valid

—Marion, 1987, p. 18

But what happens when a child refuses to follow the rules? How does one go about enforcing compliance to the limits once they are set? Dreikurs and Solz (1990) discourage the use of punishment and rewards, believing that those techniques overemphasize the dominance of one individual over another, have no place in a democratic society, and destroy children's intrinsic motivation to behave in acceptable ways. Instead, they recommend the use of ***natural*** and ***logical consequences.***

NATURAL CONSEQUENCES

Two common examples of natural consequences (and ones that the author's children can recount word for word) are (1) forgetting one's lunch and (2) failing to wear a jacket while playing outside on a chilly day. In an example of the first scenario, Kenta leaves his care provider's home in the morning and forgets to take his lunch with him. (This has been an ongoing problem. However, following the guidance principles above, Kenta's caregiver has worked with him to determine a good place to set his lunch and he knows that remembering to take it is his responsibility.)

What are the natural consequences of Kenta's action? He probably will be hungrier than usual when he arrives back at his caregiver's home after school. He also will probably remember to take his lunch the next day. If his provider, on the other hand, either (a) delivered the lunch to school or (b) dwelled on the situation after he returned from school, she would be skewing the effectiveness of the natural consequences of Kenta's behavior. In the first situation, she negates their contract that he was responsible for remembering his own lunch, and in the second, she effectively "punishes" him for his forgetfulness, making him feel ineffective and less confident that he'll be able to remember the lunch the next day.

In a second scenario, ignoring the advice of the recreation director, Detra leaves her warm jacket inside when she goes out after school to play baseball on a chilly March day. An hour in the outfield and she returns quite cold, commenting that SOMEONE should have brought her coat out to her when she got stuck out there for so long. However, the adult in charge answers, quite calmly, "No, Detra, it was your responsibility to take your coat outside or to ask someone to come in and get it for you. I will give advice about the weather but I will not take from you your right to face the consequences of your own decisions." Bailing Detra out would have taught her that someone else—not she—was responsible for her comfort (and also convinced her that, in fact, she isn't capable of taking care of herself); adding a statement such as "I told you that you'd need your coat" sends the same message. Natural consequences do not contain editorial comments and all by themselves they can be very effective teachers.

LOGICAL CONSEQUENCES

In some cases, however, natural consequences can be dangerous. No one would encourage a youth worker to send children into the ice, snow, or rain without a coat, and forgetting one's medication or one's inhaler can have disastrous effects. In these situations, adults need to help children to remember the necessary items by brainstorming memory aids. *Logical* consequences are the alternative. These also must not be enforced as punishment and should not be accompanied by sermons or threats. Rather, they involve a structuring of events so that consequences naturally flow from the misdeed.

If, for example, Priya has not finished putting away the game she's been dawdling over for 20 minutes by the time the play supervisor leaves for the outdoor playground, she will logically need to stay inside with the program supervisor and finish the task. This is not "punishment" (unless it is presented as such); it is just the logical consequence of failing to act in a timely manner.

In the same manner, if 8-year-old Marcus spills paint on the table beside the easel, it is logical that he needs to help clean it up. And if he splashes paint on the children sitting on the table, or pours paint in their hair, it is also only logical that he should assist in the cleanup of *that* mess, as well as in the explanation that will need to be given to the parents. (It is probably also logical that Marcus be refused access to the paints for a period of time if the paint was intentionally applied to his friends' hair.) Logical consequences must be related to the behavior to be effective—requiring Priya to help make snacks because she missed the outdoor play period is not logical, nor is asking Marcus to clean all the tables in the room following the paint incident. It is important to be sure that expectations and responses are appropriate to the child's developmental level and to adjust them if they are not. Ask the youngsters—if it's not a fair consequence, they'll tell you!

Other strategies may be needed if a child's behavior continues to be a problem or if the behavior presents a threat to the safety and/or well-being of the other children. Limiting free time immediately following an infraction is often effective, especially if it is accompanied by the requirement that the child remain inside (or at least away from the other children) and in the company of a staff member during that period. This is a good time to review the cognitive modification strategies described above. Discuss the broken rules with the child and work together to figure out possible options for how to handle the situation if it occurs again. Removing privileges is next, trying to relate the privileges revoked to the infraction committed. If the child continues to break program rules and a major improvement does not seem to be taking place, it is time to involve the parents.

Involving Parents

When the techniques described above are not effective in improving a child's behavior, the child's parents should be asked to a meeting. Depending on your relationship with the family, the situation at home, and any number of things, this request may produce a reaction from total cooperation to outright unwillingness to help. In some cases, children receive punishment when they return home after such a meeting, so the interpersonal skills the caregiver brings to the meeting may positively influence the outcome of this session.

Because positive reinforcement seems to be more effective than harsh punishment for misbehavior (Ames, Ilg, & Baker, 1988; Damon, 1990; Dreikurs & Solz, 1990), setting up a daily behavior record based on changed behavior in the program is a good approach. In addition to providing a visual reminder of the behavior goals, the concept of shared responsibility for behavior management is a good model for parents, who can be encouraged to set up positive behavior charts at home with appropriate rewards for even small improvements. Once again, match the rewards for improved behavior to the rules or guidelines in question. (Logical consequences can be *positive* as well as *negative!*)

For example, if the problem was the repeated use of offensive language while playing chess with a younger child, the original consequence might well have been "no chess with William." This works as a negative consequence, of course, only if the older child *likes* playing chess with William. Let's assume for the moment that he does. If the foul language continues during chess games with others, the consequence becomes "no chess." If it spills over into other games or activities, the consequence becomes "no games with other people." Solitaire, whether with cards or on a computer screen, holds only so much fascination, so a logical reward for a day with no outbursts could be an hour of playing a game with another person. This can be gradually increased in time and in numbers of children, depending on the success of the previous play session.

Certain kinds of behaviors, such as repeated hitting, destruction of material, use of tobacco or alcohol or other drugs, stealing, and so on, harm the environment for other children and should be met with strong measures, such as suspension or exclusion from the program. Often, children, especially older ones, do not want to participate in recreational or care programs and have little motivation for following group rules. For them it becomes extremely important to create an attractive and interesting place to be, for threat of exclusion is effective at changing behavior only if it is viewed as a punishment, not a reward. More is said about designing physical environments in Chapter 8.

It is also important to build relationships with parents and families *before* you need to address behavior problems. Unfortunately, some parents may view programs for school-age children as a service, like pay-per-view television, dry cleaning, or car parking. They want to purchase the service and forget about it (Seligson & Allenson, 1993). In subsidized programs, parents pay a reduced rate or none at all, and in some drop-in programs the children walk in and out of their own accord. In these cases, the motivation for parents to be partners with program leaders may be low. Partnerships with parents must be *developed*. Skillful interpersonal relations and the creation of program policies that address parent values and needs will go a long way toward encouraging parent support and involvement. Developing policies is discussed in Chapter 13.

Assuming that rapport has already been developed with the parents of the child in question and a positive behavior record/positive consequences contract has failed to improve the child's behavior, it is now time to create a written set of behavioral criteria that the child must follow to stay in the program. Ideally, this contract will be developed by a team including a parent or other trusted adult, the child, and a member of the program staff who is close to the child. Behavior needs to change immediately, and consequences must be spelled out clearly. A time frame for exclusion should also be part of this written contract (for example, on the next occurrence of the behavior, the child will be excluded for a day, then a week, then a month). If temporary exclusion does not work, parents should be informed that they must find new arrangements within a certain time frame and helped to find a program that is more suitable for their child.

As a child and youth worker, you have a profound effect on every child with whom you come in contact. Your efforts to help children grow and develop in their ability to respect and get along with other people, to resolve conflicts, and to solve problems will have long-lasting effects on their self-concept and effectiveness as social beings. It is essential that you continue to work on your own personal development, building knowledge, skills, and sensitivity. In this way, your efforts to guide behavior will be appropriate for the children in your care, allowing you to produce an environment of caring, harmony, and mutual respect.

SUMMARY

To guide the behavior of school-age children effectively, adults should understand the factors that contribute to the way children behave. Developmental characteristics play a part, as well as individual family experiences and individual differences. The guidance system, consisting of children, adults, and the environment, plays an important role in influencing behavior. The ideas of Piaget, Kohlberg, Damon, Freud, and Bandura contribute to the development of an environment and a way of interacting with children that promotes prosocial behavior and self-help skills. Essa, Marion, Gordon, and Fink each developed techniques for guiding children's behavior, and Dreikurs and Solz identified four mistaken goals that children sometimes pursue in their quest for a feeling of belonging. Child and youth workers using these concepts can build their own interactional structure that optimizes their ability to work with the children in their care and the children's parents to set limits and encourage appropriate behavior within the school-age setting. Problem solving and conflict resolution must be *taught;* the program for school-agers is an ideal place to practice these skills.

REVIEW QUESTIONS

1. Identify three factors that contribute to the way children behave in group situations.

2. What are the three components of a guidance system?

3. Compare some developmental characteristics of 5- to 7-year-olds with those of 11- to 12-year-olds that might make guidance of mixed-age groups a challenge.

4. Give three examples of prosocial behavior and three of antisocial behavior.

5. Distinguish between modeling and instructing.

6. Develop three rules that meet Marion's criteria for "good limits."

7. What would be a logical consequence of children's failing to put away the Monopoly pieces before leaving for the day with their parents?

CHALLENGE EXERCISES

1. How can the social contract theory be used to design an effective guidance system?

2. Write an outline for a parent education program designed to reduce the number of hours children watch videos and television programs with violent content.

3. Interview a child or youth worker about behavioral contracts. Do these workers use them? How do the workers involve parents? Are the contracts effective?

4. Call programs for school-age children or your local school district and inquire about the use of conflict-resolution training in their schools. Interview a child about the process. Summarize your findings and share with your class.

TERMS TO LEARN

aggressive instinct
altruism
antisocial behavior
behavior management
behavior modification
cognitive modification strategies
complete inadequacy
conflict resolution
discipline
guidance
guidance system
logical consequences
mistaken goals
model
natural consequences
prosocial behavior
punishment
reinforce
retaliation and revenge
reward
struggle for power
undue attention
unlearned

REFERENCES
··················

Ames, L. B., Ilg, F. L., & Baker, S. M. (1988). *Your ten- to fourteen-year-old.* New York: Dell.

Bandura, A. (1969). *Principles of behavior modification.* New York: Holt, Rinehart & Winston.

Bandura, A. (1973). *Aggression: A social learning analysis.* Englewood Cliffs, NJ: Prentice Hall.

Beall, K. (1996). *Insights* (Newsletter). Gilroy, CA: Gilroy Unified School District.

Damon, W. (1990). *The moral child.* New York: Free Press.

Dreikurs, R. S., & Solz, V. (1990). *Children: The challenge.* New York: Plume Books.

Essa, E. (1990). *A practical guide to solving preschool behavior problems.* Albany, NY: Delmar.

Fink, D. (1995). *Discipline in school-age care: Control the climate, not the child.* Nashville, TN: School-Age NOTES.

Freud, S. (1957). *Civilization and its discontents* (2nd ed.). London: Hogarth. (Original work published 1930)

Friends School of Minnesota. (1997). Conflict resolution training manual. 3244 34th Avenue South, Minneapolis, Minnesota 55406.

Gordon, T. (1974). *Teacher effectiveness training.* New York: David McKay.

Leach, P. (1994). *Children first.* New York: Alfred A. Knopf.

Levin, D. E. (1994). *Teaching young children in violent times: Building a peaceable classroom.* Cambridge, MA: Educators for Social Responsibility.

Lorenz, K. (1966). *On aggression.* New York: Harcourt Brace & World.

Marion, M. (1987). *Guidance of young children* (2nd ed.). Columbus, OH: Merrill.

Seligson, M., & Allenson, M. (1993). *School-age child care: An action manual for the 90s and beyond.* Westport, CT: Auburn House.

CHAPTER EIGHT

Environments for Care of School-Age Children

There is no one best out-of-school arrangement for all families. A wide variety of provisions will probably always be necessary in each community to meet diverse and changing needs. Some children will spend only part of an afternoon or a few afternoons a week in care; others will need supervision before and after school each day and for as many as 9 or more hours during school holidays and vacations. The facilities that house these children will also be varied. Some children will go to private homes after school; others to multipurpose rooms, classrooms, or portable buildings on their school playground; still others to unused gymnasiums or warehouses. But all these facilities will have one thing in common: Once they have been transfigured with imagination and love, they can become great places for children.

This chapter is about environments for children. Environments for out-of-school care should reflect the variety of cultures present in your community and the diversity of their interests and experiences. Many of the ideas presented here will be useful to Scout leaders, coaches, church-school teachers, camp directors, or other youth workers, but the main focus is on settings for school-age child care. These programs themselves come in a variety of forms, and they may be housed in many different kinds of buildings. Some of the most common settings are reviewed below.

Settings for School-Age Child Care

PRIVATE HOMES

Licensed or registered family child-care facilities are usually housed in one of two ways. Either the family members share living space with the children who

145

arrive each day, or a separate portion of the family home, often a converted family room or garage, is set aside for their exclusive use. In the first case, one or two rooms may contain books, games, art supplies, and other materials intended primarily for day care children's use. The children should also have access to the family kitchen, living rooms, bathroom facilities, and an outside play area. The caregiver may set certain "inside" and "outside" times, or allow the children to move freely from one place to another throughout the time they are there.

In other settings, caregivers have made major modifications to a family recreation room, garage, or basement, creating a substantial area dedicated to the children's use. In some cases, entrances and exits have been designed so that children in care need never enter the main house but instead have their own access to materials, the outdoors, and toilet facilities. Ideally in such a situation, a small kitchen area has also been constructed to allow the preparation of after-school snacks, cooking projects, and other activities.

SCHOOL-SITE CENTERS

Before- and after-school care sites located on school grounds also come in several forms. Programs run by school districts may be allocated a classroom for their exclusive use, although in heavily populated school districts this is unlikely. More commonly, program leaders may be offered the use of one or more regular classrooms before and after school and on holidays, if cooperation can be obtained from the teachers assigned to those classrooms in the daytime. This arrangement requires teachers to share their "territory" and sometimes give up precious preparation time, so good communication is necessary for it to work well.

Some schools establish before- and after-school centers in the school library or in a multipurpose room or gymnasium. Well-funded programs may even be able to obtain a portable classroom. (This seems to be the option most often used by school-site programs administered by agencies other than the school.) The most suitable relocatable buildings contain wheelchair-accessible bathrooms and a kitchen area. Programs housed in classroom space, whatever its form, should also have access to the school playground, the library, and the gym or multipurpose room.

CHURCHES, MOSQUES, OR SYNAGOGUES

Programs housed in buildings used for religious education or worship may find that sharing space with the owners is the only option. This may not be a major problem, however, since such facilities often sit unused during weekdays. Some wonderful facilities can be obtained this way, often affording both cozy rooms and larger halls for program use than can be obtained in private homes or public buildings. However, just as in school classrooms, sharing space requires good communication. More will be said about that later.

PERMANENT OR RELOCATABLE BUILDINGS NOT ON SCHOOL SITES

Some programs have the luxury of occupying a building that can be used exclusively by school-agers or at least has a separate area or room set aside for that purpose. This allows program staff and children to construct an environment that is just right for them. Many more options can be exercised in such a setting than in a shared facility, although careful planning is necessary to carry these ideas to fruition. Some large purpose-built centers have been designed by architects, presumably with good intentions, who appear never to have watched children play and work together. It is imperative that school-age children and the professionals who care for them be consulted in the design phase to keep that from happening to *your* building.

Environments for Care of School-Age Children

Both indoor and outdoor environments should be designed to meet the unique physical needs of school-age children and to encourage independent play and creativity. Indoor space should be large enough that children can work and play without crowding each other or interfering with one another's activities; adequate storage space allows you to keep accessible those things that are used often while storing away equipment and materials you need less frequently.

Both indoor and outdoor settings should accommodate a variety of play equipment as well as provide sheltered areas for quiet play. Ideally, outdoor areas should provide adequate space for sports, group games, and more individual activities such as bicycle riding, jump rope, and roller skating. Indoor spaces should allow the types of individual and group activities school-age children need and enjoy, such as reading, doing homework, listening to music, playing board games, making crafts, or cooking (California Child Care Resource and Referral Network, 1986). This can be done with permanent climbing structures and indoor lofts or with movable dividers or cardboard boxes. The important thing is that children have choices and that they be encouraged to take initiative and explore their interests. One guideline is to provide twice as many play spaces as there are children on the playground: "If fifty children are on the playground, then there should be one hundred places where children could be doing something. Children who can be actively playing in designated spaces will have fewer problems getting along, and fewer chances to be doing something they should not be doing" (Pratt, 1995, p. 5). Because children grow significantly between the ages of 5 and 12, programs serving those ages should invest in furniture and permanent play equipment that accommodates a variety of sizes and offers progressive challenges (Roman, 1998).

Whatever the setting, all environments where children spend a large part of their time should have certain elements. Environments for children have been described as having three dimensions: physical, temporal, and interpersonal (Gordon & Brown, 1993). The ***physical environment*** consists of the grounds and the structure—the furnishings and equipment as well as the light, color, and sound present in those spaces. Programs for school-agers often have little control over the location of their site, but wonderful areas have been created in multipurpose rooms, warehouses, and even outbuildings on fairground sites.

The ***temporal environment*** refers to the way in which time is managed. Is the time children spend in the program strictly scheduled, with little slivers of the day allocated to particular activities, such as recording attendance, standing in line to go outside, "game time," "music time," "homework time," and so on? Or does the amount of time allotted to various program elements flex and adjust to meet children's needs? Are children repeatedly rushed to complete tasks in a specified period of time, or may they safely store partially completed projects until they have the desire or opportunity to complete them? Be sure to allow plenty of time for children to accomplish what they start.

The ***interpersonal*** dimension of the environment has to do with the nature of relationships between and among children, staff, and parents as well as between members of the related community, such as classroom teachers, nearby business people, or clergy. Are they formal or informal, inclusive or exclusive, strict or permissive, hierarchical or egalitarian? This dimension is also affected by the ages and numbers of children and staff and the styles of social interaction between and among them. When all three dimensions in the caregiving environment are carefully considered, when the environment appeals to children and meets their physical and emotional needs, the before- and after-school centers will be *nurturing, attractive, interesting,* and *safe.*

A NURTURING ENVIRONMENT

Most children, when asked, would tell you they'd rather go home after school, even to an empty house, than stay in a child-care center. One of the ways in which youth leaders can change this opinion is by providing physical arrangements and materials that make children feel welcome and that support their developmental needs. Within this cozy and comfortable environment, caregivers interact with children in honest, open ways, and show interest in their lives and relationships. A ***nurturing*** environment such as this is ***supportive*** of children and their priorities. Adults in nurturing environments communicate with body language as well as words: "We enjoy having you here; you are a valuable part of our after-school community; you have interesting things to say; we care about each of you personally."

A nurturing, supportive environment contains logical groupings of interesting areas with rich resources; there are boundaries separating noisy and quiet areas, and children can select from a variety of developmentally valid activities or just "hang out." In contrast, in a ***nonsupportive*** environment, arbitrary rules are imposed; children's movements are rigidly controlled; materials are disorganized and often in short supply. Guidance experts tell us that in supportive settings, children interact on a personal level with involved adults, have opportunities to influence the nature and arrangement of their surroundings, and are allowed to move around freely, play on the floor if they like, and

A well-designed environment allows for a variety of activities to take place simultaneously.

change activities as they wish. These environments not only invite children to stay and play, but they also foster positive adaptive behavior and promote the development of self-control and mastery (Marion, 1987).

When little thought is given to enhancing the comfort and attractiveness of a space, it frequently appears inhospitable, boring, shabby. Adults who do not understand or encourage children's need to influence their surroundings and interact with one another may appear to be hostile when they are actually fearful of losing control. The effect on the children, unfortunately, is the same. (Remember the parent helper at Disneyland in Chapter 3?)

Children in a supportive physical environment are actually *encouraged* to move around and interact with the things and the people in that environment. Furniture and materials are arranged to encourage the formation of small work groups, allow quiet and noisy activities to occur at the same time, and to permit privacy for those who wish it. Trees or equipment allow children to climb, swing, and jump from safe heights. The developmentally appropriate school-age environment should accommodate children of different ages who wish to work individually, in small groups, or in large groups and with varying degrees of independence and self-direction (Albrecht & Plantz, 1993). It might even have a separate area for older school-agers and an overstuffed sofa or a bench in a shaded area where children can curl up with their favorite caregiver to exchange confidences or seek solace. Because after-school children arrive at different times of the day than younger half-day or all-day children, separate entry and play areas can minimize interruptions and distractions to children already engaged in play.

Nurturing children also includes nurturing their interests. This requires having enough supplies for a variety of different activities to take place simultaneously, and to allow for changing interests. Let the children guide this process, and encourage them to help collect the needed material. One school-age group may want to collect rocks and minerals; another build a complex maze/house for their pet guinea pig. Football and baseball cards, milk caps ("pogs"), Barbie dolls, friendship bracelets, and marbles all have a place in a supportive environment for children. Follow the fad of the moment, and help the children collect the materials they need to build/collect/trade/play with their friends.

Nurturing environments are primarily **child centered** or **child responsive,** not **adult centered.** Adults who work with children in after-school settings must be willing to respect and listen to them. Frequently, they should follow the children's lead when planning activities, arranging furniture, purchasing supplies, even setting limits for behavior. Child-responsive programs are all about meeting children's physical, social, and emotional needs, giving wings to their ideas and interests, not about satisfying adult needs to control behavior, lead games, or solve disagreements. Some school-age professionals even warn against hiring education students or primary grade teachers or others trained in the "old-style industrial methods of elementary education," fearing that they may not be able to step out of the role for which they have been trained: "Their prior experience, with its emphasis on controlling children's behavior, runs contrary to SACC precepts. Letting children play and socialize as they please takes a good deal more self-restraint than these people can usually exercise (Seligson & Allenson, 1993).

Whether or not that is true in all cases, the people who work with school-age children must have secure enough egos to set aside their own agendas and allow children to say what matters to them, and how they want to spend their time. Self-selection, rather than staff-selection, of activities and experiences should be the usual practice; required participation in activities should be very rare and serve a clear purpose that is important to the children or the program as a whole (Albrecht & Plantz, 1993). To ignore this guideline is to doom a program to failure. Researchers describing a summer recreation program in East London showed what this might look like:

> The [program] was held in a two-room community centre with no playground. In one room a worker organises children in dramatic play. She shouts at them to sit down and pay attention, says that if they are not going to join in they may sit at one side of the room and watch others, but not do anything else. A child of about six or seven cries and says he wants to go home—home is in the housing estate just outside the door. The worker leaves the other children in order to restrain him from running out. The room is dark and hot. Later in the day the children [are] taken to a park to play. On the estate outside the centre, other children, not in the playscheme, are riding their bikes, sitting talking in doorways, and playing.
>
> —Petrie & Logan, 1986, p. 27

Keeping art supplies stocked and accessible is one way of communicating to the children that they are capable and trustworthy.

Research to learn why available care programs for school-agers are underutilized repeatedly produces the same reason from parents: Their children don't want to attend the programs in existence. Further questioning frequently elicits one or more of these three explanations: The programs are "boring"; the caregivers are "bossy"; and "I'd rather play with my friends" (Bumgarner, 1995; Coleman, Robinson, & Rowland, 1991; Zigler & Lang, 1991).

Successful programs have addressed each of these issues. Over and over it can be shown that caregivers who create supportive environments and nurture children's interests attract new families to their programs in the very best way possible: Children tell their friends.

Yet *child responsive* does not mean *child managed*. Program leaders still need to determine and implement the philosophy, goals, and objectives of the program and set the boundaries for behavior. Program leaders certainly should listen to children while planning activities, but children need adults to provide models of behavior, suggest problem-solving strategies, and give assistance in working with others toward a goal.

Homework and the Nurturing Environment   The issue of child-responsive versus adult-centered programming leads rather naturally into a discussion of homework. School-age child care is an important part of the complex process of socialization. Caregivers need to work as partners with parents and other adults to provide the role modeling, guiding, and teaching necessary to prepare children for full participation in society. When both parents work or when a lone working parent is managing a household of children, finding the time to support children's out-of-school studies and projects can be very difficult. In such

Be sure there are plenty of opportunities to work or play in solitude.

circumstances, it is understandable if parents ask caregivers to provide time, space, and encouragement for their children to complete their homework.

But how does a child-responsive caregiver ensure that children actually *do* this? Is it the job of the caregiver to be a "police person"? Should persuasive, even coercive techniques be used to assure that the homework is done before other activities are pursued? This is an issue hotly debated at workshops and professional meetings, in staff rooms, and during parent conferences, mostly without satisfactory conclusions.

Many professionals in school-age care maintain that supervising homework should not be their responsibility. In some communities, that is a valid and effective posture. In some schools, children are expected to complete all school tasks within the school day, taking home only the work they did not finish in the time allowed. In other areas, however, children are given a fairly sizable number of out-of-school assignments, and youngsters in after-school care really do need time, an appropriate place, and the necessary equipment to work on them.

Depending on the academic priorities and needs of the community in which your center is located, you will need to determine the provisions for homework necessary in your center and how much time will be allotted to doing it. This can be a real controversy and is best done in conjunction with parents and children. Schedules may need to be adjusted throughout the year as needs change. In most programs, the best arrangement seems to be to leave the motivation for completion of tasks to the teachers and parents, concentrating instead on providing support for children's efforts by providing a physical and interpersonal environment that nurtures their desire to learn.

A child-responsive approach to a homework center will probably include roomy tables and chairs, a world globe, encyclopedias, dictionaries, rulers, pencils, scissors, and other supplies; it may also include some soft pillows and a sofa or two for reading, a computer, and perhaps even music. Whenever possible, accommodate children's different learning styles, allowing them to do their homework in the way that best suits them.

Adult-centered programs tend toward large bare tables, chairs, and no talking. Many children prefer do their homework on the floor, listening to music (headphones take care of the needs of others for a quiet atmosphere). Others benefit from the opportunity to talk over strategies and ideas with their friends or even to take breaks from studying or working to chat about their day (Bumgarner, 1993). Both styles of learners need resources to complete many of the tasks they have been assigned. Once again, adults who trust children to find their own way will be most likely to see exactly those results (see Table 4-4, a listing of Gardner's Multiple Intelligences, for additional ideas about homework environments).

Try to have enough staff members present to allow children free movement between the activity/homework centers and a gym or outdoor recreation area. No child whose body is crying for physical activity should be forced to remain inside for an arbitrary period of "study time" before being allowed to go outside and play. But the reverse is also true; too many children are required to spend long hours sitting on the edge of a playground that holds no interest for them when they would prefer to be inside playing games, working on crafts, or even reading or doing their homework. Although staffing regulations vary, a ratio of one adult to eight children is a good goal, with no fewer than two adults inside or outside at a time; this distribution will allow children to move between intense and relaxed activities in a natural way.

Sometimes children with special needs have personal attendants or aides to assist regular staff to meet their unique needs. Aides need to be included in planning as part of the staff, not just left sitting off in the corner alone with their charges. Also important is for the aides to interact with other children in the program so that the children with special needs are included as part of the larger group. Children with disabilities are children first. Be sure to encourage them to play and enjoy themselves.

Long-range homework projects are often assigned to children age 9 and older. Sometimes working in groups is permitted or even encouraged by the classroom teacher, and the after-school environment is an ideal setting for this to take place. Youth workers can facilitate children's developing ability to brainstorm, plan, compromise, and complete complex tasks by listening to their ideas, making suggestions, and helping them obtain the necessary materials or tools for their projects. Sometimes one staff member can be spared for a field trip to the public library, a tug on working parents' time that often gets neglected. Most children appreciate the recognition that their school

Sharing space with another agency may allow you to purchase equipment cooperatively.

responsibilities are serious. In these and other ways, when children's homework needs are considered in the planning of a before- and after-school environment, the "police" aspect of homework supervision may disappear completely.

The Challenge of Shared Space   Children and staff in programs for school-agers deserve to have a place of their own to go before and after school as well as during the holidays and summer vacations. However, space is in short supply in many communities, and out-of-school programs often find themselves housed in shared space such as a multipurpose room, gymnasium, cafeteria, recreation center, or even a classroom. School-agers who have lived with shared facilities often report feeling like second-class citizens; their long-term projects are moved or even destroyed, personal possessions left in cubby holes disappear, artwork is torn from walls. Even if the space you use is also used by other organizations, when your children are present, they should be able to feel that the area is "all theirs."

One way this can be accomplished is by negotiating a shared-use agreement with the other agency or groups using the facility (Bellum, 1990a). A roundtable discussion and brainstorming session with representatives from each group can prevent uncertainties, resentments, or unfair situations from developing later on. If possible, arrange to have at least one child from your program present for this discussion; children often think of possibilities adults forget ("Will the bathrooms be unlocked?" "Can we use the computer?"). Be sure you know exactly how many hours a day you will have exclusive use of the room and when you may also enter for preparation or meetings. Decide together who will be responsible for cleaning, purchasing bathroom supplies, securing building maintenance, and providing security. How much space do you have for storage? This is important if you will be creating and dismantling the environment every day or even every week. Does the landlord (often a church or a school) have the right to "bump" your program for special events or meetings? If so, where will you go?

You can use equipment owned by your program as bargaining tools, and your generosity might result in permission to use equipment or resources belonging to one of the other groups using the facility or the landlord agency itself. For instance, photocopiers, computers, telephones, fax machines, or laminating machines could be shared by several groups, even purchased jointly if the trust level is high enough. Creative problem solving can go a long way in developing ways to share the cost of supplies or utilities equitably. Once the terms are settled, get them in writing. Memories can be unpredictable, and staff can change. If possible, arrange to have periodic meetings with all users of the facility to work out any difficulties that may arise later.

The ideas presented in this chapter for making the program feel friendly—especially encouraging mutual respect and tolerance—should be kept in mind when working in shared space. Get to know your neighbors, especially if others who use the facility are lukewarm or hostile to your use of the space. Go out of your way to meet the administrators, teachers, secretaries, janitors, parents, parishioners. Share information, invite them to potluck dinners and special events. Win them over with your commitment to the community and to high-quality out-of-school care.

Once the negotiations are complete and you know where and when you will be housed, how much storage space you will have, how much freedom you have to use wall space or move furniture, you must design your environment for flexibility and portability. Interest areas can be created as kits that can be set up quickly and stored easily—large plastic storage boxes are helpful here. Clearly marked labels on the ends of each box can help staff and children select the interest areas they wish to use each day. Allocate staff time for retrieving materials from closets and setting up furniture, unrolling rugs, laying out supplies, and hanging up banners, artwork, or posters, then storing them all at the end of the day or the week. Do not give in to the temptation to cut corners and leave everything in boxes or on carts; no matter how portable it is, the environment should make children feel that it was designed especially for them if they are going to enjoy being there.

AN ATTRACTIVE ENVIRONMENT

Most children spend their school days in fairly structured classroom settings, with assigned seating, scheduled activities, and a series of assignments to complete. Effective programs for school-agers offer a change from this, allowing children a chance to relax, socialize, and choose the way they wish to spend their time. An attractive, homelike environment will reflect the personalities

A multipurpose room site presents a real challenge to program design.

and cultures of the children in it, and it will change over time with their interests and needs.

One way to learn what environments youngsters consider attractive is to visit their bedrooms at home. Younger children tend make nests on the floor or their bed using pillows or stuffed animals; some create thematic play areas with action figures. Older children make statements on the walls with posters, T-shirts, CD-cases, or bumper stickers. Siblings sharing rooms often create boundaries with bookcases or lines of possessions, or cooperate in the creation of larger floor spaces by moving desks or beds to one side of the room.

Actual field trips to bedrooms are probably impractical, so talk with children about what can be done with the space at hand to make it cozy and comfortable. Brainstorm freely at first, with no discussions or arguments; just list all the ideas on a large piece of paper or board for later discussion. Programs in shared space may need to transform a gymnasium, cafeteria, classroom, or auditorium into a nurturing play space every day. However, many programs do this quite successfully, with movable panels made from corrugated cardboard appliance boxes, thin sheets of Styrofoam or other lightweight material, giant hanging banners, furniture on wheels, and carts bursting with supplies, books, games, and equipment. The more challenging the setting, the more fun everyone can have transforming it into a welcoming place. Children can draw sketches, help hang draperies and wall coverings, and paint furniture. Posters of "heroes"—able-bodied and otherwise—help to set a tone for acceptance, high goals, and familiarity.

Four components of the environment that influence its attractiveness are *furnishings, light, color,* and *sound.* Another important consideration is a *provision for privacy.*

Furnishings   **Furnishings** (Including Equipment and Materials) should reflect the variety of activities that take place in a center for school-agers as well as the differing ages of the clients. Be sure there are adequate tables and different-size matching chairs so that each child can find room to play a board game, study or do homework, read a book, or draw. But also provide softer furnishings—cushions, beanbag chairs, overstuffed chairs or sofas, throw rugs, and gymnastic mats. Fabric wall coverings, banners, posters, and paintings add texture and interest. They should be topical and colorful and should reflect the children in the program. Be prepared to adapt the environment creatively for children with disabilities as they become part of your program.

Basic equipment should include outdoor sports equipment such as several different kinds of balls, bats, skipping ropes, hula hoops, tug of war ropes, Pogo sticks, portable goal nets, and yo-yos. Have supplies for indoor activities such as board games, magnets, mixing bowls, measuring cups or scales, sewing machine, sponge and brushes, paints, colored chalks, interlocking plastic blocks, a globe, and a set of encyclopedias. Koralek et al. (1995, p. 201) suggest that program staff ask the following questions when selecting materials and equipment for an out-of-school program:

1. Will it interest the children?
2. Do the children have the skills to handle it?
3. Will it challenge the children to think and explore?
4. Does the material reflect the children's ethnicity, show people with disabilities engaged in meaningful tasks, or allow both boys and girls to see themselves in nonstereotyped roles?
5. Is the item durable and in good condition?
6. Does it help achieve your goals for children?

Table 8-1 lists a set of goals for children in out-of-school programs and links them with materials and activities that support those goals. By developing such a chart for your own program, you can identify equipment and materials that you "must have" or "would like to obtain" and work toward acquiring them. This wish list of desired materials and equipment should be developed with the children and purchased as the budget allows.

Light and Color   Light and color can set moods that contribute to the emotional well-being of the children and adults in a child-care environment. Be sure there is adequate light wherever children play and work; also, the *nature* of the light-

TABLE 8-1   Selecting Activities and Materials to Meet Program Goals

Goals	Possible activities	Suggested materials
Stimulate children's imagination and creativity	Reading, storytelling, acting, painting, dressing up, building, playing house, adventure play, cutting and pasting, modeling	Paint, wet sand, building blocks, music, pencils and crayons, cars, trains, animals, dolls, construction materials
Enrich language development	Talking, asking questions, listening, recalling experiences, having discussions about home and everyday life	Tape recorders, microphones, puppet theatres, dollhouses
Form the basis of mathematical understanding	Describing, comparing, explaining, classifying, matching, sorting, combining, dividing, pairing	Sand, water, building blocks, wood, collections of objects, construction materials, puzzles, number games
Enable children to come to terms with aspects of their own lives and to express their feelings	Engaging in "playing house," writing or telling stories, conversing, listening to others, reading	Dramatic play materials, paper and writing materials, paint, multicultural books and dolls, pictures, puppets
Encourage the development of manipulative skills	Cutting, sticking, sorting, piecing together puzzles, building with manipulatives, blocks, or wood, cooking, printing, painting	Dough, clay, wood, pencils, crayons, puzzles, paints and water, construction and cooking materials, rubber stamps
Offer the chance to explore and enjoy natural materials	Walking and working out of doors, collecting, sorting, planting, weeding, harvesting, painting with natural materials, making collages	Water, clay, wet and dry sand, wood, earth (soil), leaves, fabric, corks, shells, stones, gardening tools
Develop muscular strength and coordination	Building, climbing and balancing, running, skipping, pushing, pulling, jumping, playing with balls, woodworking, rolling, hopping, throwing, crawling, swimming	Climbing and gymnastics equipment, balls, bats, tumbling mats, access to swimming pool, lake, river, or seaside, woodworking tools
Establish the use of symbols and patterns that form the basis of reading and writing	Painting, writing stories, imaginative play, piecing together puzzles, writing names of objects	Pictures, posters, puzzles, written names, paint, stories, pencils and crayons, beads, and pegboards
Help children to respect and enjoy companionship of other children and adults	Conversation, imaginative and adventure play, sharing jokes, long-term building projects	Things to share (e.g., climbing frame, road layout, home corner), joint activities (e.g., singing, outings, stories), construction materials
Create habits of listening and concentrating	Singing, learning rhymes, listening to stories, taking part in conversations	Songs, rhymes, stories, music, games, telephone, sound games
Extend children's understanding of science and the world around them	Problem solving, reading, cooking, doing investigations and experiments, talking to guest speakers	Books, water, magnets, lenses, mirrors, wood, living and growing things, visitors
Respond to children's continued need to explore through their senses	Modeling, playing with different materials, making collages, listening to music, matching scents and sounds	Fingerpaint, dough, water, dry and wet sand, sounds, scents, wood, music

Source: Adapted from Bradford Social Services, 1995, pp. 14–15.

ing fixtures is particularly important in an indoor after-school environment. Most children arriving in the afternoon will be coming from school, where they will in all probability have been working for several hours under uniform (and probably flickering) fluorescent lights or high-pressure sodium vapor lighting, both of which can cause eye fatigue and stress (Hales, 1994; Olds, 1988).

Natural light may be the best choice for room illumination if there are adequate windows to provide it. If not, incandescent or tungsten lamps, alone or in conjunction with fluorescent fixtures, can offer a refreshing change from classroom lighting, and the color of the light they produce is more pleasing to the eyes. Individual desk and table lamps placed strategically can add color and interest to the room. If you must live with tube fittings, try replacing the fluorescents with full-spectrum or color-corrected lamps, which radiate a warm light. Several studies replacing old fluorescent lights with full-spectrum lighting have shown significant benefits to health and academic performance It is also important to change fluorescent tubes as soon as they begin to flicker, an early sign of deterioration (Sudjik, 1985). Rooms with large banks of windows should have curtains, draperies, or blinds to reduce glare from early morning or late afternoon sun.

Color has been known for many years to influence mood. Color consultants can create an air of calm reassurance in a hospital or a cheerful, stimulating atmosphere around a factory assembly line simply by their selection of color for wall coverings and furniture. The successful use of color in a school-age setting requires that you not only balance colors but also distribute them well. If you have the option, use a light hue for walls and floor coverings, then allow children to help you plan accents with more intense hues in the furnishings, throw pillows, wall hangings, or accessories. These things can be changed as desired without major redecorating (Healey, 1982; Time-Life Books, 1988).

Sound   Some settings, such as cafeterias and gymnasiums, have such a characteristically high noise level that viewing a photograph of children playing in these environments will cause people to clap their hands to their ears in sympathy. Yet many before- and after-school programs must operate daily under such conditions.

Other sound disturbances can be created by vocal dramatizations such as those stimulated by action figures, fashion dolls, or road building and block play; computer sound effects; or music played on portable "boom boxes." To help with sound overlap and intrusion, the walls of rooms with bright acoustics can be lined with cloth, or sound can be muffled by the use of appliance boxes and large pillows. Programs trying to offer quiet activities in noisy locations (e.g., plagued with traffic or gymnasium noise) might want to build acoustic dividers by covering sheets of Styrofoam with mattress padding or foam; soft music can help here, also. Good planning of the environment includes separating loud and quiet activities with bookcases or other dividers, directing speakers away from other people, and using headphones whenever possible. Be conscious of the effect sound can have when it spills over into someone else's area and involve the affected children in the problem-solving process.

PERSPECTIVE

Women Who Make a Difference for the Love of Children

THREE WOMEN TACKLE CRIME, GANGS AND HOMELESSNESS*

Ellen Sherman

DOLORES BEALL

On a sunny Sunday afternoon in the fall of 1985, Dolores Beall of Dallas, Texas, drove to church in her new car. As she parked in front, she noticed a group of six teenage boys hanging out. Fearful that these kids might be responsible for recent vandalism in the parking lot, she made a preemptive strike. "I drove up with my radio playing loud and screeched my brakes," Dolores recalls. "I got out and told them they better not touch my car." At 6 feet tall, Dolores Beall is a commanding presence. On a whim, she invited the boys to join a marching band she had organized for the homecoming parade of a local college.

To Dolores's surprise, one of the boys showed up at the church for practice and brought along some friends. For a month a dozen kids met twice a week to perfect the routine. Three boys learned to play the field drums Dolores had bought at a pawn shop. And one day, during an outdoor rehearsal, they gained 20 new members as children age 7 to 17 simply stepped into the formation.

The parade went off without a hitch. And after it was over, the kids continued to congregate at the church where they had spent so many hours having fun.

Dolores kept coming back too. She talked with the kids for hours and listened to their needs and worries. She always tried to find solutions. If one child was having trouble learning to read, she brought in books and coached one-on-one. If another was hungry, she gave food. Without planning to, Dolores had created a safe place for poor kids of Dallas, many of whom had been abused or neglected. Nearly all of them werer in search of the home they never had.

*Note: This article is excerpted, only one story is printed here.

"These kids have it rough, especially the teenagers," Dolores says. "Without guidance, a lot of them head in the wrong direction."

For three years Dolores carried on her volunteer efforts informally. Then, in March 1988, something happened that brought everything into focus. As she drove down a neighborhood street, she saw three children walking along the side of the road. She recognized one of them from the marching band. The 9-year-old girl was carrying her 2-year-old sister, and their 7-year-old brother followed with milk and disposable diapers. They were returning home after spending the night at a friend's house because their mother had disappeared days before.

"Too often disadvantaged kids are expected to assume adult responsibilities," she says. "No child should have to do that."

Dolores revved up her volunteer operation and moved from the church basement to a two-bedroom house, which she rented for $270 a month. She applied for nonprofit status and gave her mission a name: The I Am That I Am Center. "It's a tongue-twister, but it means: I'm a child. Don't make a grown-up out of me," Dolores says.

The center became a one-stop shop for neglected kids. They'd show up after school for help with homework or anything else. They learned everything from proper nutrition to good hygiene to job-hunting skills.

Dolores's friends and church members got involved too, donating time and expertise. She arranged field trips to local businesses, which gave the children a glimpse of working life. She reached out to celebrities, asking people like TV comedian Jamie Foxx and boxing champion Joe Frazier to visit the center. And they did.

Today, 13 years later, Dolores is still going strong. Monetary donations from individuals and corporate foundations meant the center could move to a nicer building. For the 5,000 or so children who have passed through its doors, Dolores is the mother they so desperately need.

One 13-year-old boy avoided a fight by using the conflict resolution techniques he learned from Dolores. "I'm real proud of myself for not fighting," the boy told her.

When Sharon Woodberry was a teenager, she hung out with drug dealers and gang members. "Ms. Beall showed me my potential," she says. It took long hours of studying, but Sharon earned a spot in the National Honor Society. She attended college on an academic scholarship and became an accountant. "Ms. Beall never gave up on me," she says. "I'll never forget it."

Source: Family Circle, (1998, March) pp. 20–22.

Provision for Privacy   One of the most frequently voiced complaints from youngsters interviewed about their child-care settings is that they are never able to get away from the other children and "just be alone." In a home setting, most of us find it possible to slip away from the action occasionally, even if it is only to a bedroom or a secluded corner of the garden. Privacy and alone-time are especially important for children who exhibit what Howard Gardner (1993) calls *intrapersonal intelligence*—a strong sense of the self and a desire to understand it better. Forcing introspective children to join groups and interact after they've just spent 6 to 8 hours in a classroom is inconsiderate and unwise.

Children need to be alone sometimes, and it is important to have more than one place for that to happen. A common solution is to have a designated "quiet area," usually stocked with books and magazines, soft seating, and a plush rug. This is fine, unless two children want to read together and plan to do so out loud. Another option is to have one or two comfortable chairs situated away from other activity areas, possibly with a reading lamp on a side table. A third approach, used in home settings for generations, is to drape a sheet or blanket over a table to make a tent. Folding foam pads, or Japanese-style *shiki-butons* can also be arranged on their sides to create interesting walls for children to climb inside. These hide-away spots can provide restful places for reading and homework or for playing quiet board games with a friend. At the same time, however, all areas must be within someone's earshot or line of sight. There is a fine line between privacy and a dangerous lack of supervision.

Finally, simply having a place to be alone and quiet will not assure that children who need to be alone will necessarily manage to do so. School-age youths are often so intensely involved in social development that if large group activities are always happening, they will always choose to engage in them. Program planning that includes periods of "down time" with no planned activities ensures that this developmental need to think, unwind, and mull things over can be met (Bellum, 1990b).

AN INTERESTING ENVIRONMENT

Interesting—that is a value-laden word. What is interesting to one child may be boring to another; in fact, it undoubtedly will be. So an *interesting* environment must offer a wide variety of activities for youngsters, ranging from quiet solitary pursuits to noisy large group games.

Most child-development professionals agree that the goals of school-age care programs should be clearly differentiated from those of the educational institutions in which the children spend the bulk of their days. Bergstrom (1984) suggests that out-of-school time is well spent developing the "other 3Rs"—resourcefulness, responsibility, and reliability. School-agers, described by Erikson as balancing *industry versus inferiority,* are especially interested in feeling productive and useful, doing real work rather than pretending, using adult tools and learning adult skills.

Planning activities that offer children these opportunities is one way of ensuring that the program is interesting. Construction projects, inside and outside the children's own center, can do this. Service projects such as gardening, window washing, making aprons or beanbags for a nearby preschool, or similar pursuits allow children to develop and practice a variety of new skills while simultaneously connecting them with community needs. Remember, however, that goal-oriented and community service activities are important, but a steady diet of them can lead to burnout; children need time to pursue their own interests, make new friends, and enjoy one another's company—in other words, time simply to be children.

Variety of Materials   Make sure you have a sufficient quantity and variety of play materials. Provide lots of **open materials** that have no single "correct" outcome. These include blocks, clay, paints, and what facility designer Jim Greenman (1992) calls **loose parts**—"materials that can be used together, combined, collected, sorted, separated or pulled apart, lined up, dumped, etc." Other examples of loose parts include rocks, sticks, leaves, paper, cardboard, poker chips, bottle caps, nuts, bolts, screws, or washers. Send home notes asking for miscellaneous stuff, provide milk crates and shoeboxes to keep it in, and stand back.

Room Arrangement and Interest Areas   Flexibility is important, but there is also merit in arranging the environment with relatively permanent boundaries and traffic patterns. If certain areas are designated for quiet study and reflection, for instance, it is easier for children to know where to go for solitude and where *not* to sit while excitedly planning a project or outing. A well-arranged physical space with clear limits suggests intersting things to do, but it also helps children match their behavior to the setting. Children wishing to engage in noisy activities should be able to do so without disturbing the rest of the group; painting or cooking activities should be located near a source of water. The reading and writing area needs adequate light, and computers, tape players, or compact disc players need a power outlet.

Usually, a more effective use of space is to turn bookcases and dividers edgeways from walls as area boundaries rather than leaving them parallel to the walls with large open areas in the middle of the room. Turn sofas and chairs at angles around a rug with their backs to other interest areas, facing one another to encourage conversation. There should be plenty of tables, floor mats, chairs, and shelves.

As you plan your room layout, also consider the active ways in which school-age children move from one place to another. Provide clear, spacious pathways to the outside area, to the bathrooms, and to all doors and especially to fire exits. Allowing 12" to 18" around all furniture and other permanent objects in the room will reduce unnecessary bumps and accidents. Figure 8–1 shows two ways this can be done. A good way to plan room arrangement is to draw the available space on graph paper. Each piece of furniture, divider, and so forth can then be drawn to scale and cut out so it can be moved around on the paper until a satisfactory arrangement is found. This method can save lots of sore backs and sharp words.

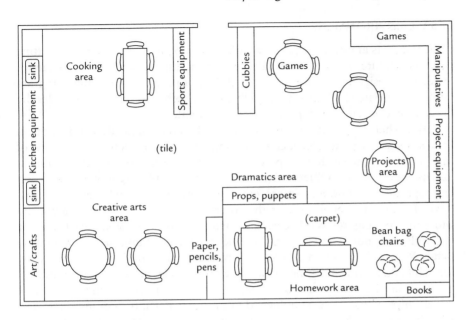

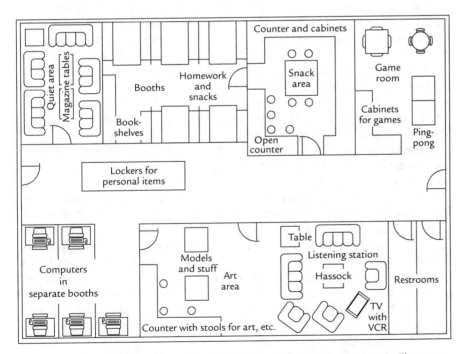

FIGURE 8-1 Sample Floor Plans Careful planning of furniture arrangement will encourage interaction and creativity. *Source:* Eddowes, E. A., & Ralph, K. S. (1998). *Interactions for development and learning.* Columbus, OH: Merrill and Decker, C. A., & Decker, J. R. (1997). *Planning and administering early childhood programs* (6th ed.). Upper Saddle River, NJ: Prentice Hall.

A SAFE ENVIRONMENT

When parents are asked what they look for in a before- or after-school setting for their children, "safe" is usually first on the list. It can be a challenge for caregivers designing environments for children to create an appealing program with appropriate challenges for rapidly growing school-agers that provides the level of security and safety parents need and want.

But what do parents mean by "safe?" To understand this and begin to develop a safety plan, consider safety from several perspectives. One view of the subject might be that keeping children safe means to protect them from disease and injuries. Objectively, few caregivers would argue with this as an appropriate goal; however, interpreting that view too narrowly could lead to a severely restricted environment that permitted no climbing or running, no stove top cooking, no woodworking, certainly no rock climbing, bike riding, or rollerblading, not even visits to the toilet facilities without an accompanying adult. We've all seen child-care settings where the rules rattle on and on: "Only one child on a swing at a time, no walking up the slide, no water in the sandbox, no sand on the concrete. Don't climb the tree, don't run, don't stack those blocks higher than your shoulder, don't bring water into the home corner." Children who are kept *this* safe might as well be wrapped in a cocoon of cotton batting; they certainly are not going to learn how to live in the real world, and they are also not going to enjoy themselves or want to come back again and again. In this realm of safety, a balanced and interesting program may actually *create* some risk of injury to children. To respond adequately to parents with this view of safety, the subject of **risk management** must be thoroughly examined by program staff before embarking on any new activity with children. Rather than avoiding any activity that carries a risk of injury, children and staff should discuss policies and procedures to minimize the likelihood of damage.

A second view of safety might concentrate on protecting children from dangers present in the outside community, such as being hit by a car on the way home from school; tormented or injured by bullies or gang members; influenced by peers who might encourage the use of drugs, tobacco, alcohol, or other addictive agents; or abducted by someone with ill intent. To avoid such danger is the primary reason many parents place their children in after-school programs, sometimes at considerable financial hardship: to protect their children from the real or perceived dangers of traveling home from school alone, arriving to an empty house, and spending several hours unsupervised until their parents return from work. This is an area of safety where well-managed after-school environments, even drop-in programs, can be very successful. In fact, programs that teach refusal skills and conflict-resolution techniques, and offer drug, alcohol, and tobacco education can actually *reduce* risks to children when they leave the program to spend time in their own neighborhoods, not just while they are in the program itself.

A third view of safety addresses the importance of protecting children from emotional injury. This approach focuses on the interpersonal relationships within the center itself. In an emotionally safe program, caregivers speak to children using honest, reflective, and nonjudgmental language, and children are taught that put-downs, racist or sexist remarks, and other belittling language will not be tolerated. Some children may have the option of spending before- and after-school time with friends, neighbors, or family members, but parents who recognize that this emotional safety aspect is not present in those environments may enroll them in after-school programs instead. The sad reality is that these children may face the very same psychologically damaging interactions in child-care settings that their parents are trying to avoid. This is especially likely when caregivers are inexperienced, lack confidence, or are faced with supervising too many children in too small a space with too few resources. Many adults feel most safe when they are in control, and attempting to maintain control can cause people to use disrespectful or intimidating words when talking to children. This is an element of safety not always addressed by program leaders and one that deserves a great deal of thought.

All three of these areas of safety can and should be addressed by out-of-school program planners and staff. The steps that need to be taken include (1) setting the standards for supervision and practices, (2) training children to use new or specialized equipment, (3) reducing hazards in the play environment, and (4) responding to accidents and injuries.

Setting the Standards for Supervision and Practices   To administer and implement a safe program for school-agers, program directors must provide training, guidance, and support to staff members and volunteers. This includes developing procedures for handling potentially hazardous activities, such as walking to restrooms or playgrounds, crossing streets, using electrical equipment or sharp tools, or playing outdoors in extremely hot or cold weather. Such standards may include developing a buddy system, requiring children to wear colored T-shirts or name tags, and washing hands before and after eating, after toileting, or playing outside. It may also include posting safety checklists or supplying all-weather first-aid kits.

Involve children in making or reviewing safety rules at the beginning of any potentially dangerous activity, such as remembering to wear helmets during skating and cycling. All staff should be trained in basic first aid and child abuse reporting procedures, and the adult-child ratio should be such that no adult is ever left alone with the children or unable to supervise their activities adequately. The center should have written procedures for managing children during earthquakes, hurricanes, tornadoes, or fires; all staff members should be trained in those procedures, and the procedures should be posted prominently on the wall.

Staff members must be educated about interpersonal relationships and how to talk with children in ways that communicate respect and caring, even while the adults are setting limits or responding to unacceptable behavior. To learn how to become responsible members of society, children need to see models of positive social behaviors, attitudes, and skills. Their life outside your program may not provide these models; they may even be subject to violent and other antisocial behavior that may leave them with damaging emotional scars. Group control techniques commonly used in some school-age programs, such as "time out" and "use your words," may restore order quickly, but they do not help children feel safe and nurtured, nor do they teach them the behaviors necessary for developing a peaceful and empowering out-of-school environment (Levin, 1994). The framework in Table 8-2 shows how children's feelings and skills can be positively affected by thoughtful planning of an interpersonal environment.

Training Children to Use Specialized Equipment   School-age children are growing rapidly in their ability to do real work with real tools. As they become interested in doing so, they should eventually be allowed to use staplers, hole punchers, paper cutters, blenders, microwave ovens, hotplates, sewing machines, wood-burning kits, soldering irons, hammers, saws, or sharp knives. However, none of these or other potentially dangerous tools should be used without adequate training and supervision. Because children's use of such equipment differs from one household to another, no assumptions can be made about previous experience. Adaptive versions of some household tools and appliances may be available for children with physical limitations. Be sure to ask parents of children with disabilities how they manage these things at home.

Each child should be carefully checked out with each piece of equipment before being allowed to use it for the first time. Some programs send questionnaires home to parents, inquiring about children's knowledge of cooking or construction activities, and they use that information to develop guidelines for ages at which children may begin to use certain tools. Even after learning how to use potentially dangerous equipment, however, no child should be left using it unsupervised. It is probably not necessary to stand directly over children once they demonstrate competency, but an adult should always be nearby in case of problems or questions.

Reducing Hazards in the Play Environment   In addition to developing guidelines and teaching children about safe practices, all child and youth workers need to be vigilant in their search for potentially dangerous situations in the environment. Don't leave this job to the director. Athletic coaches fill in gopher holes on playing fields and determine that children are wearing the right kinds of shoes; Scout leaders watch for poison ivy and snakes; school-age child-care workers should be looking for frayed electrical cords, broken chairs or tables or windows, sharp objects sticking out of walls or furniture, backpacks obstructing the doorway, potholes in playground surfaces, and loose swing ropes or rusty chains. Teach children to watch for hazards, too, and keep an active "fix-it" list to communicate needs to the program leader.

Selecting Hazard-Free Art Materials   When providing art materials for school-age children, it is important to balance their need to explore more complex art forms and media against the potential for health hazards. In general, art safety organizations discourage the use of pastels, chalk, charcoal sticks, powdered clay, powdered tempera paint, plaster of Paris or instant papier-mâché, all

TABLE 8–2 A Developmental Framework for Planning Violence Prevention
for Young Children

How children are affected	What children need
Sense of trust and safety is undermined:	**An environment that feels safe:**
I am not safe.	I am safe here.
The world is a dangerous and scary place.	Adults will keep me safe here.
I have to fight and be strong to keep myself safe.	I can learn how to keep myself safe.
	I must not do things to make others feel unsafe here, and others mustn't violate my sense of safety either.
Sense of autonomy and empowerment are undermined:	**An environment that teaches positive ways to be separate and powerful:**
Muscle and might, fighting, guns, and weapons are what you need to be autonomous.	There are many ways I can function as a capable and autonomous person.
Fighting and weapons are what people use to affect the world.	Here are all the ways I can have the effect I want without violence (or helplessness).
If I'm not strong enough, then I am helpless, and I had better be "pretty" so I will be rescued.	There are many ways I can participate in decisions that affect my daily life.
Sense of mutual respect and interdependence is undermined:	**An environment that teaches how to respect and rely on others:**
Violence is a normal and central part of human interactions.	It is possible to be heard and respected by others and to hear and respect them.
To need help or to help others is to be weak and vulnerable.	There are many mutually beneficial and cooperative ways people can interact and still be safe and competent.
We all need to look after and take care of ourselves.	Here is what it feels like and here is what I do to live and work with others as part of a mutually caring community.
Ability to understand experience and construct new skills is undermined:	**An environment that promotes the active transformation of experience into personally meaningful ideas and skills:**
I spend my play time imitating the violence I have seen, and my toys will help me do it.	I can control my play and use it to experience power, control, mastery, and understanding.
Entertainment violence [TV, Nintendo, videos] is an activity of choice when I have free time.	There is a whole range of satisfying and meaningful ways I can use my free time.
There's no way I can figure out the violence I have seen; it just happens.	There are ways I can work through the violence I have seen so I feel safe and in control.

Source: Levin, D. E. (1994). *Teaching young children in violent times: Building a peaceable classroom.* Cambridge, MA: ESR.

of which create dust that can easily be inhaled and can cause respiratory problems. Sanding dry clay pieces carries the same risk. Replace these items whenever possible with their dustless equivalent, such as oil pastels; dustless chalk; crayons; talc-free, premixed clay; liquid paints; and papier-mâché made from black-and-white newspaper mixed with library paste. Instead of sanding clay projects, wipe them with a damp cloth. Aerosol sprays also carry respiratory dangers, and due to a high risk of theft, must be kept in locked cabinets.

Other art supplies that programs are encouraged to avoid include anything containing solvents, such as epoxy, airplane glue, permanent felt-tip markers, shellac, rubber cement, oil-based paints, and mentholated shaving cream. As much as possible, advisers suggest purchasing nontoxic paste and glue, water-based inks and paints, vegetable and plant dyes, and water-based markers (American National Red Cross, 1992; Babin, Peltz, & Rossol, 1992).

As with any potentially dangerous activities, however, completely avoiding these materials may result in a watered-down (literally!) art program, and children may miss the opportunity to explore their creative talents. Certain arts and crafts projects declared in one publication to be "not suitable for the child care setting" include airbrushing, ceramic glazing, silk screening, stained glass, metal casting, acid etching, enameling, photo developing, soldering, and woodburning (American National Red Cross, 1992). All of these sound like great fun, and under the right circumstances would be entirely appropriate in programs for school-agers. So use good judgment. Be aware of the risks. Be sure if you use any of the dust-producing materials or solvent-based products that you do so in a well-ventilated area, preferably outside. Mix powdered tempera, plaster, or papier-mâché away from the children and wear a dust mask. Teach older children appropriate safety precautions and ask them to help you watch younger children so they can be protected from hazards created by older children's activities. Always supervise children when they are using any potentially harmful materials or equipment, and always be aware of those children who may be especially vulnerable to environmental hazards, such as children with asthma.

Using a Safety Checklist   Develop a safety checklist or use the one in Appendix 2. Inspect the child-care setting thoroughly at the start of each term and periodically thereafter. If you find a risky behavior or hazard, note it on a separate sheet of paper; let this become a "fix-it" list. Share your findings with other staff members, administrators, landlords, and children. Good safety practices become a habit, and the more eyes and ears there are on the job, the safer your environment will become.

Responding to Accidents and Injuries   Develop policies and procedures for responding to accidents and injuries. Does the closest adult respond to an injury and carry through to contacting parents, or is there a designated person who will take over? Even minor occurrences should be treated and recorded in order to trace later symptoms and prevent future injury. A simple way to handle minor injuries is with an "Ouch Report," a simple half-page form completed

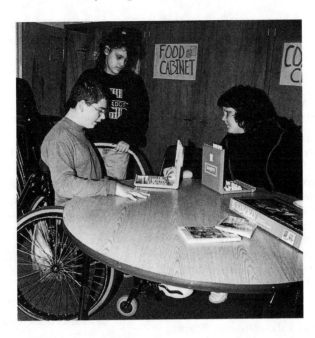

Be sure that furniture is arranged so that it allows access by children in wheelchairs or on crutches.

in duplicate. One copy is given to the parents at the end of the day, and the other is placed in the child's file. More serious injuries should be recorded on a full-page Accident or Injury Report. In addition, all accidents and injuries should be recorded in a log, one line per occurrence. Sample forms are contained in Appendix 1.

In addition, children with special needs may have additional health and safety concerns. Be sure to have, in writing from a parent and/or doctor, any such information and appropriate responses. Examples are diabetic insulin reaction (when to give orange juice or sugar), bee sting allergy, asthma attack (when to use inhaler), how (or whether) to do cardiopulmonary resuscitation (CPR) on a child confined to a wheelchair.

The ADA and Environments for School-Agers

The Americans with Disabilities Act (ADA) sets certain standards and recommendations for physical environments to be accessible and appropriate for children with special needs. You should become familiar with those guidelines and follow them as closely as the facility and finances allow. Sometimes administrators find this process overwhelming, but it doesn't have to be. In general, if the basic ideas presented in this chapter are carried out, and the individual needs of *every child in the program* are considered in planning spaces, schedules, and activities, the intent of the ADA will probably be furthered far better than slavishly adhering to building specifications and legal code without understanding their purpose.

SUMMARY

Out-of-school child care takes place in a variety of settings, including private homes, school sites, houses of worship, and purpose-built facilities. All environments have three dimensions—the *physical* environment, the *temporal* environment, and the *interpersonal* environment. To meet the physical, socioemotional, and cognitive development needs of the children they serve, school-age programs should be *nurturing, attractive, interesting,* and *safe.* Nurturing environments are supportive and child responsive. Homework and other controversial issues, when addressed within a nurturing environment, can be settled so that they reflect the needs of the local community. Sharing space, while always a challenge, is simplified when the same principles are applied. Light, color, sound, and provision for privacy all contribute to the attractiveness of the environment. Interesting environments offer a variety of activities allowing children opportunities for increasingly challenging experiences. Safety should be considered from a variety of perspectives, all of which require thoughtful planning, staff training, and administrative support. All staff members should be familiar with the provisions of the Americans with Disabilities Act and be sure that the facility meets them.

REVIEW QUESTIONS

1. Describe four settings commonly used for before- and after-school care.
2. What are the three elements present in all environments?
3. Explain the difference between a child-responsive and an adult-centered environment. Give an example of each type of response to a group of children who ask if they may build a "fort" in the corner of the day care room.
4. Do you think programs for school-agers should have a special "homework time?" Why or why not?
5. Give four examples of open materials.
6. Explain how room arrangement can influence children's behavior.
7. What are the three perspectives on safety presented in the chapter?

CHALLENGE EXERCISES

1. Visit three out-of-school programs and sketch their floor plans. Evaluate the plans using the guidelines presented in the chapter. Summarize your findings.

2. Interview four caregivers in out-of-school programs and four parents on the subject of homework in these programs. Compare their views.

3. After first securing permission to do so, evaluate a school-age child-care facility using the safety checklist in Appendix 1. Review your findings with a member of the staff. Summarize.

TERMS TO LEARN

adult centered
child centered
furnishings
interpersonal environment
intrapersonal intelligence
loose parts
nonsupportive
nurturing
open materials
physical environment
risk management
supportive
temporal environment

REFERENCES
••••••••••••••••

Albrecht, K., & Plantz, M. (1993). *Developmentally appropriate practice in school-age child care programs.* (2nd ed.). Dubuque, IA: Kendal/Hunt.

American National Red Cross. (1992). *Child care course: Health and safety units.*

Babin, A., Peltz, P., & Rossol, M. (1992). *Children's art supplies can be toxic* (Fact sheet). New York: Center for Safety in the Arts. Available angelababin@worldnet.att.net

Bellum, D. (1990a). *Challenges of shared space.* San Francisco: California School Age Consortium.

Bellum, D. (1990b). *New ideas for childcare veterans.* San Francisco: California School Age Consortium.

Bergstrom, J. M. (1984). *School's out—Now what? Creative choices for your child's time.* Berkeley, CA: Ten Speed Press.

Bradford Social Services. (1995). *The "out-of-school" handbook.* Bradford, W. Yorkshire, UK: City of Bradford Metropolitan Council.

Bumgarner, M. (1993). *Improving the understanding of learning styles in prospective early childhood education teachers through self-study and observation.* Unpublished doctoral dissertation, Nova Southeastern University, Ft. Lauderdale, FL.

Bumgarner, M. (1995). Student interviews of parents and children in a variety of after-school arrangements. Gavilan College course project.

California Child Care Resource and Referral Network. (1986). *Child care centers: Designing for children's needs* (Information packet). San Francisco, CA.

Coleman, M., Robinson, B. E., & Rowland, B. H. (1991, Summer). School-age child care: A review of five common arguments. *Day Care & Early Education,* 13–17.

Gardner, H. (1993). *Multiple intelligences: The theory in practice.* New York: Basic Books.

Gordon, A., & Brown, K. (1993). *Beginnings and beyond* (3rd ed.). Albany, NY: Delmar.

Greenman, J. (1992). *Equipping the developmentally appropriate center.* Childcraft.

Hales, D. (1994) (catalog). Kids! 6-10 school lighting, after-school topics, and other topics. *Working Mother, 17*(4), (2), 68.

Healey, D. (1982). *Living with color.* New York: Rand McNally.

Koralek, D., Newman, R., & Colker, L. (1995). *Caring for school-age children.* Washington, DC: Teaching Strategies.

Marion, M. (1987). *Guidance of young children.* (2nd ed.). Columbus, OH: Merrill.

Olds, A. (1988). Places of beauty. In D. Bergan (Ed.), *Play as a medium for learning and development* (pp. 181–185). Portsmouth, NH: Heineman.

Petrie, P., & Logan, P. (1986). *After school and in the holidays: The responsibility for looking after school children.* London: University of London Institute of Education.

Pratt, D. (1995). Enriching your outdoor environment. *CSAC Review, 8*(3), 1, 5.

Roman, J. (Ed.). (1998). *The NSACA standards for quality school-age care.* Boston, MA: National School-Age Care Alliance.

Seligson, M., & Allenson, M. (1993). *School-age child care: An action manual for the 90s and beyond.* Westport, CN: Auburn House.

Sudjik, D. (1985). *The lighting book.* New York: Crown.

Time-Life Books. (1988). *Living spaces for children.* Alexandria, VA.

Zigler, E. F., & Lang, M. E. (1991). *Child care choices: Balancing the needs of children, families, and society.* New York: Free Press.

CHAPTER NINE

Cooperative Program Planning

The "Curriculum" of School-Age Child Care

When planning is discussed in texts for classroom teachers or child-care providers, the word *curriculum* is often used. Sometimes it is defined; sometimes it is not. This term is also used freely by child-development instructors in college classes when we talk about what we do in early childhood centers or out-of-school programs. Sometimes we can explain what we mean by curriculum; often we cannot. Try for yourself. Just exactly what *is* curriculum? What does it do? Where do we get it? Why do we have it? Not an easy task, is it?

It is unfortunate that such a popular word, discussed at length and with intense feeling by so many people, should be so elusive. The *Oxford American Dictionary* defines curriculum as "a course of study." The National Association for the Education of Young Children expands that definition to include "the content children are to learn, the processes through which children achieve the identified curricular goals, what teachers do to help children achieve these goals, and the context in which teaching and learning occur" (National Association for the Education of Young Children, 1991, p. 21). It is sometimes described informally as "everything we do in our program."

For the purposes of this book, and for the school-age environments in which most of you will work, the last definition may actually be the best. Programs for school-agers should not replicate or slavishly extend the classroom day. What takes place in these programs certainly often includes "teaching and learning," but it is not, nor should it be, the same thing as the formal "course of study" occurring in conventional classrooms. When we talk about curriculum in an out-of-school program, we include *all the experiences and activities in which children and adults engage, the context from which they emerge, and the socioemotional climate in which they take place.* This includes the spontaneous activities as well as the preplanned ones; ideally, out-of-school curriculum *emerges* from the interests of the children and adults within a program, and each activity is continued for as long as needed to satisfy that interest or complete the tasks the participants set for themselves.

Why Plan?

Why, one might ask, should we plan at all? If curriculum is "emergent," why not just let it emerge? A partial answer is that by planning ahead we can provide an environment that encourages this emergent curriculum. One way to do this is to develop activity areas within the programs that are "ready to go" and can be used without advance arrangements. These activity centers provide the core of many after-school programs, and most children find a certain security in the consistent availability of certain activities, including board games, arts and crafts projects, quiet reading, constructions, listening or writing, or dramatic play.

To be effective, these activity areas must be well maintained and stocked, and obsolete materials removed or rearranged. In some programs, staff and children develop individual centers together and arrange them within the space available to create the kind of atmosphere they want for their specific program; then they stock the centers with supplies and use as desired. Chapter 8 on environments discussed these important permanent activity areas in detail.

In addition to having access to activity centers, children also enjoy spur-of-the-moment sports, indoor and outdoor games, projects, and outings. These, too, should be regular components of a well-rounded program.

However, while child-initiated and *spontaneous* activities are important, there are valid arguments for staff and school-agers getting together to plan major parts of their program ahead of time. The routines of before- and after-school programs should be peppered with interesting long-range projects and activities to keep children engaged. Summer out-of-school programs that meet all day every day for several months will need to reserve buses, purchase tickets for field trip destinations, and purchase equipment and supplies for projects. Even youth sports and community service organizations, whose schedules, activities, and fund-raising projects are most commonly adult-initiated and planned, benefit from the buy-in and innovative ideas that result when team members and participants are included in the planning process.

Thinking about activities and experiences in advance allows for *scheduling of key areas; acquisition of materials, equipment, and supplies;* and *allocation of adult staff.* In addition, advance planning helps children to *learn important skills; enjoy the anticipation of events or activities;* and *contribute their ideas about when, where, and how the events will take place.* Advance planning also gives staff time for thoughtful consideration of how to include any children with special needs who may be in the program. Finally, advance planning permits program staff to include components in the planning process and during the activities themselves that *promote the stated goals of the out-of-school program.*

Whether your program has as its goal supervision and care of school-age children, athletic training and competition, or leadership and community

After-School Activities a Must

Marian Wright Edelman, Children's Defense Fund President

Georgia and Michael Stetson of Columbus, Ohio, both 32, are a married couple with two children—one of school-age—and, between them, make $35,000 a year. Eleanor Booze of Decatur, Ga., is a 41-year-old single mother raising a 12-year-old daughter on $50,000 a year.

What do these working parents have in common? Like so many, they need somewhere for their children to go after school. Parents' need for high-quality, affordable after-school activities crosses lines of age, income, marital status, gender, and geography. Regardless of these circumstances, parents want their children to be safe, in the company of caring adults, insulated from bad peer influences, and engaged in productive activities.

Georgia and Michael only found care for their son Michael, 6, after months of searching. While they feel fortunate to have found a quality program, the cost is stretching an already tight budget.

Eleanor was able to pay a little more for an after-school program. But she didn't have time to pick up Danielle, 12, from school, drive 30 minutes to the after-school project, and then return to work. Fortunately, she found an after-school program operating right at Danielle's school. So many working parents face the same dilemmas every day. There are about 24 million children ages 5 to 14 in America with a working parent, and typically they spend less than two-thirds of the time their parents are working in school.

Even mature children benefit from constructive, organized after-school activities with improved school performance and stronger social skills. The number one substitute for good after-school programs is television. When children watch more than three hours a day, as many do, negative outcomes—including less reading and more aggressive behavior—are increasingly likely. Studies also have revealed that latchkey children are at much greater risk for truancy, stress, poor grades, risk-taking behavior, and substance abuse. Children who spend a lot of time on their own and who begin taking care of themselves at a very young age face even greater risk. So it's not surprising that juvenile crime peaks between 3 p.m. and 8 p.m., and that it triples from 2 p.m. to 3 p.m., the hour when schools usually let out.

We all learned the saying that idle hands are the devil's workshop. Today, the economy gives many parents little choice about working, so we have to renew our efforts to occupy our children's hands with constructive activities. As a nation, we need to help parents by investing in quality after-school activities that give children positive alternatives to television, drugs, alcohol, too early sexual activity, possible pregnancy, gangs, and idleness. While many states, cities, and communities have done an excellent job of caring for children after school, we *need* to do more, and we *can* do more. Our children can't afford to wait.

service projects, adult staff who pay attention to the seeds planted during activity planning can reap a plentiful harvest. This means that children should not just be *included* in the process but also *listened to.* The process of planning, in itself, provides a model of involvement that is likely to continue throughout the activity; engagement, focus, and communication are important goals of this process.

If involving children at the ground level is a new concept for your program, it may take some time to develop an environment of mutual trust in which ideas and opinions can be freely offered and exchanged. Some children are not accustomed to listening or being listened to, to respecting or being respected, or to working with others in constructive ways. Helping children develop these skills and attitudes will take time, but it is time well spent.

SCHEDULING KEY AREAS

Many activities require specific features of a program environment, such as a sink, a computer, a table, a chalkboard, the basketball court, and so forth. With advance planning, you can assure that these **key areas** are available on the date needed and reserve them. Some kind of procedure should be developed so that children and staff *not* participating in the activity have warning, and can negotiate different dates and times if they desire. This helps teach children the habit of considering the needs of others. The same kind of reservation process is also advisable for the use of special purpose equipment that may be needed during the planning or preparation of the activity, such as felt pens and a dry erase board, the photocopy machine, or the basketball. A simple form, such as the one shown in Figure 9-1, serves this function very nicely.

ACQUIRING MATERIALS, EQUIPMENT, AND SUPPLIES

Perhaps the activity being planned needs equipment that the program does not own or supplies and materials that will cost money. Advance planning allows staff and children to participate in a **scrounging mission,** which in itself requires planning and the development of certain problem-solving and communication skills. Often, equipment can be borrowed and supplies or materials obtained through donations and trades. If that is not possible, the planning process will need to include fund-raising, a necessary component of every active program.

ALLOCATING STAFF

For activities to be successful and safe, pay attention to **allocation of staff.** Sometimes, program staff members initiate activity ideas or are present when someone suggests an activity they'd like to do. In other cases, the idea may come directly from the children, who plan it pretty much on their own. In either case, be sure that an adult will be available if needed when the activity is actually happening. Staff-child ratios and group sizes must always be appropriate so that the needs of children will be met. These ratios vary according to the ages and abilities of the children but should be within a range of 1:10–1:15 for children age 6 and older and 1:8–1:10 for children under 6. Keep group sizes small when children are learning a new skill or doing something that requires careful supervision, and never allow groups to be larger than about 25 to 30 children.

Occasionally, parents or community members are invited to lead outings or special projects; sometimes, the nature of the event is such that the youngsters can manage on their own. It is still a good idea to be sure that the project is entered on the staff planning calendar, just to make sure that a member of staff will be available to participate if necessary.

Activity Area /Equipment Reservation Request

Date needed: _____

Staff in charge   _____

Youth in charge   _____

Activities area(s) needed _____

_____

_____

Equipment needed   _____

_____

_____

Description of proposed activity: _____

_____

_____

_____

_____ / _____

Signature of requesting person/date

FIGURE 9–1 Activity Area/Equipment Reservation Request

ENCOURAGING CHILDREN TO CONTRIBUTE THEIR IDEAS

One of the strongest arguments for planning activities in advance is to make sure that the children who want to take part in it have input. Perhaps a member of staff suggests a skate day—nothing wrong with that, in and of itself. However, scheduling a skate day without consulting the children first might result in a conflict with an after-school softball tournament, or fall on a day when several students are studying for a social studies quiz and would not be able to participate. Some children have music lessons or outside activities that cause them to leave their after-school program earlier on certain days. They would certainly like to have some influence on the dates and times when interesting things are going to happen. Finally, youngsters can often identify resources in the community that can be utilized in a particular project, such as the location of empty boxes, folding chairs, puppet theaters, or someone who has lots of fabric scraps.

There is another reason that children should be active participants in the planning process, especially children over 7 or 8 years of age. During this period of development, children benefit from opportunities to build interpersonal skills and learn how to accomplish more complex tasks. These tasks can include the activities being planned or even the planning process itself. Also, children are often the most creative source of ideas about how to adapt an activity to include a friend with disabilities. Whether they succeed at everything they suggest or try, older school-age children benefit when they receive accurate feedback on their ability to work at useful tasks. Planning that takes place without regard for their opinions, especially if it is perceived as a message that they "don't count" or "can't do it," undermines their sense of worth and can result in discouragement and negativity. Spirits may plummet, and behavior problems sometimes follow. It's far more helpful to include children in the planning from the earliest stages than to risk alienation and opposition later.

LEARNING IMPORTANT SKILLS

Planning for any future activity demands certain steps. If I plan a road trip with my family, I need to figure the mileage between cities, estimate driving time, and reserve motels or campsites at appropriate spots along the route. I will also need to calculate how many meals we will eat on the road (how much food to pack) and in restaurants (how much money to bring). The number of pairs of socks, the correct warmth of outer clothing, and how many paperback novels all must be calculated if the trip is to be a success.

Planning a bake sale, a puppet show, a trip to a local museum, a tournament season, or a construction project requires the same kind of thinking into the future—speculating on elapsed times, calculating a budget, considering the needs of all participants, allocating resources, raising funds. Projects of this size demand a certain amount of order and organization; if these elements are missing, complications or disappointments may occur. These unfortunate results may serve as natural consequences, resulting in better projects later, especially if a staff-led evaluation follows the debacle. However, in many cases, such circumstances can be avoided with careful planning.

In addition to teaching basic planning skills, group process of any kind offers rich opportunities for youngsters to work on the developmental tasks of childhood. Robert Havighurst identified these tasks for children between 5 and 12 to include freeing oneself from primary identification with adults and beginning to establish independence from adults in all behavior areas; forming friendships with peers, accepting oneself as a worthwhile person; clarifying the adult world and the child's world; learning rules; beginning to identify with same-sex social contemporaries; learning more realistic ways of studying and controlling the physical world (see Table 4-3). Repeated activity planning, especially if done in groups, contributes to the development of these skills as well.

ENJOYING THE ANTICIPATION OF THE EVENT OR ACTIVITY

One of the greatest pleasures in life for many people is looking forward to something enjoyable. Even though I have enjoyed many spur-of-the-moment trips to the cinema or amusement parks, I can still remember the deliciousness of savoring the *idea* of going to see a film alone with my father when I was about 10. We planned it one evening, peering together at the theater announcements in the newspaper. When we had decided on the film, we looked at my father's appointment diary. Thinking very hard, we found a day and time some 2 weeks in the future that did not conflict with his lodge night or bowling or with my music lesson. Then we talked about where we would eat—a picnic in the park or soup in a cafe? And what would we buy at the snack bar? Could I please have a chocolate bar? And maybe an orange drink? More than 30 years have passed since that event, and I have long since forgotten what was playing the night we went to the theater. However, the planning, the negotiating, and the delightful anticipation as night after night we talked about our "night out"—they are with me still. All children deserve to have such experiences. Too often youth workers surprise children with outings, projects, or activities, and expect them to change gears from whatever they were doing and "get involved." Certainly I have been guilty of that mistake and have lived long enough to regret making it.

Sometimes it is the anticipation of a desirable-sounding activity that will bring a child back to an out-of-school program often enough to make friends, begin to fit in, and perhaps even to start enjoying himself. At the very least, children deserve to know what to expect when they come to the after-school program site; sometimes expectation, rather than triggering an emotional high, serves to reassure children that there is some consistency in their world. A posted schedule of activities and outings that are planned in advance is one way of providing that security.

FURTHERING THE STATED GOALS
OF THE OUT-OF-SCHOOL PROGRAM

Professor Joan Bergstrom, author of *School's Out* (1984), a handbook for parents of school-age youngsters, has suggested that out-of-school time is best spent developing what she calls the "other 3Rs"—resourcefulness, responsibility, and reliability. Table 8-1 in this text lists a sampling of one program's goals; some help to develop these characteristics, and others relate more to school success. Goal setting is discussed later in this chapter; whatever the goals for your program, thoughtful activity planning can help you ensure that the program offers a variety of different opportunities for their attainment.

Planning the Year

Program planning takes many forms. Some of it may be scratched out on a paper napkin in a fast-food restaurant, quick jottings about activities that occur to you when you least expect them. Some of it is simply carried over from previous years if the program being planned is an ongoing one. Some planning cannot take place until the children are present, but you should have some tentative planning completed before they arrive.

A necessary precursor to activity planning is laying out the calendar year. Usually this is done by the program staff, then revisited and revised later with the help of the children. The most effective method I have seen for year-long calendar creation is to use a very large roll of paper tacked horizontally on a long wall—about 10 or 12 feet in length, at eye level (see Figure 9-2). Using broad felt-tip markers, the starting and ending dates of the year are indicated at the beginning and end of the paper, and it is divided into calendar months with vertical lines. Months can then be divided into five-day weeks (unless your program is also open weekends, in which case those days should also be reflected) and the hours of operation indicated. Holidays, vacation days, and special commemorations are then indicated (staff or children's birthdays, Groundhog Day, Valentine's Day, and so on; some of these will be determined by the cultural and ethnic makeup of the community and others that you don't think of will be remembered by the children).

In addition to dates that are celebrated, indicate dates that trigger a change in programming, such as beginning and end of school terms, holidays and half days, teacher-training days, and others. On those days, you will have more children for longer hours; that will affect both staffing and activity planning. If your program serves children from more than one school, these days may differ for different children. Post school district calendars, individual school calendars, and hours of operation on the wall near your calendar strip. In some communities, public libraries and other useful resources operate during limited hours. It is helpful to post on the wall as well the days and hours such resources are open. Every member of the planning team should have a list of the goals and objectives of your program to be sure that they keep these goals in mind as they propose projects, activities, and trips. As dates for long-term and short-term projects are determined, enter them on the planning calendar as a horizontal line, starting and ending on the appropriate dates. This kind of planning format is called a **Gant chart.**

IDENTIFYING GOALS, OBJECTIVES, AND LEADERSHIP STRATEGIES

A separate planning process, possibly at an all-day workshop with program administrators, parents, and staff, is necessary to develop the program goals, which should reflect the overall philosophy and mission of the out-of-school program. Goals differ from one program to another. An after-school center located on-site at a highly academic elementary school may stress arts and

Year at a Glance

SEPTEMBER	OCTOBER	NOVEMBER	DECEMBER	JANUARY

· Magic Fish
· Crow Boy
 	
· Poems - - - - - -
· Review 1st Grade
  Curriculum - - - - - - - ►
 	
○ Just Read - - - - -
	· Johnny Appleseed
	
	· Continue with
	  2nd Grade Curriculum - - - - - - - - - - -
		· Legend of the
		  Blue Bonnet
			· Miss Rumphius	· The Mitten
				· Cloudy with
				  Meatballs

· Writing Sentences
  including capitals,
  punctuation, nouns,
  verbs, adjectives
· Slingerland Sentence Dictations - - - -
·Paragraph Writing - - - - - - - - - - - - - - -
· Journals - - - - - -
		· Expanding
		  Sentences
				· Slingerland Spelling
				  Rules: l-l-l, silent e,
				  y rule - - - - - - - -

· Numbers · Calendar · Story Problems · Time · Money · Graphing · Organizing Data - - - - · Equations and Patterns - - - - - - - -	· Predicting and Patterns - - - - - - - ►	· Strategies - - - - - - - - - - - - ► · Fact Families - - - - - - - - - - ►		· Collections/Sorting · Place Value · Estimating - - - - - - - - - -

· Growth	· Sound Energy - - - - - - - - - - - - ►
	  (make musical
	  instrument at
	  home)
	
	·Talk About Touching - - - - - - - - - - -
				· Weather/Water Cycle
				· Light and Heat
				  Energy

· All About Me
 	
· Community Workers - - - - -
  | · Mapping - - - - -
○ Community of Caring - - - - -
		· Family/Ancestors	· Celebrations
			  Around the
			  World
			- - - - - - - - ►
				· Black History

FIGURE 9-2 Long-Term Planning Can Be Done With a Gant Chart

crafts, music and movement, and other creative activities to relieve stress and provide outlets for individual expression. Alternatively, a drop-in youth center at an inner-city recreation center may encourage children to participate in team sports and emphasize responsibility, regular attendance, and skill building. One Girl Scout training manual stresses the goals of teaching values, decision making, leadership skills, and respect for others (Girl Scouts of Santa Clara County, 1992) whereas a guide for staff of after-school programs, published by Project Home Safe, encourages the development of self-concept and independence, cognitive skills, physical development, life skills, and community involvement (Albrecht & Plantz, 1993).

Year at a Glance

FEBRUARY	MARCH	APRIL	MAY	JUNE
· Ugly Duckling	· Sylvester	· Mr. Rabbit & the Lovely Present	· Amelia Bedelia · One Fine Day · Bedtime for Frances	
		· Story Writing		
			· Geometry · Symmetry	
· Measurement	· +, −, ×, ÷			
· Animal Growth · Metamorphosis	· Changing Earth/ · Dinosaurs		· Ocean Life	
· Presidents		· Human Wants and Needs		

ENSURING A BALANCED, INTEGRATED CURRICULUM

All quality assessments of school-age programs examine the *breadth* of activities available to children. It is important to offer a wide variety of activities from which youngsters may choose and to create a curriculum that is both *balanced* and *integrated*. A balanced curriculum means that there are daily opportunities for a number of different kinds of activities, such as active physical play, creative arts and dramatic play, quiet activities, and socializing as well as enrichment activities that support the development of basic academic skills and higher-level thinking (Sisson, 1995). There should also be a balance between indoor

In addition to being developmentally appropriate, out-of-school curriculum must authentically reflect the demographics of the region served by your program.

and outdoor activities, small- and large-motor activities, teacher-directed and child-initiated activities, and quiet and loud activities. Such differentiated programming offers opportunities "to enhance the cognitive, linguistic, social-emotional, ethical, physical, and creative development of each child" (Arns, 1994, p. 40). It also encourages children of different ages and abilities to play together and to grow and develop at whatever stage is appropriate for them.

An integrated curriculum draws on several different subjects or developmental areas at the same time. For example, writing a letter to a pen pal requires a child to reflect on his or her personal experiences as well as the reader's interests. This integrates socioemotional development (self-knowledge and empathy) with language development (writing) and possibly, depending on how far away the pen pal lives, cognitive development (geography). Group cooking projects typically incorporate math and science with interpersonal relations; if they are offered as part of a nutrition and fitness awareness focus, physical education, health, and self-esteem are integrated as well.

It is important for program goals to reflect the microsociety of the center itself and also of the wider community. Historically, different geographical regions vary somewhat in values and expectations for the childhood years; additional variations within a region may derive from cultural and ethnic diversity in the community. Be sensitive to families' needs and desires for their children, and be sure to include those as you develop the goals for your program.

Not all programs for school-agers are primarily goal based. Other models include resource based, club or group based, and challenge based (Musson,

1994). However, in practice, all programs have an *intent,* and that intent can be translated into a philosophy and a set of goals. Once the overall goals are determined, break-out sessions can be held to identify specific objectives that contribute to the attainment of these goals. Finally, activities and leadership strategies that will help children achieve the identified objectives should be listed and kept in mind throughout the entire planning process.

Planning the Season

Season planning may seem unnecessary at first. After all, the seasons are obvious, aren't they? Not necessarily, and not to everyone. Even long-term residents of the Midwest may forget to take the possibility of snow into consideration if they are planning a January outing in August, and inexperienced activity planners may need a reminder that large containers of cold drinking water would be a good idea during outdoor summer activities almost anywhere. Rain is common in certain places during October; in other regions, summer storms may need to be planned around. To help in weather-related planning, use color-coded strips of paper or thickly drawn lines to indicate the likely weather patterns during certain months. Some commercial calendars indicate weather-related activities in their featured photographs, and these can be pasted above or below the calendar strip as reminders or activity suggestions.

Planning the Month

Two kinds of monthly calendars are useful for program planning: (1) the kind that parents take home and post on their refrigerators and (2) the kind on which the staff record their more detailed activity plans. Detailed planning by program staff needs to take place before the reminder calendar can be produced.

MONTHLY STAFF PLANNING CALENDAR

Once the basic structure of the program year has been plotted on the planning calendar, it is time to involve the children and parents in brainstorming activities, projects, and outings that they would like to suggest for the year. The best way to accomplish this is with a combination of questionnaires sent home with children and small discussion groups, during which a staff member or an older child keeps track of all suggestions. If too many activities are suggested, you may need to vote for the most popular, or cluster similar activities together into one, or offer some activities specifically for small groups. (Certainly it should *never* be a requirement that every child participate in every activity.) If you have children in your program who have an individual education plan designed to address a disability, try to incorporate some of those goals in your overall program planning.

Part of the brainstorming process should include deciding on a good time for these activities. Some, such as kite flying or planting vegetables, are more obviously suited for certain times of the year. Kites can be constructed when it is raining, but the windy days of early spring are usually best suited for flying. Many indoor projects, such as sewing, construction, or mask making, can be used as relief from winter doldrums, and supplies can be pulled out or put away as desired during the long wet days of fall or winter. They may also be enjoyed when the temperatures rise and hot playgrounds send children indoors for shelter. You might want to schedule certain outings, such as attending a play or sporting event, before or after other related events (such as putting on a puppet show or forming a softball team).

It is important that this planning process does not leave children or staff with the impression that all projects, outings, or activities *must* be entered on the calendar in order to happen—nor that planned activities can never be scratched or rescheduled. This would result in an inflexible program that would soon lose its appeal.

Activity planning is an ongoing process, and although many activities are made far more successful by advance planning, some do not need to be planned ahead at all. It might be a good idea to schedule a planning meeting once a month with all interested children and staff. In this meeting you will evaluate activities once they are over, add new activities or events to the schedule, and reconsider or reschedule previously planned events. Keep this meeting short; an hour is long enough. To keep these sessions interesting and lively, consider having children take turns leading them.

Once the initial long-term planning is complete, monthly staff planning calendars can be created for each of the months of the program year. Begin by entering holidays, school minimum days, teacher work days, birthdays, and other special days. Then, working as far into the year as is feasible, transfer the suggested activities from the Gant chart to the appropriate monthly calendar and identify responsible staff and children for each activity. Include dates for making arrangements, sending home and collecting permission slips, and re-minding children to bring skates, bicycles, or other needed equipment from home. If special accommodations are needed for an outing (like a van with a lift or large-print materials), be sure to request them well ahead of time. Monthly calendars can be placed in a loose-leaf notebook and updated as new ideas emerge. Once a month, information resulting from the planning process should be transferred from the staff planning calendar to a parent/child calendar and sent home.

MONTHLY PARENT/CHILD CALENDAR

You can use an ordinary commercial calendar and neat handwriting for the monthly calendar or use computer software that allows the insertion of text and graphics into each day's square. A sample parent-child calendar is shown in Figure 9-3. Transfer important dates from the yearly calendar to the monthly

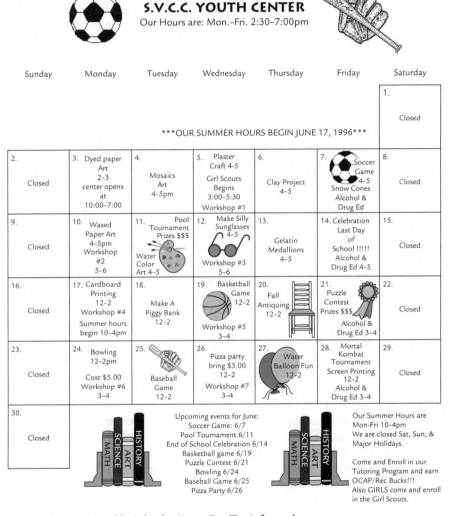

FIGURE 9-3   A Monthly Calendar Keeps Families Informed

calendar: birthdays, holidays, minimum days, and others. Identify dates such as special outings, deadlines for sign-ups, and fund-raisers; also, highlight some of the month's activities and projects. If parents or other volunteers work in your program, identifying the days on which they are scheduled to work will help them remember their commitment. If snacks and/or meals are served, it is better to create a separate menu calendar than to include that information with the program details. The menu calendar can be printed on the reverse side of the activity calendar.

Planning a Week

So far, the planning process has focused primarily on activities and events that require a fair amount of lead time in order to arrange for equipment, materials, special purpose areas, or advance reservations. The yearly planning process looks at the entire program and attempts to ensure that the program is balanced, integrated, and organized. The monthly plan takes note of important dates and staffing. However, it is the day-to-day flow of the school-age program that directs weekly planning and requires that it be kept current.

Weekly planning, when done regularly, can encourage creative thinking among staff and children. A simple theme, built around an individual's interest or discovery (for example, the birth of puppies or a local athletic or artistic event) can lead to research, gathering of materials, cleaning/rearranging projects, or other endeavors that were not considered during the year-long or even monthly planning process.

Some after-school programs do their weekly planning on Fridays, which otherwise may tend to be long, difficult days. Even children who are highly motivated to study or engage in sports after school may become less enthusiastic at the end of the week, and these Friday planning sessions can provide them with a focus. Friday planning also allows children and staff the weekend to locate material they need for a project, and furnishes something for children to look forward to on Monday. Planning for the week can also be done when children arrive at the beginning of the week, especially if the activities being planned do not require extensive preparation.

Begin by reviewing the monthly calendar with the children. After activities have been confirmed or canceled and any adjustments to interest areas have been decided on, record the activities on a weekly planning sheet, which can then be posted for everyone to see.

Although yearly and monthly planning takes into account major events and dates, which should also be recorded on the weekly planning sheet, weekly plans include regular activities and changes to the usual routine, special visitors, new materials or projects that will be available in interest areas, or projects that are continuing from previous weeks. An example of a weekly planning sheet is shown in Figure 9-4.

Planning a Day

Programming needs are different when the length of the program day varies. For example, an athletic coach may plan a particular schedule of activities for a weekly 2-hour practice session (warm-ups, laps, drills, and scrimmage). However, when he or she plans a week-long summer camp, the wise coach will vary the activities and the length of time spent on each and may also offset focused skills training with team-building activities and other enjoyable pursuits to keep the team motivated.

MONDAY 4.	TUESDAY 5.	WEDNESDAY 6.	THURSDAY 7.	FRIDAY 8.
2:30 p.m. Nancy-sign in Kammi-snack	ELECTION DAY 2:30 p.m. Nancy-snack Kammi-sign in	1:30 p.m. MINIMUM DAY Nancy-sign in Kammi-snack	1:30 p.m. MINIMUM DAY Nancy-snack Kammi-sign in	1:30 p.m. MINIMUM DAY Nancy-sign in Kammi-snack
3:00 p.m. Nancy-group 1 Christmas magnets Kammi-group 2 Christmas magnets	3:00 p.m. Nancy- group 2 Fieldtrip Kammi- group1 Fieldtrip	2:00 p.m. Nancy/Kammi HOLIDAY SAFETY VISIT FROM FIREMEN	2:00 p.m. Nancy-group 2 make fire extinguisher out of can Kammi-group 1 make fire extinguisher out of can	2:00 p.m. Nancy-group 1 paper mâche Christmas bulb Kammi-group 2 paper mâche Christmas bulb
4:00 p.m. Nancy-group 1 homework Kammi-group 2 homework	5:00 p.m. Nancy- group 2 small snack Kammi- group 1 small snack	4:00 p.m. Nancy-group 1 small snack Kammi-group 2 small snack	3:30 p.m. Nancy-group 2 outdoor freeplay Kammi-group 1 outdoor freeplay	3:30 p.m. Nancy-group 1 Twister Kammi-group 2 Twister
4:30 p.m. Nancy- continue homework Kammi- freeplay	5:30 p.m. Nancy- group 2 homework Kammi- group 1 homework	4:30 p.m. Nancy-group 1 homework Kammi-group 2 homework	4:00 p.m. Nancy-group 2 homework Kammi-group 1 homework	4:00 p.m. Nancy-group 1 freeplay Kammi-group 2 freeplay
5:00 p.m. Nancy- paperwork Kammi- small snack	6:00 p.m. Nancy/Kammi Close	5:00 p.m. Nancy-continue homework Kammi-freeplay	4:30 p.m. Nancy-freeplay Kammi-continue homework	4:30 p.m. Nancy-freeplay group 1 vs. group 2 Kammi- Wheel of Fortune
5:30 p.m. Nancy- continue paper Kammi- story time		5:30 p.m. Nancy- paperwork Kammi- group 1 & 2 story time	5:00 p.m. Nancy-group 2 small snack Kammi-group 1 small snack	5:30 p.m. Nancy- paperwork Kammi- small snack
6:00 p.m. Nancy/Kammi Close		6:00 p.m. Nancy/Kammi Close	5:30 p.m. Nancy- group 1 & 2 story time Kammi-paperwork	6:00 p.m. Nancy/Kammi Close
			6:00 p.m. Close	

FIGURE 9–4 Weekly Planning Sheet

In much the same way, experienced after-school program planners take note of the times of day and the length of time children will be in their program and make appropriate and special accommodations for those different circumstances. Many such programs operate on split-day sessions, operating for an hour or two before school then closing until 2:00 or 3:00 in the afternoon when they open again until 6:00 or 7:00 p.m. Other programs remain open all day, serving a mixed age group before and after the regular school day and kindergarten children during the half day that they are not in class. A third

Sometimes two kinds of play will overlap. Here girls in dress-up clothes comment on a friend's painting.

scenario combines children who are on- and off-track in year-round schools; these schools might have 6- or 9-week sessions followed by 2- or 3-week breaks. And nearly all programs face periodic teacher-training days or school holidays that require children to stay at the out-of-school center for 8 hours or longer. Still others offer evening activities or even overnight "camp-outs." Each of these scenarios should be planned separately and recorded clearly on the monthly and weekly calendars.

Remember to consider the varying developmental and individual needs of all the children as you plan their program day. (It may help to review the earlier sections in this book on developmental stages, special needs, guidance issues, and issues facing today's children.) Quality programs are paced to meet differing children's needs, they balance time for quiet activities with more active pursuits, and they permit several different kinds of activities to take place simultaneously. Allow for changes in plans; be flexible enough to reschedule an event that couldn't happen due to illness or an unexpected conflict, and to cancel cheerfully an activity that loses its appeal between the time it was planned and the time it is to take place. Plan backup projects that can be set up quickly.

Planning an Activity

When you are considering a specific activity, a helpful strategy is to develop a plan sheet that includes all the program features necessary for success. In ad-

```
┌─────────────────────────────────────────────────────────────┐
│                        Activity Plan                          │
│                                                               │
│   Title of Activity:                    Date:                 │
│   Where it will take place:                                   │
│   Group size:                           Time of Day:          │
│   Staff contact role:                                         │
│   Goals(s)                                                    │
│   Objectives:                                                 │
│                                                               │
│              1.                                               │
│                                                               │
│              2.                                               │
│                                                               │
│              3.                                               │
│                                                               │
│   Material/equipment needed:                                  │
│   Special accommodations needed:                              │
│   Procedures, if applicable:                                  │
│                                                               │
│   Costs:                                                      │
│                                                               │
│   Evaluation:                                                 │
│                                                               │
└─────────────────────────────────────────────────────────────┘
```

FIGURE 9-5   Activity Plan

dition to providing an organized record of the planning process, written plans allow program staff to record evaluative comments following the event, and these may be helpful the next time a similar activity is undertaken. They also permit future program participants to benefit from the planning and experience of others, even of staff members and children who may no longer be present. An activity plan form designed for use in programs for school-agers is shown in Figure 9-5.

Planning Long-Term Activities

My own children, who spent from 3 to 6 years each in school-age child care, still remember with affection the activities and inquiries they took part in that took several weeks or even months to complete. Sometimes these activities were school related (nearly all California children construct a replica of a mission during fourth grade, and two of our four replicas were constructed primarily during parent work hours). Other times, activities were suggested by one of the other children in the program. These activities tended to spill over into our daily lives (such as digging into the attic trunk for beanbag fabric for the carnival or hauling tools to school for the vegetable garden) and provided opportunities for growth and learning that are still apparent today.

Writers on the subject of modern childhood often comment on the paucity of opportunities many children have for developing problem-solving strategies, for developing a sequence of steps to the construction of a project, for maintaining a focus over several weeks or months, or for seeing a project through from planning to completion (Gardner, 1993; Goleman, 1995; Katz & Chard, 1989; Leach, 1994). Long-term projects provide practice in all these skills and also create an interesting reason to go to day care each afternoon.

Most long-term projects seem to grow naturally from someone's interest. For example, when my son was in sixth grade, the director of his after-school center created a corner of the room labeled "Australia" in which children could sequester themselves when they didn't feel like being sociable. Several children, interested in enhancing the decoration and environment of the area, submerged themselves into a lengthy study of Australian flora and fauna, writing to the Australian tourist board for posters and spending hours designing and crafting stuffed wallabies, kangaroos, wombats, kookaburras, and gum trees.

Some activities require field trips. Others beg for outside speakers or library research. Wherever the project leads, embrace it. It's probably going somewhere useful (more suggestions for long-term project ideas appear in Chapters 10 and 11).

Evaluating Activities

Monthly planning meetings should include an evaluation of activities and projects that have taken place during the previous few weeks. In addition, collecting feedback in a timely manner before memories fade is useful, especially if the activity is a new one to your program. Some of this can be done informally, by simply recording comments made by the children during the event. A more formal evaluation session can be scheduled for the day immediately following an activity, perhaps during a snack or other time when most of the participants are sitting together anyway. Sometimes you might develop simple evaluation forms for children to complete anonymously, and it is always a good idea to solicit positive suggestions for improvement. This request sends an important message— that program participants play an important role, not just in developing and implementing program activities but also in evaluating them and making suggestions for improvement.

SUMMARY

Programs for school-age children should involve staff, children, and parents in their planning. Early planning allows for scheduling of key areas; acquisition of materials, equipment, and supplies; and allocation of adult staff. It helps children to learn important skills, enjoy the anticipation of events or activities, and contribute their ideas about when, where, and how the events will take place. Planning lets program staff promote the stated goals of the program. Plan the year first, taking into consideration goals, objectives, leadership strategies, and local holidays. Then plan the month, the week, the day, and the activity. Curriculum should be balanced and integrated, driven primarily by children's and staff's interests. Long-term activities can offer children valuable experience in problem solving and following through. The curriculum planning process concludes with an evaluation.

REVIEW QUESTIONS

1. Why is it important to plan an activity?

2. Describe and define balanced and integrated curriculum. What opportunities do these curriculum styles offer children?

3. What definition of curriculum does this text suggest for school-age programs for school-agers?

4. When is the best time to evaluate an activity? Why? Please give an example.

5. What developmental task of childhood does Robert Havighurst identify that children can learn from strengthening their basic planning skills when they are between the ages of 5 and 12?

CHALLENGE EXERCISES

1. Plan a week's schedule that reflects a balanced and integrated curriculum and also the cultural and ethnic diversity in the community.

2. Write a one-month lesson plan for the following:
   a. Drop-in center (open Monday through Friday)
   b. After school care program
   c. Family child care home

3. Choose a school-age child-care center to observe. Drop in and observe for half an hour each day for 2 or 3 days. Can you tell what the curriculum is based on?

4. Visit two programs for school-agers and observe the centers' planning calendar for the month, week, and day. Summarize your findings.

5. Ask an after-school program staff member for a summary of the best and worst activities they can remember planning. Ask what made them work or what could have made them better.

6. Plan and participate in an activity with a small group of school-age children. Discuss and evaluate the activity with the participants; write a summary.

TERMS TO LEARN

allocation of staff
curriculum
emergent curriculum
Gant chart
key areas
scrounging mission
spontaneous

REFERENCES

Albrecht, K., & Plantz, M. (1993). *Developmentally appropriate practice in school-age child care programs* (2nd ed.). Dubuque, IA: Kendal/Hunt.

Arns, B., et al. (1994). Kid's Time: *A school-age care program guide.* Sacramento: California Department of Education.

Bergstrom, J. M. (1984). *School's out—Now what? Creative choices for your child's time.* Berkeley, CA: Ten Speed Press.

Gardner, H. (1993). *Multiple intelligences: The theory in practice.* New York: Basic Books.

Girl Scouts of Santa Clara County. (1992). *A guide to troop/group leadership.* San Jose, CA: Girl Scouts of Santa Clara County.

Goleman, D. (1995). *Emotional intelligence.* New York: Bantam Books.

Katz, L., & Chard, S. (1989). *Engaging children's minds: The project approach.* Norwood, NJ: Ablex.

Leach, P. (1994). *Children first.* New York: Alfred A. Knopf.

Musson, S. (1994). *School-age care: Theory and practice.* Don Mills, Ontario, Canada: Addison-Wesley.

National Association for the Education of Young Children. (1991, March). Guidelines for appropriate curriculum content and assessment in programs serving children ages 3 through 8. *Young Children,* 21–38.

Sisson, L. (1995). *Pilot standards for school-age child care.* Washington, DC: National School-Age Care Alliance.

CHAPTER TEN

Inside, Outside, Upside Down

Outdoor Activities With School-Age Children

Organized Outdoor Games

One of the cornerstones of out-of-school care for children is recreational games, both indoors and out. After sitting in school for 6 or 7 hours, children need to move, and this is a good way to begin an afternoon session. Because you may end up organizing and leading outdoor games almost every day during good weather, it is important to develop a repertoire of different games that can be played with large groups. Even the most enthusiastic participants of the current "popular" game, whether it is "Duck, Duck, Goose" or "Steal the Bacon," eventually tire of it when it is played day after day. Many books are available with instructions for outdoor games. Two excellent ones are *Outdoor Action Games for Elementary Children* (Foster & Overholt, 1994) and *School-Age Ideas and Activities for After School Programs* (Haas-Foletta & Cogley, 1990).

When you work with school-age children, it is important to participate in the games as well as to organize them. Don't worry that you're not in great physical shape, that will change! More important than your skill is your good humor and your enthusiasm. Many school-age children are unaccustomed to regular exercise and may even be overweight. Enjoyable games that require vigorous movement can go a long way toward offsetting this trend and may even kindle an interest in sports among some children. Another thing to remember is that school-age children need to participate in deciding what games are played, for how long, and how often. They can actually do much of the organizing, too, if you model the process and encourage them to take a larger and larger role.

Most games can easily be adapted to include children with special needs, even though Annie's walker slows her down or Jamal doesn't really grasp the

It's more fun for many children if their group leaders participate in play with them.

rules. Encourage all children to help each other play together. Doing this not only promotes inclusion of the children with disabilities but it also makes participation more fun for all the other children who aren't athletic "stars."

It is also important to consider the ethnicity and culture of the children in your program. Seek out ways to develop curriculum activities that are respectful of cultural values and offer children an opportunity to learn skills and traditional games from their own and others' cultures. One good source of these activities is workshops and conferences; a new resource is the growing number of Web sites devoted to multicultural topics, such as the Native Child Web site depicted on the following page. Other web sites that may be helpful include "My Home Town" (http://www.magmacom.com/%Emtooker/cities/cityintr.htm—a page for children adopted from China to learn about their hometowns and home provinces), "Japanese Friendship Dolls" (http://www.clas.ufl.edu/users/jshoaf/ Jdolls/friendship.htm), and Boston University's "African Resources for the K-12 Classroom" (http://www.sas.upenn.edu/African_Studies/K-12/African_ Resources_BU.html). The last resource can also be obtained by writing to Boston University African Studies Center, 270 Bay Street, Boston, MA 02215.

Outdoor games can include circle games ("Duck, Duck, Goose," "Telephone," "A Tisket a Tasket"), team sports, or individual "silly stuff" (like "Follow the Leader," "Water Balloon Pop," or the "Bunny Hop"); you can also provide equipment for children to toss beanbags, jump rope, or play sets of giant dominoes. Some programs might want to schedule certain days when children bring their roller blades, skateboards, or bicycles and adapt favorite games to be played on wheels.

Figure 10–1 Native Child Web Site. The URL for this site is http://www.nativechild.com/core.html

In addition to these ideas and those to follow, descriptions of group games can be found in manuals for adult leaders of Camp Fire, Scouts, YMCA/YWCA, or other youth organizations. Other helpful sources are books written for elementary physical education instructors. One such text is *Children Moving* (Graham, Holt/Hale, & Parker, 1998) and its accompanying manual of lesson plans, *On the Move* (Holt/Hale, 1998). Search libraries for other sources of games. The following were adapted from *Cooperative Games for Indoors & Out*, by Jim Deacove (1974).

VOLLEY-UP

Two groups on either side of a volleyball net try to keep the volleyball aloft for as many hits as possible. A good goal is to get to 100. One player starts by serving from the end of the court and the ball has to go over the net from one side to the other, as usual. Three successive hits by one side are permitted. The last player to touch the ball on a dropped ball or unsuccessful hit is the one to serve it into play again (you might want to limit this to three successive tries). One person serves as a score-keeper to **tally** the hits.

STOP AND GO

This is a variation on softball that develops skills and involves all the players. Use a bat and ball and set up bases as usual. All remotely feasible positions are assigned, including just one batter. Everyone is a team when the scoring is tallied. The batter stays up and hits. The hit is chased and stopped or caught. When caught or stopped, the person fielding it shouts, "Got it!" The batter running around the bases stops wherever he or she is, even if on the basepath between bases. The person fielding the ball becomes the third baseman and everyone moves up a position, including the fielders, left, center, right, first right, second right, and so on, depending on the number of players. If the infield catches the ball, everyone moves up one place. The catcher becomes the batter. If the ball is caught rather than fielded, the one catching it becomes the next batter and the first batter stays on the basepath as far as he or she ran before the ball was caught.

Individuals can therefore work for themselves both when at bat and in the field, but they also work to add more enjoyment for everyone by trying their best to field or catch the ball. Scoring is done this way: Everyone on the basepath tries, in sequence, to get around the bases to home base. Each runner who makes it to home counts as one run. The runner who scores goes out into the field and enters the batting order. He or she can bat twice if he or she fields the ball or catches it and moves up again.

The whole team scores the number of runs achieved in one inning. An inning is over when you get the same number of hits as there are players playing. If ten people are playing, then ten hits make up an inning. Three innings allow you a chance to see what kind of a score you can get. The number of players can vary as for any baseball game. You need at least a batter, a catcher, a

Follow the leader is a game that can be played with children of varying ages.

pitcher, and a few fielders. You can play without a catcher if you have a good backstop. There are no strike-outs or walks. Each batter stays up until she is given a pitch she can hit, and of course she can also wait for a pitch she likes best. There is no reward or competitive inducement to this game, and when you play it you will notice that even children who don't usually care to play softball tend to play better and have more fun.

SCRAMBLE

This game is a variation on musical chairs except that the object is to make sure that no one is left out. As Jim Deacove, the author of *Cooperative Games,* says: "Our **cultural conditioning** gets us worrying about getting ahead in the musical chairs of society and all the time our hearts are worrying about those who don't get a chair. It would be nice if we could build a society that made sure anyone got a chair."

The game works nicely with 10 to 15 players, but more or fewer can play, depending upon what you use as the chair. You can literally use a chair, but you can also use a tree stump, a board on a box, a tree, a small circle drawn on the ground, or whatever you wish. Assign four corners of the playing area, naming them North, South, East, and West. Everyone but the caller is scattered around the four areas, and the caller describes an activity they must engage in while he waits for the right moment—hopping, walking, running, crawling on all fours, and so on.

Now the caller runs around the playing area, and suddenly calls out one of the areas. He may shout, "North!" At once, the players in the North area scramble to the chair, stump, tree, or whatever, and try to get a place on it. Everyone must somehow manage to get on the object and hang on. Everyone has to help the scramble work. A time limit of 30 seconds can be made if you wish. The caller calls the time, and if everyone is still on the object, the game is won, and the first on board becomes the caller. If everyone cannot get aboard, the caller resumes running around the playing area, and the children resume their activity. This can be made even more interesting by calling two areas or even three. Be sure to use large and sturdy objects as the base.

TAG AND FREEZE TAG

Don't forget old standby games like tag. Freeze tag is just like regular tag except when you get tagged you're frozen, and you stay frozen until someone who's not frozen tags you. If you get tagged three times, you're "It." If everyone gets frozen, then whoever has been tagged the most is "It."

Growing a Garden

Some children may be fortunate enough to have worked in a family garden, but for many more, nurturing plants is a new and wonderful adventure that they can explore with their friends at the out-of-school center. A good way to begin is to take a walk with the children, talk about the idea of growing living things, and find out whether they would like to try it. Some may want to grow flowers; others will prefer vegetables. Either is fine, and both are even better. Don't expect everyone to be enthusiastic. It is far better to have a small group of dedicated gardeners than a larger group who have to be talked into going outside to pull weeds on a hot day.

If no garden area has previously been allocated to your program, walk around the grounds with some of the children, selecting several areas that seem suitable. It is a good idea to do this at different times of the day and in different types of weather, to assure adequate sunshine, access to water, sufficient drainage, and safe routes for walking. If your program is located at a school site, ask the principal of the school for the correct procedure to request the use of one of the areas. Sometimes it is necessary to prepare a presentation to a school site council or the board of trustees, but often the on-site administrator can approve your project.

Suggest that children write letters to plant nurseries, hardware stores, or parents requesting the donation of child-sized tools, soil amendments, and seeds. Sometimes local gardening club members will join you for a session and teach children about composting, preparing soil for planting, mulching, cultivating, or other techniques that will assure success. Service clubs such as Rotary, Lions, or the Elks may also be willing to help, and retired community members often enjoy assisting children with such enterprises. Formulating and

PERSPECTIVE

Attitude Adjustment Time

From the highway, the wetlands appear as a vast wasteland surrounding the oil refineries off Highway 4. Yet, inside the marsh, hardy varieties of plant and animal life thrive. There's silky cattail, coyote brush, red-tipped pickleweed and the orange dodder "vampire" plant that sucks the life out of all surrounding plants. Fish, wild birds and other creatures are also abundant.

Another colorful species frequently visits the marsh and thrives: middle school girls. For them, the marsh is a habitat where they can get away from the sometimes overwhelming pressure to be pretty, popular and unassuming. In the marshland, they can be brave, inquisitive, adventurous and free-spirited. They can get dirty and tramp around in the soggy pathways without worrying about how they look or what other people—especially boys—will think.

Today, the marsh rang with the happy sounds of an all-girl science club. Competing with the cries of gulls, girls shrieked, giggled and screamed as they crossed a channel via an elevated wooden walkway complete with stairs that some of the girls built last year. But it wasn't all fun and games. Accompanied by three educators and a parent, they looked for signs of animal life and collected interesting plant species to take back to school. They also answered a stream of scientific questions about their soggy environs.

"How do you know when you're going to hit water?"

"'Cause you see a boat?"

"No, because the plants get taller."

Suddenly some of the girls hit tall plants—and water. "Eeeek!" they yelled. "Oh, no! We've hit the ocean."

They call themselves the GWA. It stands for Girls With Attitude, and they've got plenty to go around. But they don't want people to get the wrong idea. Overall, they say, it's a pretty good attitude.

The students encompass a variety of ethnic backgrounds, shapes, sizes, interests and social groups. The all-girl, after-school science club was started last year by their teacher, Ana Pittioni, who wanted to do something special for these "spirited, spunky, interesting people."

"I think it's great," says student Rajesh Singh. "Boys always think they rule. But, here, girls can rule."

"It's nice to have no boys in the wetlands," chimes in classmate Rebecca Politas. "If guys were here, the girls would go, 'Oooh, it's gross to be in the mud,' but without boys we can help each other and not be embarrassed. Guys think girls are sissies and girls don't want to show them that we can be tough."

"Normally, guys make us do all the work and take all the credit," Meta Griffin adds. "And when they act macho and cool, a lot of girls act dumb around the guys."

"This is more than just a science club," says Pittioni. "These girls need someone to talk to about the way they feel. They sometimes feel teased and harassed by boys, and they want someone to talk about it with so they don't feel like they're tattling all the time.

"They need to talk about the differences between boys and girls, standing up for their own needs inside and outside of the classroom, peer pressure and the way the media distorts the image of women. They need to look at different body shapes and see that they're really okay. They need to learn about how they can be more active in their education and get into good classes. They need to learn how to work with teachers and get teachers' attention in appropriate ways."

The idea for GWA came to Pittioni via Project PLANET (Partnership for Learning and Accessing New Educational Technology), a NASA science program in which students use satellite data to study the wetlands. When Pittioni took her class to the marsh, she noticed that the boys were eager to roam and explore, while the girls were much more reticent, worrying about their hair, makeup and clothing getting messed up. They felt inhibited and overshadowed by their male classmates, and responded by non-participation and complaining that the marsh was dirty and stinky.

"When I asked them to explore the marsh they said, 'I can't do that in front of a boy,'" recalls Pittioni. "They said, 'We can't wear these boots. We can't get dirty.'"

She decided to hold a field trip at the marsh just for girls, during which she noticed a major attitude adjustment. "They were excited and interested. They waded through the sloughs in waders. They were different people."

She applied to the American Association of University Women (AAUW) for a fellowship to start an all-girl science club. In addition to $10,000 in funding, she received a trip to Washington, D.C., for AAUW training. While there, she met with researchers who had conducted the AAUW *Girls in the Middle* study which describes how schools can help middle school girls succeed.

Despite the funding, "it was a challenge getting GWA off the ground," recalls Pittioni. "We started with three active sixth-graders who did some networking. Now we have between 25 and 30 students, with a balance of sixth, seventh and eighth-graders."

Under her leadership, the girls have visited San Francisco's Exploratorium; researched the environment on the Internet; and conducted experiments to measure salinity, ammonia and dissolved oxygen in the marshland.

They have also entered a relationship with the "Save the Bay" campaign, sponsored by the Chesapeake Bay Foundation, which has hosted canoe trips for the girls.

When asked if her work in the GWA club goes above and beyond the call of duty, Pittioni muses, "It's important for teachers to have personal relationships with kids. High student achievement and personal relationships go hand-in-hand."

As the field trip drew to a close, Pittioni offered some parting words for the girls who were somewhere between childhood and adulthood: "Stick up for yourselves and stick up for each other. If you see someone being teased or some being hurt, stick together. If you do, you'll find that things will be much easier."

---

writing letters and tracking down addresses can fill many hours of the rainy season, and build motivation for the project when the planting season finally arrives. During this time it might also be fun to visit a garden center or commercial garden and talk with the owner about suitable plants for your area.

PLANTING AND CULTIVATING

Small gardens can be contained in several large tires, or boxes can be made from railroad ties or similar material. Many plants benefit from being started inside before it is warm enough for outdoor gardening, and in some areas it might even be necessary to build a greenhouse. Cut-down milk cartons, clear plastic liter-sized bottles, and concentrated juice cans make good containers for seed nurseries. During the weeks while the seeds are germinating, tools are being located, and the plot is being secured, children can draw pictures of their fantasy garden and eventually develop a realistic plan. If you live in a rural or semirural area, rodent screens under the planting boxes are a good idea, as are fences to keep out passing dogs; pathways between rows will help to protect the plants from enthusiastic feet and allow accessibility for friends who use wheelchairs. Gardens grown in the middle of the city have an attraction for passersby, and benches set on the edges of the garden will sometimes fill up with teachers or community workers eating lunch or taking a break from work.

EXTRA BENEFITS OF GARDENS

Long-term projects such as gardening produce many rewards besides flowers and vegetables. Walking in a garden at the end of a long day can have a mellowing effect on parents, children, and caregivers, and the lessons learned from patiently removing pesky weeds and watering thirsty vines day after day will last forever. In addition, planning and maintaining a garden teaches research and organizational skills that can be used later in school or community projects.

During the growing season, children can share their project with friends and family; if the garden is close to a school or preschool, school-agers can host field trips to the garden. Harvest time can be celebrated with a feast made from vegetables grown by the children, served on tables decorated with their own flowers. The looks on the youngest children's faces will be worth all the muddy footprints left on the center floor. Extra flowers can be dried and sold in bunches; excess vegetables can be donated to a food bank. Older children can lead younger ones in matching games made from the pictures in seed catalogs, and they can teach one another the names of the different plants. The children at one center made picture frames and stationery using dried flowers from their own garden. Another group planted herbs in a big barrel by the front door and sold fresh clippings to their parents as they came to pick them up in the evening. You could also plant a ***windowsill garden.***

A number of helpful gardening books are available. The following are especially good for children's projects: *Linnea's Windowsill Garden* (Bjork & Anderson, 1988), *Rainy Days Grow It for Fun* (Robson & Bailey, 1991), *Best Kids' Garden Book* (Elving, 1992), and *Gardening from Garbage* (Handelsman, 1993).

Parachute Activities

What is it about parachutes? Children (and many adults) love being inside them, under them, running in circles watching the silk fronds billow, and collapsing in laughing heaps among the folds when they finally deflate and fall. School-supply houses sell colorful parachutes designed specifically for children's play, but many school-age centers are still enjoying surplus-store parachutes that were once carried in military airplanes. Either type is a good investment.

Most parachute play consists of placing six to twenty children around the outside of a parachute where they each take firm hold of the edge and either walk around in circles or lift the parachute up by rhythmically bouncing their hands up and down. Most parachute games can be played in a gym or cafeteria, but children may be allowed to be more boisterous if the games are played on a soft grassy area. Here are some enjoyable things to do with parachutes.

BOUNCE THE BEACH BALL

Throw a beach ball on top of a taut parachute. By moving the edge of the chute up and down in a "wave," children can move the ball around the edge of the parachute, or they can attempt to move it to the center of the chute. Sometimes there is a hole that can be the target, and you can also play this game with a smaller ball. This can be a two-team challenge—one group tries to get the ball

Parachutes are a favorite with all ages.

in the middle, while the other group tries to keep the ball toward the edge. Also try using a smaller, lightweight ball.

SLITHERING SNAKES

All players take off their shoes and sit on the grass in a circle, with the parachute covering their legs but pulled fairly tight. One person is declared "It" and remains under the chute, in the "lake." Slithering under the "water," "It" touches someone on the foot and pulls that person under the water. Now both of them slither around looking for a new victim. The last person to be selected becomes the new "It."

PARACHUTE CAVE

This is a favorite game on a hot day. Everyone stands around the parachute and pulls it taut. Using a rhythmic up-and-down movement, players gradually fill the parachute with air and raise it higher and higher until it billows full. Then, on the count of three, the children bring the edges of the chute down to the ground, duck under it, and sit down, with the chute wrapped around their backs and tucked under them. By rocking back and forth just right, the children can eventually learn to keep the parachute afloat around them for 10 or

Children in child-care settings delight in the same kinds of water play as children at home.

15 minutes. It's nice and cool in there. Other ideas can be found in books and videos sold by the supply houses that sell parachutes.

Water Fun

Running through sprinklers on a sunny day . . . sitting in two inches of cool water and reading a book . . . making a dam or stepping stones across a creek . . . sailing milk-carton boats down the gutter. These and other delightful pursuits in and around water have been enjoyed by children for generations, and children who spend their days in child-care settings should have opportunities to experience them, too.

Many of the children in school-age care are unaccustomed to "playing"—with water or with anything else. It may take creative leadership to bring out the little boys and girls trapped inside the sophisticated young people in your program, but rest assured, once you find them, they'll be there to stay. Make sure everyone has a change of clothes or obtain a washer and dryer, so children won't be worrying about ruining their clothes. Be sure the day is reasonably warm. Here are some more things school-age children have been known to enjoy doing with water:

Make large hoops out of coat hangers and craft pipe cleaners. Dip them in a soap solution and make giant bubbles. You can also use plastic straws (blow, don't suck!), plastic strawberry baskets, and serving spoons with holes.

Soap solution: ⅔ cup liquid dish soap to 1 gallon of water. For stronger bubbles, add 1 tablespoon glycerine (available in cake decorating sections of grocery or craft stores).

Fill a large galvanized tub with water (you can buy these at animal feed stores) and float apples on it. Take turns trying to remove an apple from the water with your mouth (for the uninitiated, this is called "bobbing for apples").

Dig a ditch and fill it with water. (This activity can take all day.)

Fill a water table with water and do "big kid" kinds of things with it— whatever those are.

Take the hose out to a dirt patch and make mud. Play in it.

Make water balloons. Throw them on the ground and watch them burst.

Water the garden. Water the plants. Fill a birdbath.

Dump a pile of sand on the ground. Make sand castles.

Working With Wood

Many preschools have put away their woodworking tools, and fewer parents amuse themselves in garage workshops than in years past. Budget cuts have even restricted the offering of woodshop in many middle schools and high schools. But working with wood is a very satisfying activity, and many patterns for simple projects such as birdhouses, planters, or letter racks still exist in public libraries, although you may need to request a book from the main branch. If no one on staff feels confident enough to teach a woodworking workshop, try asking parents, or contacting a branch of the 4-H, Scouts, or Camp Fire Inc. to ask whether they have a suggestion. You can also check local middle and high schools for teachers who may have taught woodshop in the past or who still pursue the craft. Staff members and children can learn together. A great resource for nonwoodworkers is *Woodworking for Young Children,* by Skeen, Garner, and Cartwright (1984).

START SMALL

It is a good idea to begin small, with miscellaneous scraps of wood and the creation of art sculptures rather than diving immediately into a structured project. This allows children to become comfortable using hammers and nails and with the safety precautions necessary to use woodworking tools. Five- to seven-year-old children are often perfectly happy to experience the process of sawing, hammering, and gluing wood together without being too concerned about the outcome. Older youngsters may appreciate assistance in building specific projects, such as birdhouses (Challand, 1985).

Lumber yards that cut wood to order can sometimes provide free wood scraps. If children have several different kinds, sizes, and shapes of wood as well as different sized nails, they will be more interested. Hand saws, drills, screwdrivers, and chisels can be introduced one at a time, and projects can be designed to provide practice with these tools. Activity leaders might want to supply the younger children with chunks of balsa and other soft woods that can be cut with a small **coping saw** and glued together. Harder wood, hammer and nails, and **crosscut saws** can come later.

A search through magazines, books, and pamphlets can be made by children who want to try making finished projects. Learning how to enlarge patterns and transfer them to the wood is a logical next step; then follows measuring, cutting, fastening the pieces together, smoothing with sandpaper, and applying a finish. Encourage good workmanship rather than speedy production. One of the advantages of an out-of-school program is that children can take advantage of long stretches of time and do a really careful job.

TRY LARGER PROJECTS

After children get the hang of small projects, they might want to tackle larger ones. Perhaps they could build a playhouse or a tree house, or a puppet theater. One college student remembers his satisfaction at age 10 when he used strips of plywood to build a complex exercise area for the center's pet hamster. Modeled after a mouse maze, it contained nooks and crannies in which the creature could sleep as well as interesting areas to explore. Open at the top and accessible from the hamster's cage, it provided hours of enjoyment for both rodent and children.

Somewhere in your community you might have a retired cabinet maker or furniture refinisher who can teach the fine points of wood construction or finishing. With patient and gentle guidance from their teacher, three 10-year-olds at one center covered a kitchen work area with ceramic tiles. Their sense of competence soared, and they proudly showed off their work to visitors for many months. Be sure there is adequate ventilation whenever paint, varnish, or other solvent-based products are used; if possible, schedule these activities out of doors. Other good resources for woodworking activities include *Woodworks* (Brown, 1984), *Carpentry Is Easy When You Know How* (Check, 1974), and *If I Had a Hammer: Woodworking with Seven Basic Tools* (Lasson, 1974).

Raising Animals

In some before- and after-school environments, animals can be included in the curriculum. Whether the animals are small and caged, such as guinea pigs, hamsters, snakes, or iguanas, or much larger such as sheep, pot-bellied

Some children cannot have pets where they live; often they love to spend hours caring for the animals at their after-school center.

pigs, ponies, or ostriches running in larger enclosures, children will never forget their animal friends and will learn many valuable lessons from helping to care for them.

Visits from veterinarians, local farmers and ranchers, dog or cat breeders, 4-H members, or Future Farmers of America can be used to develop an interest in animal care among your group. Sometimes speakers from a pet rescue organization or wild animal rehabilitation group can bring in injured animals and talk about the care necessary to return their patients to the wild.

Pets arrive in child-care settings from a variety of sources. Sometimes one of the staff members or parents has a pet that he or she can no longer care for at home. School-age children like to earn money, and the acquisition of a center pet could become the goal of a fund-raising effort. An advertisement can be placed in a local newspaper. It is important that before any animals are brought into the center, however, local health regulations are reviewed, the cost of required immunizations and possible neutering are considered, and the source of funds for the animal's feed is defined. Obviously, if you share your facility with other people, they will also need to be consulted. Once the kind of pet has been determined, make a visit to the public library with a few children to borrow books about caring for the animal. Together, plan where the pet will live and discuss how the cleaning, feeding, and exercising will be managed. Rearrange the furniture as necessary to accommodate the cage and supplies, or make arrangements to build fencing and a shelter. After all these considerations are dealt with, enjoy the new addition to your program!

Many different types of animals have been cared for in school-age child-care programs:

birds	hamsters	cats	dogs	chickens
horses	mice	rabbits	snakes	gerbils
fish	iguanas	frogs/toads	turtles	ducks
guinea pigs	sheep	heifers	ostriches	pot-bellied pigs

A good reference for looking after your pets is *The Complete Book of Pet Care* (Roach, 1995).

Hiking/Cycling/Skating

Children who spend as many as 6 or 7 years in child care are dependent on high-quality programs to offer them a wide variety of experiences. Whenever possible, try to find ways to allow the children in your program to enjoy the same kinds of activities and pursuits that their friends outside the center get to enjoy; help them to develop lifelong habits of healthy play. They should have opportunities to swim, ride bikes or scooters, skate, skateboard, roller blade, jump on sticks or spin hula hoops, or participate in whatever outdoor activity is popular at the moment.

If it is safe to do so, schedule frequent jaunts around and out of the neighborhood. Some children may walk, but others may prefer to skate or ride their bicycles. These trips can be designed in a variety of ways—searches for **collage material,** garbage pickup, scavenger hunts, or simply explorations and adventures. For everyone to enjoy these outdoor activities, keep the group size small and allow the leaders to plan them on fairly short notice. One way to avoid inconveniencing parents who may not always arrive for pickup at the same time is to set aside 1 or 2 days a week for these kinds of "away" activities. Involve both parents and children in deciding which days they should be and what time the group should return. Then, the day before a hike or outing, have interested children sign up for the event and take home a reminder notice. Be sure also to plan an interesting activity for those who cannot participate and must remain at the center.

Team Sports

Sometimes children in out-of-school care are unable to participate in recreation leagues organized for softball, soccer, football, swimming, hockey, or other team sports. School-age center staff can sometimes make the difference by coordinating between parents, coaches, and teachers to assist with transportation to and from practices or by organizing a team that practices at the center itself. Inquire into the recreation activities in your community and see what sports are offered, where, and when. If you have enough children within an age group, fielding your own team and participating in the community league may be the easiest approach, although it may not be practical for a staff member to coach the team. See whether a parent or community volunteer can take that role. You will need to work closely with parents on every step of this process, as they may be required to pay league fees, provide uniforms, and transport children on weekends. Perhaps there is a way the school-age program can raise money to help with some of these needs; it may also be feasible for staff members to participate in the weekend games.

Whether or not participation in organized athletic leagues is possible, allowing the children to organize team sports after school can be a very enjoyable endeavor. If your program does not have money for equipment, allow them to bring their own or request donations from community agencies. Locate a rule book for the sport of the month and encourage the children to refer to it. If they request help with skills and a staff member knows how to develop skill-building activities, go for it. Generations of youngsters enjoyed pickup basketball games and softball in spare lots long before parents began organizing leagues; the after-school program is a perfect environment to allow these pastimes to develop naturally if the interest is there.

Other Outdoor Games

Other outdoor activities, most of which can be set up within the school-age center grounds, include Ping-Pong (table tennis), shuffleboard, croquet, miniature golf, and ten-pin bowling. Try to obtain real game sets, not the "kiddie" versions. They can often be found in the bargain section of the Sunday want ads. It can be fun to keep score and develop tournaments. Perhaps you might want to invite local experts to teach game-specific skills, but don't let competition overcome enjoyment. As in all areas of curriculum, enthusiastic youth leaders are the key to finding enjoyable things to do out of doors and engaging the interest of the children in them.

The suggestions for outdoor activities given in this chapter are only examples. Following the interests of the staff and children in your program and the expertise of volunteers in your community, you can incorporate many other activities into your curriculum.

SUMMARY

Children who participate in out-of-school programs after school need lots of physical activity to develop normally and build lifelong habits of healthy living. Organizing outdoor games and activities takes planning and preparation by center staff. It also takes an enthusiastic attitude and a willingness to participate along with the children. Outdoor activities such as gardening, woodworking, and animal husbandry provide opportunities for children to engage in long-term commitments and see the results of their efforts. Athletic activities such as team sports or swimming, hiking, cycling, skating or skateboarding may take special arrangements, but they can add a great deal to the value of a program for school-agers.

REVIEW QUESTIONS
....

1. Why are recreational games an important part of the program for school-agers?
2. What does Jim Deacove mean when he compares musical chairs to our society?
3. List four possible sources of free gardening equipment or supplies.
4. Describe three things you can do with a parachute.
5. How can children in after-school care participate in team sports?

CHALLENGE EXERCISES
....

1. Lead a group of 10 school-age children in a game that most of them do not know. How did it go? Describe in a few paragraphs what steps you went through to explain the rules, demonstrate the play, and clarify confusion.

2. Call your local Chamber of Commerce and ask for a list of service clubs in your community. Which clubs could be the source of supplies or equipment for outdoor activities?

3. Draw a sketch of a site with which you are familiar. Where might you put a small garden? Explain why it is important to select several sites before approaching the school or agency administration for permission to plant a garden.

4. What problems might you run into when you decide to plan a bike day at your center? How could you handle each of the problems you think of?

TERMS TO LEARN
....

collage material
coping saw
crosscut saw
cultural conditioning
tally
windowsill garden

REFERENCES
....

Bjork, C., & Anderson, L. (1988). *Linnea's windowsill garden*. New York: R & S Books.

Brown, W. F. (1984). *Woodworks*. New York: Atheneum.

Challand, H. J. (1985). *Science projects and activities*. Chicago: Children's Press.

Check. (1974). *Carpentry is easy when you know how*. London: Marshall Cavendish.

Deacove, J. (1974). *Cooperative games for indoors and out*. Perth, Ontario, Canada: Family Pastimes.

Elving, P. (1992). *Best kids' garden book*. Menlo Park, CA: Sunset.

Foster, D., & Overholt, J. (1994). *Outdoor action games for elementary children*. West Nyack, NY: Parker Publishing.

Graham, G., Holt/Hale, S., & Parker, M. (1998). *Children moving: A reflective aproach to teaching physical education*. Mountain View, CA: Mayfield.

Haas-Foletta, K., & Cogley, M. (1990). *School-age ideas and activities for after school programs*. Nashville, TN: School-Age Notes.

Handelsman, J. (1993). *Gardening from garbage*. Brookfield, CT: Millbrook Press.

Holt/Hale, S. A. (1998). *On the move*. Mountain View, CA: Mayfield.

Lasson, R. (1974). *If I had a hammer: Woodworking with seven basic tools*. New York: E. P. Dutton.

Roach, P. (1995). *The complete book of pet care*. New York: Macmillan.

Robson, D., & Bailey, V. (1991). *Rainy days grow it for fun*. New York: Gloucester Press.

Skeen, P., Garner, A., & Cartwright, S. (1984). *Woodworking for young children*. Washington, DC: National Association for the Education of Young Children.

CHAPTER ELEVEN

Rainy Day and Snowy Day Projects

Especially Engaging Things to Do Inside

On bad weather days, children come through your door already weary of being inside. They've probably been cooped up for hours and subjected to one planned activity after another, during which they most likely had very little to say about what they did, where they did it, or with whom. What most adults generally feel like doing after a day like that is collapsing into a comfortable chair with the newspaper or a good book, enjoying a time of peaceful re-generation before facing people or activities. Many youngsters say they feel the same way.

Sadly, school-age program managers often believe that **structured programming** is more important than usual on these occasions to keep school-agers' pent-up high spirits under control. Staff members may plan a full afternoon of interesting group activities and then become frustrated or discouraged when the children don't want to participate in them. It is important for school-age children to have opportunities both for a transitional "un-stress" period and for long periods of **unstructured play,** even on rainy or snowy days. The importance of play cannot be understated in a program for school-agers:

> Play gives children opportunities to develop in acceptable ways and build self-esteem. Play is also one of the most important ways in which children develop social skills. They learn to take turns, negotiate, share materials, understand how a friend feels, and express their emotions. In addition, play helps children try out grown-up roles and overcome their fears.
> —Koralek, Newman, & Colker, 1995, vol. 2, p. 144

Having said that, we must also note that some children, left with no structure at all, have trouble focusing on a self-directed activity or pursuit. They act bored and may even exhibit behavior problems; so it is important to offer them a wide variety of things to do and to be watchful of individuals who need physical activity or just a change of page. Never coerce children into participating if they would rather not. *Coaxing* is OK, but *requiring* participation is a sure way to destroy the fun. It is the job of the school-age child-care professional to **engage** children's interest. Sometimes this takes the form of modeling interest yourself. Demonstrate for bored children how to reach out and try new things, but also allow children merely to observe if that is their choice. Another helpful technique is to interest one or two class leaders in a project or game. Usually other children will join in if the leaders appear to be having fun.

Organized Active Games

Organized indoor games are a good way to help children burn excess energy on days when weather does not permit outdoor play. Be sure to keep ideas fresh, and ask the children to suggest games they especially like to play. Sources of indoor games are similar to those of outdoor games (Chapter 10). Also, search libraries for books of "party games" or "parlor games." Following are a few to try.

INDOOR HIDE AND SEEK

Hiding places large enough for children are hard to come by in most after-school programs, so the child who is "It" hides his or her eyes while each child hides an object. The objects must be things that will be recognized when found, such as stuffed animals, trucks, or blocks; they must be in plain sight when "It" is close to them. All other parts of the game, such as counting to 100 (or some other agreed-on number) and running for base, are the same (children will need to set ground rules about where they stand while their objects are being located so that there is an element of reason in the dash to "base"). Certain areas may need to be placed off limits before play begins. Another variation on Hide and Seek is Four Corners, in which everyone crowds into one of the four corners of the room; depending on the arrangement of your center, there may be more than four corners. The person who is "It" hides his or her eyes during this process, then calls out a name and races the called person to base.

LEAPFROG

Players line up, one behind another. The first player squats down, knees bent, hands on knees, head down. The second player now places their hands on the first player's shoulders, spreads both knees wide, and jumps over the first player. The third player jumps over the first two, one at a time. The fourth player jumps over the first three, and so on. When all players are squatting in a row, the last player leaps over all of them, and the first one begins again. This can continue all over the room, for as long as the players wish.

FREEZE DANCE (STATUES)

Twelve-year-old Deborah described this game to me: "Someone ("It") turns on some music and everyone dances around. Then the person who's "It" turns off the music and everyone freezes. Anyone who moves is out. The last person to be out is "It." No one wants to be out because they like to dance so everyone works really hard to stay still, even though they're usually laughing so hard they can't." This is a game that many children with disabilities can play as gleefully as their peers.

Cooking and Science Activities

FOOD PREPARATION

One of the most motivating statements a school-age staff member can make is "Let's cook." Not only is there an obvious reward at the end of the task, but most children enjoy the social interaction inherent in the process as well as the opportunity to pour, measure, stir, and shape ingredients. If you have access to a sink and counter space, food preparation can be a daily event. Pizza, popcorn, cheese balls, soups, pies, pasta, brownies, pretzels, peanut brittle—there is no end to the cooking projects in which children can participate. In fact, with a little instruction at the beginning of the program year, older children can plan, organize, and supervise food projects that allow younger children to participate and learn future leadership roles. Food can be purchased with money earned through fund-raising projects, included in the program budget, or donated in turn by parents.

Learning to do simple tasks in the kitchen, such as separate an egg, grate cheese, or pop popcorn, can be the focus of a whole cooking activity. Or children can do experiments with different types of foods, such as toasting whole wheat, white, and rye bread to see which takes the longest (D'Amico & Drummond, 1995). Making foods from scratch that are usually purchased ready-made can also be interesting. Shake whipping cream in jars until it becomes butter; and spread the butter on hot slices of bread made from flour that the children have ground themselves (Bumgarner, 1984). Mix cereal squares together with pretzels, nuts, and Worcestershire sauce, then toast to create a crispy snack mix. Cooking activities, in addition to being enjoyable, also teach basic math and science concepts that will be useful later in children's lives. Following are three recipes that have received "thumbs up" from school-agers:

Pizza From Scratch

1 tablespoon (package) dry yeast

1 cup warm water

2 tablespoons vegetable oil

¼ to ½ teaspoon salt

3 to 4 cups flour

Wash hands and have all ingredients ready. In a medium-size bowl, dissolve yeast in warm water. Allow to stand for 10 minutes to start bubbling, then stir well. (To speed along the fermenting process, you can add up to one tablespoon sugar or honey to the warm water.) Stir in remaining ingredients, adding just enough flour to form a stiff dough, one that requires your hands to get it mixed and pressed into a ball. Knead dough on a floured surface for about 5 minutes until warm and elastic. Rinse the bowl in hot water if necessary to remove flour residue, dry with a paper towel, then spray with vegetable oil. Turn ball of dough around in the bowl to coat, then cover with a towel and let it rise in a warm place about 1½ hours, or until doubled in size. Punch ball down and divide into two pieces. Roll out each piece and place on a greased 12" to 14" pizza pan or cookie sheet and push to the edges, forming a rim around the outside. Brush dough with vegetable oil. (All or half the dough can also be frozen for use another day.)

To make pizza, spread with prepared pizza sauce (you can buy that in the supermarket or make it from scratch) and any toppings you wish (favorites seem to be browned and drained ground beef or sausage, sliced mushrooms or olives, ham and pineapple, or pepperoni). Top with 1 to 2 cups grated mozzarella cheese. Bake at 425°F for 15 to 20 minutes, until crust is golden brown. Cool slightly and cut into wedges. Enjoy!

Hot Dog Bean Soup
. . . .

1 cup navy beans, soaked overnight in 8 cups of water

1 large onion, finely chopped

2–3 carrots, diced

2 stalks celery, diced

1 teaspoon salt

1 tablespoon flour

1 cup hot water

2 tablespoons molasses

1 teaspoon mustard

3–6 fat-free frankfurters, sliced

Drain beans and cover with fresh boiling water. Add onion, carrots, celery, and salt and cook over low heat until beans are tender, at least 2 hours. (Add more water as necessary to keep from sticking.) Remove ½ cup beans from pan and squash them into a creamy texture with a spoon. Stir in flour and 1 cup hot water until smooth. Return flour/bean mixture to pan, add molasses and mustard, and stir until blended. Continue cooking until soup thickens, about 5 to 10 minutes. Add hot dogs, heat through, and serve.

Extra-Rich Peanut Butter Cookies
....

Beat together

½ cup soft margarine

½ cup brown sugar★

½ cup granulated sugar★

Add

1 beaten egg

1 cup creamy peanut butter

1 teaspoon vanilla flavoring

Sift together in a separate bowl

1½ cups flour

½ teaspoon salt

½ teaspoon baking soda

Stir sifted ingredients into first mixture. With sugared hands, roll dough into small balls, approximately 1 inch in diameter. Set about 1 inch apart on an oiled cookie sheet. Press flat with a fork or glass. Bake at 375°F for about 15 minutes.

A number of good books are available for school-age cooks. Three of these are *The Science Chef,* by Joan D'Amico and Karen Eich Drummond; *Kids' Cooking: A Very Slightly Messy Manual,* by The Authors at Klutz Press; and *Kids in the Kitchen: 100 Delicious, Fun & Healthy Recipes to Cook and Bake,* by Sarah Bracken and Micah Pulleyn.

SIMPLE SCIENCE PROJECTS

Children learn about the world by playing in it. Many simple science experiments and projects lend themselves to out-of-school settings and often provide a way for children to understand some of the ideas being taught in academic classrooms. A trip to the local library can provide books on topics of interest; many of these will suggest ways to demonstrate the ideas presented in the books. Children may suggest their own experiments by their questions: I wonder if this floats? How can you tell a worm from a caterpillar? Which is harder, a diamond or a piece of glass?

★Press out any lumps first.

Science activities appeal to children of all ages.

Remember: It is the *children* who are supposed to be doing the science, not the adults. Staff in the program can support the process by creating an environment that nurtures inquiry and by helping children locate resources, tools, and materials. They can also assist wherever there is a possibility of accidents. However, the school-agers should lead the inquiry forward and, wherever possible, set up the experiments themselves. Otherwise, it's just like being in school. Following are some science projects that school-age children may enjoy doing together:

The Egg-Eating Bottle
. . . .

Materials

An egg

A bottle with a neck slightly smaller than the egg

A piece of paper

A match (and an adult to help with the lighting)

Steps

1. Place the egg in cold water in a pan; bring the water to a boil and cook the egg for about 10 minutes, until hard boiled.
2. Cool the egg, then remove shell and skin.
3. Make sure the egg will rest on the top of the bottle without falling through (a quart-sized milk bottle or wine carafe will usually work).

Once the older children see how the volcano eruption is caused, they can demonstrate it for younger children.

4. Wrinkle up the piece of paper and put it into the bottle.
5. Light the match and drop it into the bottle so that it sets the paper on fire.
6. Quickly fit the egg into the neck of the bottle. The egg will be sucked into the bottle!

Explanation   As the paper burns, it uses the oxygen in the air. Placed in the neck of the bottle, the egg seals the opening so that no more air can get in to replace the oxygen used by the burning paper. The air pressure inside the jar drops, and the egg is sucked in (adapted from Walpole, 1988).

The Erupting Volcano
• •

Children age 6 to 8 seem to enjoy this activity best. Older children may not find it as exciting as it sometimes shows up in intermediate science curricula. If that is the case, the fourth-, fifth-, or sixth-grade children could plan the construction of the volcano and combine the ingredients the first time; then the younger children can play with the effects.

Materials

A volcano shape made out of wire covered with papier-mâché, or a pile of gravel or sand.

A hidden center made out of a plastic water bottle with a fairly wide top, or use a narrow-topped bottle and a funnel.

Glass measuring cup

Baking soda

Vinegar

Large pan or tray to contain volcano and the mess it will make.

Steps

1. Build the volcano with the plastic bottle in the center. (This can be as simple or as complicated a process as the children wish. In one center, the volcano construction and painting took nearly a week; the resulting realistic model was later incorporated into a model train board.)

2. Place volcano on tray (or build it on a large flat surface that will contain spills).

3. Place about ¼ cup of baking soda in the bottle, using the funnel if necessary.

4. Using the measuring cup, pour about ½ cup of vinegar into the bottle and stand back. (This process can be made more realistic by adding red food coloring to the vinegar.)

Explanation   Placing baking soda and vinegar together causes a chemical reaction that results in carbon dioxide gas, or foaming bubbles. This is similar to the process that happens in real volcanic eruptions, which are caused by extremely hot gases exploding through weak spots in the earth's crust (adapted from Wood, 1994).

Making a Magnetic Compass

Materials

Bar magnet

Steel sewing needle

About 8–10 inches of fine thread

Pencil or pen

Drinking glass or jelly jar

A piece of paper about 1 × 2 inches

Steps

1. Thread the needle and tie a knot in one end of the thread. Leave the other end free so it can be pulled through the paper. Fold the paper in the middle to make a 1-inch square. Now spread the paper a little and push the needle through the center fold from the inside. Gently pull the thread

through the paper so the knot is not pulled through. Take the needle off the thread.

2.   Magnetize the needle by stroking it 20 to 30 times *in the same direction* across one end of the magnet.

3.   Tie the free end of the thread around the middle of the pencil and lay the pencil across the top of the glass. The length of thread should suspend the paper about an inch above the bottom of the glass.

4.   Make the paper into an upside down V and insert the needle horizontally through the center of both parts of the paper. Lower the paper inside the glass again so that it and the needle are suspended by the thread and held up by the pencil. If the needle is free to turn, it will align itself north and south.

Explanation   The earth is a huge magnet. One magnetic pole is near the North Pole, and the other near the South Pole. A magnetic field is made up of lines of force that travel in a circular pattern from one pole to the other. In the experiment, the needle turns a few times, then aligns itself north and south with the lines of force in the earth's magnetic field (adapted from Wood, 1994).

You can find excellent science books for children, often in the local public library. Here are four especially good ones: *What? Experiments for the Young Scientist,* by Robert W. Wood; *How? More Experiments for the Young Scientist,* by Dave Prochnow and Kathy Prochnow; *Science Projects and Activities,* by Helen J. Challand; and *175 Science Experiments to Amuse and Amaze Your Friends,* by Brenda Walpole.

Learning to Use a Sewing Machine

Simple straight-sew and zigzag sewing machines often languish in garages, basements, and attics; see if you can round up a few for your program. Get some outside instruction if necessary, or invite a member of the retired community to come and give sewing lessons. Following simple safety instructions, children (and staff) can be taught how to thread the machine and practice sewing straight seams. In just a few hours, most children are ready to make something "real." Some useful projects for out-of-school programs include beanbags, shopping/book bags, simple curtains, furniture slipcovers, covers for tables to turn them into puppet theaters or forts, tablecloths or sets of napkins for special occasions. These require only the simplest of construction techniques and are fun to make.

After completing several projects with straight seams, children who want more challenging projects might enjoy visiting a fabric store and selecting simple craft patterns. Most stores include directions for making decorator pillows, simple stuffed toys, Christmas stockings, or other whimsical items. Collect fabric scraps, thread, buttons, scissors, and other supplies by requesting them in notes sent home with children or by asking their classroom teachers to request donations. (Teachers may have suggestions of their own; children in one program sewed simple skirts, capes, and hats for a school play.) After the initial learning phase, make sewing projects a free-choice option.

Making Jewelry

With every passing school year there seems to be a new friendship bracelet, necklace, or pin in style. Establishing a jewelry-making center to allow children to construct the fashion of the year can lead to the creation of more complex jewelry projects. Some youngsters will enjoy spending several afternoons threading beads, tying knots, or twisting plastic strands to decorate their ankles, wrists, necks, and clothing or those of their friends.

Younger children may be content to dye macaroni with food coloring, threading it on string, but older children will be more interested in working with colored wooden or plastic beads or shrinkable colored plastic, or tying repetitive macramé-like knots to form their adornments. Teen magazines are good sources of craft ideas, or you can invite junior high or high school students to lead jewelry-making workshops. Collect supplies at yard sales and flea markets; ask children's parents for their discards. Previously worn jewelry with broken catches or broken chains with working clasps can be taken apart and reconfigured. Some children will even enjoy organizing the found materials into egg cartons or muffin tins. Some programs have sold repaired and re-crafted jewelry as a fund-raising project.

Dramatic Activities

Authors Louisa May Alcott and the Brontë sisters wrote their first stories during long winter evenings. Long winter days at the school-age child-care center can also be productive if staff and children work together to create dramatic productions.

FANTASY PLAY

One way to pique children's interest in drama is to create dramatic play areas suited to the school-age child. Different from household settings usually seen in preschools, this area of the center may have various furnishing at different times throughout the year. Boxes of theatrical *props*[1] can be developed that suggest certain themes. With a ***prop box,*** an *ice cream shop* can be created with ice cream scoops; a box of cones; containers of toppings, nuts, and cherries;

---

[1] This theatrical abbreviation for "property" refers to movable items used on the set of a theater production, especially those handled by the actors.

aprons and hats; and materials to make menus. Children can serve imaginary ice cream made out of balls of pink, white, or brown yarn, or prepare real ice cream snacks for their friends. A *restaurant prop box* could contain tablecloths and napkins, cutlery, flowers, salt and pepper shakers, and other table equipment. Food packages and posters help identify the type of food served: ethnic, health food, fast food, or pizza. Children can develop a *service station* with a box of work clothes and hats, oil cans and rags, paper towels, plastic spray bottles, miscellaneous tools, and posters from local garages or tire stores. Children exploring these materials may be able to track down one or two real tires with axles to work on with a lug wrench. *Office prop boxes* can be made from plastic or cardboard file boxes purchased from office supply or stationery stores. They may contain file folders, envelopes and pads of paper, pens, pencils and holders, clear plastic tape and dispensers, a telephone, staplers, stamps, hole punches, and other office supplies. Larger objects, such as telephones and a computer, could be permanently situated in a corner of the classroom where they can be used by children throughout the program day.

This realistic dramatic play offers valuable opportunities for children to interact with others, exercise their imaginations, share and take turns, and try out new roles (Myhre, 1993). Children can also integrate their imaginary play with other activities taking place in the program. For example, the "office workers" might enjoy typing thank-you letters to volunteers or designing fund-raising posters. "Restaurant workers" could provide a special meal for Valentine's Day or other celebration. "Service station mechanics" might offer to check the brakes or lubricate their friends' bicycles before a ride around the community. Ideally, these ideas would flow naturally out of the play and be initiated by other children rather than by the adult staff.

STAGING A PLAY

Children's use of the dramatic play area may go no further than enjoyable hours spent in fantasy play, but it may also lead to a suggestion by someone: "Let's put on a play." Plays can be staged with memorized parts or with some children reading the script and other children acting it out or operating puppets. Some effective plays are taken directly from stories children already know; others are made up by the children. Some children are content to use only the costumes and props provided by the program; others develop elaborate schemes and bring in lots of materials to set the scene.

Dramatic ventures may arise on the spur of the moment, and they need only amuse the children who wish to participate in them or observe. They don't need to be very complicated at all. Sometimes, however, they may turn into big productions, and that, for the most part, is all right, too. Some program staff members, staying up all night sewing costumes or painting sets the night before a play, might think things got out of hand (and they probably *did* if the adults are doing the costumes instead of the youngsters!); but once it is all over, they are usually ready to start again.

SPECIALIZED PROP BOXES

Some out-of-school programs have taken prop boxes beyond the realm of merely suggesting dramatic play activities. They have developed interesting collections of materials that are portable (for taking to the park, for example) and easy to store in cupboards or on shelves.

The use of prop boxes enhances curriculum, both indoors and out, and offers individualized choices of activities for the children. Prop boxes are especially valuable for programs that must recreate their environment every day, such as sites in cafeterias, gymnasiums, at parks, or in other shared space; they can reduce behavior problems caused by a lack of interesting things to do. The director of one program for school-agers that is housed in portable classrooms uses prop boxes as a way to expand the classroom into the outdoors. Children are invited to select a prop box and take it outside with them. There they can set up a "mini-classroom" using supplies and equipment contained in the box. Interesting props for outside boxes include magnifying glasses (for looking at insects, leaves, or toes); small gardening shovels and rakes; bats, balls and mitts; beanbags and folding targets; bubble solution and straws; and modeling clay.

Select containers and supplies that are durable and require little or no maintenance; and keep them lightweight and easily accessible. Great prop boxes can be made from cardboard file carriers with finger holes at each end, or from clear plastic housewares boxes with tight-fitting lids. Brainstorm ideas with children and staff, and remember to keep the contents simple so they will be cost effective. Good sources for prop material include flea markets, service club stores, parent donations, and a variety of community resources (hospitals, fire department, post office, police department, and others).

A special kind of prop box developed by one out-of-school program is known to its charges as the "Five O'Clock Box." About that time of the day, explains program director Maureen O'Hanlin, some children's parents start arriving to take them home, and the children need to clean up the projects that have occupied their attention that day. Before the "Five O'Clock Box" system was invented, program staff had to choose between asking the children who stayed the latest to put away material left out by children who had gone home earlier, or make them wait for their parents in a neat but boring room.

Their creative solution to this dilemma was to engage everyone in cleaning up before the majority of parents arrived, usually between 4:30 and 5:00 p.m. Then, when the room was returned to order for the next day, they would bring out the "Five O'Clock Boxes." These are plastic boxes of small games and objects that are interesting to play with but do not make a big mess. Two or three children can take out a box together and the individual games can be quickly returned to the box as each youngster leaves. Examples of good materials for Five O'Clock Boxes include string and diagrams for playing cat's cradle, plastic handheld puzzles, the miniature Etch-A-Sketch, travel games in resealable plastic bags, and decks of cards and card game books. Colored pencils and small coloring books, magnifying glasses and tiny objects to magnify, and magnets and metal objects can all be packaged into interesting pastimes for those last few minutes of the day. Marking each game or object with colored inventory dots that correspond with the box from which it came simplifies cleanup when parents arrive. Here are some other curriculum prop box ideas (O'Hanlin, 1997):

QUIET BOX
books to read
blankets
Walkman™
cassette story tapes
word search books
crossword puzzles
notebooks

GAMES BOX
small jigsaw puzzles
handheld computer games
string and cat's cradle
    instructions
jacks and ball
bag of marbles

BLOCK BOX
cars
animals
carpet
foam blocks
colored unit blocks

ART BOX
beads and string
art supplies
tabletop easel
laptop easel
plastic containers w/tops
watercolors
origami paper and idea book

MUSIC BOX
multicultural instruments
tape recorder and tapes
earphones
ribbons for dancing
material for making simple
    musical instruments
rhythm instruments (oatmeal
    box drum; orange juice can
    rattle)

WRITING/DRAWING
writing paper and pens
rulers, protractors
templates
colored pencils
crayons
felt pens

HOMEWORK BOX
dictionary
atlas
pencil sharpener
ruler
erasers

BEAUTY BOX
curling iron
rollers
blow dryer
mirrors
clips
hot rollers
hair products

PUPPET MAKING

Making puppets is also a great indoor activity. There are many different kinds of puppets, and children of all ages can make some kind of puppet to enjoy. If you are not familiar with different kinds of puppet construction, locate a book at the public library. With a group of children, practice making stick puppets, paper bag puppets, or sock puppets. If older children are in the group, you might introduce them to papier-mâché techniques and suggest that they make the heads of characters from a favorite story. Ask your sewing machine experts to make simple bodies for the puppets. Facial features and clothing can be cut out of fabric scraps and glued on.

PUPPET PLAY

Sometimes the children who like to make puppets are not the same children who want to put on puppet shows; there may need to be some group decision making about who owns a puppet once it is made. Some of the puppet builders might agree to make a selection of characters that will remain in the center for others to use in their productions. Puppets are great for fantasy play. Don't restrict their use to formal presentations. Some children talk to the puppets and develop complex dialogues with puppet characters. For them, an audience would only get in the way. A box of puppets and a small puppet theater that sits on a table can be the source of a great many hours of entertainment.

Large Constructions

Many children like to build things. If the materials are lightweight—such as cardboard, Styrofoam™ sheets, or fabric—the constructions can be quite large and impressive. A young friend of mine recalls spending several weeks during sixth grade building and decorating a set of interconnected tunnels made from appliance cartons and held together with duct tape. The oldest boy at the child care center, he retreated inside his "house" whenever he felt overwhelmed by the younger children, but occasionally he actually allowed his young friends to play inside it. Other uses for large boxes include dollhouses, mailboxes, ships, fantasy corner furniture, and reading centers.

If puppets are popular at your center, a puppet theater may be the object of a construction project. Refrigerator boxes are good for this. The result doesn't have to be terribly sturdy or long-lasting. The construction process is the main point, and if the theater eventually gets bent and squashed—well, there are more boxes at the appliance store.

Programs that operate in large spaces, such as multipurpose rooms, can use children's building projects to provide privacy or permit different activities to take place at the same time. In fact, children often suggest this kind of project themselves. Dividers can be made from Styrofoam sheets, or from light wood frames covered with cloth or burlap. Even large banners hanging from suspended horizontal poles can be construction projects: Large pieces of felt can be cut into shapes and glued onto sheets of burlap or other cloth. Younger children usually need suggestions, but older children prefer to make and carry out their own plans without much assistance (or interference) from adults. If

Due to budget cuts, many school-age children have few opportunities to experience cooking projects during the regular school day.

they know it's all right to come up with ideas for projects, they probably will; and if they need you, they'll tell you. A nurturing environment allows this kind of creativity to happen.

Literature-Related Activities

Plays and puppet shows can be written by the children, and sometimes they enjoy dramatizing stories they are reading in school. As children begin to read more and more, they begin to make connections between what they read and other parts of their lives and they may enjoy sharing their favorite stories with other children. Classroom teachers use *literature webs* to build an integrated curriculum; out-of-school program staff can use the same process to help children amuse themselves in constructive ways.

Think of a web as a selection of related concepts. The core concept or idea (it can also be the title of a book) is written in the center of a piece of paper, and lines are drawn forming a set of spokes going away from it (Figure 11-1). The second level of ideas, or *web strands* (Freedman & Reynolds, 1980), represent different categories of information related to the core concept. If relationships exist between various web strands, they can be connected with *strand ties.* Sometimes a second level of ideas, or *strand supports,* is added to represent information or facts that add meaning or relevance to the web strands. In the

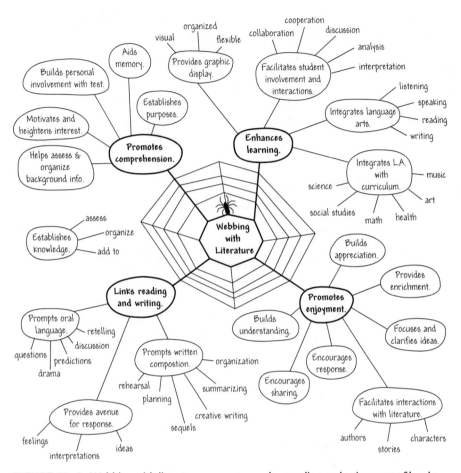

FIGURE 11–1 Webbing with literature promotes understanding and enjoyment of books.

book *Webbing with Literature: Creating Story Maps With Children's Books* (1991), author Karen Bromley explains that diagramming literature themes enhances readers' understanding and appreciation of literature and helps children identify important issues in the books they read.

Figure 11-2 shows a web of activities relating to Konigsburg's *From the Mixed-up Files of Mrs. Basil E. Frankweiler*. The learning concepts illustrated in the web were identified by a parent who led the activities during a summer-long out-of-school program (a detailed description of the activities is presented in Chapter 5 of this book). Activity webs such as these can be built by children or by children and staff together as ways to extend the enjoyment of a book. In these situations, the learning concepts tend to be discovered as the children's interests lead them forward rather than being determined in advance of the activities.

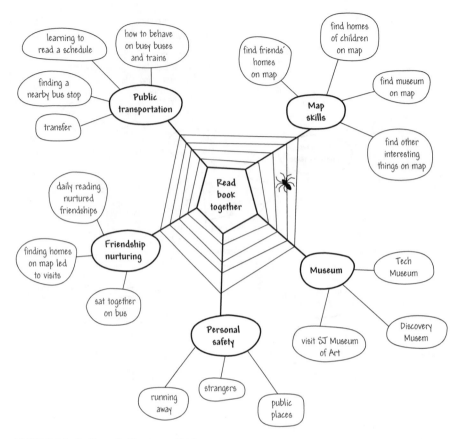

FIGURE 11–2 Sample Literature Web

Writing Letters; Global Friendships

Making friends in other countries can be a horizon-broadening experience. Talk the idea over with the children, then make inquiries among the children themselves, their parents, your friends, and your professional colleagues. Most of us know someone who has traveled out of the country and who has friends or relatives who might know a teacher who has a class that might be interested in exchanging letters. Other good contacts are ministers of local churches and teachers at the local community college, especially if they have an international student adviser.

Once you have found a place to send the letters, help the children learn proper letter-writing style. Be sure they put their home address and the date on the top of the letter, start it with Dear New Friend or something similar, and end the letter with a ***complimentary close***, such as "Your friend," and their name. Children usually need help brainstorming the things they should write about. A "group think" can be helpful here, as children suggest topics and list them on the board for everyone to use. It might be a good idea to have everyone

A map showing the location of pen pals' homes teaches geography while enhancing the pleasure of receiving letters.

write a rough draft of his or her letter first, then help each other with spelling, grammar, and punctuation. Last, they will write a final, ink version to mail. It is also fun to take pictures of each child to enclose with the letters. Be sure to help with addressing, especially if the letters are going to a country in which English is not the standard language. Make sure to have a return address on each envelope. A trip to the post office to purchase postage and mail the letters is an obvious next step. You could even put together a package to send to the children overseas; it might contain an issue of a local newspaper, information about your out-of-school program, and essays or pictures from the children about things they like to do or visit.

While they are waiting for their answers, children might enjoy learning something about the country where their letters are headed. Provide them with a world map or globe and encourage discussion about the location of the country, its neighbors, and what kinds of things the residents might do there. Bring in magazine stories and geography books or make a trip to the public library to borrow books about the country. A bulletin board can be developed as the children's knowledge grows.

You can nurture the children's interest in the project by bringing in literature, music, or news articles about the area. Letters take about a week to get to Europe or Australia from most of the United States and a week to come back. Letters to India, Africa, Asia, or the Middle East will probably take longer. It may be a month or more before the first answer comes. However, the long wait is usually worthwhile. Programs that have initiated international pen pals in years past report that some of the children end up with lifelong friends.

SUMMARY

Children who have been in school all day need opportunities to unwind in their after-school program. For some children, unstructured play is the best choice; these children benefit from being allowed to read, listen to music, chat with their friends, or just be still and quiet for a time. Others, after a brief interlude, are ready to participate in group activities or games. On days when weather doesn't allow outdoor play, school-agers may appreciate some adult leadership in organizing things to do. Children of the TV generation may not be familiar with traditional indoor games or pursuits. Adult staff can serve valuable roles as both resource agents and participants as they introduce new games and activities.

REVIEW QUESTIONS

1. Explain why structured programming may not be appropriate in after-school programs on bad weather days.

2. Describe two ways of encouraging rather than requiring children to participate in activities.

3. Name three things you can do in the kitchen without a recipe.

4. What is a prop box and what can you do with one?

CHALLENGE EXERCISES

1. Locate someone in the community who has a skill that school-age children might like to learn. Coordinate with the director of an after-school program to invite this person to teach the children the skill. Observe and comment on the session.

2. Think about how you liked to spend your time on rainy days after school. Which of the activities you enjoyed could also be enjoyed in a center for school-agers?

3. Develop a literature web for a school-age children's book. Plan three activities and demonstrate them in class.

TERMS TO LEARN

complimentary close
engage
literature web
prop box
structured programming
unstructured play

REFERENCES

Bromley, K. (1991). *Webbing with literature: Creating story maps with children's books.* Boston: Allyn & Bacon.

Bumgarner, M. A. (1984). *Organic cooking for (not-so-organic) mothers.* Morgan Hill, CA: Chesbro Press.

Challand, H. J. (1985). *Science projects and activities.* Chicago: Childers Press.

D'Amico, J. D., & Drummond, K. (1995). *The science chef.* New York: Wiley.

Freedman, G., & Reynolds, E. (1980). Enriching basal reading lessons with semantic webbing. *The Reading Teacher, 33*(6), 677–684.

Koralek, D., Newman, R., & Colker, L. (1995). *Caring for school-age children.* Washington, DC: Teaching Strategies.

Myhre, S. (1993, July). Enhancing your dramatic-play area through the use of prop boxes. *Young Children,* 6–11.

O'Hanlin, M. (1997). Lecture on prop boxes at Gavilan College.

Prochnow, D., & Prochnow, K. (1993). *How? More experiments for the young scientist.* Blue Ridge Summit, PA: TAB Books.

Walpole, B. (1988). *175 science experiments to amuse and amaze your friends.* New York: Random House.

Wood, R. W. (1994). *What? Experiments for the young scientist.* San Francisco: TAB Books.

CHAPTER TWELVE

Working With Older School-Age Children and Teens

One of the most significant challenges for out-of-school programs, especially those that offer traditional before- and after-school care, is designing environments and planning activities that appeal to children beyond fifth grade, generally age 10 and above. Many of these children have been in some kind of group care since early childhood; in most cases, they would prefer to go home, even alone, after school. They know all the board games, they are tired of the routines, and they want a more individualized and private way to spend their time.

The arguments against self-care presented in the introduction to this text are primarily targeted at this group of youngsters. Few parents believe that their 7- or 8-year-old children are old enough to leave unsupervised; even if they allow these children some modicum of self-care, they usually feel uneasy about it. But a 12-year-old? A 14-year-old? Fewer than 50 years ago, children that age in this society were earning wages—and some still are. It seems a bit of a stretch to tell these youngsters and their parents that they are not old enough to take care of themselves after school.

However, our world is different from the one our grandparents lived in, and today's preadolescent children and young teens are far more vulnerable to violent crimes and drug and alcohol habits spawned by boredom and stress than were their forebears. Most of the crimes perpetrated by and against teenagers in the United States take place between 3:00 and 8:00 p.m. (Cannon, 1997; Whitaker & Bastion, 1991), and the after-school habits of unsupervised 10-year-olds may predispose them to be included in those statistics. There are fewer wholesome and safe activities for them to participate in with their friends than there were 20 or 30 years ago, and fewer parents or grandparents available to keep an eye on them near home as they try their wings.

Communities that have developed programs for older schoolchildren have seen a decrease in vandalism and school failure (University of Wisconsin Cooperative Extension, 1994). Many parents in these communities, who have previously spent most afternoons worrying about and communicating with their school-age children, are now able to concentrate on their jobs. This increase in parental ***productivity*** is another outcome of school-age programming that is encouraging increasing numbers of businesses to provide financial support for out-of-school options in their communities (Wong, 1995; Work/Family Directions, 1998).

Some Differences in Programs for Older Children

Programs that are effective in serving the needs of older youngsters look different from other programs for school-agers. One Pennsylvania community experimented with care for older children when the school district moved fifth and sixth graders from local elementary schools into a newly constructed middle school. In a description of their program, director Tracy Yanouzas explained that she and her staff had begun with little specialized knowledge, but gradually came to understand school-age programming quite differently from the way they had viewed it before. First, "Don't call your program child care!" she cautions. "Have your kids think of a catchy name, ***logo,*** and ***mascot***" (Yanouzas, 1993). Many programs for older children use the word *club* rather than *care,* and they design environments that feel and sound more like cafes, coffee houses, or gymnasiums than after-school centers. Another lesson her staff learned was that the games, activities, and art projects they had used in the elementary program were no longer appropriate. The older children wanted new games, new challenges, and new rules.

CLUBS

One popular approach to program planning for older children is to designate 2 or 3 days a week to be "club" days. (This is different from including *club* in the name of the program.) Clubs are interest groups, led by adults or teens who have a particular skill or interest in a subject. Popular clubs for older children include dance, computers, drama, painting, karate, cooking, basketry, math, playing musical instruments, rocket building, or competitive sports. Some programs allow children to select the club they wish to attend each time they meet, but most encourage youngsters to stay with the same club for a period of weeks, even months. Some programs hold clubs on only 1 or 2 designated days a week; they ask parents not to pick up their children early on those days so they can finish whatever they start.

Many clubs operate much like a short class, with the leader teaching certain skills that take several weeks to develop and culminate in some kind of a product. For example, one program's cooking club put on a "1950s diner" evening for their parents. A common ending to a drama club session would be

Older school-agers may spend most afternoons doing homework.

a play or a puppet show. A sewing club might have a fashion show or make stuffed animals for a children's center or hospital. In this model, the sports club might include studying statistics, history, and creative writing as well as learning to play the sport.

To develop a selection of enthusiastic leaders for clubs as well as ideas for club topics, add "interest areas" to your employment application. The topics selected are not necessarily a determining factor in hiring, but they provide you with a list of activities that staff might enjoy developing into the club concept.

It's important with older children to offer fewer structured options on club days. Not all older children want to participate in group activities, so allow them to play games, read, do homework, or listen to music. If some youngsters lose interest in a club and don't want to participate, let them drop out until the next set of clubs begins, then make a different selection. For them to miss several meetings, then start again, especially if they do it frequently, can be disruptive. Clubs should last only 45 minutes to an hour on the days that they meet. That's plenty of time for children to become engaged in an activity and complete a task. Much longer than that, program directors report, and the participants' enthusiasm and enjoyment start to diminish.

ROLE OF THE STAFF

Staff members moving into programs for older children also find they have a different interpersonal role to play from the one they played before. As in programs for younger children, it is important for them to research and plan new and interesting activities to engage the program participants; however, they are also asked to teach athletic skills and new dance steps, take groups to the library, help children practice speeches and parts for the school play, even plan "the perfect outfit" for the sixth-grade promotion dance.

A ROOM OF THEIR OWN

Some programs differentiate care for older children in their regularly established after-school programs by allowing children of different ages to group together at various times during the day or week. The availability of their own space can be extremely morale-boosting to youngsters. Children's advocate and writer Don Bellum describes a program housed in a large multipurpose room with a sign in one corner that reads, "Third graders, teachers, and parents only. All other children KEEP OUT!" (Bellum, 1990). One family child-care provider allowed fifth and sixth graders to clean out an unused workshop in her back garden and turn it into a clubhouse. It now serves as a site for special "older kid" meetings and planning sessions, a homework retreat on fair afternoons, and a quiet place to read for one or two children at a time. Because the workshop was designed with large windows, line-of-site supervision is not a problem. And even though their caregiver can keep an eye on them, the children value the opportunity to have a space that is all theirs.

An after-school program housed in three portable buildings on a school site in northern California designates 4:30 as the time each afternoon when children above fourth grade retreat into one of the buildings for "club time." During that period, the older children may choose to work on long-term projects, read, do homework, or talk quietly in a conversation area. Their group leader is an avid photographer, and a year or so ago he set up a film enlarger in a closet for a 6-week introduction to photography workshop. It's still there. During long gloomy winter afternoons, this older group can often be seen peering at negatives and contact sheets and designing collages or cropping images for enlargements, the results of which decorate two of the building's walls. A do-it-yourself snack center in the same portable provides a place to take a break or a focus of activity for some children; a well-equipped art corner appeals to others (Willyoung, personal communication, 1997).

This program recognizes the value of mixed-age groupings for certain activities, especially sports and games, yet it also communicates to the older children that they have the right to unique interests, tastes, likes, and dislikes. Once again, flexibility is the key; it's important for older children to have their space, but it's counterproductive to the program if they are cliquish or snobbish about it. Sometimes (subject to approval from their peers) older youngsters in the California program invite a younger friend to visit during club time or they

Effective programs for older youths provide a variety of ways for them to develop new skills and friendships.

may accompany a younger sibling or buddy into one of the two remaining buildings after 4:30 to assist with a project, help with homework, or just hang out. This interaction is encouraged by adult staff members. It doesn't take away from the older children's privileged privacy, but it helps to maintain relationships between the different age groups.

Key Characteristics of Programs for Older Children

In addition to having dedicated space and time with their peer group, older school-age children have other developmental needs. Experienced out-of-school program designers agree that successful programs for older children (1) actively involve the youngsters in planning, (2) are flexible and offer a wide variety of activities, (3) permit participants to challenge their skills, develop new abilities, and experience safe risks, and (4) provide links with community agencies, services, businesses, and opportunities (Bellum, 1990; Musson, 1988; Yanouzas, 1993).

INVOLVE YOUNGSTERS IN PLANNING

All out-of-school programs should encourage participation from children in the planning process. However, as children grow and develop in their ability to solve problems of time, space, and personal interaction, the tasks of planning future activities should gradually be handled more and more by the participants and less and less by the program staff. For example, when planning a bicycle outing for a group of second and third graders, the group leader might sketch the streets to be traveled; remind children to bring such important necessities as helmets, sturdy shoes, water bottles, and light jackets; and write the permission slips. The children may have suggested the outing in the first place or may make some suggestions about when and where they would go, but the adult is still basically running the show.

A bicycle outing for seventh and eighth graders, however, will be far more successful if the participants are encouraged actually to plan the route, develop a menu for the picnic lunch, and brainstorm lists of things that could go wrong, need to be brought, and so on. The group leader now serves as a facilitator, occasionally asking a question or making a suggestion, but the activity is pretty much in the hands of the cyclists themselves.

BE FLEXIBLE

Even when youngsters plan their own activities, they may change their minds about participating or decide to postpone the activity until another day. Preteens and teenagers' moods are highly changeable, influenced by circumstances of the school day, affairs of the heart, media coverage of local and national events, the weather, even their hormones. It's a good idea to have backup plans for everything and to keep a good sense of humor.

Flexibility also includes being willing to change the location of an activity if someone else needs the spot, or figuring out how to get along when certain supplies or equipment are missing, broken, or being used. Modeling flexibility is an important role for child and youth workers; the problem solving that goes along with it encourages creativity and spontaneous thought.

OFFER A WIDE VARIETY OF ACTIVITIES

Older school-agers are constantly seeking new challenges. Playground games that engaged them when they were 6 and 7 years old have become too predictable and boring; the daily routine, important for providing a sense of security in their earlier years, now seems deadly dull. After-school programs have a tremendous opportunity to provide children with activities that may be unavailable to them in financially beleaguered school districts or in the limited amount of time they spend with their families. The rest of this section offers ideas to try.

Request donations of musical instruments and advertise for a retired musician; then form a band or an orchestra. A participant in the School-Age Care online newsgroup (SAC-L@postoffice.cso.uiuc.edu) described listening to classical music with children in her program in the Ukraine; with some explanations and repetitions, the youngsters learn to love it ("Not just the *sounds* of a rave," she writes, "but the *music*" (Teterin, personal communication, 1997). Her program provides a music studio where youths can record their own songs, and once or twice a year they prepare performances for the whole community. Even without a proper studio, however, a computer and a synthesizer can provide a group of budding musicians with many hours of enjoyable experimentation. It may not be classical, but it will certainly be memorable.

Invite a local scientist or mathematician to run a science or math club one after-noon a week, or to coach youngsters in their design of science fair projects. NASA is actively entering into partnerships with many schools and after-school pro-grams. One of their goals in doing this is to expand opportunities in math and science for women and people from diverse cultural backgrounds, a goal that fits perfectly with the mission of school-age programming. Why not set up a math lab area with manipulatives, calculators, rulers, and other equipment; then contact NASA employees, parents, or college students to volunteer 1 or 2 hours a month to come by for the last hour of the day to help students with math homework? Alternatively, the older students in your program could staff a homework lab for younger children in the program.

Invite the local community theater to put on their next play at your center, and offer to build the sets and sew the costumes. Many communities have active amateur theater groups that are scrounging for venues. One dance studio, for example, hosted the production of a musical review based on a 1930s radio show. Their part of the bargain was to build a temporary stage, provide rehearsal space, make costumes, and staff the box office. Many lasting friendships grew out of this partnership, and the studio gained several new paying customers who hadn't even known the studio existed until they attended a performance of the play. This sort of collaboration could work equally well in an after-school pro-gram or youth center.

Design a center that invites older youngsters to stay. Most older school-agers, especially teens, enjoy settings that are decorated in a theme, such as a pool hall, a coffee house, or a 1950s malt shop. The way a program feels when you walk through the door is almost as important as what happens once you get there. Older children, especially teens, also like to have a personal impact on their environment. If they are allowed to decorate the space they've been pro-vided, they are far more likely to enjoy being in it. If you can obtain permission to paint walls, build temporary dividers, or add floor coverings, there is no limit to what you and they can do. But very creative environments have also been designed without hammering a nail. Here are some examples:

- Inflate a rubber raft and fill it with pillows. Create a "river" of blue carpet or butcher paper, and surround it with river rushes and overhanging trees made from cardboard tubes and construction paper.
- Set up a dome tent. Equip it with folding camp chairs, pillows, books, and homework supplies; hang an electric light from the ceiling. Place it on a tarpaulin, and add a picnic bench, ficus tree, or hammock.
- Use a combination of cardboard appliance cartons and Styrofoam boards to create a separate room within a room. Paint it or decorate it with artwork

Young Teens Still Need After-School Supervision

Susan Reimer
Baltimore Sun, 9/30/97

My son, now 13, believes he has outgrown the need for after-school supervision while his father and I work. And apparently the federal government agrees.

Since he is no longer 12, he is no longer eligible under the Dependent Care Tax Credit, so his father and I no longer qualify for the modest tax break we received for the huge checks we have been writing for day-care services and camps all these years.

This tax credit never amounted to more than a few hundred dollars a year, and it was not the reason we provided for his care after school, but it was an endorsement for our thinking that 6 was not the right age for a child to come home to an empty house.

Well, 13 isn't the right age, either. And not just because he might absent-mindedly leave the toaster oven on and burn the place down.

Two recent reports show that kids do more than watch too much television when unsupervised after school. Half of all violent juvenile crime occurs between 2 p.m. and 8 p.m. on school days, according to one of these reports. Most babies born to unwed teenage mothers are conceived in the girl's bed after school, according to another.

And the children most at risk are middle-school kids—caught in the dead zone between elementary-school after-care programs and high-school after-school activities. The children with the most unformed decision-making capacity—and the ones most likely to act on it—are left to their own devices.

Meanwhile, their parents are caught between one branch of government that issues dire warnings about after-school mayhem and another branch that withdraws even token encouragement to pay for the supervision of these kids.

Talk about your mixed messages. What are we thinking?

The dependent-care tax benefit dates back to 1954, written into law apparently out of compassion for widowers, widows, divorced parents or working mothers whose husbands were incapacitated. It amounted to only $12 a week—low even for the 1950s—

and was phased out once the family income reached $5,100 a year.

During the 1960s and the 1970s, it was liberalized and expanded and, in 1976, Congress changed it to a tax credit instead of a tax deduction so it would benefit families—presumably low-income families—that did not itemize their deductions.

Today, the tax credit is criticized for benefiting the middle class more than low-income families—another fact that illustrates the muddled thinking on this topic.

Middle-class kids are just as likely to make bad decisions as poor kids, because risk-taking is a function of adolescence, not economics. Just ask the parents of the children in the wealthy suburban subdivision near my home who discovered that their kids were taking turns breaking into each other's houses for liquor, sex and car keys while the moms and dads were at work.

The problem with the dependent-care credit is not that it benefits the wrong families. The problem is that it doesn't benefit all families long enough. In 1988, Congress adjusted the eligibility down from age 15 to under 13.

Likewise, the benefit has shrunk over time. The sliding scale that governs the family income has not been adjusted for inflation since 1981, and the qualifying child-care payment (which amounts to about $1.15 per hour, per child) has not been increased since 1982.

At the same time, middle-school sports programs disappeared because of the high costs of liability insurance, uniforms and coaching. And community-based after-school programs dried up along with the funds that paid for them.

And every year, more of the neighborhood mothers who might have kept an eye on the neighborhood kids return to work. More working parents, who might have taken some financial encouragement from the dependent-care tax credit, rationalize that their world-wise 13-year-olds are old enough to be left alone for a couple of hours after school.

They are not.

This is not to say that all kids will become teen-age "super-predators," as conservative pundit William J. Bennett fears, if they are left alone between 3 p.m. and 6 p.m. Or that all girls will drag boys off the bus and under their pink rosebud coverlets.

And I don't believe a modest tax credit requiring a mountain of record-keeping will motivate parents to joyously pay for after-school jailers for their kids.

But let's not kid ourselves. The tax code in this country reflects our social priorities—for good or ill—and it should reflect our commitment to look after kids who are not young adults, but tall children. The government has an immediate and a long-term stake in the supervision—nay, the nurturing—of our teens.

My son is embarrassed that he is not allowed to come home to an empty house.

Congress should be ashamed to think he ought to.

Teens enjoy decorating their own space.

or construction paper creations, or cover it with cloth. Furnish it with sofa, comfortable chair, coffee table, and board games.

- Ask youngsters to bring in unused activity items from home. Search for a pool table, a piano, a dart board, an air hockey game, or similar items.

Make homework an integral part of the program. Unlike younger children, who can probably finish their homework once they return home in the evening, most older students cannot. After fifth or sixth grade, several hours of studying and completing out-of-class assignments are generally expected of all American schoolchildren. By setting up an area that is conducive to study and quiet work, you show that you think this is an important endeavor. By being available to help resolve questions and confusion, you can assist parents with this important task. Program staff need to consult with parents and decide whether a certain amount of time should be dedicated strictly to homework and when, or whether, it is their role to facilitate the process. It's also important to provide the tools these older students will need in order to do their homework, which becomes more academically challenging and specific than it was in the early grades. Have one or more computers available, if possible, and develop reference libraries that include copies of textbooks when you can.

CHALLENGE CHILDREN'S SKILLS

Providing a wide variety of activities may offer opportunities for youngsters to grow and learn, but only if you exercise creativity as you help the children plan those activities. Simply buying new and different board games or teaching new sports is not enough. Competition is a natural characteristic of most older school-agers. It can get out of hand and be hurtful to some children, but a certain amount of competition can spur most youngsters to new growth.

Developing pro-social behaviors is another goal that can be achieved during out-of-school time. One program set up a system (devised by the youngsters themselves) to award variable numbers of points for a selection of useful activities around the program—sweeping the floor, vacuuming the carpet, tutoring a younger child, sorting out the game closet, alphabetizing the last month's supply receipts, and so on. Points were recorded and collected to purchase prizes or buy privileges such as sitting at the program director's desk to do homework, 10 minutes of telephone usage, a banana split, or other small awards.

Cooking, woodworking, sewing, generating computer graphics, learning a foreign language—there is an endless number of interesting things that older children can be exposed to and encouraged to learn. Program staff can share their own interests and also bring in experts from the community. Hobbies provide many adults with countless hours of pleasurable activity, and most began these spare-time pursuits in middle or late childhood.

PROVIDE LINKS WITH COMMUNITY AGENCIES

Some programs for older children connect with community service clubs or recreation departments to develop competitive athletic or other activities during out-of-school time. If the program can't field an entire team, perhaps they can join together with youngsters from another after-school program to do so. Some children may enjoy participating in or leading a Scout troop, 4-H project, or Camp Fire club; inquiries to local youth-serving-organization staff members may reveal ways they can do so. These associations have been working with middle school and high school children for decades and have a lot to offer school-age programs. Another approach is to work with some of these groups to fill a community need. For example, you could adopt a street or a park, then plant trees, bushes, and flowers. Organize a monthly street or park patrol to clean up litter and keep an eye on things. Work with schools or the arts community to paint murals on areas that are vulnerable to graffiti.

Many of these opportunities exist for alliances between out-of-school programs and community civic organizations. For example, members of the Teen Scene Club in Charles County, Maryland, join with children in an after-school activity program at the local public library to participate in reader's theater presentations, to plan and host afternoon teas for library trustees, and to publish a library newsletter (ERIC/EECE, 1992). Eight after-school programs in Boston were able to offer a science component as the result of a partnership between the Museum of Science and the Boston MOST Initiative (Shortt, 1997). The 4-H clubs in Missouri are working with the public schools to open computer labs after school and in the evenings (McClain, personal communication, 1998). Other possibilities for partnerships include collaborative training, workshops and conferences, and shared curriculum. Tap into the energy and idealism of young people. Involve them in community issues, such as homelessness, vandalism prevention, and safety.

Individual community service opportunities that may appeal to older school-agers include volunteering as library pages, hospital candy stripers, or preschool aides. The administration of your out-of-school program will need to develop guidelines for how youngsters will be transported to and from these activities and perhaps how the fee schedule will be adjusted for hours they are away from the center. But these are merely details and shouldn't be allowed to get in the way of helping them learn to take a gradually more expansive and responsible role in their community.

Special Challenges—Full-Day Programs and Programs for Teens

EXTENDED-DAY PROGRAMS FOR OLDER CHILDREN

Longer days in the summer or when year-round schools are off-track provide opportunities for school-agers to plan and undertake projects that take several days or weeks to complete. Snow days or other kinds of winter emergency closings do also and have the added stress of requiring everything to be done inside. Some programs are open for 10 or more hours a day under these circumstances, so it's important to have a rich collection of ideas and projects ready for these days before they arrive.

For example, collect miscellaneous inexpensive trinkets throughout the year in a "prize box." Good things to put in the box include free pens and pencils, souvenir cups, hats, and novelty items of all kinds. When children are cooped up for long hours, play Jeopardy or Wheel of Fortune or Bingo. The oldest youngsters can take turns organizing the games and keeping score, letting participant children select their own prizes as they win individual rounds of play. Perhaps this could even be operated like a carnival, with children turning in two or three collected small prizes for one of greater value. Obviously, you can't over-use this activity or you'll run out of prizes and it will cease to be fun, but it's a good activity once in a while.

Long inclement days provide good opportunities to get out the Monopoly board, the chess and checker sets, the woodburning kit, and the bead looms. Some of these old hobby/activities from years gone by are ideal for days with long time frames. Supply a bookcase with especially gripping books for reading, either out loud in small groups or individually, and collect popular magazines for days when homework is simply not an issue. Keep a running list of things to do "when there's time." Recruit a group of bored youngsters to help you put magazine article sheets in file cabinets, or sort out the parts to all the games, or send for all the free things you've collected offers for.

Rich Scofield (1993) suggests planning projects for older children that

- develop a new skill
- advance to the next skill level
- give a feeling of personal satisfaction and accomplishment
- give something to the community
- help persons in need

Long-range projects that lend themselves well to long summer (or winter) days and incorporate some of these goals can include (1) writing and putting on a play, musical performance, or talent show; (2) publishing a newsletter for parents, community, or school pals; (3) redecorating the whole environment; (4) setting up a penny carnival for needy children; (5) forming a basketball (volleyball, soccer, softball) team and learning to play *really well;* and (6) making puppets, building a puppet theater, and presenting shows for community children.

Summer activities offered by the U.S. Army School-age and Teen programs include recreational and enhancement activities for children of military personnel such as specialty "camps" (e.g., drama, cheerleading, computers), sports clinics, open recreational periods, classes, and trips to local points of interest. With additional staff and training, certain sites also offer horseback riding, rock climbing, water sports, and others. Any of these ideas could be incorporated into most school-age programs for older children, and the U.S. Army School-Age and Teen program staff are willing to share what they have learned. If you have access to the Internet, check out their Web site:

www.per.hqusareur.army.mil/odsper/cfsd/asat/princ/summer.htm

School-age programs can play an important role in the growth and development of mid-aged children. To be able to do so, however, they need to develop attractive programming options that appeal to these age groups. Careful planning and appropriate activities will keep older children interested and engaged, provide them with opportunities to develop new skills and extend others, and prepare youngsters for the transition into responsible self-care when their families agree it is time for them to move on.

OUT-OF-SCHOOL PROGRAMS FOR TEENAGERS

In 1990, the Carnegie Council on Adolescent Development convened a 26-member Task Force on Youth Development and Community Programs to examine community-based youth-development organizations. They were trying to determine how, or even if, existing community organizations met the needs of adolescents during the nonschool hours. This investigation was driven by a growing body of research indicating that young teens are increasingly at risk for crime, violence, and substance abuse.

According to statistics collected by the National Victim Center, 1 in 5 students and nearly 1 in 3 males among inner-city high school students have been shot at, stabbed, or otherwise injured with a weapon at or in transit to or from school in the past few years. Almost 1 in 13 of all high school students (7.4%) carried a gun to school in 1993–94; 13.8% joined a gang; and 35% threatened to harm another student or a teacher. The risk of violent victimization is greater for a 12-year-old than for anyone age 24 or older (National Victim Center, 1995). And whereas the illegal consumption or sale of drugs and alcohol among schoolchildren may not, in itself, be violent, such behavior often leads to violent acts (Whitaker, 1991).

According to the Carnegie report, by the age of 15, "substantial numbers of American youth are at risk of reaching adulthood unable to meet adequately the requirements of the workplace, the commitments of relationships in families and with friends, and the responsibilities of participation in a democratic society" (Carnegie Corporation of New York, 1990). The recommendation of the Carnegie Corporation is this: "Communities must build networks of affordable, accessible, safe, and challenging youth programs that appeal and respond to the diverse interests of young adolescents."

In the years since the Carnegie report was published, many communities have responded to the challenge. In a summary of the report, *A Matter of Time: Risk and Opportunity in the Nonschool Hours,* the task force made specific recommendations. Community programs, they directed, should do the following:

- Tailor their program content and processes to the needs and interests of young adolescents.
- Recognize, value, and respond to the diverse backgrounds and experience of young adolescents.
- Extend their reach to underserved adolescents.
- Actively compete for the time and attention of young adolescents.
- Strengthen the quality and diversity of their adult leadership.
- Reach out to families, schools, and a wide range of community partners in youth development.
- Enhance the role of young adolescents as resources in their community.
- Serve as vigorous advocates for and with youth.
- Specify and evaluate their programs' outcomes.
- Establish strong organizational structures, including energetic and committed board leadership.

—Carnegie Corporation of New York, 1990

Among the key recommendations made by the Carnegie report was that schools and youth-serving organizations need to link with families, health care organizations, and the media to support "safe, appealing growth-promoting settings for middle schoolers during the out-of-school hours" (Carnegie Corporation of New York, 1990). In 1996, the American Business Collaboration for Quality Dependent Care, a national coalition led by 21 major corporations, provided funding for research and development of resources that will help to increase the supply of quality programs for middle schoolers. In addition, the coalition invested $500,000 to develop a model middle school program that can be repeated nationwide. This vote of confidence and commitment by the business community is an important indicator that improved and expanded out-of-school programs for adolescents will soon be appearing throughout the nation.

One program that has already answered the challenge is L.E.A.P.—Leadership, Education and Athletics in Partnership. This program is a comprehensive, community-based program that serves nearly 700 children from eight economically disadvantaged neighborhoods in Connecticut. Delivered through community-based after-school sessions and summer programs, L.E.A.P. works closely with school curriculum to reinforce literacy and academic achievement goals. This is an important factor in programs for adolescents, as research consistently shows a relationship between school failure and vandalism, drug/alcohol usage, and violence (Carnegie Corporation of New York, 1990; Tygart, 1988; Whitaker, 1991).

One of the most innovative and probably the most important characteristic of the L.E.A.P. program is that it works toward preventing problems facing poor young children at the same time it addresses the out-of-school needs of adolescents. College and high-school students are trained to work as counselors for younger children. After training, one college student is paired with a high school student to work with a group of eight gender- and age-matched children from a targeted neighborhood. While the L.E.A.P. program is primarily literacy-based, program designers recognized the need for children to develop socially outside the classroom environment as well, so arts workshops, athletic leagues, wilderness camping trips, and visits to other cities are incorporated into the year-round program. In the L.E.A.P. program, both group leaders and group participants benefit: Younger children develop skills and interests that will buffer them from many *at-risk* situations and behaviors; older participants receive valuable training in leadership, curriculum development, conflict resolution, and interpersonal relations.

Teens need opportunities for safe risks. Growing and stretching is one of their major developmental tasks, and if they don't have chances to do it with supportive adults to help them, they'll do it without that guidance. Depending on the community, tasks such as chopping and stacking wood, lighting campfires or fireplace fires, carving soap or wood, learning to shoot a bow and arrow, and using power tools all might fall under this heading. Native Americans have historically taught 10- to 16-year-old children the tasks and responsibilities of adulthood. In fact, throughout most societies of the world, this has always been an important time for young people. Instead of simply "hanging out," they can be spending valuable time in out-of-school programs, developing important skills they'll need in the coming years. Plan activities for long summer days such as hikes, rock climbs, or horseback riding; bring in speakers or other community resources to teach map-reading skills, outdoor safety, and care of specialized equipment.

Adolescents also need safe and interesting places to go at night. An unfortunate knee-jerk response to the frightening statistics in the Carnegie report was for many cities to institute curfew laws. Justifying the wholesale sweep of under-age youngsters from the streets as being "for their own good," city after city began to round up teens found to have no immediate destination after 9:00 or 10:00 p.m. In some cases, communities could demonstrate a slight drop in juvenile crime and crimes perpetrated against juveniles after initiating curfews. But a second result was more quickly evident—a loud and collective wail from teenagers and their parents that "there's nothin to do" and especially "there's nothing to do that doesn't cost money." In other words, young people on their way to or from sporting events, films, restaurants, pool halls, bowling alleys, or coffee houses were exempt from the curfews; those without the financial means to attend those events or places were picked up by the sweep.

In an effort to reduce the number of adolescents in public places at night, an effort that was well-meant and supported by research, curfew and antiloitering laws curtail what for many teens is a primary source of entertainment: "hanging out." City administrators who are listening to their young people are finding ways for their youth to do this safely. Members of the League of California Cities discussed the issue at a statewide conference in 1995 and concluded that "the teen years were the missing element in many city and school programs" (Zinko, 1995, p. 1). Encouraged by assurances from teens that "if you build them we will come," communities all over the state opened teen centers, under-18 clubs, and kids-only coffee houses. Unfortunately, a year later, many of them had closed, unused and sometimes vandalized by the very youngsters they were intended to serve.

What went wrong? In many cases, although cities initiated planning teams and task forces, they didn't spend enough time talking to the youths they believed would be using their new centers. One or two representatives from the local high school were usually asked for input, but rarely were the vast majority of local teens polled. If they had asked, what would they have heard? What do teens want in a youth center? In communities that did ask the questions, the responses were fairly consistent:

"It has to have music."

"Dancing is cool, especially with strobe lights, and so is gymnastics."

"Be sure there's a hangout room, lots of free food, good restrooms, telephones, and an arcade."

"I like to play pool—can it have some pool tables, and a Coke machine?"

"We'd do our homework there if we could do it in a happening place—not a quiet room like the library."

"Lots of us don't have computers at home. It should have computers we can use."

The facility also has to be accessible by public transportation or by walking, and the decorating should be supervised, if not carried out, by the teens themselves. For teens to feel that their opinions matter, they must be participants in every step of the developmental process.

And what about adult leaders? Even after all that planning, the selection of staff can make or break a teen center. One 16-year-old phrased it like this: "They'd have to have cool adults to regulate everything" (Zinko, 1995). Peter Benson and Carl Glickman, authors of *All Kids Are Our Kids: What Communities Must Do to Raise Caring and Responsible Children and Adolescents* (1997), would agree. Their book contends that successful young people have specific **assets** in their lives—such assets as parental support, community involvement, motivation and self-esteem. Adults who are assets to adolescents love and support them, are approachable and available when kids have something to talk about, and will take the time to talk seriously on just about any topic. According to research cited in Benson, Galbraith, & Espeland's *What Kids Need to Succeed* (1995), the most successful young people have three or more of these adults in their lives to whom they can turn for advice and support.

Not too surprisingly, what youths say they want in teen center programs closely parallels the findings of the Carnegie Corporation and other research groups. The Carnegie report identified the needs of young adolescents that can be addressed by community organizations as opportunities to (1) socialize with peers and adults, (2) develop skills that are relevant now and in the future, (3) contribute to the community, (4) belong to a valued group, (5) feel competent.

Clearly, communities need to continue to work closely with young people and school-age professionals to develop successful networks of affordable, accessible, safe, and challenging youth programs that appeal to the diverse interests of teens from all sectors of society. As the programs emerge, out-of-school professionals will need to be there to assure that each one is successful.

SUMMARY
. . . .

Developing out-of-school programs for older school-agers is challenging because the interests of this age group are different from those of younger children and there is a widespread perception that these children do not need care in the hours before and after school. Successful programs help youngsters develop a new skill or advance to the next skill level, give a feeling of personal satisfaction and accomplishment, and link program participants to their community in some way. Even more challenging are programs that operate all day during school vacations and holidays, and programs designed for children over 13. These programs must incorporate youth participants in environmental design, program planning, and evaluation of activities; they may need to seek funding from the business community to survive. Research supports the need for community linked programs for older youngsters, as these can reduce teen involvement in drugs, alcohol, and violent crime.

REVIEW QUESTIONS

1. What is meant by the term *older children* in this chapter?

2. Identify three characteristics of programs for older children that differentiate them from those for younger school-agers.

3. What was the most common community reaction to the publication of the Carnegie report?

4. List four positive ways to structure time for older school-agers during extended-day programs.

CHALLENGE EXERCISES

1. Locate a teen center in your community. Visit it during the hours when teens are using it. Describe the environment, the activities, the interaction between staff and teens. Does it appear to be a place youngsters enjoy being?

2. (a) Interview two small-business owners about older school-age children in their communities. Has this group been identified by the community as a "problem"? If so, why? (b) Determine whether there are programs for older youngsters in the community. Do you think there is a relationship between (a) and (b)?

3. Read the local news section of five consecutive issues of your community newspaper (you can find them in the public library). Highlight every time the word "teen" is used. Make a table identifying the topics discussed and their incidence. Summarize your findings.

TERMS TO LEARN

at-risk
logo
mascot
productivity

REFERENCES

Bellum, D. (1990). *New ideas for childcare veterans.* San Francisco: California School Age Consortium.

Benson, P., Galbraith, M., Espeland, P. (1995). *What kids need to succeed.* Minneapolis, MN: Free Spirit.

Benson, P., Glickman, C. (1997). *All kids are our kids: What communities must do to raise caring and responsible children and adolescents.* Jossey-Bass.

Cannon, A. (1997, September 11). Study: Juvenile crime in prime time. *The Daily News.*

Carnegie Corporation of New York. (1990). *A matter of time: Risk and opportunity in the nonschool hours.* Waldorf, MD: Carnegie Council on Adolescent Development.

ERIC/EECE. (1992). Library latchkey children. *ERIC Digest, EDO-PS-92-1.*

Musson, S. and Gibbons, M. (1988). *The new youth challenge: A model for working with older children in school-age child care.* Nashville: School-Age Notes.

National Victim Center. (1995). *School Crime: K–12.* Available http://www.hvc.org/infolink/info43.htm

Scofield, R. (1993, April). Summer, older kids and projects. *School-Age Notes.*

Shortt, J. (1997). *Creative solutions: The MOST initiative* (Vol. 3, No. 1). Boston: National Institute on Out-of-School Time, Wellesley College.

Tygart, C. (1988). Public school vandalism: Toward a synthesis of theories and transition to paradigm analysis. *Adolescence, 23*(89), 187–200.

University of Wisconsin Cooperative Extension. (1994). *Preventing problem behaviors and raising academic performance in the nation's youth: The impacts of 71 school-age child care programs supported by the CES Youth-at-Risk Initiative.* Madison, WI.

Whitaker, C., & Bastion, L. (1991). *Teenage victims: A national crime survey report.* Washington, DC: Bureau of Justice Statistics, U.S. Department of Justice.

Willyoung, A. A personal communication (1997).

Wong, R. (1995, November/December). American business collaboration leads corporate support. *Child Care Bulletin.*

Work/Family Directions, I. (1998). American Business Collaboration for Quality Dependent Care takes lead in developing national model after school program for middle schoolers. (Online press release).

Yanouzas, T. (1993, June). Middle school-age care. In S. Krampitz (Ed.), *Kids,* p. 3. Storrs: University of Connecticut Cooperative Extension/National Network for Child Care.

Zinko, C. (1995, December 10). In the wake of new curfew laws, cities are responding to teen-agers' gripes that they have nothing to do. *San Jose Mercury News,* pp. 1, 31.

CHAPTER THIRTEEN

Legal and Budget Issues, Policies, Procedures, and Personnel

The unique scheduling and staffing needs of programs for school-agers usually lead site directors to work directly with children. This can make life easier, as managerial decisions are frequently made by the same people who implement them, or harder, because meeting the immediate needs of children may cause directors to postpone paperwork or other administrative duties. (The worst case is when directors put paperwork first!) Unlike programs for younger children, where administrative and teaching duties are usually separated, staff working in school-age programs may find that lines of authority and responsibility are drawn less clearly, and the teaching staff may be more often included in decision making. It is important that, especially given this multiplicity of tasks juggled by director and line staff, there be enough people to go around. Be sure that staff-child ratios and group sizes always permit the staff to meet the needs of children and youths; their safety and well-being must come before balancing the budget, at least during the program day.

The integrated nature of school-age-program administration often means that the management function takes place at the centers as much as it does in centralized offices. For this reason, all members of the staff must understand the program philosophy, goals and objectives, and priorities. These should be reviewed each year with them. A benefit of this knowledge is a greater opportunity for **shared decision making,** in which both staff and management contribute to developing policy and finding solutions to administrative challenges (Figure 13-1).

Be sure to support families' involvement in your programs by including them in decision making as well. If you offer an orientation session for families at the beginning of each year and for each new family, and nurture communication throughout the year, you may discover that they can offer valuable insight and information.

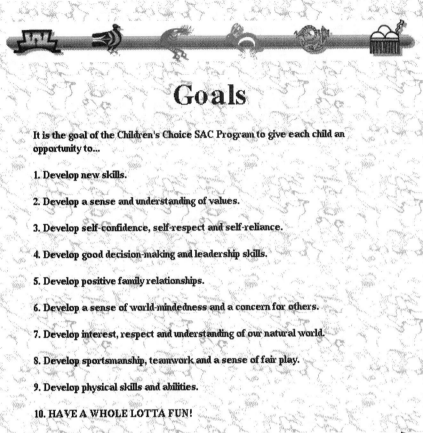

Goals

It is the goal of the Children's Choice SAC Program to give each child an opportunity to...

1. Develop new skills.

2. Develop a sense and understanding of values.

3. Develop self-confidence, self-respect and self-reliance.

4. Develop good decision-making and leadership skills.

5. Develop positive family relationships.

6. Develop a sense of world-mindedness and a concern for others.

7. Develop interest, respect and understanding of our natural world.

8. Develop sportsmanship, teamwork and a sense of fair play.

9. Develop physical skills and abilities.

10. HAVE A WHOLE LOTTA FUN!

Figure 13–1   A Clear Set of Goals Helps Staff Develop Program Priorities   This list is posted on New Mexico's Children's Choice School-Age Care Program Web site for the convenience of parents and potential clients. *Source:* www.tarnet.com/childschoice/info.html.

The site director should have specific knowledge of child-care administration. Most colleges and universities offer coursework that will prepare directors to hire and supervise staff, develop and oversee a budget, understand legal and liability issues, and determine a philosophical direction for curriculum development. Figures 13-2 and 13-3 present recommended competencies for various levels of leadership in school-age programs. In no way does this chapter provide that administrative training; rather, it presents an overview of the kinds of administrative issues that exist in school-age settings and should be read by anyone working in out-of-school programs.

LEVELS OF RESPONSIBILITY

Program Administrator

Overall direction of the program

- developing a mission, goals, and policies for the program
- program implementation and evaluation
- administration, including fiscal management
- organizational development, including management of human resources

Site Director

Daily operations of the program

- supervising staff
- communicating with families
- building relationships with the host community
- overseeing all program activities

Senior Group Leader

Supervision and guidance of children in the program

- program planning
- communicating with families
- supervising support staff
- relating to the community

Group Leader

Supervision and guidance of children in the program under the direction of a Senior Group Leader

- same as the Senior Group Leader

Assistant Group Leader

Supervision and guidance of children under the direct supervision of a Group Leader

Figure 13–2 In 1998, the National School Age Care Alliance published this recommended hierarchy of responsibilities within a school-age program. Titles vary, so the responsibility assumed by that staff member will determine the qualifications required. *Source:* The NSACA Standards for Quality School-Age Care.

MINIMUM QUALIFICATIONS

Position	Experience	Education	Professional Preparation
Program Administrator	One year	Associate's or Bachelor's Degree in Related Field	Six credit hours: ■ child and youth development (3) ■ administration (3)
		———*or*———	
	Two years	Bachelor's Degree in Unrelated Field	Twelve credit hours: ■ child and youth development (3) ■ administration (3) ■ other areas related to sac programming (6)
	Eighteen months	AA Degree or two years of college in a related field or equivalent certification	Nine credit hours: ■ child and development (3) ■ other areas related to sac programming (6)
Senior Group Leader		Bachelor's Degree in related field	
		———*or*———	
	Three months	Bachelor's Degree in unrelated field	Six credit hours: ■ child and youth development (3) ■ other areas related to sac programming (3)
		———*or*———	
	Six months	AA Degree or two years of college in related field or equivalent	Six credit hours: ■ child and youth development (3) ■ other areas related to sac programming (3)
		———*or*———	
	One year	AA Degree or two years of college in unrelated field	Six credit hours: ■ child and youth development (3) ■ other areas related to sac programming (3)
Group Leader	None	Bachelor's Degree in a related field	
		———*or*———	
	Three months	Bachelor's Degree in unrelated field	Three credit hours: ■ child and youth development
		———*or*———	
	Six months	AA Degree in related field	
		———*or*———	
	Nine Months	AA Degree or two years of college equivalent	Three credit hours: ■ child and youth development
		———*or*———	
	Eighteen months	HS Diploma or GED	Six credit hours: ■ child and youth development (3) ■ other areas related to sac programming (3)
Assistant Group Leader	None	Minimum age 16	See section on orientation and in-service training

Figure 13–3 Recommended Minimum Qualifications for Staff in School-Age Programs. *Source:* The NSACA Standards for Quality School-Age Care.

Licensing and Regulations

....

Licensing is the process by which an individual, organization, or corporation procures from the appropriate state agency a license to operate a school-age child-care program. The purpose of having licensing requirements is to assure *minimum standards* for all licensed programs. Many out-of-school programs, such as service organizations, athletic teams, homework clubs, or drop-in centers, have historically been exempt from licensing because they operate infrequently or for specific, noneducational purposes. These programs may be covered under an umbrella of regulations through their association with a parent agency.

In addition, many programs for school-agers are covered by previously existing *early childhood legislation,* which stipulates required square footage, ratios of adults to children, number of bathrooms, diaper-changing procedures, and so on. As unique school-age programs develop to fill unmet needs, state legislators are gradually writing special regulations to govern them. According to one report, 15 states had separate regulations for preschool and school-age care in 1992, up from only five states that had such regulations in 1988 (Seligson & Gannett, 1992).

But determining who governs your program and locating a copy of the regulations may be a lengthy task. For example, a program operated on school grounds by a private agency may be governed by the Department of Social Services, the Department of Human Services, or the Department of Child and Family Services, depending on the state in which the program is operated (Seligson & Allenson, 1993). The same agency, whichever it is, may operate other programs under contract with the State Department of Education, which would then be the governing agency for those programs. But if the local school district administers the program, whether or not it is located on the school grounds, the agency governing the school district would be the one specifying the regulations for the after-school program. A legal manual for administrators of school-ager programs has been developed by the School-Age Child Care Project at Wellesley College (Cohen, 1984). However, you may want to discuss specifics of local requirements with directors of other programs for school-agers in your community, both on and off school grounds, and funded by both private and public money.

Licensing regulations address generally the same areas in each state: organization and administration, staffing, physical environment and equipment, health and safety, program, discipline, and parent rights. Educational agencies and professional organizations take over where licensing leaves off, usually recommending lower adult-child ratios, enhanced environment and programming, and stipulating guidelines for parent and community participation. It is important for staff of these programs to be current with local licensing laws, contract funding terms and conditions, and the recommendations of professional organizations in order to ensure legal compliance and a high-quality out-of-school program.

What to Look for in a Quality School-Age Care Program

ASK THESE QUESTIONS ON YOUR VISIT TO THE PROGRAM:

- What qualifications do the staff and director have? What ongoing training are staff required to attend, and are staff encouraged to attend trainings offered by professionals in the field of school-age care? Are staff specifically trained to work with this age group?

- How does the program's environment look? Are there separate areas for different age or interest groups? Are there areas for kids to have some private space? Is it generally clean and orderly? Are you inclined to stay?

- What types of activities are planned for the kids? Is there good balance between indoor/outdoor, large group/small group, active/quiet, and staff-directed/child-directed activities? Is there time for kids to just hang out? Are activities planned to meet the development needs of all children in the program? Will the program meet the needs and interests of your particular child?

- What are the program philosophies and goals? Do these match your ideas? Ask to have a copy of the program's handbook to check out all the important information on billing, payments, pickup, safety, etc.

- What is the staff-to-child ratio? The ratio should never exceed 15-to-1. Lower ratios (10-to-1) promote higher quality standards.

- What is the rate of staff turnover? Continual changes in staff can create program instability.

- What meals or snacks are served? Are they nutritious and well balanced? Is there enough food served to meet the needs of this age group?

- Do they have a state-issued DSHS license that is current? (Note—programs that are run by Park and Recreation Departments or school districts are exempt from licensing but should meet basic health and safety standards.)

- Will the director give you names of parents in the program to call and ask questions? Do they allow open visits by parents?

- What is the program's discipline policy? Does this fit into your ideas and beliefs? If your child has special needs in this area, will they be met by the program?

- What is your child's first impression of the program—your first impression? Is the overall atmosphere and sound of the kids and staff a happy and inviting sound? Are they having fun?

- What are transportation policies? What vehicles do they use?

- What community resources does the program utilize? Quality programs get out in their community and regularly invite featured speakers to visit.

- What are the policies on TV viewing? Quality programs use the TV for special occasions only!

Source: Compiled by School's Out Consortium/WASACA, 1118 Fifth Avenue, Seattle, WA 98101, (206) 461-3602.

Developing Admission Agreements

Once the director and staff have determined which regulations and recommendations govern their program and have designed a program to meet them, they must explain those requirements to parents along with any other stipulations necessary for the health of the program. This is done by the means of **parent handbooks** and **admission agreements.** Parent handbooks explain the details of the program and outline the responsibilities of both the administering agency and the parents; admission agreements serve as an acknowledgment of those details and a contract for care. Be careful as you prepare these documents

Remember that most parents are running on a tight schedule when they drop off or pick up their children.

to remember that a ***family-centered program*** is most helpful to the children you will serve. It is important to confer with parents and children as you develop program details and guidelines to assure that their needs will be met. Programs that ignore parents' working hours, commute time, and need for child care during school holidays and teacher in-service days add stress to already stressed families. Your program will be far more effective (and successful) if it is seen as an advocate rather than as an adversary of parents.

Liability: Who Is Responsible?

A reasonable area of concern to private agencies and individuals operating any kind of business is ***liability,*** or the potential for lawsuits. Three legal principles usually apply in legal actions involving child-care programs (Decker & Decker, 1997):

1. *Employee Liability:* Employees are hired to perform certain types of duties, and are expected to be educated adequately to perform those duties as well as to understand the expectations of the employer. When employees act within the scope of the employer's expectations, they are not liable for the results of their actions. However, when they act beyond them or fail to act up to them, they are considered negligent, and they *are* liable.

2. *Employer Liability:* Except for the above-mentioned negligence, employers are liable for all actions of their employees carried out while they are at work.

3. *Board Liability:* Boards of directors are responsible for the actions of all employees hired by the board, as the board essentially becomes the "employer."

Liabilities vary, depending on many factors. The form of ownership of the agency, its tax status, and whether the program falls under the Civil Rights Act or the various Education for All Handicapped Children acts and amendments will define exactly what the expectations are of all individuals involved in the school-age program.

In terms of ownership, school-age centers can function as proprietorships, partnerships, or corporations. **Proprietorships** are businesses owned by one person, who assumes full responsibility for debts, taxes, and legal issues. **Partnerships** involve more people and depend for their stability on the continued interest, either financial or emotional, of all members of the partnership. Each partner is held responsible for his or her own taxes, but liability and decision making is shared with other partners.

Corporations are sometimes formed to limit the liability of individuals wishing to operate a school-age program or center. Corporations may be for-profit or non-profit and are governed by a board of directors. Corporations identified as *for-profit* run essentially like proprietorships; their main purpose is to make a profit. Stockholders in the corporation pay taxes on this profit, as does the corporation itself. Private *nonprofit* corporations are permitted to make a profit, but that is not their main goal, and they must put any profit back into the program. Generally, out-of-school programs organized as non-profit corporations serve a specific population or geographic area that could not support a program on tuition and fees alone.

The owner of the building in which the program is housed, the driver who runs the van service between schools and the school-age center, even the independent contractor who provides piano lessons or coaches a soccer team—each of these individuals has varying degrees of legal exposure. It is important to learn what is expected of your program and the people working in it and to understand clearly your potential liability. For example, make sure you don't inadvertently violate ADA or other civil rights laws by having policies or admission requirements that are discriminatory. A good idea is to ask a local attorney or legal aid volunteer to present a workshop to staff and parents to be sure everyone understands his or her rights and obligations.

Funding and Finances

Programs for school-agers obtain their start-up and operating funds in a variety of ways. They may be sponsored by youth-serving organizations such as YMCA and Boys and Girls Clubs, or by churches, parks and recreation departments, housing associations, military bases, or government agencies.

State-funded programs may be supported fully, or their funding may be partial, with contributions from local funding sources expected to make up the difference. Privately owned school-age centers receive most of their income from parent-paid tuition and fees. Some programs may receive start-up funding from a public or private agency, then must operate on a combination of private and public funds. Nearly all school-age centers participate in some kind of fund-raising to assure adequate funds for supplies, field trips, and "extras." Sometimes benefactors can be found in the community who will sponsor specific expenditures that match their community service goals. If a local service organization sponsors a grant-writing workshop, be sure to attend. Take advantage of the tips offered to learn how to apprise such benefactors of your needs.

Budget development is a specialized skill, and successful *fiscal management* and planning are crucial for the success of any community program. Anyone having responsibility for budget building and management of funds must learn the process and confer with appropriate financial advisers for the first few years. Community colleges and business schools often advertise courses in business administration, and community colleges sometimes offer specialized coursework for child-care management.

Understand the goals and objectives of your program so you can prioritize expenditures. When you need to decide whether to use this year's funds to resurface the playground, purchase a new computer, or add services for 12- and 13-year-olds, referring to a *mission statement* can make the decision much easier. Be sure your program has one.

Two Sample Mission Statements

To enhance the economic stability of County families by offering affordable, high quality, developmentally appropriate before and after school and vacation care at County elementary schools
— Prince William County, Virginia School Age Care Program

To provide each child an environment where he/she is able to develop a positive self image and to offer peace of mind to our families through loving care and communication.
— Children's Creative Learning Centers, Sunnyvale, California

Transportation and Parking

How will the children arrive at your out-of-school program? They can come in a variety of ways—by private car, in vans operated by schools or school-age programs, alone or with their parents on public transportation, on foot, even in taxis and limousines. Consider the various routes and means by which your children will be traveling so you will provide adequate parking, turnaround space, greeters, or traffic control. An urban program may need to be situated near a public transportation hub or run its own shuttle bus; programs situated on school sites may want to negotiate with the school district for automobile access to the portable building or classroom where the program is located. One child-care agency received major start-up funding from a local transportation agency because they were willing to locate at the intersection of a bus route, light rail, and train depot. However, when the administrators discovered that over 70% of their clients drove their own cars to the center, they had to enlarge the parking lot and turnaround area (Seipel, 1997).

Getting Along With Your Neighbors

Being a good neighbor can be considered both a legal and a financial responsibility. For example, when you are designing a new program for school-agers, be sure that fences, driveways, parking lots, and drive-throughs are planned with the needs of local residents in mind. Of course, you will obtain the necessary permits and permissions to construct such items, but you must also pay attention to traffic patterns, footpaths, noise, and visual impact. If your center is situated in a residential area, get to know one or more families before completing the plans. Sometimes a chat over a fence (or over a cup of coffee) can save hours of wrangling at public meetings. Even the color of the building can become an issue; residents have been known to bring suit against child-care centers painted in primary colors amidst a group of paler buildings. If your program operates in a business district, consider how the comings and goings of parents and children will affect nearby merchants. It may be helpful to join the local chamber of commerce or other business association. Working with people on community projects provides opportunities for relationships to develop that may make future negotiations easier to accomplish.

Once your after-school program is open, monitor the times of day when children's spirited voices can be heard in neighbors' homes and yards, and do whatever is necessary to keep arrivals and departures from impacting negatively on the neighborhood. Let the community know the positive impact of organized school-age care programs through public service announcements and visits to service clubs, churches, and other neighborhood agencies. Involve children and staff in community cleanup days and other activities so that if conflicts do arise, neighbors will already associate faces, names, and personalities with the program. It is much easier to resolve problems when the disputants see one another as human beings rather than merely representatives of faceless institutions.

Developing a Policies and Procedures Manual

The art of writing a guidebook for policies and procedures is to combine clear directions with as many possibilities for potential problems as everyone in the organization can think of. Generally, the board will set policy; and the director, in collaboration with his or her staff, will develop the procedures for implementing the policy (Sciarra & Dorsey, 1995). For example, the board may establish a policy to admit all children between the ages of 6 and 12 who can benefit from the program. The director then meets with staff and possibly parents to develop the procedures necessary to accomplish the children's enrollment, including planning publicity; designing, distributing, and reviewing registration forms; and informing parents that their child has been accepted or placed on a waiting list. Here, again, you must keep up to date on the implications of ADA and other antidiscrimination laws.

Procedures need to be clear and unambiguous; but if they are overly detailed, they won't be read or followed. Certain components of a policies and procedures manual—such as a mission statement, program goals and objectives, job descriptions, staff orientation, training, and evaluation—should be revisited every few years and adjusted as necessary. For cost reasons, these manuals are not generally distributed to parents; however, they should be available for review if requested, and every staff member with decision-making responsibilities should have a copy.

Setting a Schedule

Programs for school-agers that include kindergarten children operate over a large portion of the day. Other programs may meet before and after school when school is in session and for extended days only during school holidays, vacations, and teacher in-service days. Some programs serve several different schools that may be on different calendars; others serve only one school or schools from one district that all follow the same schedule. In either case, you will need to make a policy decision about whether your program will provide care and activities when school is not in session, and how early and late it will be open. Three sample schedules are shown in Figure 13-4.

Referring to the goals, objectives, and mission statement of your program will help here. For example, if a goal is to relieve parents from some of the stress of worrying about their children's welfare while they are at work, consider how they will feel if the program does not operate during the summer, or during winter break, or during teacher in-service days. Even major holidays are workdays for retail workers, parents who are employed in the fields of recreation or transportation, or those in a medical profession. If your board decides to remain open for most of the public holidays and all other times when school is closed, you will need to hire enough staff members to allow for rotation of holidays and vacations among employees. If the program closes during days when parents must work, you might want to compile a list of licensed care providers who will take school-age children, and assist parents to find alternative arrangements.

Hours of operation will determine your staffing pattern. Programs that open more than an hour before school starts and stay open until 6:00 or 7:00 in the evening will need to employ several part-time people, and possibly also

Before- and After-School Day	
Before School	
7:00–8:00	Children arrive; do quiet activities, such as games, puzzles, or block play; or work on homework.
8:00–8:15	Time for cleaning up and gathering belongings for school.
8:15	Children leave for school; kindergartners walked to classroom.
After School	
11:30	Kindergartners picked up from classroom; things put in cubbies.
11:45–12:15	Outdoor active play, free play, or planned activity.
12:15–12:45	Clean up for lunch; eat lunch; clean up after lunch.
12:45–1:15	Planned activity for kindergartners (art, music, science, health, language, or math-readiness games).
1:15–1:30	Story time.
1:30–2:00	Rest or quiet time.
2:00–3:00	Quiet activities for those who are awake; sleepers rise when ready.
3:00–3:30	Arrival and sign-in of older children.
3:30–4:00	Snack available; free choice of indoor activity and play areas or outdoor play.
4:00–4:15	Group-meeting and planning time; staff set up activities.
4:15–5:00	Planned activities, clubs, homework.
5:00–6:00	Activity cleanup; individualized activities, free play outdoors or in gymnasium; prepare to go home.
6:00	Center closes.

continued

Figure 13–4 Sample Schedules for School-Age Child-Care Programs. *Source:* California Department of Education. (1996). *Kidstime.* Sacramento.

institute split shifts. Early morning routines may include more caregiving than after school later in the day, which will often be a time for homework and active play. Children who arrive at the child-care center before 7:00 a.m. may need some time and a quiet place to nap or awaken gradually. They may also

Extended Afternoon

2:00–2:15	All children in the program arrive at the same time, or children leave for a field trip.
2:15–2:30	Group-planning time.
2:30–3:00	Planned activities, clubs, homework.
3:00–3:15	Snack.
3:15–5:00	Planned activities, clubs, homework.
5:00–6:00	Activity cleanup; individualized activities, free play outdoors or in gymnasium; prepare to go home.
6:00	Center closes.

Full Day

7:00–9:30	Free choice of activity areas, games, and materials for self-directed artwork.
9:30–10:00	Snack available; clean up activity areas.
10:00–11:30	Planned activities, clubs, projects; free-play choices available.
11:30–12:30	Lunch and cleanup.
12:30–1:30	Rest or quiet activity.
1:30–3:00	Planned activities, clubs, long-term projects; free-play choices available.
3:00–3:30	Snack; group-planning time.
3:30–5:00	Planned activities, clubs, long-term projects; free-play choices available.
5:00–6:00	Cleanup; activity areas and materials available.

Figure 13–4   Sample Schedules for School-Age Child-Care Programs *(Continued)*

need a snack or breakfast before starting school. Staff who work these early hours should be aware of the nurturing aspect of their role and be willing to read stories or snuggle with youngsters as they prepare for the day. Don't expect these to be the same people who participate in lively games 9 hours later.

Year-round/Intersession

The schedule is similar to the full-day schedule, except that children who attend only the before- and after-school program need to be integrated into the full-day program. When the SAC program is on a school site, the schedule, particularly outdoor or high-noise-level activities, needs to be synchronized with the elementary school program to avoid disturbing children doing quiet work. The integration of children in after-school care begins at approximately 3:00 p.m., when the children are dismissed from the elementary school program and they rejoin the children in the year-round intersession program.

7:00–8:00	Snack and quiet time for both groups of children.
8:00–8:15	Cleanup; before- and after-school group leaves for elementary school.
8:15–3:00	Same as full-day schedule for children on intersession.
3:00–3:30	Children on intersession may do physical education or other recreational activities with part of the staff; after-school children come in and may do homework or other quiet activities.
3:30–4:00	Snack and group-planning time for the whole group.
4:00–5:30	Planned activities, clubs, projects, free-play choices available.

Figure 13–4 *Continued*

SUMMARY

There is usually more overlap between the responsibilities of management and staff in programs for school-agers than in programs serving younger children. Shared decision making is more effective if all members of staff understand the program philosophy, goals and objectives, and priorities. Site directors of school-age care programs should be knowledgeable about licensing regulations, liability issues, and fiscal matters. Directors may work with a governing board, teachers, and parents in the development of admission agreements and a policies and procedures handbook. Other matters that will need to be understood and overseen by program directors include transportation and parking, community relations, and the development of program calendars and schedules that serve parent needs.

REVIEW QUESTIONS

1. Explain how the role of a site director in a program for school-agers may differ from that of a director of a program for younger children.

2. Describe what is meant by shared decision making.

3. List three things a director can do to improve the attitude of neighbors toward having a school-age program in their midst.

4. What is the difference between the role played by state licensing regulations and the terms and conditions of a funding agency?

CHALLENGE EXERCISES

1. Request a copy of a parent handbook from a program for school-agers. Try to identify within it the philosophy, goals and objectives, and priorities of the program. If they are not listed specifically, see if you can figure out what they are from the text of the handbook. Summarize.

2. Obtain the yearly calendar from two school-age programs serving the same school district. Are they open the same number of days? What are their policies on minimum school days and school holidays or vacations? Interview a parent from each program about the availability of child care during summer vacations in their community.

3. If possible, attend a parent, staff, or board meeting for a program for school-agers. List the agenda items and the kinds of solutions that were reached at the meeting.

TERMS TO LEARN

admission agreements
corporations
early childhood legislation
family-centered program
fiscal management
liability
minimum standards
mission statement
parent handbooks
partnerships
proprietorships
shared decision making

REFERENCES

Cohen, A. (1984). *School-age child care: A legal manual for public school administrators.* Wellesley, MA: School-Age Child Care Project.

Decker, C. A., & Decker, J. R. (1997). *Planning and administering early childhood programs* (6th ed.). Upper Saddle River, NJ: Prentice-Hall.

Sciarra, D. J., & Dorsey, A. G. (1995). *Developing and administering a child care center* (3rd ed.). San Francisco: Delmar.

Seipel, T. (1997, February 16). Child care falls short as a transit lure. *San Jose Mercury News,* p. 1.

Seligson, M., & Allenson, M. (1993). *School-age child care: An action manual for the 90s and beyond.* Westport, CT: Auburn House.

Seligson, M., & Gannett, E. (with Cotlin, L.). (1992). Before- and after-school child care for elementary school children. In B. Spodek & O. N. Saracho (Eds.), *Yearbook in early childhood education: Vol. 3. Issues in child care* (pp. 125–142). New York: Teachers College Press.

Totten, J., & Romberg, R. (1997). *Personnel Guide for childhood educators.* Auburn, CA: Darleemel Publications.

CHAPTER FOURTEEN

Developing Partnerships With Families and the Community

Out-of-school programs hold a unique place in the field of child and youth work. By their very nature, programs that are designed for children during the hours when their parents work operate at times when parents are not usually available to participate. School-age child care is an indispensable service for thousands of parents, especially single working parents or two-parent families who are juggling work or school responsibilities with child rearing. Yet, as valuable as this care is, the parents who depend on it so desperately may normally have very little contact with the program director or staff who spend several hours of each day with their children.

Some children arrive at the program by bus, van, or taxi before and after school; then they are picked up by a rushed relative or neighbor at the end of the day. Others ride in car pools with rotating drivers who also rush to their evening responsibilities. Even if parents are able to come into the center to fetch their children, out-of-school staff members may be involved with other children and unable to carry on extended conversations with the parents.

In other types of programs, such as athletic, enrichment, or service clubs, the coaches, dance or piano instructors, Scout leaders, or other adults are usually involved in setting up for or clearing away after the day's activities or interacting with children or other staff when parents are present. Conversation is often difficult at these times as well. Regardless of the difficulties, regular, open communication between families and out-of-school staff is essential. Without it, neither member of the parenting-socializing team has the whole picture, either of the child or of the program.

The Concept of Partnership in Out-of-School Programs

Chapter 5 discussed the role of adults in the socialization of children. The message of that research is that if children in out-of-school care are to receive a consistent, positive set of messages about themselves and how things work in their society, their adult leaders must become working partners with their families. One author described it this way:

> Caregivers may know more about child development and group care, and about how the child spends the school day, but parents know much more about the child's history, personality, home life, and culture. A good partnership is based on cooperation, the sharing of knowledge, and mutual respect.
> —Bellum, 1990, p. 4

On the most basic level, families and out-of-school programs enter into a partnership when the children are first enrolled in the program (Seligson & Allenson, 1993). This is a *contractual partnership* in which parents agree to give money, vouchers, or at least permission to attend in exchange for peace of mind about their children's safety, and the out-of-school program agrees to provide some kind of child-care or enrichment service. If nothing is done to foster a relationship between the adult who contracts for service and the program providing that service, this is as far as the partnership will go.

However, if nurtured, this legal relationship can grow into a *committed partnership* in which each party recognizes the importance of the other in contributing to the growth and development of a young human being and works to optimize those contributions. This process of nurturing family partnerships begins with the all-important first contact and continues throughout the year with every interaction between staff and family members.

Setting the Tone at the First Contact

Parents inquire about school-age child-care programs at various times during the year. They may be preparing for a job change or relocation of residence, changing work hours or commuting arrangements, or planning ahead for a child who will be attending elementary school in the coming year. First contacts may come at inconvenient times, often taking the form of telephone calls in the middle of group activities or drop-in visits while staff is in planning meetings. A helpful strategy is to develop a brief script and a packet of informational material that can be quickly pulled from a file and handed to a visitor or mailed to a caller. The next step is to arrange for an appointment and tour at a more convenient time.

When you are meeting with a first-time parent or other family member, remember that this person will not know your program philosophy. Explain that first, before getting into details about your admission agreements, rules, and scheduled hours. Provide the visitor with a copy of your mission statement and a description of the program goals and objectives. If parents decide that your philosophy matches their own, you can progress to a more detailed discussion of specifics, either individually or at the first parent meeting in the fall.

Reassure prospective clients that you are accessible and that communication between your program and their family is important to you. Encourage them to study the material you have provided and to ask any questions that occur to them before enrolling their child. This is also a good time for you to find out a little about the child you will be serving as well as the rest of the family. Identify any special needs that must be accommodated or contributions that family members can make to the program. Asking briefly about the new child's family can communicate your interest without seeming intrusive; you can learn which community services they might use and how they can participate in the program.

New residents will appreciate information you have compiled on bus routes, enrichment and athletic programs, or other services provided for families in your community; even long-time residents may be unaware of certain children's activities or resources. Acknowledging and nurturing the heritage of culturally and linguistically diverse children during this period will help to develop connections between home and school (Novick, 1996) and go far in ensuring that children and their parents feel valued and secure.

Admission and Enrollment Policies and Parent Handbooks

Chapter 13 discussed the development of admission and enrollment policies. It is important that these written materials be clear and reflect program philosophy, including relationships with parents, educational and developmental goals, and discipline guidelines. However, it is also important that they reflect your concern for real parent needs, such as having the center open on school holidays that are not usually included in the business holiday calendar and maintaining hours that are long enough to serve parents who commute some distance to work.

Enrollment contracts should contain clear instructions for parents who wish to take their children on extended vacations yet maintain their child's enrollment slot; this must be done without depriving the program of needed funds. Contracts should also set guidelines for termination of services by either party. A complete fee schedule should be included in the enrollment packet.

Parent handbooks should be developed as these will contain information parents need for reference throughout the year. Typical inclusions are a current program calendar and schedule, sign-in and sign-out procedures, guidelines for late pickup of children and payment of fees, procedures for emergencies and illness, discipline guidelines, procedures for meals and snacks, and any materials parents are expected to supply.

Keep parents informed by setting aside an area for news, coming events, and special information.

Back-to-School Night and Parent Conferences

Some out-of-school programs schedule an open house before school begins in the fall so families can visit their site and meet with program staff and children. These gatherings are primarily social in nature and let program staff and returning families welcome newcomers before the stressful first week of school. To accommodate working parents, the events should be scheduled after normal program hours. Car pool maps can be posted as well as sign-up sheets for workdays, potluck suppers, snacks, or fund-raising activities. After a welcoming evening such as this, when the program gets underway, new children and families are already feeling involved and have familiar faces to greet them as they arrive each day.

Consider holding parent-staff conferences once or twice a year to talk in greater depth about the children or the program and discuss any difficulties or issues that have arisen. In programs at school sites, these meetings may be scheduled in conjunction with parent-teacher conferences, allowing parents to sign up for the after-school conference on the same day they visit their children's classroom teachers. In some cases, a leader from the after-school program may accompany parents to the teacher conference if circumstances suggest it. Children do not always function the same way in formal classroom environments as they do in less structured out-of-school settings; sometimes, the entire parenting-caregiving team talking together can identify areas of need that elude the notice of any one individual. At the very least, school-age program staff can serve as advocates and facilitators for parents who are new to or uncomfortable in dealing with school systems, and the conference process can help to identify areas where this advocacy might be welcome.

Father/Male Involvement in Out-of-School Programs

The need to involve men should not be overlooked when you are developing partnerships with families. Elsewhere we have discussed the changing family structures and the increasing number of children who live in single-parent households, reconstituted or blended families, foster-parent homes, extended families with relatives, and other family configurations. An important yet often overlooked change in family dynamics is the increased role of fathers and other male family members in the active parenting of children (McBride, 1996).

Traditionally, school parent-teacher conferences were between the teacher and one parent, usually the mother, because they were most often scheduled during the normal work day. Increasingly, schools are recognizing the need to schedule these events in the evenings. The shift may have been primarily a response to women joining the workforce, but the result has been that many more men now participate in this important interchange.

There is sometimes a perception that fathers of children from single-parent homes, especially those of "low-income" and "high-risk" backgrounds, avoid participating in child rearing and therefore do not need to be included in conferences or considered in the scheduling of activities such as conferences, back-to-school nights, and other events. According to several studies, this perception is wrong (Gary, Beatty, & Weaver, 1987; Levine, 1993; McBride, 1996). Research findings show that regular and consistent interaction between children and their fathers is alive and well in over 60% of the families studied. However, this male involvement is not limited to fathers alone.

Increasingly in single-parent families, the male role is filled by grandfathers, uncles, mothers' boyfriends, stepfathers, foster fathers, and other men. Focusing program interactions primarily on parents may exclude these important people and communicate to them that their role is unimportant. An effective approach is to identify who the significant men are through informal conversations with children and parents and encourage them individually to participate in program activities. These relationships take time to develop, so be patient; but repeat your invitations each time an event is scheduled until all significant family members feel included.

PERSPECTIVE

Our Schools Are No Longer Safe for Children

- In 1995, 14.6% of students ages 12 through 19 reported being victimized at school (Chandler, Chapman, Rand & Taylor, 1998).

- 1,084 school-age children were killed by firearms in 1996 (Federal Bureau of Investigation, 1997).

- In 1994, juveniles age 12 through 17 were 2.7 times as likely as adults to be victims of violent crimes (Sickmund, Snyder & Poe-Yamagata, 1997).

- One in five students—and nearly one in three males—among inner-city high school students have been shot at, stabbed, or otherwise injured with a weapon at, or in transit to or from, school in the past few years (Sheley, McGee & Wright, 1995).

- 13.1% of violent crimes and almost 18% of simple assaults occurred inside school buildings or on school property in 1994 (Bureau of Justice Statistics, 1997).

- 25% of inner-city school students report carrying a weapon in school, and 44% report carrying weapons out of school (Sheley, McGee & Wright, 1995).

- 31% of inner-city high school students have been arrested at least once (Sheley, McGee & Wright, 1995).

- While only 4% of inner-city high school students report use of hard drugs, 13% report either dealing drugs or working for a drug dealer *(Sheley, McGee & Wright, 1995).*

- 57% of violent crimes committed by juveniles occur on school days, even though only about half of the days in a year are school days. In fact, 1 in 5 violent crimes committed by juveniles occur in the four hours after school (Sickmund, Snyder & Poe-Yamagata, 1997).

OVERVIEW

Our nation's schools, once a protected haven for learning and growth, are no longer safe for teachers or students in many of our nation's communities. From overt violent acts, such as homicide and assaults, to concealed crimes, such as child sexual abuse, violence in schools affects everyone—teachers, parents, children and the whole community. Victims of violent crime in the school, like victims elsewhere, may suffer physical ailments, withdrawal from peer relations, and display indifference to learning. They also may be more likely to abuse alcohol or drugs, which contributes to lack of learning, growth and development, and hinders the effective education of children.

Today, the problems in our schools are firearms, weapons, substance abuse and gangs. Many people equate school violence with large urban areas; however, violence has invaded suburban and rural schools as well. Not only public schools, but private schools are also involved.

Firearms

Guns in schools have increased to the point that approximately one in four major school districts now use metal detectors to reduce the number of weapons brought into schools by students (Wheeler & Baron, 1993). The juvenile offenders who are arrested for weapons violations are sometimes fellow students, and other times non-student peers, who threaten and attack students, administrators and teachers. According to a 1994 survey conducted by the National Parents' Resource Institute for Drug Education, almost one in thirteen (7.4%) of all high school students carried a gun to school in 1993–1994, and 35% threatened to harm another student or a teacher (Manning, 1994)...

Drug and Alcohol Abuse

Almost three out of four students reported that drugs were available at school in 1995 (Chandler, Chapman, Rand & Taylor, 1998). While illegal consumption or sale of drugs and alcohol among school children may not, in itself, be violent, such behavior often leads to violent acts. A *National Crime Survey Report* found that 37% of violent crime offenders ages 16 to 19 were perceived by their victims to be under the influence of drugs and/or alcohol (Whitaker & Bastian, 1991). . . .

Gangs

28.4% of students in 1995 reported that street gangs were present in their schools compared to 15.3% in 1989 (Chandler, Chapman, Rand & Taylor, 1998). Organized youth gangs are not limited to large, inner-city areas as is commonly believed, and membership crosses all racial and ethnic boundaries. According to a survey conducted by the National Parents' Resource Institute for Drug Education, 13.8% of American high school students joined a gang during the 1993–1994 school year (Manning, 1994). With these younger gang members attending school, schools themselves have become prime recruiting grounds. Gang members stake out their turfs in their territory, including the neighborhood school grounds (Wheeler & Baron, 1993).

Sexual Crimes

Sexual crimes against children cause extreme victimization—both immediately and often well into adulthood. The principle reason reported for revocation of teacher certificates is sexual misconduct (Whiteby, 1992). Such crimes are commonly called concealed crimes since they often go unreported because child victims are frequently silenced by their perpetrators with either threats or intimidation. . . .

SCHOOL SAFETY AS A POLICY

What can be done to provide a safer school environment? In the National School Safety Center (NSSC) resource paper, *School Crisis Prevention and Response,* it is noted that courts have held that schools are expected to provide a physical environment conducive to the purposes of an educational institution, although a school may not be expected to ensure nor guarantee the safety of its students (Wheeler & Baron, 1993). The paper goes on to state that the right to safe schools includes the right of students and staff to:

- Protection against foreseeable criminal activities;
- Protection against violence or student crime which adequate supervision can prevent;
- Protection against potentially dangerous students who are identifiable;
- Protection against dangerous persons admitted to school in a negligent manner; and
- Protection from negligently selected, retained or trained school administrators, teachers or staff.

The National School Safety Center recommends that a security plan be prepared and that the following general security measures be taken to lessen the chances of school violence:

- A local school security committee or task force comprised of school officials should be established by school districts. Planning for needed safety measures and their implementation should be performed by this task force, including regular review of safety and security measures.

- Crime prevention expertise should be developed and greater responsibility taken by school administrators in working with the school board and districts.
- A comprehensive crisis management plan should be developed by schools which incorporates resources available through other community agencies.
- Regular updates on safety plans and in-service training should be conducted to keep school staff informed. The training should include certified staff, classified staff, part-time employees and substitute teachers.
- Volunteers from the community, as well as parents, should be used to help patrol surrounding neighborhoods and supervise the campus before, during and after school.
- Access points to school campuses should be monitored during the school day. Access should be limited where possible. A single visitor entrance should be monitored by a receptionist or security officer and visitors should be required to sign in and wear an identification pass. Delivery entrances should also be monitored closely.
- Students should be taught to report suspicious individuals or unusual activity. They should also be taught to take responsibility for their own safety by learning personal safety and conflict resolution techniques.
- A curriculum committee focusing on teaching students non-violence, pro-social skills, conflict resolution, law-related education, and good decision-making should be established.
- Plans should be made to establish alternative schools to handle problem students. When these offenders are expelled from school there must be other programs in place to keep them off the streets where other violent incidents may be perpetrated.

Efforts such as these require the support of parents, administrators, social workers, criminal justice professionals and community leaders working together.

Source: Infolink: School Crime K–12. © 1998 National Center for Victims of Crime, Arlington, VA.

267

Family Fun Nights, Parent Meetings, and Parenting Assistance

Workers in many out-of-school programs have discovered that parent involvement in the day-to-day operation of the program, always difficult for working parents, increases when parents become comfortable with the program staff and get to know the other parents and families in the program. One way to facilitate this process is with monthly pizza parties or family fun nights. Some programs meet off-site; others order food and ask each family for a small contribution; in still other communities, preparation of the meal is a shared event.

These evenings work best if they are scheduled when there is a low calendar conflict. Find out when practice occurs for the sport of the season; what night the school is holding award ceremonies, or school-site council meetings, or whatever other regular event might conflict. Remember to list the date in the monthly parent calendar and send home reminders a few days before the monthly event. Inquire whether individual families need help with transportation, child care, or translation, and develop "buddy pairs" among the families who can assist with one or more of those needs.

Some of the program's social events should be just that—social. Think of them as opportunities for building friendships and eventually partnerships. At other times, the children might like to present plays, puppet shows, or musical productions for their families. Still other evenings might include a short business meeting where you can present ideas for future activities that would benefit from family input to the planning process. Some programs schedule one or two evening sessions a year devoted to *parenting assistance,* inviting speakers to discuss issues such as homework, competitive sports, conflict resolution, or other topics that are suggested by the parents themselves.

Other ways in which out-of-school programs can assist parents in resolving parenting or child-development issues include acquiring and organizing a lending library of books on topics of interest to parents, maintaining a section of the parent-communication bulletin board devoted to parenting topics, and listening to parents who need someone to talk to when they run into difficult times with their children. Sometimes all a parent needs to hear is that other parents are facing the same challenges.

Some family members will choose not to confide their frustration. In fact, many people find it difficult, even intimidating, to speak with teachers or caregivers about their children, even when things are obviously not going well. Fortunately, very few parents can ever hear too much about their children, especially if the information is positive and useful, so sometimes the best way to help is to communicate your interest by sharing anecdotes about daily events while respecting parents' privacy.

Day-to-Day Communication

Communication is clearly the key to building committed partnerships. Successful programs find many different ways to facilitate this communication. Individual conferences, parent handbooks, and family evenings have already been mentioned. Some programs also develop voice mail systems or online Web sites that list their location, hours, goals, procedures, and coming events (see Figure 14-1). Marsha Faryziarz, director of school-age programs for the Greater Burlington YMCA in Vermont, offers the following suggestions (Faryziarz, 1995).

NEWSLETTERS

Weekly or monthly newsletters are an excellent way to inform parents about coming events, past successes, and a variety of other things. However, parents receive newsletters and flyers from many sources, so they should be brief, informative, and interesting. Have children take turns doing the artwork, or include an article on individual children each time, to keep parents looking for a story on their child. Include important dates, procedural or schedule changes, and upcoming events. Arrange the information in a clear, easy-to-read format. Keep extra copies around for families whose original never made it home.

PERSONAL CONVERSATIONS

Sometimes it's good just to chat. Faryziarz suggested surprising parents by asking them how their day was, without mentioning their child at all. Compliment them on something they do well as parents. Parents need affirmations as much as children do.

TELEPHONE CONTACT

Periodically, take a few minutes during the workday to call parents and ask them if they have any questions or concerns they have forgotten to share with you. Don't do this too often or it will be an intrusion, but once or twice in a school year it sends the message that you care about their child and the whole family. Encourage them to call you during the day as well if they want to discuss something that does not lend itself to end-of-the-day conversation.

NOTES

A short note in a child's backpack saying something nice about that child can give a parent a wonderful lift. Share an interaction you noticed between the child and other children, or a special accomplishment. Extend the "eyes" of a parent who misses seeing much that happens during the child's day.

PICTURES

Invest in an instant-developing camera and ask each family to donate one roll of film each year. Once a week, post photos of children's activities on the

PARENT INFORMATION

WELCOME TO THE CHILDREN'S CHOICE

SCHOOL-AGE CARE (SAC) PROGRAM

We are happy to welcome you and your child into our Children's Choice family. It is the mission of Children's Choice to develop and maintain a model school-age child care program which will serve as a source of training and support to other school-age child care providers. You and your children are now a vital part of this working model.

As part of a collaborative process, the City of Albuq, Albuq Pub Schools, Sandia Base E.S., and Children's Choice will also provide after-school enrichment classes such as drama, dance, chess, art, computers, life skills, etc.

Albuquerque City Council

Albuquerque Public Schools

The goal of this Parent Information is to share with you Children's Choice goals, policies, procedures and other information. Please take time to read the information thoroughly. If you have further questions, please do not hesitate to call us. The voice mail number for Children's Choice is 505-296-2880, and the cellular phone number is 505-235-6328.

Figure 14–1   A Web Site Can Enhance Communication With Parents

bulletin board, and send several pictures home with each family throughout the year. When photos are taken down from the bulletin board, have children arrange them in a scrapbook with artwork and descriptions of the activities that are pictured. Bring the books to family fun nights and keep them in the room where children can share them with their families.

Parents and staff who work together to develop partnerships can create out-of-school programs that foster children's development in all areas. The keys to success are respect, understanding, and communication.

Resolving Parent-Staff Differences

In spite of our best efforts to develop a climate of open communication and committed partnership, parents and staff will occasionally disagree about such things as program policies, peer relationships, or discipline strategies. Dealing with direct disagreements requires ***respect*** and ***discretion*** (Katz, Aidman, Reese, & Clark, 1996). Respect parents' rights to their views and avoid direct conflict with cultural beliefs or practices. Before discussing disagreements in detail, be sure you know your program's policy for resolving conflicts with families. Are teachers free to work out the solution directly with parents or should the program director be included? Should the child participate in some or all of the process or should the adults discuss the situation in private?

Always use discretion about where and when children and their families are discussed and where you discuss conflicts with parents. Never talk about children or their families in public or social settings; don't discuss one child with another or with another parent. Confidentiality is extremely important if you are to maintain the trust between families and program staff. Handled respectfully and discreetly, the resolution of differences between a program and a family can be a positive experience, and it can serve as a model of constructive behavior for the children at the center of the conflict.

Developing Community Partnerships

Nurturing relationships with the families of children served by your program is important, but so is working within the wider community. Individual members of each community—such as business owners, members of the clergy, librarians, city council members, and teachers—all have a stake in developing high-quality out-of-school programs for school-age children, even if they don't at first understand or recognize that importance.

COMMUNITY PARTNERSHIPS IMPROVE CHILDREN'S FUTURES

One way of emphasizing the importance of community support for out-of-school programs addresses the future of our society:

In popular cultures and in the actions of prominent citizens, there are few positive messages to children and youth and much that undermines the values of honesty, human dignity and service to others. The result is that too many children are entering adulthood without the skills or the motivation to contribute to society. They are poorly equipped to reap the benefits or meet the responsibilities of parenthood, citizenship and employment. What consequences await them, and what future awaits the rest of us?

Investing in children is no longer a luxury—or even a choice. It is a national imperative as compelling as an armed attack or a natural disaster.

—National Commission on Children, 1991, p. 2

COMMUNITY PARTNERSHIPS REDUCE CRIME

Another, perhaps more pragmatic approach, simply communicates the short-term outcomes of school-age care in communities where it exists. For example, unsupervised or "latchkey" children have been found to be at greater risk of truancy from school, stress, receiving poor grades, risk-taking behavior, and substance abuse (Dwyer et al., 1990). Children who spend more hours on their own and those who began self-care at younger ages were found to be at the greatest risk. Additionally, the occurrence of vandalism, graffiti, and violent crime is greater at certain times in communities where unsupervised children exist in large numbers.

Data compiled on eight states by the Federal Bureau of Investigation in 1997 identified the peak hours for violent juvenile crimes as 3 p.m. to 8 p.m. The authors of this report (Fox & Newman, 1997) called for after-school programs that provide responsible adult supervision, constructive activities, and insulation from peer pressure during these high-crime hours:

In the afternoons, we used to have sports, drama and music. We had violins, and now it's violence. We've closed down ball fields. We've closed down community centers. We have disinvested in childhood and kids literally have too much time to kill.

—Fox, cited in Cannon, 1997, p. 7

One assistant principal in Jacksonville, Florida, struggling to convince a school board to open an after-school program in their community, took a more direct approach. At 7:20 a.m. one morning, he carried his camera and tape recorder around to several schools. There, nearly two hours before school doors opened, he photographed unsupervised children playing on school property and climbing on dangerous equipment parked nearby, asked why they were at the schoolyard so early, and taped their replies. Most of the children explained that their mothers had gone to work and they were tired of sitting at home. When the educator presented his slide/tape show to the board, he finally succeeded in persuading them that their community needed a program (Levine, 1980).

Community programs such as this community fair increase awareness of the ethnic diversity in communities. The children enjoy practicing for the performance and take pride in their native heritage.

COMMUNITY PARTNERSHIPS THAT WORK

Many excellent examples exist of community partnerships. For example, in Morgan Hill, California, two drop-in sports programs developed by one community agency resulted in a youth center being built by another. It began as a simple, weekly, evening game of pickup basketball in a high school gym. The popularity of the high school program, known as Friday Night Jams, led the sponsoring organization, El Toro Youth Center, to develop a daytime version of the same thing for younger children.

Following the success of these two programs, city leaders in the nearby town of Gilroy decided to turn an abandoned power company warehouse into an after-school activity and tutoring center. Located in a gang-ridden area of the community, the South County Youth Center offered a safe haven for children whose parents were still at work and whose homes were lonely and often frightening. Several agencies formed a funding consortium; assisted by a network of volunteers, a small paid staff provides an attractive smorgasbord of activities, including athletics, arts and crafts, field trips, computer training, music, and assistance with schoolwork. In 1997, the Gilroy Rotary Club made the youth center the focus of a fund-raising effort and helped the staff purchase

CREATIVE SOLUTIONS: THE MOST INITIATIVE

- Seattle MOST leveraged funds for new programs. By bringing together the children's Museum, Seattle Housing Authority, and the YMCA, MOST initiated a partnership that received federal funds to create a new YMCA school-age program in a public housing community.

- Together, Chicago MOST and the Chicago Park District have transformed over 40 drop-in recreational programs in diverse neighborhoods into high-quality after-school programs.

- Chicago MOST fostered "Friendship Circles": connections among school-age programs in different neighborhoods that expose children and staff to diversity. Through Friendship Circles,

over 500 children and staff come together to share activities.

- A partnership between Boston MOST and Boston's Museum of Science added a science component to eight established after-school programs.

- MOST involved the federal AmeriCorps organization to improve school-age care programs in Boston. Among seven program sites, typical AmeriCorps efforts included managing volunteers at a large school-based program and informing parents about school-age programs within a housing development.

—Shortt, 1997, p. 227

the building they had been renting from the public utility company. Examples such as these show the power of communities and funding agencies who work together.

In 1994, DeWitt Wallace-Reader's Digest launched a program to develop community-based coalitions in five cities. The models that were developed as a result of the MOST (Making the Most of Out-of-School Time) initiative illustrate creative ways in which public and private funding can be combined to increase programs for school-age children, as shown in the box.

COMMUNITY PARTNERSHIPS TAKE TIME

Developing partnerships, with parents or with communities, takes time, patience, and interpersonal skills. However, while separately each out-of-school program can touch dozens of children's lives, when each of us collaborates with parents and communities, we can impact the lives of thousands—not a bad day's work. Writing in a state school-age consortium newsletter, the project coordinator for a child-care planning council expressed her frustration at the time required to forge community partnerships at the same time she acknowledged their value:

> How many hours have I spent in meetings this week, I ask myself. I've met with the network of providers, the local Chamber of Commerce and attended a Community Developing Block Grant (CDBG) priority funding hearing.

What has been achieved? A heightened awareness of child care issues facing providers, a partnership with private business to meet the child care needs of our employed community and the potential creation of private/public partnership to save $50,000 for child care scholarships in CDBG priorities.

—Sinai, 1995, p. 1

SUMMARY

Developing partnerships with parents requires open and frequent communication. Beginning with the first contact, out-of-school programs need to develop ways to help parents get to know the program staff and other families served by the program and keep them informed of changes and upcoming events. It is also important to develop partnerships with communities. This is time-consuming, but the effort put into working collaboratively with community agencies and organizations can pay off in a high-quality out-of-school program with strong connections to the neighborhoods it serves.

REVIEW QUESTIONS

1. Why is it more challenging to get parents involved in out-of-school programs than in early childhood programs or classrooms?

2. List three ways in which program staff can facilitate communication with parents.

3. What is meant by *contractual* versus *committed* partnerships?

4. List three successful community partnerships described in the chapter.

CHALLENGE EXERCISES

1. Talk to a program director and find out what strategies are used in his or her program to develop partnerships with parents.

2. Research examples of community partnerships with programs for school-agers in your community.

3. Search the Internet for a Web site designed by or for a school-age child-care program. Bring a printout of it to class.

TERMS TO LEARN

committed partnership
contractual partnership
parenting assistance

REFERENCES

Bellum, D. (1990). *Parent involvement and communication.* San Francisco: California School Age Consortium.

Cannon, A. (1997, September 11). Study: Juvenile crime in prime time. *The Daily News,* p. 7.

Dwyer, K. M., Richardson, J. L., Danley, K. L., Hansen, W. B., Sussman, S. Y., Brannon, B., Dent, C. W., Johnson, C. A., & Flay, B. R. (1990). Characteristics of eighth-grade students who initiate self-care in elementary and junior high school. *Pediatrics, 86,* 44–45.

Faryziarz, M. (1995, May 1995). Working with parents. *School-Age Notes.*

Fox, J. A., & Newman, S. (1997). *Fight crime: Invest in kids.* Boston, MA: Northeastern University.

Gary, L., Beatty, L., & Weaver, G. (1987). *Involvement of black fathers in Head Start. Final Report submitted to the Department of Health and Human Services, ACYF, Grant No. 90-CD-0509.* Washington, DC: Howard University, Institute for Urban Affairs and Research.

Katz, L. G., Aidman, A., Reese, D. A., & Clark, A. M. (1996). *Preventing and resolving parent-teacher differences* (EDO-PS-96-12). Champaign, IL: ERIC Clearinghouse on Elementary and Early Childhood Education.

Levine, J. A., with Seltzer, M. (1980, September). Why are these children staying after school? (And why are they so happy about it?). *Redbook,* 32.

Levine, J. A. (1993). Involving fathers in Head Start: A framework for public policy and program development. *Families in Society, 74*(1), 4-19.

McBride, B. A. (1996). *Father/male involvement in early childhood programs.* Champaign, IL: ERIC Clearinghouse on Elementary and Early Childhood Education.

National Commission on Children. (1991). Investing in children. Practical Parenting Partnerships brochure. Jefferson City, MO: Missouri Department of Elementary and Secondary Education.

Novick, R. (1996). *Developmentally appropriate and culturally responsive education: Theory in practice.* Portland, OR: Northwest Regional Educational Laboratory.

Seligson, M., & Allenson, M. (1993). *School-age child care: An action manual for the 90s and beyond.* Westport, CT: Auburn House.

Shortt, J. (1997). *Creative solutions: The most initiative.* Boston, MA: National Institute on Out-of-School Time.

Sinai, J. (1995). Why collaborate? *CSAC Review, 8*(1), 1.

CHAPTER FIFTEEN

Ensuring Program Quality

Program Improvement and Accreditation

Quality in an Expanding Field

When my husband and I separated in 1981, my first major challenge was finding someone to help me care for my two children, age 6 and 9. When I searched the telephone yellow pages and the newspaper advertisements for before- and after-school care programs, I discovered that there were no school-site centers in my community. In fact, there were *no* child-care centers at all that would accept a child over 5 years, 9 months of age. Fortunately for me and my family, our town was (and continues to be) rich in licensed family child-care providers who gave my little ones nurturance and security during that difficult time and kept them engaged and happy.

However, by the time I was seeking before- and after-school care for my youngest child in 1989, our community had sprouted six school-site programs and two large corporate child-care centers; in addition, two preschools had added portables to serve school-age children. In 1998, while organizing a school-age professional development conference, I counted 14 school-age center-based programs and five after-school recreation/resource programs in the same town. The number of family child-care homes has grown in almost the same proportion.

As a parent, I applaud the increase in child-care spaces; but as a child-development professional, I know that rapid growth brings with it special challenges. These include finding trained staff, understanding the community's changing needs, and maintaining quality while keeping up with demand for increased services. This chapter addresses those issues, which face all of us as we enter the 21st century.

Rapid Growth Brings Challenges

The growing need for supervision and care of school-age children during their out-of-school time has encouraged many agencies and organizations to establish before- and after-school care and recreation programs in thousands of cities. Each year, new programs open and already existing programs expand. A broad examination of U.S. out-of-school programs completed in 1993 reported "significantly improved" opportunities for working parents to find a safe environment for their school-age children during non-school hours (Seppanen et al., 1993). The same trend exists in other nations, both industrialized and developing (Evans & Myers, 1994).

This is good news. Research has shown that children who participate in high-quality school-age programs are more likely to show improvements in social behavior, ability to handle conflicts, leadership skills, range of interests, academic performance, and school success (Howes, 1987; Mayesky, 1980; Posner & Vandell, 1994; Sheley, 1984). Similarly, these children are less likely to be retained in the same grade, placed in special education programs, or exhibit behavior problems or vandalism in and around schools (California Department of Education, 1996). Therefore, an increase in opportunities for children to attend out-of-school programs is a positive and desirable step.

However, simply increasing the *quantity* of programs and spaces is not enough. Researchers specify *high-quality* programs when they report social and behavioral improvements for children in out-of-school care. To meet the broad needs of children, families, and society effectively, programs must be designed thoughtfully and based on knowledge of the communities and families they serve. In addition, all programs for school-age children should be administered and implemented by people with a solid understanding of school-age children's development and characteristics. Unfortunately, a wide gap exists in most communities between the number of well-trained child and youth workers and the number needed to design and staff these new and expanding programs.

As program directors search for qualified employees or encourage existing employees to seek advanced education, they discover that opportunities for training and certification requirements vary considerably from place to place. Certainly it is important for us to provide a variety of educational options and career ladder entry points in order to recruit staff members who represent a diversity of backgrounds and experience. However, for employees to feel equitably treated and able to envision a career in the field, it is also necessary to develop some common ground in job descriptions and expected competencies.

In California, guidance came from the Advancing Careers in Child Development project of Pacific Oaks College and Children's Center. In this project, private and public agency representatives met with community and 4-year college faculty for several years to develop a matrix of job titles and educational requirements for early childhood education programs. The Department of Education of the University of California, Irvine, in collaboration with the Child Development Division of the California Department of Education, conducted a School-Age Care Professional Development Project. This project considered ways to offer training and certification opportunities to school-age care staff that focus on the skills they need to serve children between the ages of 5 and 14. Project participants proposed that a school-age care emphasis be added to the early childhood professional development matrix (Department of Education, 1998). This matrix stipulates the training and experience required for the various levels of the Child Development Permit—the credential required for anyone employed in California's state-funded child-care centers. Other states are proposing similar structures, which will eventually lead to a greater consistency of hiring patterns within the field (Michael Morrow, personal communication, 13 July 1998) as well as increasing the level of compensation and recognition (Joan Costly, Center for Career Development at Wheelock College).

Another critical need during periods of rapid growth is communication—communication between parents and programs, between programs and the state oversight agencies, and between programs and other programs. Without organization or communication, school-age care and out-of-school programs seem to spring independently from nowhere—some great, some not so great. How can parents select a high-quality program for their children? How can school-age staff in Boston learn what wonderful things are happening in Portland? How can legislators develop public policy to help guide and finance the development of a coherent system of out-of-school programs for our children? As in any profession, some kind of organization is necessary to create a network through which practitioners can have dialogues with one another and support continuous review and improvement of school-age care and recreation programs.

In many areas, regional groups have developed to address these and other issues resulting from rapid growth in program offerings. Informal or formal professional organizations that focus their discussions on the needs of school-age children can be extremely helpful in formulating policy, facilitating communication, and encouraging legislative and financial support for programs. Local workshops and conferences add to training opportunities for school-age staff and also increase the networking opportunities for everyone who participates.

School-Age Child Care: A Profession in the Making

A fairly common practice is to hire college and university students to work in before- and after-school programs. If you are reading this book for a college class, you may already be working in a program yourself or be considering it. Program directors who hire students are doing so for many good reasons: students tend to be young and enthusiastic, so they are appealing to the children with whom they work; by hiring students with interests and specialized knowledge in art, drama, athletics, or science, program administrators can feel more confident that their children will be enjoying a balanced curriculum. Students also tend to like the odd scheduling that before- and after-school programs require, including early mornings, split shifts, and flexible scheduling. Finally, students are usually willing to work for the almost embarrassingly low wages paid by most out-of-school programs.

Ellen Gannett, of the National Institute on Out-of-School Time, calls these employees "pass-through people" because, like many other staff members who are working in out-of-school programs, they may remain in the field only until they get a "real job"—a teaching position or one related to whatever they are studying in college (Gannett, 1995).

Even though we understand that students and other pass-through employees may work in school-age care programs for only a few years, they should still be recognized as important members of the staff and as such, need education and training. Ellen Gannett addressed this issue at the National Institute for Early Childhood Professional Development Conference in San Francisco in June 1995. She noted that these staff members eventually go on to become parents with children in need of school-age care, to be voters, and to be members of the business community; therefore, their education on school-age issues will not be wasted. While they spend time with children in out-of-school programs, they will be better able to meet their needs; once they move on, they will more likely become advocates of quality school-age programming:

> So the importance and benefits of training "pass-through" people is not just how they can be more effective in our programs today but also their role as our supporters later. These are not wasted dollars when we send college students to training for licensing requirements even though they will stay with the program for a short time.
>
> —Gannett, 1995, p. 1

Without reducing the importance of so-called pass-through employees, if we are to develop high-quality school-age child-care programs, we must also recruit and train a core of career-oriented staff members. One identified characteristic of high-quality child care is consistent and committed staff. We would be unrealistic to expect college students, working part-time on their way to a degree, to continue to work odd hours and for inadequate pay once they graduate. (In fact, it will be difficult to convince any child and youth workers to make long-term educational and career commitments to school-age care until the work they do is recognized by others as having value and is rewarded accordingly. Pay and recognition are important issues that must be addressed by local and national school-age organizations.) High-quality out-of-school programming must have both a rich cadre of enthusiastic, energetic, even if temporary, activity leaders and a permanent core of well-educated, committed professionals.

Consider some differences between two people who can both be found in the faculty workroom of an elementary school at 4:00 p.m. one afternoon. Imagine for a moment that both these school employees are 29 years old, hold B.A. degrees, and work with children of about the same age. One of them is a third-grade teacher; the other works in the after-school program. In most communities, the teacher will have a work space and mailbox in the school office building, will receive employment benefits such as health care and a retirement plan, is encouraged to attend professional development workshops as part of his or her paid obligation, has a reasonable expectation of increased salary as

In order to attract and keep high-quality staff in school-age programs, it will be necessary to develop a career ladder that includes increased pay for increased experience, education, and responsibility. Here Worthy Wage campaigners march in the streets of Seattle during the 1998 National School Age and Recreation Conference.

the years go by, and is respected by parents as an educational authority. It is unlikely at the present time that many school-age child-care workers experience any of these fringe benefits. The teacher, it can be argued, would be considered by most observers to be a professional. The school-age worker would, in all likelihood, not be. If society is to acknowledge, respect, and compensate appropriately the people who protect and care for our school-age children, these caregivers must be perceived as professionals.

There is no definition of ***profession*** that actually lists the fields or positions included in that category, but certain identifiable characteristics set some occupations apart from others. According to the *International Encyclopedia of the Social Sciences,* "professions" are traditionally distinguished from "occupations" by having a shared body of knowledge embracing a generalized cultural tradition; an intellectual component; formal technical training accompanied by some institutionalized model of validating both the adequacy of the training and the competence of trained individuals; and "some institutional means of making sure that such competence will be put to socially responsible uses" (Sills, 1968, p. 556). Going a step further, it appears that for the occupation of school-age care to be recognized as a profession there needs to be

1. A shared body of knowledge that includes both theory and practice
2. Identified standards and competencies for school-age practitioners
3. A system of peer-reviewed validation, as recognition that standards are being met

Fortunately, these elements already exist. Since 1978, the School-Age Child Care Project at Wellesley College has been studying how families care for their school-age children when school is not in session. In 1982, the research team published *School-Age Child Care: An Action Manual,* which provided information gathered from 100 school-age child-care programs around the country and guided other communities through the process of designing, developing, implementing, and operating programs for school-age children. Encouraged by the enthusiastic response to their work, the team continued to serve as a clearinghouse for information about existing programs and turned to other areas of research, such as state legislation and funding and the availability of postsecondary education for school-age staff. Now known as the National Institute on Out-of-School Time (NIOST), the organization offers training, technical help, and program-quality audits. NIOST provides a wide variety of publications and reseach reports and also manages national initiatives directed at improving the quantity and quality of school-age care (National Institute on Out-of-School Time, 1998).

In 1988, the National School-Age Child Care Alliance was formed, tying together the many regional and state school-age child-care organization coalitions that had begun around the country. In the United Kingdom, the Kids Club Network began about the same time. Regional, national, and international conferences followed, providing opportunities for experts and local practitioners to exchange ideas and dreams. Books appeared that focused on working with school-age children; colleges and universities developed coursework; states began identifying regional needs and requesting child-care funds designated for school-age programs; legislators began promulgating regulations governing out-of-school programs. In the past decade, dozens of national and international conferences have allowed school-age practitioners to share the work being done in their communities. The "shared body of knowledge" is growing, and the task ahead is to consolidate this information and disseminate the best of it throughout the field.

The Role of Professional Organizations in Program Quality

In most recognized professions, the function of developing and disseminating knowledge, **standards,** and expectations is done through professional organizations. Several specialized coalitions already exist in the field of early childhood education and care. Some of them have a very long history, and are highly respected throughout the world. A list of some of these groups is included in Appendix 3. However, until 1988, none of these organizations specifically addressed the needs and development of school-age care at the national level. The National School-Age Care Alliance (NSACA) filled that void. NSACA is a national umbrella organization that brings together the collective wisdom and experience of many of local networks; it is specific to school-age care and recreation. The NSACA network develops and promotes national standards for school-age programs, connects care providers locally and nationally, offers

Preparing a site for an accreditation visit can raise staff morale and create a sense of excitement.

opportunities for professional development and interaction, and helps shape public policy. Working at the local level and also in the public arena, NSACA representatives act as advocates for the needs of school-age children and connect the people who work with them.

One of the major roles taken by NSACA has been to collaborate closely with the National Institute on Out-of-School Time to listen to school-age care professionals and to foster discussion about promoting quality in school-age programs. Recognizing the variations in state and local regulations, standards, and opportunities for training, representatives of NSACA saw clearly that the improvement process must come from inside the field rather than externally from government agencies. The organization leaders turned, therefore, to school-age professionals, parents, experts, and youngsters as they began to develop a set of standards. Focus groups met around the United States to review and comment on the proposals at each stage. As a result, the project concluded with a high level of agreement.

In focusing on the concerns of children, NSACA representatives looked at the need both for accreditation and for professional development and recognition in this growing field, and created a set of standards that put children first. The NSACA Standards, discussed later in this chapter, focus on five elements of quality: human relationships; indoor and outdoor environments; activities; safety, health, and nutrition; and administration (National School-Age Care Alliance, 1997).

Assessing Program Quality

Two important tools used in the fields of child development and education for ensuring and improving program quality are *assessment* and *accreditation*. **Program assessment** is a process that allows program staff to "step back from the program and get some objectivity" (Seligson & Allenson, 1993, p. 277). For a single site, this examination can be as simple as a one-evening information-gathering session followed by a potluck meal with the staff and parents; in other circumstances, it can be a rigorous, six-month process that includes children, parents, staff, and community members and culminates in a written report. Thinking about the program in a methodical fashion, considering the various aspects of each day or week or the whole year and asking the various stakeholders in the program how they feel about each of these aspects can be extremely helpful. Self-assessment is an important tool in determining areas of strength and areas that need strengthening; it is an important first step in building program quality.

One limitation on self-study is the difficulty sometimes encountered of getting a clear picture of how your program compares to other programs. Another is that the parents, staff, and administration may not agree on the goals and objectives of the program or how well the curriculum or environment reflects those important missions. Once you have gathered information from the various groups, it is helpful to measure yourself against a set of external standards.

As the international awareness of the positive effects of high-quality school-age programs has grown, researchers have identified characteristics that excellent programs seem to have in common. Several organizations have used this information to develop instruments and procedures specifically to evaluate school-age programs (Albrecht & Plantz, 1993; Harms, Jacobs, & White, 1996; National Out-of-School Alliance, 1995; Sisson, 1995). In 1994, the Australian federal government disseminated a draft national standards document for school-age programs; the Kids Club Network in the United Kingdom began piloting their instrument in 1996 (National Out-of-School Alliance, 1995). In the United States, the Army worked with the Council for Early Childhood Professional Recognition to publish an assessment system and set of competency standards—the Council for Early Childhood Professional Recognition. They added the *School-Age Care Environment Rating Scale* to their selection of environmental checklists (Harms et al., 1996), and, drawing on ten years of research and discussion with each of these groups, NSACA in 1998 published *Standards for Quality School-Age Care* (National School-Age Care Alliance, 1998).

An effective way to assure continued growth toward quality is to study one of these sets of evaluative criteria and work through it with a team of people who care about your program. By examining the components of the program carefully and comparing them periodically to external guidelines, you will identify areas of need (which change over time) and the program can grow toward excellence. It is important, however, to train participants in the self-study process at the beginning of the evaluation period. Rosa Andrews, president of the North Carolina School-Age Care Coalition and the Improving Quality Project Director for the 4-H School-Age Care Project at North Carolina State University, describes well-implemented training as being "extremely motivating. . . . The training . . . prepared our programs to evaluate themselves and make program improvements. . . . I think any time providers have the opportunity to network together and gain explanations and information in their field the outcome is positive" (Andrews, personal communication, 1998).

Accreditation of School-Age Programs

The next step in the journey toward high-quality programming is **accreditation.** This is a process, common in the educational community, by which programs first measure themselves against a set of commonly agreed-on standards, then invite a team of external examiners to visit their site and do the same. The two sets of findings are then compared. If accreditation status is awarded, it is a verification that the program does, indeed, meet the standards. If the visiting team members, also known as **validators** or **endorsers,** do not agree with the findings of the program self-study, accreditation will be delayed until agreed-on improvements or changes in the program can be made. The award of accreditation status assures parents and community members that administrators of a school or child-care program have thought through a broad range of issues and offer a coherent and appropriate program to their children.

Programs with areas that need improvement can use information provided by the visiting team to guide them in their goal setting. Rosa Andrews reports that "motivation is very definitely created through this process. The excitement that this kind of quality is possible is contagious . . . [and] the process empowers the staff to ask for what they need to improve their programs" (Andrews, personal communication, 1998).

State-mandated licensing, required in most areas, is a necessary and helpful process for assuring a reasonable level of program safety and effectiveness, but it requires programs to meet only a *minimum* set of standards. Even self-study using a generally accepted assessment tool is limited by the ability of a program to critique itself honestly. The accreditation process encourages school-age care programs to see themselves through the eyes of others and to strive for continued growth toward higher quality. Becoming accredited by an organization that has high standards shows that a program is performing with a "high degree of excellence and meeting model standards" (Sciarra & Dorsey, 1995, p. 35).

Accreditation criteria are developed by professionals who have visited many programs and conferred with researchers and program staff to analyze the components that result in program quality. Two accreditation options available to out-of-school programs are the National Association for the Education of Young Children (NAEYC) Early Childhood Program Accreditation process,

Accredited by the
National Academy
of Early Childhood
Programs

FIGURE 15-1   **NAEYC
Accreditation Symbol**

administered by the National Academy of Early Childhood Programs; and the National Improvement and Accreditation System, jointly developed by the National School-Age Care Alliance (NSACA) and the National Institute on Out-of-School Time (NIOST).

NAEYC EARLY CHILDHOOD PROGRAM ACCREDITATION

Although developed primarily for use with children up to age 5, this accreditation system can also be used by school-age programs. Until recently, it was the only accreditation process available for them. NAEYC accreditation involves three steps: (1) self-study, (2) validation, and (3) accreditation decision. During the first phase, which may take as long as a year, program staff and parents conduct a self-assessment to determine how well their program meets the criteria of the Academy. Next, they plan and implement the needed improvements and write a report, which is submitted to the Academy. Following the review of this report, trained validators make an on-site visit to verify the accuracy of the program description. Programs are not required to demonstrate absolute compliance with the criteria, and the three-person commission that makes the accreditation decision considers both the program description provided by the applicant and the validators' report (National Association for the Education of Young Children, 1997). The NAEYC accreditation symbol appears in Figure 15-1.

The characteristics of quality examined by the NAEYC accreditation process have been summarized in a descriptive document that poses the following questions:

1. Are the children in the program generally comfortable, relaxed, and happy, and involved in play and other activities? Happy, relaxed children who are enjoying themselves as they play and learn are one of the best signs of a good program. See if there is an ample variety of materials for children of this age group.

2. Are there sufficient numbers of adults with specialized training in early childhood development and education? The younger the child, the more individualized attention is needed. The Academy's criteria recommend that all groups have at least two teachers [and that] . . . 4- to 5-year-olds should be in groups of 16 to 20 children. Specialized training in child de-

velopment and early education helps assure that staff understand how children grow and learn so they can be more effective teachers and caregivers.

3. Do adult expectations vary appropriately for children of differing ages and interests? Groups for infants and toddlers will look quite different from groups for older children. Toys and materials should vary by age as should teachers' expectations for children. In addition, teachers and caregivers should recognize and respect individual differences in children's abilities, interests, and preferences.

4. Are all areas of a child's development stressed equally, with time and attention being devoted to cognitive development, social and emotional development, and physical development? Good programs help children learn *how to learn;* to question why and discover alternative answers; to get along with others; and to use their developing language, thinking, and motor skills.

5. Do the staff meet regularly to plan and evaluate the program? Planning should reflect a balance of activities between vigorous outdoor play and quiet indoor play. Activities should allow ample time for children to work and play individually or in small groups, with the focus on activities that are child initiated as opposed to teacher directed. Flexibility, however, is also key. Staff should be willing to adjust the daily activities to meet children's individual needs and interests.

6. Are parents welcome to observe, discuss policies, make suggestions, and participate in the work of the program? Close communication between parents and staff is vital. Staff should regularly discuss highlights of the child's experiences with parents and show respect for families of varying cultures and background.
   —National Association for the Education of Young Children, 1997

The National Center for the Early Childhood Work Force examined 92 child-care programs in three northern California communities between 1994 and 1996 to document (1) changes in program quality resulting from participation in the NAEYC accreditation process, (2) the impact of various support models on programs' achievement of accreditation, and (3) the extent to which NAEYC accreditation contributes to building a skilled, stable workforce.

Although recognizing that the number of accredited centers in the study was quite small (23 out of the 92 centers studied), a preliminary review of findings presented in the executive summary suggests that NAEYC accreditation is successfully achieving its primary goal of improving and recognizing program quality (National Center for the Early Childhood Work Force, 1997).

For information about the Academy's accreditation process, or to receive accreditation materials, contact

National Academy of Early Childhood Programs
NAEYC
1509 16th Street, N.W.
Washington, DC 20036-1426
Phone: 202-232-8777 or 800-424-2460
Fax: 202-328-1846

NSACA NATIONAL IMPROVEMENT AND ACCREDITATION SYSTEM

Elements of the System   Seeing a need for a system of assessment and accreditation specifically designed for school-age programs, the National School-Age Care Alliance worked with the National Institute on Out-of-School Time School-Age Child Care Project at the Center for Research on Women at Wellesley College to develop *The NSACA Standards for Quality School-Age Care,* published in 1998 (Roman, 1998). The NSACA accreditation symbol appears in Figure 15-2.

These standards form the core of a nationwide program improvement and accreditation project. The standards are based on the *ASQ (Advancing School-Age Child Care Quality) Program Observation Instrument and Questions for the Director,* by Susan O'Connor, Thelma Harms, Debby Cryer, and Kathryn A. Wheeler. *The NSACA Standards* encourage a step-by-step approach for school-age programs to use as they examine five major areas: Human Relationships; Environment; Activities; Safety, Health and Nutrition; and Administration. Each of these areas is described below.

HUMAN RELATIONSHIPS   People who spend hours together each day affect one another's lives. An examination of the elements of interaction can sometimes identify attitudes, behaviors, and assumptions that lead to a less-than-optimum experience for adults and children. Do children value one another's unique characteristics, or do they form cliques that freeze out people who do not share their views? Do child and youth workers really listen to children and respect their feelings about things they care about? Through a series of questions, the standards seek to identify whether staff, children, and families are relating to one another in positive and helpful ways.

ENVIRONMENT   The indoor and outdoor environments should be examined to assure that they meet the needs of children, support a wide range of activities, and allow children to be independent while they explore their interests. Children who spend many hours a day in an organized out-of-school program need an environment that supports their play and development needs and that can be reshaped from time to time as those needs change.

Unless opportunities for such activities are included in their out-of-school programming, many children growing up today may never be able to build tree forts or explore their neighborhoods with friends. If children are to develop

FIGURE 15-2 **NSACA Accreditation Symbol.** Providers showing this logo have proven their commitment to "providing safe places for children to learn and grow.

healthy connections with their society and their culture, the environment in which they spend their time should provide the same opportunities for emotional, physical, and cognitive development that self-selected play environments did for their parents and grandparents.

ACTIVITIES   The curriculum of out-of-school programs should not duplicate what children experience in the regular daily classroom. Ideally, activities will be child-initiated or self-selected and include opportunities for active physical play, creative arts, quiet activities and socializing, and academic enrichment. The schedule should be flexible enough to allow youngsters to move smoothly from one activity to another at their own pace. The standards address scheduling; variety of activities, materials, supplies, and equipment; and developmental needs of the children in the program.

HEALTH, SAFETY, AND NUTRITION   Most states address health and safety criteria through licensing standards. However, the accreditation process expands on licensing by encouraging programs to serve healthy foods, support older children's need to eat varying amounts at different times, and allow them to influence the process of menu building.

ADMINISTRATION   Accreditation standards for administration include the requirements covered in most state regulations for licensing, but they expand beyond them. Group sizes and ratios of adults to children are addressed, as are provisions for older children to move slightly out of the direct supervision of adults. Do staff support and encourage family and community involvement in the program? This is measured by examining how staff orient family members to the program goals and activities, how they communicate with parents and community members, and how much staff encourage children and families to give input and be involved in the program activities. This criterion also addresses staff qualifications for working with children at several levels of responsibility, their training on the job, and their compensation.

The Accreditation Process   The NSACA Program Improvement and Accreditation project began with the distribution of pilot standards to school-age care programs and professional organizations all over the United States. The initial pilot, which was conducted with 74 programs, helped gather information on how the system and standards could be revised and strengthened. A second pilot was conducted with the revised standards, which were then approved by the NSACA board and published in January 1998.

The revised standards are the basis of the self-study process and of the accreditation process itself (see Figure 15-3). The ASQ (Advancing School-Age Quality) process consists of five steps. After completing the ASQ, programs that wish to apply for accreditation will send a program description to NSACA, which will then schedule an endorsement visit for the site. In the program description, program teams evaluate themselves against the standards and develop an improvement plan. Endorsers will rate the programs on the

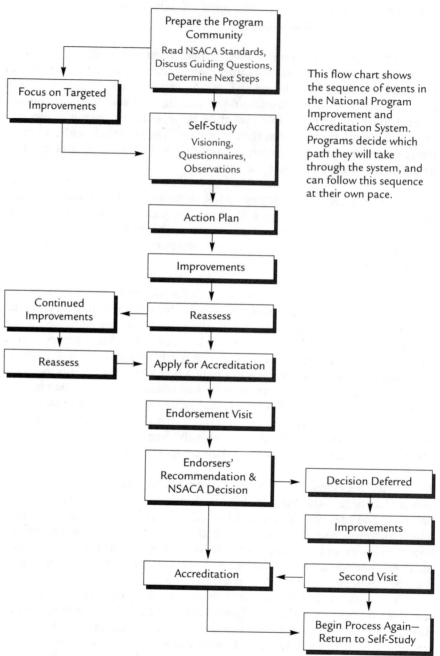

NSACA Program Improvement and Accreditation
Steps in the Process

Prepare the Program
Community

Read NSACA Standards,
Discuss Guiding Questions,
Determine Next Steps

Focus on Targeted
Improvements

Self-Study

Visioning,
Questionnaires,
Observations

Action Plan

Improvements

Continued
Improvements

Reassess

Reassess

Apply for Accreditation

Endorsement Visit

Endorsers'
Recommendation &
NSACA Decision

Decision Deferred

Improvements

Accreditation

Second Visit

Begin Process Again—
Return to Self-Study

This flow chart shows
the sequence of events in
the National Program
Improvement and
Accreditation System.
Programs decide which
path they will take
through the system, and
can follow this sequence
at their own pace.

FIGURE 15–3   **NSACA Improvement and Accreditation Program**

standards by a combination of observations, on-site documentation reviews, and interviews. The endorsers will then submit a report to NSACA, which will make the final decision.

Essentially a peer review system, the NSACA accreditation process is a bold step toward assuring quality in school-age child care. The complete NSACA Program Improvement and Accreditation kit, which includes self-study materials and a video, became available in Spring 1998. Programs in communities where an NSACA regional office was in place began applying for accreditation in September 1998. For more information about the NSACA accreditation process or to receive accreditation materials, contact

The National School-Age Care Alliance
1137 Washington Street
Boston, MA 02124
Phone: 617-298-5012
Fax: 617-298-5022
E-mail: staff@nsaca.org

SUMMARY

In response to a pressing need for safe environments for school-age children, many agencies and organizations have established care and recreation programs in the last decade. In our enthusiasm for increasing the *quantity* of school-age care programs, however, we must not forget the importance of *quality* in those programs. By using a program assessment or accreditation process, program managers, staff, parents, and children can examine and improve components of their program. The NAEYC accreditation process, originally developed for use in programs for children up to age 5, examines staff-child interaction, curriculum, physical setting, and health and safety. The NSACA quality assurance process was developed specifically for school-age care programs. Five areas examined by the National School-Age Care Alliance Standards for Quality School-Age Care include human relationships; environment; activities; safety, health, and nutrition; and administration. Following a 2-year pilot study of the instrument and the process, school-age programs began to seek accreditation through NSACA in 1998.

REVIEW QUESTIONS

1. What kinds of outcomes have been associated with high-quality school-age programs?

2. Distinguish between *assessment* and *accreditation*.

3. Why is it important to review the components of a school-age program continually?

4. What distinguishes the NAEYC accreditation process from that of NSACA accreditation?

5. Identify the five areas examined by the NSACA Standards document.

CHALLENGE EXERCISES

1. Inquire in your community to learn whether any of the school-age care programs have completed a self-study assessment process. Meet with the director to discuss the process and its outcomes. Summarize and share your findings with the class.

2. Obtain a copy of the NSACA standards. Select one or more *keys of quality* and describe

what a program might look like that met each of them. Compare your description to your observation notes from site visits made in the past. Discuss.

3. Explain why training is just as important to "pass-through" employees as to career-oriented school-age child-care staff.

TERMS TO LEARN
··················

accreditation
endorsers
profession
program assessment
standards
validators

REFERENCES
················

Albrecht, K., & Plantz, M. (1993). *Developmentally appropriate practice in school-age child care programs* (2nd ed.). Dubuque, IA: Kendal/Hunt.

California Department of Education. (1996). *School-age care in California.* Sacramento: Child Development Division.

Department of Education, University of California at Irvine. (1998). *School-age care in California: Addressing the needs for training, certification, and professional development.* Irvine.

Evans, J., & Myers, R. (1994). Childrearing practices: Creating programs where traditions and modern practices meet. *Coordinators' Notebook: An international resource for early childhood development.* Issue No. 15, 1994. Haydenville, MA: The Consultative Group on Early Childhood Care and Development.

Gannett, E. (1995). Difference between training "pass-through" staff and "career oriented" staff. *School-Age Notes, 15*(11), 1–2.

Harms, T., Jacobs, E. V., & White, D. R. (1996). *School-age care environment rating scale.* New York: Teachers College Press.

National Association for the Education of Young Children. (1997). *NAEYC early childhood program accreditation: A commitment to excellence.* (Brochure). Washington, DC: Author.

National Center for the Early Childhood Work Force. (1997). *NAEYC accreditation as a strategy for improving child care quality.* Washington, DC: Author.

National Institute on Out-of-School Time. (1998). *Working together for quality care after school.* Boston, MA: Author.

National Out-of-School Alliance. (1995). *Aiming high: KCN's quality assurance scheme for out of school clubs.* London: Bellerive House.

National School-Age Care Alliance. (1997). Caring, stimulating, responsive. In National School-Age Care Alliance (Ed.), *NSACA, A professional support network for quality care.* Boston, MA: Author.

Roman, J. (Ed.). (1998). *The NSACA standards for quality school-age care.* Boston, MA: National School-Age Care Alliance.

Sciarra, D. J., & Dorsey, A. G. (1995). *Developing and administering a child care center* (3rd ed.). San Francisco: Delmar.

Seligson, M., & Allenson, M. (1993). *School-age child care: An action manual for the 90s and beyond.* Westport, CT: Auburn House.

Seppanen, P., Love, J., deVries, D., Bernstein, L., Seligson, M., Marx, F., & Kisker, E. (1993). *National study of before- and after-school programs.* Portsmouth, NH: RMC Research Corporation.

Sills, D. (Ed.). (1968). *International encyclopedia of the social sciences* (Vol. 12). New York: Macmillan.

Sisson, L. (1995). *Pilot standards for school-age child care.* Washington, DC: National School-Age Care Alliance.

Safety Checklist

Use this checklist to find hazards. Whenever a hazard is found, fix it if you can. If you cannot fix it, make a note of it and plan to get it fixed.

Safety checks should be done at least once a month. Having different people do the safety checks helps find more hazards. The more people who are involved in watching for hazards, the more they will help fix hazards whenever they see them. Safety is everyone's business!

General Indoor Areas

Yes No

☐ ☐ Guns, projectile toys, darts, and cap pistols are not kept in the child care setting.

☐ ☐ Floors are smooth and have nonskid surfaces. Rugs are skid-proof.

☐ ☐ Doors to places that children can enter, such as bathrooms, can be easily opened from the outside by a child or by an adult.

☐ ☐ Doors in children's areas have see-through panes so children are visible to anyone opening the door.

☐ ☐ Doors have slow closing devices and/or rubber gaskets on the edges to prevent finger pinching.

☐ ☐ Glass doors and full-length windows have decals on them that are at the eye levels of both children and adults.

☐ ☐ Windows cannot be opened more than 6 inches from the bottom.

☐ ☐ All windows have closed, permanent screens.

☐ ☐ Bottom windows are lockable.

☐ ☐ Walls and ceilings have no peeling paint and no cracked or falling plaster.

☐ ☐ The child care setting is free of toxic or lead paint and of crumbly asbestos.

☐ ☐ Safety covers are on all electrical outlets.

Adapted, courtesy of the American Red Cross, from *The American Red Cross Child Care Course,* Health & Safety Units, 1990, pp. 38–44. This checklist is authorized for use by individual child care providers. All other usage is strictly prohibited without the express approval of the American Red Cross.

Yes **No**

☐ ☐ Electrical cords are out of children's reach. Electrical cords are placed away from doorways and traffic paths.

☐ ☐ Covers or guards for fans have openings small enough to keep children's fingers out.

☐ ☐ Free-standing space heaters are not used.

☐ ☐ Pipes, radiators, fireplaces, wood burning stoves, and other hot surfaces cannot be reached by children or are covered to prevent burns.

☐ ☐ Nobody smokes or has lighted cigarettes, matches, or lighters around children.

☐ ☐ Tap water temperature is 120° Fahrenheit or lower.

☐ ☐ Trash is covered at all times and is stored away from heaters or other heat sources.

☐ ☐ Drawers are closed to prevent tripping or bumps.

☐ ☐ Sharp furniture edges are cushioned with cotton and masking tape or with commercial corner guards.

☐ ☐ Emergency lighting equipment works.

☐ ☐ Regular lighting is bright enough for good visibility in each room.

☐ ☐ Enough staff members are always present to exit with children safely and quickly in an emergency.

☐ ☐ All adults can easily view all areas used by children.

☐ ☐ Pets are free from disease, are immunized as appropriate, and are maintained in a sanitary manner.

☐ ☐ Poisonous plants are not present either indoors or outdoors in the child care areas.

☐ ☐ All adult handbags are stored out of children's reach.

☐ ☐ All poisons and other dangerous items are stored in locked cabinets out of children's reach. This includes medicines, paints, cleansers, mothballs, etc.

☐ ☐ Pesticides are applied only to surfaces that children cannot reach and surfaces not in direct contact with food.

☐ ☐ A certified pest control operator applies pesticides while observed by a caregiver.

Yes	No	
☐	☐	Cots are placed in such a way that walkways are clear for emergencies.
☐	☐	Children are never left alone in infant seats on tables or other high surfaces.
☐	☐	Teaching aids such as projectors are put away when not in use.
☐	☐	A well-stocked first aid kit is accessible to all caregivers.

Toys and Equipment

Yes	No	
☐	☐	Toys and play equipment have no sharp edges or points, small parts, pinch points, chipped paint, splinters, or loose nuts or bolts.
☐	☐	All toys are painted with lead-free paint.
☐	☐	Toys are put away when not in use.
☐	☐	Children are not permitted to play with any type of plastic bag or balloon.
☐	☐	Toy chests have air holes and a lid support or have no lid. A lid that slams shut can cause head injuries or suffocation.
☐	☐	Shooting or projectile toys are not present.
☐	☐	Commercial art materials are stored in their original containers out of children's reach. The word *nontoxic* appears on the manufacturer's label.
☐	☐	Rugs, curtains, pillows, blankets, and cloth toys are flame-resistant.

Hallways and Stairs

Yes	No	
☐	☐	Handrails are securely mounted at child height.
☐	☐	Handrails are attached to walls for right-hand descent, but preferably are attached to the walls on both right and left sides.
☐	☐	Doorways to unsupervised or unsafe areas are closed and locked unless the doors are used for emergency exits.

Hallways and Stairs, CONTINUED

....

Yes   No

☐   ☐   Emergency exit doors have easy-open latches.

☐   ☐   Safety glass is used in all areas of potential impact.

☐   ☐   Caregivers can easily monitor all entrances and exits to keep out strangers.

☐   ☐   Stairways and hallways are clear of objects that can cause a fall.

Kitchen and Food Preparation and Storage Areas

....

Yes   No

☐   ☐   Caregivers always wash hands before handling food.

☐   ☐   Trash is always stored away from food preparation and storage areas.

☐   ☐   Refrigerator temperature is monitored by thermometer and is kept at or below 40° Fahrenheit.

☐   ☐   All perishable foods are stored in covered containers at 40° Fahrenheit or lower.

☐   ☐   Hot foods are kept at 140° Fahrenheit or higher until ready to be eaten.

☐   ☐   Pest strips are not used.

☐   ☐   Cleansers and other poisonous products are stored in their original containers, away from food, and out of children's reach.

☐   ☐   Nonperishable food is stored in labelled, insect-resistant metal or plastic containers with tight lids.

☐   ☐   Refrigerated medicines are kept in closed containers to prevent spills that would contaminate food.

☐   ☐   Food preparation surfaces are clean and are free of cracks and chips.

☐   ☐   Eating utensils and dishes are clean and are free of cracks and chips.

☐   ☐   Appliances and sharp or hazardous cooking utensils are stored out of children's reach.

☐   ☐   Pot handles are always turned towards the back of the stove.

☐   ☐   An ABC-type fire extinguisher is securely mounted on the wall near the stove.

Adapted, courtesy of the American Red Cross, from *The American Red Cross Child Care Course,* Health & Safety Units, 1990, pp. 38–44. This checklist is authorized for use by individual child care providers. All other usage is strictly prohibited without the express approval of the American Red Cross.

Yes	No	
☐	☐	All caregivers know how to use the fire extinguisher correctly and have seen a demonstration by members of the fire department.
☐	☐	There is a "danger zone" in front of the stove where the children are not allowed to go.
☐	☐	A sanitarian has inspected food preparation and service equipment and procedures within the past year.
☐	☐	Trash is stored away from the furnace, stove, and hot water heater.
☐	☐	Kitchen area is not accessible to children without constant adult supervision.
☐	☐	Caregivers do not cook while holding a child.
☐	☐	Hot foods and liquids are kept out of children's reach.
☐	☐	Stable step stools are used to reach high places.

Bathrooms

Yes	No	
☐	☐	Stable step stools are available where needed.
☐	☐	Electrical outlets have safety covers or are modified to prevent shock.
☐	☐	Electrical equipment is stored away from water.
☐	☐	Cleaning products and disinfectants are locked in a cabinet out of children's reach.
☐	☐	Toilet paper is located where children can reach it without having to get up from the toilet.
☐	☐	There are enough toilets so children do not have to stand in line.
☐	☐	Caregivers and children always wash hands after toileting.
☐	☐	Paper towels and liquid soap are readily available at the sink.
☐	☐	Thermometers are used to check that water temperatures are between 120° and 130° Fahrenheit or lower.
☐	☐	Cosmetics are stored out of children's reach.
☐	☐	Bathtubs have skid-proof mats or stickers.
☐	☐	Children are never left unsupervised in or near water.

Playground

Yes	No	
☐	☐	The playground offers a wide range of parallel and interactive activities.
☐	☐	All surfaces underneath play equipment are covered with 10 to 12 inches of impact-absorbing material such as sand, wood chips, or pea gravel, or with a manufactured energy-absorptive surface which is under and extends at least 6 feet on all sides of the equipment.
☐	☐	Surfaces are raked weekly to remove litter, sharp objects, and animal feces.
☐	☐	Stagnant pools of water are not present.
☐	☐	All pieces of play equipment are at least 8 feet apart.
☐	☐	Boundaries such as railroad ties, low bushes, benches, or painted lines separate play equipment from walking areas.
☐	☐	Bike or trike riding areas are separate from other equipment.
☐	☐	Playgrounds are fenced in.
☐	☐	Exposed concrete or hard anchoring material is covered.
☐	☐	There are no sharp edges, loose connections, exposed nails, or bolt ends.
☐	☐	Equipment is appropriate to the size and development of the children.
☐	☐	The playground is designed for safety. Caregivers remind children regularly of playground safety rules.
☐	☐	Swing sets are placed 9 or more feet from other equipment and at least 8 feet from walls, fences, walkways, and other play areas.
☐	☐	Swings are hung at least 1½ feet apart from one another.
☐	☐	Slides have an 8 to 9 foot run-off space.
☐	☐	Slides are no taller than 6 feet and have side rims at least 2½ inches high.
☐	☐	Slides have an enclosed platform at the top for children to rest on and get into position.
☐	☐	Slide ladders have flat steps and a handrail on each side.
☐	☐	Slides have a flat surface at the bottom to slow children down.
☐	☐	Metal slides are shaded to prevent overheating.

Adapted, courtesy of the American Red Cross, from *The American Red Cross Child Care Course,* Health & Safety Units, 1990, pp. 38–44. This checklist is authorized for use by individual child care providers. All other usage is strictly prohibited without the express approval of the American Red Cross.

Yes	No	
☐	☐	Wood slides are waxed or oiled to prevent rough surfaces.
☐	☐	The slide incline is equal to or less than a 30° angle.
☐	☐	Steps and rungs are 7 to 11 inches apart and are evenly spaced for easy climbing.
☐	☐	Climbing or swinging bars stay in place when grasped.
☐	☐	The maximum height of play equipment is 6 feet.
☐	☐	Climbers have regularly spaced footholds from top to bottom.
☐	☐	The tops of climbers have a "safe way out" for children.
☐	☐	Playground equipment has no openings 4⅜ to 9⅛ inches to entrap a child's head.
☐	☐	Rungs on climbers are painted in bright or contrasting colors for easy visibility.
☐	☐	Swings with canvas sling seats are available for children over age 5.
☐	☐	Swings have no "S" or open-ended hooks.
☐	☐	The points at which swing seats and chains meet are enclosed in plastic tubing.
☐	☐	Hanging rings are less than 5 inches or more than 10 inches in diameter (smaller or larger than a child's head).
☐	☐	Seesaw equipment is designed to prevent pinching.
☐	☐	Wooden blocks or parts of a rubber tire are placed beneath the ends of seesaws to prevent feet from getting caught.
☐	☐	Merry-go-rounds are installed so that a child cannot fit head or body beneath the turning platform.
☐	☐	Sandboxes are located in the shade, have smooth frames, and are covered when not in use.
☐	☐	Sandbox sand is raked at least every 2 weeks to remove debris.
☐	☐	Pools are fenced in and closed to trespassers. They have been inspected and their safety equipment, sanitation, procedures, and supervision have been approved.
☐	☐	Play areas are free of trash cans and poisonous plants and berries.
☐	☐	Play areas have clean drinking water and lots of shade.
☐	☐	Caregivers can easily view the entire play area.

Playground, CONTINUED

....

Yes No

☐ ☐ Caregivers closely supervise high risk areas such as climbing equipment.

☐ ☐ Adult seating near the high risk areas is provided to encourage adult observation.

☐ ☐ Children learn how to use sports equipment and how to use the proper safety equipment for each sport.

☐ ☐ Children learn water safety and they are always watched by adults when they are in or near water.

☐ ☐ Children over 5 years of age should know how to swim.

☐ ☐ The caregiver gives specific safety instructions such as "Don't climb the tree" or "Stay inside the fence."

☐ ☐ The caregiver looks around the playground for broken glass and other debris before permitting children to play.

☐ ☐ A well-stocked first aid kit is accessible to all caregivers during outdoor play.

Swimming Pools

....

Yes No

☐ ☐ All pools and ponds are enclosed with four-sided fencing that is resistant to climbing, is at least 5 feet high, comes within 3½ inches of the ground, and has openings no greater than 3½ inches.

☐ ☐ Fence openings have self-closing latching gates with the latch at least 55 inches from the ground.

☐ ☐ Walk areas around the pool have a nonskid surface.

☐ ☐ The pool and pool maintenance have been inspected and approved by the local health department within the past year.

☐ ☐ Small, portable wading pools are not used for group water play.

☐ ☐ Equipment is available and used every two hours while children are in the water to test and maintain the pH of the water between 7.2 and 8.2

☐ ☐ Water temperatures are maintained between 82°F and 93°F while the pool is in use.

Adapted, courtesy of the American Red Cross, from *The American Red Cross Child Care Course*, Health & Safety Units, 1990, pp. 38–44. This checklist is authorized for use by individual child care providers. All other usage is strictly prohibited without the express approval of the American Red Cross.

Emergency Preparedness

Yes	No	
☐	☐	All caregivers have roles and responsibilities in case of fires, injury, or other disasters.
☐	☐	One or more caregivers certified in infant and child first aid and where children swim or children with disabilities are in care, one or more caregivers certified in infant and child CPR are always present.
☐	☐	All first aid kits have the required supplies. The kits are stored where caregivers can easily reach them in an emergency.
☐	☐	Caregivers always take a first aid kit on trips.
☐	☐	Smoke detectors and other alarms work.
☐	☐	Each room and hallway has a fire escape route clearly posted.
☐	☐	Emergency procedures and telephone numbers are clearly posted near each phone.
☐	☐	Children's emergency phone numbers are posted near the phone and can be easily taken along in case of an emergency evacuation.
☐	☐	Emergency procedures include the following: ■ How to phone emergency medical services (EMS) system ■ Transportation to an emergency facility ■ Notification of parents ■ Where to meet if the child care setting is evacuated ■ Plans for an adult to care for the children while a caregiver stays with injured children. This includes escorting children to emergency medical care.
☐	☐	All exits are clearly marked and free of clutter.
☐	☐	Doors and gates all open out for easy exit.
☐	☐	Children are taught to tell if they or anyone else is hurt.
☐	☐	Children are taught the words *stop* and *no*. Caregivers avoid using those words unless there is danger.
☐	☐	Children are taught their own telephone number, address, and parent's work numbers.
☐	☐	Children are taught how to phone EMS (911).
☐	☐	Children are taught how to Stop, Drop, Roll, Cool in case their clothes catch fire.
☐	☐	Children are taught to turn in any matches they find to an adult.

Vehicles

....

Yes   No

☐   ☐   All vehicles work well.

☐   ☐   Everyone, during every ride, uses age-appropriate safety restraints.

☐   ☐   Staff helps to unbuckle and buckle-up children at drop-off and pickup.

☐   ☐   Drivers use child-resistant door locks when the vehicle is in motion.

☐   ☐   All vehicles are locked when not in use.

☐   ☐   A well-stocked first aid kit is in the vehicle for every ride.

☐   ☐   The caregiver has on hand current emergency contact information when driving children.

☐   ☐   Trip plans include how to manage emergencies.

☐   ☐   Children wear identification when transported.

☐   ☐   Pickup and drop-off points are safe from traffic.

☐   ☐   Infant seats are installed correctly, with seats facing the rear of the car until the child exceeds the weight recommended by the manufacturer for facing rear.

☐   ☐   Driver knows where children are before putting vehicle in reverse.

☐   ☐   Bicycles and other riding toys are stable, well-balanced, and of the appropriate size. They do not have broken parts.

☐   ☐   Children use helmets approved by ANSI (American National Standards Institute) or Snell Memorial Foundation when riding bikes.

☐   ☐   Young bikers know traffic rules.

☐   ☐   Children do not horse around while riding bikes and do not ride in the street.

☐   ☐   Young children never cross the street without an adult. Children should know rules for crossing the street.

Adapted, courtesy of the American Red Cross, from *The American Red Cross Child Care Course,* Health & Safety Units, 1990, pp. 38–44. This checklist is authorized for use by individual child care providers. All other usage is strictly prohibited without the express approval of the American Red Cross.

Injury Report Form

Complete within 24 hours of injury. For an injured child, obtain the signature of a parent or legal guardian. File the completed form in the injured child's (or injured adult's) record. Give a copy (or a carbon copy) of the child's form to the parent.

Name of injured _____ Age _____

Date of injury _____ Time of injury _____ a.m. / p.m.

Witness(es) _____

Where injury happened _____

Any equipment or products involved _____

Name of parent notified _____

Time notified _____ a.m. / p.m.   Notified by _____

Description of injury and how it happened _____

Who gave first aid and what did they do _____

First aid given by medical personnel, telling who, what, when, and where _____

Follow-up plan for the injured _____

Injury prevention steps taken _____

Caregiver completing form _____

Date form completed _____ Parent's signature _____

Organizations Serving Child Care and Related Professions

Information dissemination is a priority of the National Child Care Information Center. To complement and not duplicate the work of other agencies, the NCCIC maintains a web site (http://nccic.org) that promotes linkages with national organizations and clearing-houses. These organizational resources include membership groups, advocacy organizations, and researchers. Many of the organizations also have Home Pages. . . . In some cases, more detailed information is provided about an organization, which can be retrieved by clicking on the highlighted name of that organization. This information is available as it is made available to the NCCIC. The National Child Care Information Center does not endorse any organization, publication, or resource.

LIST OF ORGANIZATIONS DESCRIBED
....

- American Public Welfare Association
- Center for Career Development in Early Care and Education, Wheelock College
- Child Care Action Campaign
- Child Care Institute of America
- Child Care Law Center
- Children's Defense Fund
- Children's Foundation
- Child Welfare League of America, Inc.
- Council for Early Childhood Professional Recognition
- Council of Chief State School Officers
- Ecumenical Child Care Network

- ERIC Clearinghouse on Elementary and Early Childhood Education (ERIC/EECE)
- Families and Work Institute
- National Association for the Education of Young Children (NAEYC)
- National Association for Family Child Care
- National Association of Child Care Professionals (NACCP)
- National Association of Child Care Resource and Referral Agencies (NACCRRA)
- National Black Child Development Institute
- National Center for Children in Poverty
- National Center for the Early Childhood Work Force
- National Child Care Association
- National Head Start Association
- National Indian Child Care Association
- National Institute on Out-of-School Time (formerly School-Age Child Care Project)
- National Resource Center for Health and Safety in Child Care
- National School-Age Care Alliance
- School-Age Child Care Project (see National Institute on Out-of-School Time)
- USA Child Care
- Women's Bureau, U.S. Department of Labor
- Zero To Three: National Center for Infants, Toddlers, and Families
- Interagency Task Force on Child Abuse and Neglect Clearinghouse Consortium Members

American Public Welfare Association

810 First Street, NE
Suite 500
Washington, DC 20002-4267
Phone: (202) 682-0100
Web: http://www.apwa.org/

The American Public Welfare Association is committed to developing and advocating effective public policies that improve the lives of low-income Americans. APWA provides policy research, development and analysis. Current issues include adolescent pregnancy, immigration reform, child welfare issues, and the prevention of elder abuse. The Association also provides professional training for public welfare staff.

Child Care Action Campaign

330 7th Avenue, 17th Floor
New York, NY 10001
Phone: (212) 239-0138
Web: http://www.usakids.org/sites/ccac.html

CCAC is a national advocacy organization that works to stimulate and support the development of policies and programs that increase the availability of quality, affordable child care. Current programs include: Child Care and Education: Forging the Link, the Family Support Watch (to monitor and strengthen the child care provisions of welfare reform); the Strategic Communications Plan for Early Care & Education, financing alternatives and public education.

Child Care Institute of America

3612 Bent Branch Court
Falls Church, VA 22041
Phone: (703) 941-4329

The Child Care Institute of America is a national, nonprofit organization that supports private-licensed, center based, and ecumenical early childhood programs.

Child Care Law Center

973 Market Street, Suite 550
San Francisco, CA 94103
Phone: (415) 495-5498
E-mail: cclc@childcarelaw.com

The Child Care Law Center (CCLC) is the only organization in the country working exclusively on the legal issues concerning the establishment and provision of child care. The Center's major objective is to use legal tools to foster the development of quality, affordable child care programs. Established in 1978, the CCLC serves as a statewide legal support center providing free legal training and legal services to attorneys and others who work on child care issues for low-income families throughout California. The Child Care Law Center also provides legal assistance

and information to nonprofit centers, family day care providers, parents, policymakers, community and governmental agencies, unions and employers throughout the country. In addition to its small legal staff, the Center is able to call upon attorneys who provide technical consultation and pro bono legal representation.

Children's Defense Fund

25 E Street, NW
Washington, DC 20001
Phone: (202) 628-8787
Web: http://www.childrensdefense.org

The Children's Defense Fund (CDF) is a nonprofit research and advocacy organization that exists to provide a strong and effective voice for children of America who cannot vote, lobby or speak out for themselves. The Children's Defense Fund pays particular attention to the needs of poor, minority, and disabled children. The CDF's goal is to educate the nation about the needs of children and encourage investment in children before they get sick, drop out of school, suffer damage breakdown, or get into trouble.

The Children's Foundation

725 15th Street, NW, #505
Washington, DC 20005
Phone: (202) 347-3300

The Children's Foundation is a private national educational nonprofit organization that strives to improve the lives of children and those who care for them. Through the National Child Care Advocacy Project and National Child Support Project, the Children's Foundation conducts research and provides information and training on federal food programs; quality child care; leadership development; health care; and enforcement of court-ordered child support.

Child Welfare League of America, Inc.

440 First Street, NW
Suite 310
Washington, DC 20001-2085
Phone: (202) 638-2952
Web: http://www.cwla.org/

The Child Welfare League of America (CWLA) is a federation of over 750 public and voluntary member agencies that serve children and families throughout the United States and Canada. These agencies provide a full array of child welfare services including child care. CWLA's services include developing standards in 12 service areas including child care.

Center for Career Development in Early Care and Education, Wheelock College

200 The Riverway
Boston, MA 02215
Phone: (617) 734-5200
Web: http://ericps.crc.uiuc.edu/ccdece/ccdece.html

The Center for Career Development in Early Care and Education strives to improve the quality of care and education for young children by creating viable career development systems for practitioners. The multi-faceted activities of The Center are designed to help states and localities bring about systemic change to replace the fragmented system of training that now exists. The Center is the vehicle through which Wheelock, in partnership with other national organizations and government policymakers, stimulates and further develops the concept of a dynamic career development system.

Council for Early Childhood Professional Recognition

2460 16th Street, NW
Washington, DC 20009
Phone: (800) 424-4310

The Council for Early Childhood Professional Recognition, founded in 1985, is a nonprofit corporation headquartered in Washington, DC. The Council's mission is to increase the status and recognition of early care and education professionals who care for children birth through age 5 years of age in child care centers, family child care homes, and as home visitors. As part of the Council's mission to professionalize the early child care field, a training team travels across the country to conduct workshops and seminars for early childhood educators. In addition, the Council publishes books and manuals on the trends and developments in the field.

Council of Chief State School Officers

One Massachusetts Avenue, NW, #700
Washington, DC 20001-1431
Phone: (202) 336-7033
Web: http://www.ccsso.org

The Council of Chief State School Officers (CCSSO) is a nationwide, nonprofit organization composed of officials who head the departments of elementary and secondary education in the states, U.S. extra-state jurisdictions, the District of Colum-

bia and the Department of Defense Dependents Schools. The Council's members develop policy and consensus on major education issues, which the Council advocates before the President, federal agencies, the Congress, professional and civic associations and the public. With the support of foundations and federal agencies, the Council undertakes projects that assist states with new policy and administrative initiatives and assist the federal agencies and foundations in implementing their programs. During the past eight years, the Council has adopted major policy statements around the theme "Education Success for All."

CCSSO is currently engaged in a number of national and international efforts in the areas of early childhood care and education, science and math, community service learning, connecting schools to employment, HIV and school health programs, Title I of the Improving America's Schools Act (IASA) and high-poverty schools, collaboration and integrated social and health services in schools, bilingual education, middle grade school improvement, migrant education, education and technology, state and local education leadership and school improvement, large-scale assessment, curriculum and instructional improvement, student and teacher assessment, education data and information systems, standards, and family involvement in children's learning.

Ecumenical Child Care Network

8765 West Higgins Road, Suite 405
Chicago, IL 60631
Phone: (312) 693-4040

The Ecumenical Child Care Network is a national, interdenominational membership organization whose members advocate for high quality, equitable, and affordable child care and education in churches and other religious organizations. As Christians, the Ecumenical Child Care Network challenges members to apply anti-bias/anti-racist principles in their work and in all that they do.

ERIC/EECE

University of Illinois at Urbana-Champaign
Children's Research Center
51 Gerty Drive
Champaign, IL 61820-7469
Phone: (800) 583-4135 or (217) 333-1386
Web: http://ericps.crc.uiuc.edu/ericeece.html

The Educational Resources Information Center's Clearinghouse on Elementary and Early Childhood

Education collects and disseminates research, literature, fact sheets and briefing papers on the physical, cognitive, social, educational and cultural development from birth through early adolescence. Included in the collection is information on prenatal development, parenting and family relationships, learning theory research and practice, teaching and learning and theoretical and philosophical issues pertaining to children's development and education.

Families and Work Institute

330 Seventh Avenue, 14th Floor
New York, NY 10001
Phone: (212) 465-2044
Web: http://www.familiesandworkinst.org

The Families and Work Institute is a nonprofit research and planning organization committed to developing new approaches for balancing the changing needs of America's families with the continuing need for workplace productivity. The Institute conducts policy research on a broad range of issues related to the changing demographics of the workforce and operates a national clearinghouse on work and family life. It serves decision makers from all sectors of society: business, education, community, and government. The Families and Work Institute was founded in 1989 by Dana Friedman and Ellen Galinsky. Located in New York City, the Institute carries out its work with a core staff of in-house researchers and leading experts throughout the country.

National Association for the Education of Young Children (NAEYC)

1509 16th Street, NW
Washington, DC 20036
Phone: (800) 424-2460 or (202) 232-8777
Web: http://www.naeyc.org/naeyc/

NAEYC is a nonprofit professional organization of more than 90,000 members dedicated to improving the quality of care and education provided to our nation's young children. The Association administers the National Academy of Early Childhood Programs, a voluntary, national, accreditation system for high-quality early childhood programs, and the National Institute for Early Childhood Professional Development, which provides resources and services to improve professional preparation and development of early childhood educators and fosters development of a comprehensive, articulated system of high-quality professional development opportunities. In addition to the bimonthly journal *Young Chil-*

dren, NAEYC also publishes an extensive array of books, brochures, videotapes, and posters.

NAEYC's primary goals of improving the professional practice of early childhood education and building public understanding and support for high quality early childhood programs are shared and implemented by a national network of more than 450 Affiliate Groups. For 25 years NAEYC has sponsored the Week of the Young Child to focus public attention on the rights and needs of young children.

National Association for Family Child Care (NAFCC)

206 6th Avenue, Suite 900
Des Moines, IA 50309-4018
Phone: (800) 359-3817 or (515) 282-8192
Fax: (515) 282-9117
Web: http://www.nafcc.org/
E-mail: nafcc@assoc-mgmt.com

The National Association for Family Child Care (NAFCC) is the national membership organization working with the more than 400 state and local family child care provider associations in the United States. The focus of NAFCC is to promote quality family child care through accreditation and to promote training and leadership development through specialized technical assistance.

National Association of Child Care Professionals (NACCP)

304-A Roanoke Street
Christiansburg, VA 24063
Phone: (800) 537-1118
Fax: (540) 382-6529
E-mail: admin@naccp.org

The National Association of Child Care Professionals is deeply committed to strengthening the professional skill level of child care directors, owners, and administrators nationwide, without regard to tax status or corporate structure. NACCP believes effective management is the critical link to superior child care.

National Association of Child Care Resource and Referral Agencies (NACCRRA)

1319 F Street, NW, Suite 810
Washington, DC 20004-1106
Phone: (202) 393-5501
Web: http://www.childcarerr.org

NACCRRA is a national membership organization of over 400 community child care resource and referral agencies (CCR&Rs) in all 50 states. NACCRRA's mission is to promote the growth and development of high quality resource and referral services and to exercise leadership to build a diverse, high quality child care system with parental choice and equal access for all families. The CCR&Rs it represents are the only portion of the child care delivery system which maintains daily contact with both parents and child care providers in hundreds of local communities. CCR&Rs work closely with a broad array of community leaders, including employers and unions. Increasingly, NACCRRA and its members offer innovative guidance to policy makers on service delivery and regulatory issues and strategies.

National Black Child Development Institute

1023 Fifteenth Street, NW, Suite 600
Washington, DC 20005
Phone: (202) 387-1281
Web: http://www.nbcdi.org

The National Black Child Development Institute (NBCDI) serves as a critical resource for improving the quality of life of African American children, youth, and families through direct services, public education programs, leadership training, and research.

National Center for Children in Poverty

Columbia University School of Public Health
154 Haven Avenue
New York, NY 10032
Phone: (212) 304-7100
Web: http://cpmcnet.columbia.edu/dept/nccp/

The National Center for Children in Poverty encourages interdisciplinary thinking at the national, state, and local levels and emphasizes the needs and opportunities for early intervention with young children (ages birth to 5 years) and their families in poverty, especially in providing comprehensive services and using service integration strategies.

National Center for the Early Childhood Work Force

733 15th Street, N.W., Suite 800
Washington, DC 20005
Phone: (202) 737-7700

The National Center for the Early Childhood Work Force (NCECW), formerly the Child Care Employee Project, is a nonprofit resource and advocacy organization committed to improving the quality of child care services through upgrading the compensation and training of child care teachers and providers. NCECW is recognized as the national resource clearinghouse on child care staffing issues, as well as a leader in advocating for better regulation and funding of child care services. In addition, NCECW serves as the national coordinator of the Worthy Wage Campaign, a grassroots effort to empower child care workers themselves to fight for solutions to the staffing crisis. Our goal is to create a unified and powerful voice for the child care workforce, advocating for fair and decent employment for caregivers and reliable, affordable care for families.

The mission of the National Center for the Early Childhood Work Force is to assure high quality, affordable child care services by upgrading the training and compensation of teachers and providers. The NCECW addresses its mission through policy and program development, research and evaluation, and public education activities at the national, state, and local levels.

National Child Care Association

1016 Rosser Streeet
Conyers, GA 30207
Phone: (800) 543-7161
Web: http://www.nccanet.org/
E-mail: nccallw@mindspring.com

The National Child Care Association (NCCA) is a professional trade association representing the private, licensed early childhood care and education community. NCCA has a dual advocacy for quality, affordable child care as well as the business of child care.

National Head Start Association

1651 Prince Street
Alexandria, VA 22314
Phone: (703) 739-0875
Web: http://www.nhsa.org

The National Head Start Association (NHSA) is the membership organization representing Head Start parents, staff, directors, and friends across the nation. Major activities of the National Head Start Association include education and advocacy on behalf of Head Start children, families, and programs; quarterly publication of the NHSA journal, regular policy and legislative updates, special studies and reports; two annual training conferences, and leadership institutes. NHSA focuses on issues that shape the future of Head Start, and uses its national voice to inform communities, states, corporate America, and Washington lawmakers of its concerns.

National Indian Child Care Association

279 East 137th Street
Glenpool, OK 74033
Phone: (918) 756-2112

The purpose of the National Indian Child Care Association is to create and maintain an efficient and effective organization that advocates quality child care provision for Native American children, establishes a medium for information dissemination, and through a collaborative effort, builds trust and communication between Native American Tribes to perpetuate the identification and consideration of Tribal needs through a government to government relationship and presenting these assertions with a unified voice to the government of the United States of America.

National Institute on Out-of-School Time (formerly School-Age Child Care Project)

Wellesley College Center for Research on Women
Wellesley, MA 02181
Phone: (617) 283-2547
E-mail: lcoltin@wellesley.edu
Web: http://www.wellesley.edu/WCW/CRW/SAC/

The mission of the National Institute on Out-of-School Time (formerly the School-Age Child Care Project) is to improve the quantity and quality of school-age child care programs nationally through collaborative work with communities, individuals and organizations, and to raise the level of public awareness about the importance of children's out-of-school time. The Institute concentrates its efforts in four primary areas: research, education and training, consultation, and program development.

National Resource Center for Health and Safety in Child Care

University of Colorado Health Sciences Center
School of Nursing
4200 E. Ninth Ave.
Campus Box C287
Denver, CO 80262
Phone: (800) 598-KIDS (5437)
Web: http://nrc.uchsc.edu

The Maternal and Child Health Bureau's (MCHB) National Resource Center for Health and Safety in Child Care seeks to enhance the quality of child care by supporting state and local health departments, child care regulatory agencies, child care providers, and parents in their efforts to promote health and safety in child care. The National Resource Center will achieve this goal through information services, training and technical assistance to support regional, state, and local initiatives, conferences for sharing experiences and knowledge, and development and distribution of resource materials.

National School-Age Care Alliance

1137 Washington Street
Boston, MA 02142
Phone: (617) 298-5012
Web: http://www.nsaca.org

The National School-Age Care Alliance (NSACA) is a membership organization composed of individuals and groups. Members range from state affiliates with hundreds of individual and group members to individual school-age child care staff who are new to the field and seek affiliation with a professional organization. Basic membership benefits include a newsletter for members which keeps them in touch with the national organization as well as abreast of new developments in the field, a discount to the annual national school-age child care conference, discounts to video licensing, and participation in the development of an accreditation process.

USA Child Care

KCMC Child Development Corporation
2104 E. 18th
Kansas City, MO 64127
Phone: (816) 474-0434
E-mail: usaccare@aol.com

USA Child Care is a national membership association of child care and early education providers and advocates who deliver services directly to children and families. The mission of USA Child Care is to serve as a national voice for these direct service providers to ensure quality, comprehensive early care and education that is affordable and accessible to all families.

Women's Bureau, U.S. Department of Labor

Work and Family Clearinghouse
200 Constitution Avenue, NW, Room 3317
Washington, DC 20210-0002
Phone: (202) 219-4486
Web: http://gatekeeper.dol.gov/dol/wb/

The Work and Family Clearinghouse of the U.S. Department of Labor Women's Bureau provides statistical information on the status of women in the workforce. The Clearinghouse also conducts seminars and workshops on issues relating to women, such as non-traditional jobs, work and family issues, child and dependent care, women business owners, and women's job rights.

Zero To Three: National Center for Infants, Toddlers, and Families

734 15th Street, NW
Tenth Floor
Washington, DC 20005-2101
Phone: (202) 638-1144 or (800) 899-4301 for Publications
http://www.zerotothree.org

Zero To Three, formerly the National Center for Clinical Infant Programs, is the only national organization dedicated solely to infants, toddlers, and their families. Directed by a large Board of nationally-recognized experts in a wide range of disciplines, Zero To Three both gathers and disseminates information through its publications, its journal (*Zero To Three*), the annual National Training Institute, its Fellowship Program, specialized training opportunities, and technical assistance to communities, states, and the federal government.

INTERAGENCY TASK FORCE ON CHILD ABUSE AND NEGLECT CLEARINGHOUSE CONSORTIUM MEMBERS

Juvenile Justice Clearinghouse

PO Box 6000
Rockville, MD 20850
Phone: (800) 638-8736
E-mail: look@ncjrs.aspensys.com

Military Family Resource Center

Military Family Clearinghouse
4015 Wilson Boulevard, Suite 903
Arlington, VA 22203-5190
Phone: (703) 696-5806

National Adoption Information Clearinghouse

PO Box 1182
Washington, DC 20013-1182

Phone: (703) 352-3488
Fax: (703) 385-3206

National Center for Education in Maternal and Child Health

2000 15th Street, North
Suite 701
Arlington, VA 22201-2617
Phone: (703) 524-7802
E-mail: ncemch01@gumed lib.dml.georgetown.edu

National Center for Missing and Exploited Children

2101 Wilson Boulevard
Suite 550
Arlington, VA 22201-3052
Hotline: (800) 843-5678
Phone: (703) 235-3900
E-mail: 74431.177@compuserve.com
Web: http://www.missingkids.org

National Child Care Information Center

301 Maple Avenue, West
Suite 602
Vienna, VA 22180
E-mail: agoldstein@acf.dhhs.gov
Web: http://ericps.ed.uiuc.edu/nccic/nccichome.html

National Clearinghouse for Alcohol and Drug Information

PO Box 2345
Rockville, MD 20847-2345
Phone: (800) 729-6686
E-mail: info@prevline.health.org
Web: http://www.health.org

National Clearinghouse on Child Abuse and Neglect Information

PO Box 1182
Washington, DC 20013-1182
Phone: (800) FYI-3366
E-mail: nccanch@clark.net
Web: http://www.calib.com/nccanch/

National Clearinghouse on Families and Youth

PO Box 13505
Silver Spring, MD 20911-3505
Phone: (301) 608-8098

National Information Center for Children and Youth with Disabilities

PO Box 1492
Washington, DC 20013-1492
Phone: (800) 695-0285
E-mail: nichcy@aed.org
Web: http://www.nichcy.org/

National Information Clearinghouse for Infants with Disabilities and Life Threatening Conditions

University of South Carolina
Benson Building, First Floor
Columbia, SC 29208
Phone: (800) 922-9234 ext. 201
or (803) 777-4435

National Maternal and Child Health Clearinghouse

8201 Greensboro Drive
Suite 600
McLean, VA 22102-3843
Phone: (703) 821-8955 ext. 254
E-mail: lcramer@dgs.dgsys.com

National Sudden Infant Death Syndrome Resource Center

8201 Greensboro Drive
Suite 600
McLean, VA 22102-3843
Phone: (703) 821-8955 ext. 249 or 474

National Women's Resource Center for the Prevention and Treatment of Alcohol, Tobacco, and Other Drug Abuse and Mental Illness

515 King Street
Suite 420
Alexandria, VA 22314
Phone: (800) 354-8824
Web: http://www.nwrc.org/

Office for Victims of Crime Resource Center

PO Box 6000
Rockville, MD 20850-6000
Phone: (800) 627-6872

Women's Bureau Clearinghouse

Women's Bureau
Room S3306
US Department of Labor
200 Constitution Avenue, NW
Washington, DC 20210-0002
Phone: (800) 827-5335
Web: http://gatekeeper.dol.gov/dol/wb/public/programs/house.htm

National Resource Center on Child Abuse and Neglect

63 Inverness Drive, East
Englewood, CO 80112-5117
Phone: (800) 227-5242

Credits

Index